BUSINESS ETHICS

Ethical Decision Making
Seventh Edition

O. C. FERRELL
University of New Mexico

JOHN FRAEDRICH
Bill Daniels Distinguished Professor of Business Ethics
University of Wyoming

LINDA FERRELL
University of New Mexico

HOUGHTON MIFFLIN COMPANY
BOSTON   NEW YORK

Executive Publisher: George Hoffman
Senior Development Editor: Joanne Dauksewicz
Associate Project Editor: Kristen Truncellito
Art and Design Coordinator: Jill Haber
Senior Photo Editor: Jennifer Meyer Dare
Composition Buyer: Chuck Dutton
Associate Manufacturing Buyer: Susan Brooks
Senior Marketing Manager: Mike Schenk
Marketing Coordinator: Erin Lane

Custom Publishing Editor: Luis Rosas
Custom Publishing Production Manager: Christina Battista
Project Coordinator: Janell Sims

Cover Designer: Eric Hague
Cover Image: stock.xchng

ISBN-13: 978-0-547-01254-4
ISBN-10: 0-547-01254-3
1030751

1 2 3 4 5 6 7 8 9 – CM – 09 08 07

Houghton Mifflin
Custom Publishing

222 Berkeley Street • Boston, MA 02116

Address all correspondence and order information to the above address.

Brief Contents

Contents

Preface

Perhaps no area of business has changed so rapidly in recent years as the field of business ethics. The "institutionalization of business ethics" is being felt and reflected upon by businesses and public policy decision makers. The Sarbanes–Oxley Act and the 2004 amendments of the Federal Sentencing Guidelines for Organizations have had a profound effect on business ethics programs and compliance requirements. We are seeing the repercussions of organizational misconduct through the trials of executives at Enron, HealthSouth, Wal-Mart, and other high-profile executives. This edition of *Business Ethics* reflects the latest research and knowledge on the current state of business ethics. Our extensive revision creates the most comprehensive and current business ethics text on the market. We have discovered that you want a complete teaching and learning package, and this revision provides the best available resources. We have spent a significant amount of time listening to your needs and providing the content, cases, and teaching tools necessary to help students learn the important dimensions of business ethics.

Business ethics has moved from the back room to the boardroom and the classroom over the last five years. The seventh edition has been revised to reflect these events by providing new frameworks, up-to-date examples, and cases. Business ethics issues that have become extremely relevant include concern for stakeholders, corporate governance, and the institutionalization of business ethics by government and society. Business schools are being asked to do a better job in teaching business ethics to help prepare future managers and to achieve accreditation by AACSB International by maintaining appropriate standards. More corporations are developing ethics programs and making ethics a higher priority than in previous years.

Using a managerial framework, we explain how ethics can be integrated into strategic business decisions. This framework provides *an overview of the concepts, processes, mandatory, core, and voluntary business practices* associated with successful business ethics programs. Some approaches to business ethics are excellent for exercises in intellectual reasoning but do not deal with the actual ethical decision-making situations that people in business organizations face. Our approach prepares students for ethical dilemmas that they will face in their business careers.

We have been careful in this revision to provide the most up-to-date knowledge while retaining the strengths that have made this text so successful. This book has been successful because *it addresses the complex environment of ethical decision making in organizations and real-life issues.* Every individual has unique personal values, and every organization has its own set of values and ethical policies. Business ethics must consider the organizational culture and interdependent relationships between the individual and other significant persons involved in organizational decision making. Without effective guidance, a businessperson cannot make ethical decisions while facing organizational pressures and day-to-day challenges in the competitive environment.

Employees cannot make most business ethics decisions in a vacuum outside organizational codes, policies and culture. Most employees and all managers are responsible not only for their own ethical conduct but also the decisions of coworkers and employees they supervise. Therefore, teaching business ethics as only an independent personal decision-making process fails to address the requirement that employees help develop, implement, and improve organizational ethics programs. Employees must know when to report and address ethical issues observed in the workplace. Students must learn to fit into the ethical culture of their organization and be responsible for their own decisions and uphold organizational standards.

By focusing on the issues and organizational environments, this book provides students the opportunity to see the roles and responsibilities they may face as they advance in the workplace. Our primary goal—as always—is to enhance the awareness and the decision-making skills that students will need to make business ethics decisions that contribute to responsible business conduct. By focusing on the concerns and issues of today's challenging business environment, we demonstrate that studying business ethics provides vital knowledge that contributes to overall business success.

PHILOSOPHY OF THIS TEXT

Business ethics in organizations requires values-based leadership from top management and purposeful actions that include planning and implementation of standards of appropriate conduct, as well as openness and continuous effort to improve the organization's ethical performance. Although personal values are important in ethical decision making, they are just one of the components that guide the decisions, actions, and policies of organizations. The burden of ethical behavior relates to the organization's values and traditions, not just to the individuals who make the decisions and carry them out. A firm's ability to plan and implement ethical business standards depends in part on structuring resources and activities to achieve ethical objectives in an effective and efficient manner.

The purpose of this book is to help students improve their ability to make ethical decisions in business by providing them with a framework that they can use to identify, analyze, and resolve ethical issues in business decision making. Individual values and ethics are important in this process. By studying business ethics, students begin to understand how to cope with conflicts between their personal values and those of the organization.

Many ethical decisions in business are close calls. It often takes years of experience in a particular industry to know what is acceptable. We do not, in this book, provide ethical answers but instead attempt to prepare students to make informed ethical decisions. First, we do not moralize by indicating what to do in a specific situation. Second, although we provide an overview of moral philosophies and decision-making processes, we do not prescribe any one philosophy or process as best or most ethical. Third, by itself, this book will not make students more ethical nor will it tell them how to judge the ethical behavior of others. Rather, its goal is to help students understand and use their current values and convictions in making business decisions and to encourage everyone to think about the effects of their decisions on business and society.

Many people believe that business ethics cannot be taught. Although we do not claim to teach ethics, we suggest that by studying business ethics a person can improve ethical decision making by identifying ethical issues and recognizing the approaches available to resolve them. An organization's reward system can reinforce appropriate behavior and help shape attitudes and beliefs about important issues. For example, the success of some campaigns to end racial or gender discrimination in the workplace provides evidence that attitudes and behavior can be changed with new information, awareness, and shared values.

COMPLETE CONTENT COVERAGE

In writing *Business Ethics,* seventh edition, we have strived to be as informative, complete, accessible, and up to date as possible. Instead of focusing on one area of ethics, such as moral philosophy or social responsibility, we provide balanced coverage of all areas relevant to the current development and practice of ethical decision making. In short, we have tried to keep pace with new developments and current thinking in teaching and practices. The corporate governance and ethical compliance issues that resulted in the passage of the Sarbanes–Oxley Act of 2002 are appropriately addressed. The 2004 amendments of the Federal Sentencing Guidelines for Organizations provide directions for ethical leadership and oversight responsibilities for boards of directors. Specific ethical issues including abusive and intimidating behavior, lying, conflicts of interest, bribery, corporate intelligence, discrimination, sexual harassment, environmental issues, fraud, insider trading, intellectual-property rights, privacy, and other issues that may cause social or environmental damage are covered through dilemmas, examples, and cases. Additionally, we have added a new chapter on institutionalization of business ethics to reflect legal and societal pressures for required compliance, core practices and voluntary activities to improve business ethics.

ORGANIZATION OF THE TEXT

The first half of the text consists of ten chapters, which provide a framework to identify, analyze, and understand how businesspeople make ethical decisions and deal with ethical issues. Several enhancements have been made to chapter content for this edition. Some of the most important are listed below.

Part One, "An Overview of Business Ethics," includes two chapters that help provide a broader context for the study of business ethics. Chapter 1, "The Importance of Business Ethics," has been revised with many new examples and survey results to describe issues and concerns important to business ethics. Chapter 2, "Stakeholder Relationships, Social Responsibility, and Corporate Governance," has been significantly reorganized and updated with new examples and issues. This chapter was reorganized and expanded to develop an overall framework for the text.

Part Two, "Ethical Issues and the Institutionalization of Business Ethics," consists of two chapters that provide the background that students need to identify ethical issues and understand how society, through the legal system, has attempted to hold organizations responsible for managing these issues. Chapter 3, "Emerging Business Ethics Issues," has been significantly reorganized and updated and provides expanded coverage of business ethics issues. Reviewers requested more detail on key issues that create ethical decisions. Within this edition, we have increased the depth of ethical issues and have added the following new issues: abusive and intimidating behavior, lying, bribery, corporate intelligence, environmental issues, intellectual-property rights, and privacy. Chapter 4, "The Institutionalization of Business Ethics" examines key elements of core or best practices in corporate America today along with legislation and regulation requirements that support business ethics initiatives. The chapter is divided into three main areas: voluntary, mandated, and core boundaries.

Part Three, "The Decision-Making Process" consists of three chapters, which provide a framework to identify, analyze, and understand how businesspeople make ethical decisions and deal with ethical issues. Chapter 5, "Ethical Decision Making and Ethical Leadership," has been revised and updated to reflect current research and understanding of ethical decision making and contains a new section on ethical leadership. Chapter 6, "Individual Factors: Moral Philosophies and Values," has been updated and revised to explore the role of moral philosophies and moral development as individual factors in the ethical decision-making process. This chapter now includes a new section on white-collar crime. Chapter 7, "Organizational Factors: The Role of Ethical Culture and Relationships," considers organizational influences on business decisions, such as role relationships, differential association, and other organizational pressures, as well as whistle-blowing.

Part Four, "Implementing Business Ethics in a Global Economy," looks at specific measures that companies can take to build an effective ethics program, as well as how these programs may be affected by global issues. Chapter 8, "Developing an Effective Ethics Program," has been refined and updated with corporate best practices for developing effective ethics programs. Chapter 9, "Implementing and Auditing Ethics Programs," offers a framework for auditing ethics initiatives as well as the importance of doing so. Such audits can help companies pinpoint problem areas, measure their progress in improving conduct, and even provide a "debriefing" opportunity after a crisis. Finally, Chapter 10, "Business Ethics in a Global Economy," contains new examples of international business ethics issues, conflicts, and cooperative efforts to establish universal standards of conduct.

Part Five consists of eighteen cases that bring reality into the learning process. Nine of these cases are new to the seventh edition, and the remaining nine have been revised and updated. The companies and situations portrayed in these cases are real; names and other facts are not disguised; and all cases include developments up to 2006. By reading and analyzing these cases, students can gain insight into ethical decisions and the realities of making decisions in complex situations.

The seventh edition provides five behavioral simulation role-play cases developed for use in the business ethics course. The role-play cases and implementation methods can be found in the *Instructor's Resource Manual* and on the website. Role-play cases may be used as a culminating experience to help students integrate concepts covered in the text. Alternatively, the cases may be used as an ongoing exercise to provide students with extensive opportunities for interacting and making ethical decisions.

Role-play cases simulate a complex, realistic, and timely business ethics situation. Students form teams and make decisions based on an assigned role. The role-play case complements and enhances traditional approaches to business learning experiences because it (1) gives students the opportunity to practice making decisions that have business ethics consequences; (2) re-creates the power, pressures, and information that affect decision making at various levels of management; (3) provides students with a team-based experience that enriches their skills and understanding of group processes and dynamics; and (4) uses a feedback period to allow for the exploration of complex and controversial issues in business ethics decision making. The role play can be used with classes of any size.

BUSINESS ETHICS LEARNING CENTER WEBSITE

The website developed for the seventh edition provides up-to-date examples, issues, and interactive learning devices to assist students in improving their decision-making skills. The Business Ethics Learning Center has been created to take advantage of information available on the Internet while providing new interactive skill-building exercises that can help students practice ethical decision making. The site contains links to companies and organizations highlighted in each chapter; Internet exercises; ACE (ACyber Evaluation) interactive quizzes, which help students master chapter content through multiple-choice questions; links to association, industry, and company codes of conduct; case website linkages; company and organizational examples; and academic resources, including links to business ethics centers throughout the world and the opportunity to sign up for weekly abstracts of relevant *Wall Street Journal* articles. Four Ethical Leadership Challenge scenarios are available for each chapter. Training devices, including Lockheed Martin's Gray Matters ethics game, are also available online. In addition, students have access to their own set of PowerPoint slides to help them review and master the text material.

To access the text's websites

- ◆ Go to http://college.hmco.com
- ◆ Select "Instructors" or "Students"
- ◆ Select "Go to Your Discipline" and then "Business"
- ◆ Select Ferrell/Fraedrich/Ferrell, *Business Ethics* from the Textbook Sites menus

EFFECTIVE TOOLS FOR TEACHING AND LEARNING

Many tools are available in this text to help both students and instructors in the quest to improve students' ability to make ethical business decisions. Each chapter opens with an outline and a list of learning objectives. Immediately following is "An Ethical Dilemma" that should provoke discussion about ethical issues related to the chapter. The short vignette describes a hypothetical incident involving an ethical conflict. Questions at the end of the "Ethical Dilemma" section focus discussion on how the dilemma could be resolved. At the end of each chapter are a chapter summary and an important terms list, both of which are handy tools for review. Also included at the end of each chapter is a "Real-Life Situation" section. The vignette describes a realistic drama that helps students experience the process of ethical decision making. The "Real-Life Situation" minicases presented in this text are hypothetical; any resemblance to real persons, companies, or situations is coincidental. Keep in mind that there are no right or wrong solutions to the minicases. The ethical dilemmas and real-life situations provide an opportunity for students to use concepts in the chapter to resolve ethical issues. Each chapter concludes with a series of questions that allow students to test their EQ (Ethics Quotient).

In Part Five, following each real-world case are questions to guide students in recognizing and resolving ethical issues. For some cases, students can conduct additional research to determine recent developments because many ethical issues in companies take years to resolve.

The *Instructor's Resource Manual* contains a wealth of information. Teaching notes for every chapter include a brief chapter summary, detailed lecture outline, and notes for using the "Ethical Dilemma" and "Real-Life Situation" sections. Detailed case notes point out the key issues involved and offer suggested answers to the questions. A separate section provides guidelines for using case analysis in teaching business ethics. Detailed notes are provided to guide the instructor in analyzing or grading the cases. Simulation role-play cases, as well as implementation suggestions, are included. The *Test Bank* provides multiple-choice and essay questions for every chapter in the text. A computerized version of the test bank is also available. Password-protected Power-Point slides are available at Houghton Mifflin's Online Teaching Center along with an online version of the *Instructor's Resource Manual*. Additional instructor resources can be found at www.e-businessethics.com including PowerPoint slides and an online *Teaching Business Ethics Resource Manual*. Finally, a selection of video segments is available to help bring real-world examples and skill-building scenarios into the classroom.

ACKNOWLEDGMENTS

A number of individuals provided reviews and suggestions that helped to improve this text. We sincerely appreciate their time and effort.

Donald Acker
Brown Mackie College

Donna Allen
Northwest Nazarene University

Suzanne Allen
Walsh University

Carolyn Ashe
University of Houston–Downtown

Laura Barelman
Wayne State College

Russell Bedard
Eastern Nazarene College

B. Barbara Boerner
Brevard College

Judie Bucholz
Guilford College

Greg Buntz
University of the Pacific

Julie Campbell
Adams State College

April Chatham-Carpenter
University of Northern Iowa

Peggy Cunningham
Queen's University

Carla Dando
Idaho State University

James E. Donovan
Detroit College of Business

Douglas Dow
University of Texas at Dallas

A. Charles Drubel
Muskingum College

Philip F. Esler
University of St. Andrews

Joseph M. Foster
Indiana Vocational Technical College–Evansville

Terry Gable
Truman State University

Robert Giacalone
University of Richmond

Suresh Gopalan
West Texas A&M University

Mark Hammer
Northwest Nazarene University

Charles E. Harris, Jr.
Texas A&M University

Kenneth A. Heischmidt
Southeast Missouri State University

Neil Herndon
Educational Consultant

Walter Hill
Green River Community College

Jack Hires
Valparaiso University

David Jacobs
American University

R. J. Johansen
Montana State University–Bozeman

Edward Kimman
Vrije Universiteit

Janet Knight
Purdue North Central

Anita Leffel
University of Texas at San Antonio

Barbara Limbach
Chadron State College

Nick Lockard
Texas Lutheran College

Terry Loe
Kennesaw State University

Nick Maddox
Stetson University

Isabelle Maignan
ING Bank

Phylis Mansfield
Pennsylvania State University—Erie

Robert Markus
Babson College

Randy McLeod
Harding University

Francy Milner
University of Colorado

Lester Myers
University of San Francisco

Patrick E. Murphy
University of Notre Dame

Cynthia Nicola
Carlow College

Carol Nielsen
Bemidji State University

Lee Richardson
University of Baltimore

Zachary Shank
*Albuquerque Technical
Vocational Institute*

Cynthia A. M. Simerly
Lakeland Community College

Karen Smith
Columbia Southern University

Filiz Tabak
Towson University

Debbie Thorne
Texas State University—San Marcos

Wanda V. Turner
Ferris State College

David Wasieleski
Duquesne University

Jim Weber
Duquesne University

Ed Weiss
National-Louis University

Jan Zahrly
University of North Dakota

We wish to acknowledge the many people who assisted us in writing this book. We are deeply grateful to Melanie Drever for helping us organize and manage the revision process and for preparing the *Instructor's Resource Manual* and *Test Bank*. We are also indebted to Barbara Gilmer and Gwyneth V. Walters for their contributions to previous editions of this text. Debbie Thorne, Texas State University—San Marcos, provided advice and guidance on the text and cases. Thanks go to Matt Paproth, Katie Duncan, Raghu Kurthakoti, Deepa Pillai, Benjamin Siltman, Alexi Sherrill, and Rajendran Murthy in preparing and updating cases, test banks, and chapters in this edition. Finally, we express appreciation to the administration and to our colleagues at the University of New Mexico, Southern Illinois University at Carbondale, and the University of Wyoming for their support.

We invite your comments, questions, or criticisms. We want to do our best to provide teaching materials that enhance the study of business ethics. Your suggestions will be sincerely appreciated.

– O. C. Ferrell

– John Fraedrich

– Linda Ferrell

An Overview of Business Ethics

CHAPTER 1

The Importance of Business Ethics

CHAPTER OBJECTIVES

- To explore conceptualizations of business ethics from an organizational perspective

- To examine the historical foundations and evolution of business ethics

- To provide evidence that ethical value systems support business performance

- To gain insight into the extent of ethical misconduct in the workplace and the pressures for unethical behavior

CHAPTER OUTLINE

John Peters had just arrived at the main offices of Dryer & Sons (D&S) from Midwest State University. A medium-size company, D&S manufactured components for several of the major defense contractors in the United States. Recently, D&S had started a specialized software division and had hired John as a salesperson for both the company's hardware and software.

A diligent student at Midwest State, John had earned degrees in engineering and management information systems (MIS). His minor was in marketing—specifically, sales. Because of his education as well as other activities, John was not only comfortable discussing numbers with engineers but also had the people skills to convey complex solutions in understandable terms. This was one of the main reasons Al Dryer had hired him. "You've got charisma, John, and you know your way around computers," Dryer explained.

D&S was established during World War II and had manufactured parts for military aircraft. During the Korean War and then the Vietnam War, D&S had become a stable subcontractor for specialized parts for aircraft and missiles. When Al Dryer and his father started the business, Al was the salesperson for the company. In time, D&S had grown to employ several hundred workers and five salespeople; John was the sixth salesperson.

During his first few months at the company, John got his bearings in the defense industry. For example, when Ed, his trainer, would take procurement people out to lunch, everyone would put money into a snifter at the table. The money collected was usually much less than the bill, and Ed would make up the difference. Golf was a skill that Ed required John to learn because often "that's where deals are really transacted." Again, Ed would indirectly pick up the golfing bill, which sometimes totaled several hundred dollars.

Another of Ed's requirements was that John read the Procurement Integrity Section of the Office of Federal Procurement Policy Act and the Federal Acquisition Regulation, which implements the act. In addition, John had to read the Certificate of Procurement Integrity, which procurement agents had to sign. As John read the documents, he noted the statement in Section 27(a)(2), forbidding agents to "offer, give, or promise to offer or give, directly or indirectly, any money, gratuity, or other thing of value to any procurement official of such agency; or (3) solicit or obtain, directly or indirectly, from any officer or employee of such agency, prior to the award of a contract any proprietary or source selection information regarding such procurement."

"Doesn't this relate to what we're doing, Ed?" John asked.

"Yes and no, my boy, yes and no," was Ed's only answer.

One Monday, when Ed and John had returned from sales calls in St. Louis and Washington, DC, Ed called John into his office and said, "John, you don't have the right numbers down for our expenses. You're 15 percent short because you forgot all of your tips." As John looked at his list of expenses, he realized that Ed was right, yet there was no item on his expense report for such things.

"Ed, where do I put the extra expenses? There's no line on the forms for this."

"Just add it into the cost of things as I've done," replied Ed, showing John his expense report.

As John looked at Ed's report, he noticed some numbers that seemed quite large. "Why don't we mention this problem to Mr. Dryer so that accounting can put the extra lines on the reports?" John suggested.

"Because this is the way we do things around here, and they don't like changes to the system. We have a saying in the company that a blind eye goes a long way to getting business done," Ed lectured John. John didn't quite grasp the problem and did as he was told.

On another trip, John learned the differences between working directly with the federal government procurement people and the companies with which D&S subcontracted. For example, certain conversations of the large defense contractors were relayed to D&S, and then Ed and John would visit certain government agencies and relay that information. In one case, Ed and John were told to relay a very large offer to an official who was entering the private sector the next year. In addition, Ed and John were used to obtaining information on requests for proposals, as well as other competitive information, from procurement agents. When John asked Ed about this, Ed said, "John, in order to excel in this business, you need to be an expert on knowing exactly where things become legal and illegal. Trust me, I've been doing this for fifteen years, and I've never had a problem. Why do you think I'm your trainer?"

John started reviewing more government documents and asking the other salespeople about Ed. Two replied that Ed was a smart operator and knew the ropes better than anyone at the company. The other two salespeople had a different story to tell. One asked, "Has he tried to explain away his padding of the expense reports to you yet?"

"But I thought that's what everyone does!" John exclaimed.

"Ed has been doing business with the Feds and the large defense companies for so long that he sometimes doesn't realize that the rules have changed. He's been lucky that he hasn't been caught. Watch your step, John, or you'll find yourself with dirty hands and nowhere to clean them," the second salesperson said.

At the end of another trip to Washington, DC, Ed called John into his office. "John, your numbers don't add up," he pointed out. "Didn't I tell you to add at least 15 percent to your totals for tips and miscellaneous items? Let's get with it. Do you want to be in training forever? You know that I have to sign off before you can go it alone, and I want to make sure you understand the ropes. Just between you and me, I think Dryer is finally going to make a vice president slot, which should go to me because of my seniority. So hurry up and learn this stuff because you're my last trainee. Now just sign the document with these revised numbers on them."

What should John do?

QUESTIONS • EXERCISES

1. What is Ed's ethical dilemma?
2. What are the ethical and legal considerations for John at D&S?
3. Identify the ethical conflict in this situation.
4. Discuss the implications of each decision John has made and will make.

*This case is strictly hypothetical; any resemblance to real persons, companies, or situations is coincidental.

The ability to recognize and deal with complex business ethics issues has become a significant priority in twenty-first-century companies. In recent years, a number of well-publicized scandals resulted in public outrage about deception and fraud in business and a demand for improved business ethics and greater corporate responsibility. The publicity and debate surrounding highly visible legal and ethical lapses at a number of well-known firms, including Enron, WorldCom, HealthSouth, and even Coca-Cola, highlight the need for businesses to integrate ethics and responsibility into all business decisions. Table 1–1 reflects increasing distrust of business among Americans as reported by a leading polling organization, Yankelovich Partners, Inc. A global opinion poll for the World Economic Forum concluded that public trust in companies has eroded and dropped significantly over the last few years. Public trust in national governments and the United Nations has fallen significantly too.[1] Largely in response to this crisis, business decisions and activities have come under greater scrutiny by many different constituents, including consumers, employees, investors, government regulators, and special-interest groups. Additionally, new legislation and regulations designed to encourage higher ethical standards in business have been put in place.

TABLE 1–1	American Distrust of Business	
80%	**70%**	**61%**
American business is too concerned about profits, not concerned about responsibilities to workers, consumers, and the environment.	If the opportunity arises, most businesses will take advantage of the public if they feel they are not likely to be found out.	Even long-established companies cannot be trusted to make safe, durable products without the government setting industry standards.

SOURCE: J. Walker Smith, Ann Clurman, and Craig Wood of Yankelovich Partners, Inc. *Point,* February 2005, www.RacomBooks.com; results from Yankelovich MONITOR.

The field of business ethics deals with questions about whether specific business practices are acceptable. For example, should a salesperson omit facts about a product's poor safety record in a sales presentation to a client? Should an accountant report inaccuracies that he or she discovered in an audit of a client, knowing the auditing company will probably be fired by the client for doing so? Should an automobile tire manufacturer intentionally conceal safety concerns to avoid a massive and costly tire recall? Regardless of their legality, others will certainly judge the actions taken in such situations as right or wrong, ethical or unethical. By its very nature, the field of business ethics is controversial, and there is no universally accepted approach for resolving its issues.

A survey of nearly 25,000 high school students revealed that 62 percent of the students admitted to cheating on an exam at least once, 35 percent confessed to copying documents from the Internet, 27 percent admitted to shoplifting, and 23 percent owned up to cheating in order to win in sports.[2] If today's students are tomorrow's leaders, there is likely to be a correlation between acceptable behavior today and tomorrow, adding to the argument that the leaders of today must be prepared for the ethical risks associated with this downward trend. According to another poll by Deloitte and Touche of teenagers aged 13 to 18 years old, when asked if people who practice good business ethics are more successful than those who don't, 69 percent of teenagers agreed.[3] On the other hand another survey indicated that many students do not define copying answers from another student's paper or downloading music or content for classroom work as cheating.[4]

Before we get started, it is important to state our philosophies regarding this book. First, we do not moralize by telling you what is right or wrong in a specific situation. Second, although we provide an overview of group and individual decision-making processes, we do not prescribe any one philosophy or process as best or most ethical. Third, by itself, this book will not make you more ethical, nor will it tell you how to judge the ethical behavior of others. Rather, its goal is to help you understand and use your current values and convictions when making business decisions so that you think about the effects of those decisions on business and society. In addition, this book will help you understand what businesses are doing to improve their ethical conduct. To this end, we aim to help you learn to recognize and resolve ethical issues within business organizations. As a manager, you will be responsible for your decisions and the ethical conduct of employees who you supervise. The framework we develop in this book therefore focuses on how organizational ethical decisions are made and on ways companies can improve their ethical conduct.

In this chapter, we first develop a definition of business ethics and discuss why it has become an important topic in business education. We also discuss why studying business ethics can be beneficial. Next, we examine the evolution of business ethics in North America. Then we explore the performance benefits of ethical decision making for businesses. Finally, we provide a brief overview of the framework we use for examining business ethics in this text.

BUSINESS ETHICS DEFINED

The term *ethics* has many nuances. It has been defined as "inquiry into the nature and grounds of morality where the term morality is taken to mean moral judgments, standards and rules of conduct."[5] Ethics has also been called the study and philosophy of human conduct, with an emphasis on determining right and wrong. *The American Heritage Dictionary* offers these definitions of ethics: "The study of the general nature of morals and of specific moral choices; moral philosophy; and the rules or standards governing the conduct of the members of a profession."[6] One difference between an ordinary decision and an ethical one lies in "the point where the accepted rules no longer serve, and the decision maker is faced with the responsibility for weighing values and reaching a judgment in a situation which is not quite the same as any he or she has faced before."[7] Another difference relates to the amount of emphasis that decision makers place on their own values and accepted practices within their company. Consequently, values and judgments play a critical role when we make ethical decisions.

Building on these definitions, we can begin to develop a concept of business ethics. Most people would agree that high ethical standards require both businesses and individuals to conform to sound moral principles. However, some special aspects must be considered when applying ethics to business. First, to survive, businesses must earn a profit. If profits are realized through misconduct, however, the life of the organization may be shortened. Many firms, including Arthur Andersen, Enron, WorldCom, and Sunbeam, that made headlines due to wrongdoing and scandal ultimately went bankrupt or failed because of the legal and financial repercussions of their misconduct. Second, businesses must balance their desires for profits against the needs and desires of society. Maintaining this balance often requires compromises or tradeoffs. To address these unique aspects of the business world, society has developed rules—both legal and implicit—to guide businesses in their efforts to earn profits in ways that do not harm individuals or society as a whole.

Most definitions of business ethics relate to rules, standards, and moral principles regarding what is right or wrong in specific situations. For our purposes and in simple terms, **business ethics** comprises the principles and standards that guide behavior in the world of business. Investors, employees, customers, interest groups, the legal system, and the community often determine whether a specific action is right or wrong, ethical or unethical. Although these groups are not necessarily "right," their judgments influence society's acceptance or rejection of a business and its activities.

WHY STUDY BUSINESS ETHICS?

A Crisis in Business Ethics

As we've already mentioned, ethical misconduct has become a major concern in business today. The Ethics Resource Center conducted the National Business Ethics Survey (NBES) of about three thousand U.S. employees to gather reliable data on key ethics and compliance outcomes and to help identify and better understand the ethics issues that are important to employees. The NBES found that observed misconduct is higher in large organizations—those with more than five hundred employees—than in smaller ones and that there are also differences in observed misconduct across employee levels. Reporting of misconduct is most likely to come from upper-level management, as compared to lower-level supervisors and nonmanagement employees. Employees in lower-level positions have more of a tendency to not understand misconduct or be complacent about what misconduct they observe. Figure 1–1 is based on the percentage of employees who indicated that they did observe misconduct during the past year. Each bar represents the percentage of employees who reported misconduct. Among senior managers, 77 percent of employees report observed misconduct, while among nonmanagement, only 48 percent of employees report observed misconduct.[8]

SPECIFIC ISSUES   Abusive behavior, harassment, accounting fraud, conflicts of interest, defective products, bribery, and employee theft are all problems cited as evidence of declining ethical standards. For example, Krispy Kreme, once a high-flying company, experienced a meltdown when two executives tried to manage earnings to meet Wall Street expectations. The company's stock, which had traded for $105/share in November 2000 before two-for-one stock splits, traded at $5/share in January 2006.[9] A poll by Harris Interactive found many scandal-plagued firms at the bottom

FIGURE 1–1   Employee Reporting of Misconduct by Employee Level

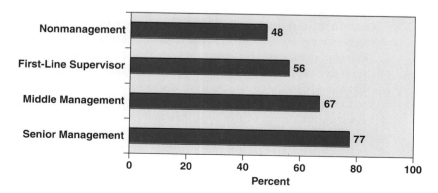

SOURCE: From *2005 National Business Ethics Survey: How Employees Perceive Ethics at Work,* 2005, p. 30. Copyright © 2006, Ethics Resource Center (ERC). Used with permission of the ERC, 1747 Pennsylvania Ave., N.W., Suite 400, Washington, DC 2006, www.ethics.org.

of its annual survey of perceived corporate reputation, including Enron, Global Crossing, WorldCom, Andersen Worldwide, and Adelphia. The survey, which ranks companies according to how respondents rate them on twenty attributes, also found that public perceptions of trust had declined considerably as a result of the accounting scandals of the early twenty-first century. Joy Sever, a Harris vice president, reported, "The scandals cost many companies their emotional appeal, the strongest driver of reputation."[10]

Martha Stewart was investigated for insider trading after she sold nearly four thousand shares of ImClone Systems stock prior to the company's announcement that regulators had rejected its application for a cancer-fighting drug. The firm's CEO, Samuel Waksal, pleaded guilty of attempting to sell his own shares in advance of the announcement and was sentenced to seven years in prison. Stewart resigned as CEO of her company, Martha Stewart Living Omnimedia, and gave up her seat on the board of the New York Stock Exchange. Moreover, shares of the stock of her company plummeted after the stock sale scandal was exposed.[11] A federal grand jury indicted Stewart on charges of securities fraud, conspiracy, making false statements, and obstruction of justice, but not insider trading. In 2004 the judge threw out the most serious of the charges against her—securities fraud. However, just one week later, a jury convicted her on four remaining charges of making false statements and conspiracy to obstruct justice, and she was sentenced to serve five months in jail and five months in home detention. She finished her jail time in 2005.

After HealthSouth Corporation was investigated for allegedly inflating earnings by $2.7 billion, eleven former employees, including all the firm's former chief financial officers (CFOs), pleaded guilty to fraud charges.[12] In 2006 HealthSouth agreed to issue stocks and warrants valued at $215 million, and the company insurers agreed to pay $230 million cash to investors. Richard M. Scrushy, founder and former chief executive officer (CEO), was acquitted of criminal charges. In addition he was convicted of six charges of bribery and mail fraud by an Alabama jury for giving $500,000 to a former Alabama governor to get a seat on the state hospital regulatory board. However, just a couple of months later, he was ordered to return $36.4 million in bonuses paid to him during the massive accounting fraud at the health-care company. Such highly publicized cases strengthen the perception that ethical standards in business need to be raised.

In government, several politicians and some high-ranking officials have had to resign in disgrace over ethical indiscretions. For example, James Traficant of Ohio was expelled from Congress and sent to jail after being convicted of accepting bribes while serving in the U.S. House of Representatives.[13] Irv Lewis "Scooter" Libby, a White House advisor, was indicted on five counts of criminal charges:[14] one count of obstruction of justice, two counts of perjury, and two counts of making false statements. Each count carries a $250,000 fine and maximum prison term of thirty years.

Several scientists have been accused of falsifying research data, which could invalidate later research based on their data and jeopardize trust in all scientific research. Bell Labs, for example, fired a scientist for falsifying experiments on superconductivity and molecular electronics and for misrepresenting data in scientific publications. Jan Hendrik Schon's work on creating tiny, powerful microprocessors seemed poised to significantly advance microprocessor technology and potentially bring yet another Nobel Prize in physics to the award-winning laboratory, a subsidiary of Lucent Technologies.[15] Hwang Woo-Suk was found to have faked some of his famous stem-cell research in which he claimed to have created thirty cloned human embryos and made stem-cell lines from skin cells of eleven people, as well as producing the world's first cloned dog. He also apologized for using eggs from his own female researchers, which was in breach of guidelines, but still denies fabricating his research.[16]

Even sports can be subject to ethical lapses. For example, Chicago Cubs player Sammy Sosa accepted a seven-game suspension for using a corked bat although he claimed it was an accident. Jimmy Johnson's crew chief, Chad Knaus, was thrown out of the Daytona 500 for illegal modifications made to Johnson's car during pole qualifying. Although Johnson finished fifth in qualifying, he had to start from the rear of the field and then went on to win the 2006 Daytona 500.[17] Additionally, several colleges and universities have been put on probation and in some cases given the "death penalty"—complete suspension of their athletic programs—for illegally recruiting or paying players.

Whether made in business, politics, science, or sports, most decisions are judged as either right or wrong, ethical or unethical. Regardless of what an individual believes about a particular action, if society judges it to be unethical or wrong, whether correctly or not, that judgment directly affects the organization's ability to achieve its business goals. For this reason alone, it is important to understand business ethics and recognize ethical issues.

The Reasons for Studying Business Ethics

Studying business ethics is valuable for several reasons. Business ethics is not merely an extension of an individual's own personal ethics. Many people believe that if a company hires good people with strong ethical values, then it will be a "good citizen" organization. But as we show throughout this text, an individual's personal values and moral philosophies are only one factor in the ethical decision-making process. True, moral rules can be applied to a variety of situations in life, and some people do not distinguish everyday ethical issues from business ones. Our concern, however, is with the application of rules and principles in the business context. Many important ethical issues do not arise very often in the business context although they remain complex moral dilemmas in one's own personal life. For example, although abortion and the possibility of human cloning are moral issues in many people's lives, they are usually not an issue in most business organizations.

Professionals in any field, including business, must deal with individuals' personal moral dilemmas because these issues affect everyone's ability to function on the job. Normally, a business does not establish rules or policies on personal ethical issues such as sex or the use of alcohol outside the workplace; indeed, in some cases, such policies would be illegal. Only when a person's preferences or values influence his or her performance on the job do an individual's ethics play a major role in the evaluation of business decisions.

Just being a good person and, in your own view, having sound personal ethics may not be sufficient to enable you to handle the ethical issues that arise in a business organization. It is important to recognize the relationship between legal and ethical decisions. Although abstract virtues linked to the high moral ground of truthfulness, honesty, fairness, and openness are often assumed to be self-evident and accepted by all employees, business-strategy decisions involve complex and detailed discussions. For example, there is considerable debate over what constitutes antitrust, deceptive advertising, and violations of the Foreign Corrupt Practices Act. A high level of personal moral development may not prevent an individual from violating the law in a complicated organizational context where even experienced lawyers debate the exact meaning of the law. Some approaches to business ethics assume that ethics training is for people whose personal moral development is unacceptable, but that is not the case. Because organizations are culturally diverse and personal values must be respected, ensuring collective agreement on organizational ethics (that is, codes reasonably capable of preventing misconduct) is as vital as any other effort an organization's management may undertake.

Many people who have limited business experience suddenly find themselves making decisions about product quality, advertising, pricing, sales techniques, hiring practices, and pollution control. The values they learned from family, religion, and school may not provide specific guidelines for these complex business decisions. In other words, a person's experiences and decisions at home, in school, and in the community may be quite different from his or her experiences and decisions at work. Many business ethics decisions are close calls. In addition managerial responsibility for the conduct of others requires knowledge of ethics and compliance processes and systems. Years of experience in a particular industry may be required to know what is acceptable. Consider the challenge faced by Harry Kraemer, the CEO of Baxter International, after fifty-three dialysis patients died during treatment in the United States, Spain, and five other countries. The dialysis filters used in each of the cases had come from a single lot manufactured by Althin Medical AB, a firm that Baxter had acquired the previous year. After investigating, Kraemer took responsibility, apologized, recalled all of Althin's dialysis filters, and ultimately decided to shut down Althin's operations, actions that cost Baxter $189 million. Kraemer later asked the company's board of directors to reduce his bonus because of the deaths. Kraemer could have made different decisions, but he put the situation in a broader context: "We have this situation. The financial people will assess the potential financial impact. The legal people will do the same. But at the end of the day, if we think it's a problem that a Baxter product was involved in the deaths of 53 people, then those other issues become pretty easy. If we don't do the right thing, then we won't be around to address those other issues."[18]

Studying business ethics will help you begin to identify ethical issues when they arise and recognize the approaches available for resolving them. You will also learn more about the ethical decision-making process and about ways to promote ethical behavior within your organization. By studying business ethics, you may begin to understand how to cope with conflicts between your own personal values and those of the organization in which you work.

THE DEVELOPMENT OF BUSINESS ETHICS

The study of business ethics in North America has evolved through five distinct stages—(1) before 1960, (2) the 1960s, (3) the 1970s, (4) the 1980s, and (5) the 1990s—and continues to evolve in the twenty-first century (see Table 1–2).

TABLE 1–2	A Timeline of Ethical and Socially Responsible Concerns			
1960s	**1970s**	**1980s**	**1990s**	**2000s**
Environmental issues	Employee militancy	Bribes and illegal contracting practices	Sweatshops and unsafe working conditions in third-world countries	Cybercrime
Civil rights issues	Human rights issues	Influence peddling	Rising corporate liability for personal damages (for example, cigarette companies)	Financial management
Increased employee–employer tension	Covering up rather than correcting issues	Deceptive advertising	Financial mismanagement and fraud	International corruption
Honesty		Financial fraud (for example, savings and loan scandal)		Loss of employee privacy
Changing work ethic		Transparency issues		Intellectual-property theft
Rising drug use				

SOURCE: "Business Ethics Timeline," *Ethics Resource Center,* http://www.ethics.org/be_timeline.html (accessed March 29, 2006). Copyright © 2006, Ethics Resource Center (ERC). Used with permission of the ERC, 1747 Pennsylvania Ave., N.W., Suite 400, Washington, DC 2006, www.ethics.org.

Before 1960: Ethics in Business

Prior to 1960, the United States went through several agonizing phases of questioning the concept of capitalism. In the 1920s, the progressive movement attempted to provide citizens with a "living wage," defined as income sufficient for education, recreation, health, and retirement. Businesses were asked to check unwarranted price increases and any other practices that would hurt a family's "living wage." In the 1930s came the New Deal, which specifically blamed business for the country's economic woes. Business was asked to work more closely with the government to raise family income. By the 1950s, the New Deal had evolved into the Fair Deal by President Harry S Truman; this program defined such matters as civil rights and environmental responsibility as ethical issues that businesses had to address.

Until 1960 ethical issues related to business were often discussed within the domain of theology or philosophy. Individual moral issues related to business were addressed in churches, synagogues, and mosques. Religious leaders raised questions about fair wages, labor practices, and the morality of capitalism. For example, Catholic social ethics, which were expressed in a series of papal encyclicals, included concern for morality in business, workers' rights, and living wages; for humanistic values rather than materialistic ones; and for improving the conditions of the poor. Some Catholic colleges and universities began to offer courses in social ethics. Protestants also developed ethics courses in their seminaries and schools of theology and addressed issues concerning morality and ethics in business. The Protestant work ethic encouraged individuals to be frugal, work hard, and attain success in the capitalistic system. Such religious traditions provided a foundation for the future field of business ethics. Each religion applied its moral concepts not only to business but also to government, politics, the family, personal life, and all other aspects of life.

The 1960s: The Rise of Social Issues in Business

During the 1960s, American society turned to causes. An antibusiness attitude developed as many critics attacked the vested interests that controlled the economic and political sides of society—the so-called military–industrial complex. The 1960s saw the decay of inner cities and the growth of ecological problems such as pollution and the disposal of toxic and nuclear wastes. This period also witnessed the rise of consumerism—activities undertaken by independent individuals, groups, and organizations to protect their rights as consumers. In 1962 President John F. Kennedy delivered a "Special Message on Protecting the Consumer Interest" in which he outlined four basic consumer rights: the right to safety, the right to be informed, the right to choose, and the right to be heard. These came to be known as the **Consumers' Bill of Rights.**

The modern consumer movement is generally considered to have begun in 1965 with the publication of Ralph Nader's *Unsafe at Any Speed,* which criticized the auto industry as a whole, and General Motors Corporation (GM) in particular, for putting profit and style ahead of lives and safety. GM's Corvair was the main target of Nader's criticism. His consumer protection organization, popularly known as Nader's Raiders, fought successfully for legislation that required automobile makers to equip cars with safety belts, padded dashboards, stronger door latches, head restraints, shatterproof windshields, and collapsible steering columns. Consumer activists also helped secure passage of several consumer protection laws such as the Wholesome Meat Act of 1967, the Radiation Control for Health and Safety Act of 1968, the Clean Water Act of 1972, and the Toxic Substance Act of 1976.[19]

After Kennedy came President Lyndon B. Johnson and the Great Society, which extended national capitalism and told the business community that the U.S. government's responsibility was to provide the citizen with some degree of economic stability, equality, and social justice. Activities that could destabilize the economy or discriminate against any class of citizens began to be viewed as unethical and unlawful.

The 1970s: Business Ethics as an Emerging Field

Business ethics began to develop as a field of study in the 1970s. Theologians and philosophers had laid the groundwork by suggesting that certain principles could be applied to business activities. Using this foundation, business professors began to teach and write about corporate **social responsibility,** an organization's obligation to maximize its positive impact on stakeholders and to minimize its negative impact. Philosophers increased their involvement, applying ethical theory and philosophical analysis to structure the discipline of business ethics. Companies became more concerned with their public images, and as social demands grew, many businesses realized that they had to address ethical issues more directly. The Nixon administration's Watergate scandal focused public interest on the importance of ethics in government. Conferences were held to discuss the social responsibilities and ethical issues of business. Centers dealing with issues of business ethics were established. Interdisciplinary meetings brought business professors, theologians, philosophers, and businesspeople together. President Jimmy Carter attempted to focus on personal and administrative efforts to uphold ethical principles in government.

The Foreign Corrupt Practices Act was passed during his administration, making it illegal for U.S. businesses to bribe government officials of other countries.

By the end of the 1970s, a number of major ethical issues had emerged, such as bribery, deceptive advertising, price collusion, product safety, and the environment. *Business ethics* became a common expression and was no longer considered an oxymoron. Academic researchers sought to identify ethical issues and describe how businesspeople might choose to act in particular situations. However, only limited efforts were made to describe how the ethical decision-making process worked and to identify the many variables that influence this process in organizations.

The 1980s: Consolidation

In the 1980s, business academics and practitioners acknowledged business ethics as a field of study. A growing and varied group of institutions with diverse interests promoted its study. Business ethics organizations grew to include thousands of members. Five hundred courses in business ethics were offered at colleges across the country, with more than forty thousand students enrolled. Centers for business ethics provided publications, courses, conferences, and seminars. Business ethics was also a prominent concern within such leading companies as General Electric, Chase Manhattan, General Motors, Atlantic Richfield, Caterpillar, and S. C. Johnson & Son, Inc. Many of these firms established ethics and social policy committees to address ethical issues.

In the 1980s, the **Defense Industry Initiative on Business Ethics and Conduct** (DII) was developed to guide corporate support for ethical conduct. In 1986 eighteen defense contractors drafted principles for guiding business ethics and conduct.[20] The organization has since grown to nearly fifty members. This effort established a method for discussing best practices and working tactics to link organizational practice and policy to successful ethical compliance. The DII includes six principles. First, DII supports codes of conduct and their widespread distribution. These codes of conduct must be understandable and provide details on more substantive areas. Second, member companies are expected to provide ethics training for their employees as well as continuous support between training periods. Third, defense contractors must create an open atmosphere in which employees feel comfortable reporting violations without fear of retribution. Fourth, companies need to perform extensive internal audits and develop effective internal reporting and voluntary disclosure plans. Fifth, DII insists that member companies preserve the integrity of the defense industry. Finally, member companies must adopt a philosophy of public accountability.[21]

The 1980s ushered in the Reagan–Bush eras, with the accompanying belief that self-regulation, rather than regulation by government, was in the public's interest. Many tariffs and trade barriers were lifted, and businesses merged and divested within an increasingly global atmosphere. Thus, while business schools were offering courses in business ethics, the rules of business were changing at a phenomenal rate because of less regulation. Corporations that once were nationally based began operating internationally and found themselves mired in value structures where accepted rules of business behavior no longer applied.

The 1990s: Institutionalization of Business Ethics

The administration of President Bill Clinton continued to support self-regulation and free trade. However, it also took unprecedented government action to deal with health-related social issues such as teenage smoking. Its proposals included restricting cigarette advertising, banning vending machine sales, and ending the use of cigarette logos in connection with sports events.[22] Clinton also appointed Arthur Levitt as chairman of the Securities and Exchange Commission in 1993. Levitt unsuccessfully pushed for many reforms that could have prevented the accounting ethics scandals exemplified by Enron and WorldCom.[23]

The **Federal Sentencing Guidelines for Organizations** (FSGO), approved by Congress in November 1991, set the tone for organizational ethical compliance programs in the 1990s. The guidelines, which were based on the six principles of the DII,[24] broke new ground by codifying into law incentives to reward organizations for taking action to prevent misconduct such as developing effective internal legal and ethical compliance programs.[25] Provisions in the guidelines mitigate penalties for businesses that strive to root out misconduct and establish high ethical and legal standards.[26] On the other hand, under FSGO, if a company lacks an effective ethical compliance program and its employees violate the law, it can incur severe penalties. The guidelines focus on firms taking action to prevent and detect business misconduct in cooperation with government regulation. At the heart of the FSGO is the carrot-and-stick approach: By taking preventive action against misconduct, a company may avoid onerous penalties should a violation occur. A mechanical approach using legalistic logic will not suffice to avert serious penalties. The company must develop corporate values, enforce its own code of ethics, and strive to prevent misconduct.

The Twenty-First Century: A New Focus on Business Ethics

Although business ethics appeared to become more institutionalized in the 1990s, new evidence emerged in the early 2000s that more than a few business executives and managers had not fully embraced the public's desire for high ethical standards. For example, Dennis Kozlowski, former CEO of Tyco, was indicted on thirty-eight counts of misappropriating $170 million of Tyco funds and netting $430 million from improper sales of stock. Kozlowski, who pleaded not guilty to the charges, allegedly used the funds to purchase many personal luxuries, including a $15 million vintage yacht and a $3.9 million Renoir painting and to throw a $2 million party for his wife's birthday.[27] Arthur Andersen, a "Big Five" accounting firm, was convicted of obstructing justice after shredding documents related to its role as Enron's auditor.[28] The reputation of the once venerable accounting firm disappeared over night, along with most of its clients, and the firm ultimately went out of business. Later the Supreme Court overruled the Arthur Andersen obstruction-of-justice conviction, but it was too late for the firm to recover. In addition to problems with its auditing of Enron, Arthur Andersen also faced questions surrounding its audits of other companies that were charged with employing questionable accounting practices, including Halliburton, WorldCom, Global Crossing, Dynegy, Qwest, and Sunbeam.[29] These accounting scandals made it evident that falsifying financial reports and reaping questionable benefits had become part of the culture of many companies. Firms outside the United States, such as Royal Ahold in the Netherlands and Parmalat in Italy, became major examples of accounting misconduct from a global perspective.

Such abuses increased public and political demands to improve ethical standards in business. In a survey of twenty thousand people across twenty countries, trust in global companies has declined significantly.[30] To address the loss of confidence in financial reporting and corporate ethics, Congress in 2002 passed the **Sarbanes–Oxley Act,** the most far-reaching change in organizational control and accounting regulations since the Securities and Exchange Act of 1934. The new law made securities fraud a criminal offense and stiffened penalties for corporate fraud. It also created an accounting oversight board that requires corporations to establish codes of ethics for financial reporting and to develop greater transparency in financial reports to investors and other interested parties. Additionally, the law requires top executives to sign off on their firms' financial reports, and they risk fines and long prison sentences if they misrepresent their companies' financial position. The legislation further requires company executives to disclose stock sales immediately and prohibits companies from giving loans to top managers.[31]

The 2004 amendment to the FSGO requires that a business's governing authority be well informed about its ethics program with respect to content, implementation, and effectiveness. This places the responsibility squarely on the shoulders of the firm's leadership, usually the board of directors. The board is required to oversee the discovery of risks and to design, implement, and modify approaches to deal with those risks.

The Sarbanes–Oxley Act and the FSGO have institutionalized the need to discover and address ethical and legal risk. Top management and the board of directors of a corporation are accountable for discovering risk associated with ethical conduct. Such specific industries as the public sector, energy and chemicals, health care, insurance, and retail have to discover the unique risk associated with their operations and develop an ethics program to prevent ethical misconduct before it creates a crisis. Most firms are developing formal and informal mechanisms to have interactive communication and transparency about issues associated with the risk of misconduct. Business leaders should view that their greatest danger is not discovering serious misconduct or illegal activities somewhere in the organization. Unfortunately most managers do not view the risk of an ethical disaster as important as risk associated with fires, natural disasters, or technology failure. Ethical disasters can be significantly more damaging to a company's reputation than risks that are managed through insurance and other methods. As Warren Buffett said in his interview in May of 2005 on Public Broadcasting Corporation's *Business Nightly News,* "We have 180,000 employees, we know there is somebody doing something wrong today, we just hope it's small and that we catch it. But that is going to happen in any large organization."

In the KPMG Forensic Integrity Survey, employees were asked whether they had "personally seen" or had "firsthand knowledge of" misconduct within their organizations over the prior twelve-month period. Roughly three-quarters of employees— 74 percent—reported that they had observed misconduct in the prior twelve-month period. Figure 1–2 shows the results of misconduct by industry; there are generally high levels of observed misconduct across all industries. Employees in highly regulated financial industries, such as banking, finance, and insurance, reported relatively lower rates of misconduct within their organizations compared with others. While

| **FIGURE 1–2** | Prevalence of Misconduct by Industry During the Prior Twelve Months |

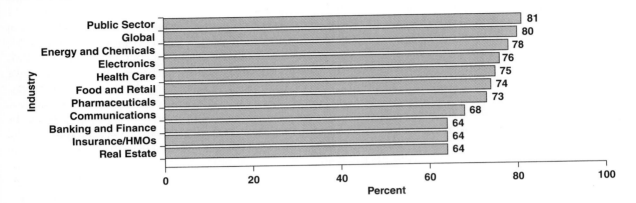

SOURCE: Copyright © 2006 KPMG International. KPMG International is a Swiss Cooperative that serves as a co-ordinating entity for a network of independent firms operating under the KPMG name. KPMG International provides no services to clients. All rights reserved. KPMG Forensic Integrity Survey 2005–2006 from http://www.kpmginsiders.com/display_analysis.asp?cs_id=148597 (accessed March 9, 2006).

employees working in the public sector, which has not been subject to many of the new regulatory mandates placed on its private-sector counterparts, reported relatively higher rates of misconduct compared with others.

DEVELOPING AN ORGANIZATIONAL AND GLOBAL ETHICAL CULTURE

The current trend is away from legally based compliance initiatives in organizations to cultural initiatives that make ethics a part of core organizational values. To develop more ethical corporate cultures, many businesses are communicating core values to their employees by creating ethics programs and appointing ethics officers to oversee them. The ethical component of a corporate culture relates to the values, beliefs, and established and enforced patterns of conduct that employees use to identify and respond to ethical issues. The term **ethical culture** can be viewed as the character or decision-making process that employees use to determine whether their responses to ethical issues are right or wrong. Ethical culture is used to describe the component of corporate culture that captures the rules and principles that an organization defines as appropriate conduct. The goal of an ethical culture is to minimize the need for enforced compliance of rules and maximize principles that contribute to ethical reasoning in difficult or new situations. An ethical culture creates shared values and support for ethical decisions and is driven by top management.

The New York Stock Exchange, for example, requires all member companies to have codes of ethics. Many firms now have ethics officers, and some firms, including UPS, Raytheon, and Baxter International, take ethics seriously enough to have their ethics officers report directly to senior management or boards of directors. The growth of the Ethics and Compliance Officer Association (ECOA) to over twelve hundred members, representing nearly every industry, to include more than 62 percent of the Fortune 100 and conducting business in over 160 countries, highlights the increasing importance of this position in business today.[32] The organization offers an intensive week-long course, Managing Ethics in Organizations, which provides practical knowledge, the fundamental theories, and general skills needed by prospective and recently appointed ethics and compliance officers and others who have responsibilities for their organization's ethics, compliance, or business conduct programs. They also offer a leadership seminar designed to examine the essential linkage between leadership, ethics, and corporate culture.[33] Most misconduct comes from employees trying to attain the performance objectives of the firm. Consider oil traders at Royal Dutch Shell who created fictitious sales that eliminated price competition and market risk for their companies. Houston-based Shell Trading U.S. Company and London-based Shell International Trading and Shipping Company trades violated futures trading rules on the New York Mercantile Exchange and resulted in a combined $300,000 in fines.[34]

Globally, businesses are working more closely together to establish standards of acceptable behavior. We are already seeing collaborative efforts by a range of organizations to establish goals and mandate minimum levels of ethical behavior, from the European Union, the North American Free Trade Agreement (NAFTA), the Common Market of the Southern Cone (MERCOSUR), and the World Trade Organization (WTO) to, more recently, the Council on Economic Priorities' Social Accountability 8000 (SA 8000), the Ethical Trading Initiative, and the U.S. Apparel Industry Partnership. Some companies will not do business with organizations that do not support and abide by these standards. The development of global codes of ethics, such as the Caux Round Table, highlights common ethical concerns for global firms. The Caux Round Table (www.cauxroundtable.org) is a group of businesses, political leaders, and concerned interest groups that desire responsible behavior in the global community.

THE BENEFITS OF BUSINESS ETHICS

The field of business ethics continues to change rapidly as more firms recognize the benefits of improving ethical conduct and the link between business ethics and financial performance. Both research and examples from the business world demonstrate that building an ethical reputation among employees, customers, and the general public pays off. Figure 1–3 provides an overview of the relationship between business ethics and organizational performance. Although we believe there are many practical benefits to being ethical, many businesspeople make decisions because they believe a particular course of action is simply the right thing to do as a responsible member of society. For example, after a small Massachusetts textile plant owned by Malden Mills burned to the ground, Malden Mills' CEO, Aaron Feuerstein, could have opted to close the plant in favor of moving the work to an overseas facility with lower wages, just as many of his competitors had already done. However, he recognized the negative impact that such a decision would have had on the plant's employees as well as the community. Thus, he chose not only to rebuild the plant but also to continue to pay its three thousand workers for ninety days while the plant was being rebuilt.[35]

FIGURE 1–3	The Role of Organizational Ethics in Performance

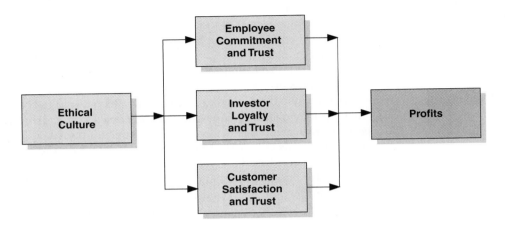

Texas Instruments, which has always been a company very concerned about ethics and ranked tenth on *Business Ethics* magazine's "100 Best Corporate Citizens" in 2006, proposed a challenge to its design team. If the team could find a way to build the new factory for $180 million less than the last Dallas factory built in the late 1990s, then Texas Instruments would locate in Dallas. The design team managed it by designing the new building with two floors, not three, and with a design that is expected to cut utility costs by 20 percent and water usage by 35 percent.[36]

Among the rewards for being more ethical and socially responsible in business are increased efficiency in daily operations, greater employee commitment, increased investor willingness to entrust funds, improved customer trust and satisfaction, and better financial performance. The reputation of a company has a major effect on its relationships with employees, investors, customers, and many other parties.

Ethics Contributes to Employee Commitment

Employee commitment comes from employees who believe their future is tied to that of the organization and their willingness to make personal sacrifices for the organization.[37] The more a company is dedicated to taking care of its employees, the more likely it is that the employees will take care of the organization. The NBES survey indicates that 79 percent of employees agree that ethics is important in continuing to work for their employer. It is also interesting to note that approximately 20 percent of employees are *not* concerned about the ethical environment of their organization.[38] This group is very complacent and has the potential for misconduct without guidance and ethical leadership. Issues that may foster the development of an ethical culture for employees include the absence of abusive behavior, a safe work environment, competitive salaries, and the fulfillment of all contractual obligations toward employees. An ethics and compliance program can support values and appropriate conduct. Social programs that may improve the ethical culture range from work–family programs and stock ownership plans to community service. Home Depot associates, for example, participate in disaster-relief efforts after hurricanes and tornadoes by rebuilding roofs, repairing water damage, planting trees, and clearing roads in their communities. Because employees spend a considerable amount of their waking time at work, a commitment by the organization to goodwill and respect for its employees usually increases the employees' loyalty to the organization and their support of its objectives. Companies like Wal-Mart responded in the wake of Hurricane Katrina not only to try to improve their image among customers and associates but also to help the community in which they operate. Wal-Mart also donated more than $15 million to relief efforts. They also established mini-Wal-Mart stores in areas impacted by the hurricane where such items as clothing, diapers, baby wipes, food, formula, toothbrushes, bedding, and water were given out free of charge to those with a demonstrated need.[39]

Employees' perception that their firm has an ethical culture leads to performance-enhancing outcomes within the organization.[40] For the sake of both productivity and teamwork, it is essential that employees both within and between departments throughout the organization share a common vision of trust. The influence of higher levels of trust is greatest on relationships within departments or work groups, but trust is a significant factor in relationships between departments as well. Consequently, programs that create a work environment that is trustworthy make individuals more willing to rely and act on the decisions and actions of their coworkers. In such a work environment, employees can reasonably expect to be treated with full respect and consideration by their coworkers and superiors. Trusting relationships between upper management and managers and their subordinates contribute to greater decision-making efficiencies. One survey found that when employees see values such as honesty, respect, and trust applied frequently in the workplace, they feel less pressure to compromise ethical standards, observe less misconduct, are more satisfied with their organizations overall, and feel more valued as employees.[41]

The ethical culture of a company seems to matter to employees. According to a report on employee loyalty and work practices, companies viewed as highly ethical by their employees were six times more likely to keep their workers.[42] Also, employees who view their company as having a strong community involvement feel more loyal to their employers and feel positive about themselves.

Ethics Contributes to Investor Loyalty

Employee commitment also helps a firm's reputation among other constituents. Companies perceived by their employees as having a high degree of honesty and integrity had an average three-year total return to shareholders of 101 percent, whereas companies perceived as having a low degree of honesty and integrity had a three-year total return to shareholders of just 69 percent.[43] Investors today are increasingly concerned about the ethics, social responsibility, and reputation of companies in which they invest, and various socially responsible mutual funds and asset management firms can help investors purchase stock in ethical companies. Investors are also recognizing that an ethical culture provides a foundation for efficiency, productivity, and profits. On the other hand, investors know too that negative publicity, lawsuits, and fines can lower stock prices, diminish customer loyalty, and threaten a company's long-term viability. Many companies accused of misconduct, including Global Crossing, Adelphia, FreddieMac, and HealthSouth, have experienced dramatic declines in the value of their stock when concerned investors divested their stocks and bonds. TIAA-CREF investor participants were asked would they choose a financial services company with strong ethics or higher returns? Surprisingly 92 percent of respondents said they would choose ethics while only 5 percent chose higher returns.[44]

To be successful, relationships with investors must rest on dependability, trust, and commitment. Investors look at the bottom line for profits or the potential for increased stock prices or dividends. But they also look for any potential flaws in the company's performance, conduct, and financial reports. Thus, many executives spend considerable time communicating with investors about their firms' reputation and financial performance and trying to attract them to the company's stock. The issue of drawing and keeping investors is a critical one for CEOs because roughly 50 percent of investors sell their stock in companies within one year, and the average household replaces 80 percent of its common stock portfolio each year.[45] Therefore, gaining investors' trust and confidence is vital to sustaining the financial stability of the firm.

Ethics Contributes to Customer Satisfaction

It is generally accepted that customer satisfaction is one of the most important factors in successful business strategy. Although a company must continue to develop, alter, and adapt products to keep pace with customers' changing desires and preferences, it must also seek to develop long-term relationships with customers and its stakeholders. While Wal-Mart has focused on low prices for customers, today there are questions about who might be hurt by Wal-Mart's quest to maintain the lowest prices possible. Nearly four in ten Americans have an unfavorable opinion of Wal-Mart today. Wal-Mart's reputation has dropped rapidly as the mass media has reported low benefits to employees, environmental issues, and ethical issues in top management. In addition, there are concerns that Wal-Mart is outsourcing American jobs to China by forcing their suppliers to move manufacturing overseas.[46] For most businesses, both repeat purchases and an enduring relationship of mutual respect and cooperation with their customers are essential for success. By focusing on customer satisfaction, a company continually deepens the customer's dependence on the company, and as the customer's confidence grows, the firm gains a better understanding of how to serve the customer so the relationship may endure. Successful businesses provide an opportunity for customer feedback, which can engage the customer in cooperative problem solving. As is often pointed out, a happy customer will come back, but a disgruntled customer will tell others about his or her dissatisfaction with a company and discourage friends from dealing with it.

The public's trust is essential to maintaining a good long-term relationship between a business and consumers. The Millennium Poll of twenty-five thousand citizens in twenty-three countries found that almost 60 percent of people focus on social responsibility ahead of brand reputation or financial factors when forming impressions of companies.[47] As social responsibility becomes more important for companies, it has been suggested that corporate social responsibility is a sign of good management and that it may, according to one study, indicate good financial performance. However, another study indicates that the reverse may be true, that companies who have good financial performance are able to spend more money on social responsibility.[48] For example, after the *Exxon Valdez* oil spill, special-interest groups and individual citizens boycotted the company. Before Chicken of the Sea and many of its competitors adopted dolphin-friendly nets to catch tuna, many consumers refused to buy tuna. Moreover, consumers may avoid the products of companies that are perceived as treating their employees unfairly. For example, Wal-Mart has been facing increasing pressure from customers and employees regarding how it treats its employees. As a direct result, it has increased the health–benefits that it offers its part-time workers.[49] Companies that subcontract manufacturing operations abroad have had to confront the ethical issues associated with supporting facilities that abuse or underpay their work force—sometimes called "sweatshops." The Gap, the number-one U.S. clothing chain, and Nike, the world's largest maker of athletic shoes, suspended orders at June Textiles Company, a Cambodian garment factory, after learning that the British Broadcasting Corporation planned to air a program alleging use of child labor at the factory.[50] Because of a large amount of negative publicity about how they operated abroad, Nike completely changed the way that it operated. Nike now has a complete website devoted to responsibility, which includes a section on workers and factories and their evolving approach, as well as the code of conduct for their factories and employees. They also have improved their monitoring and assessment of factories abroad.[51] New industry codes of conduct, such as SA 8000 (www.sa-intl.org) mentioned earlier, have been established to help companies identify and address these ethical issues. When consumers learn about abuses in subcontracting, they may boycott the companies' products.

When an organization has a strong ethical environment, it usually focuses on the core value of placing customers' interests first.[52] Putting customers first does not mean that the interests of employees, investors, and local communities should be ignored, however. An ethical culture that focuses on customers incorporates the interests of all employees, suppliers, and other interested parties in decisions and actions. Employees working in an ethical environment support and contribute to the process of understanding customers' demands and concerns. Ethical conduct toward customers builds a strong competitive position that has been shown to affect business performance and product innovation positively.[53]

Ethics Contributes to Profits

A company cannot nurture and develop an ethical culture unless it has achieved adequate financial performance in terms of profits. Businesses with greater resources—regardless of their staff size—have the means to practice social responsibility while serving their customers, valuing their employees, and establishing trust with the public. Many studies have found a positive relationship between corporate social responsibility and business performance.[54] Companies convicted of misconduct experience a significantly lower return on assets and on sales than firms that have not faced such charges. Research indicates that the negative effect on return on sales does not appear until the third year following the conviction, and multiple convictions are more harmful than a single one.[55]

There are many examples of companies that have experienced significant performance declines after the disclosure of their failure to act responsibly toward various stakeholders. Although HealthSouth Corporation's CEO Richard Scrushy was acquitted of participating in a $2.7 billion accounting fraud, but later convicted of bribery in a state court, many of his executives plea-bargained deals with the government for more lenient sentences. Moreover, the resulting damage to the firm's reputation was a disaster, and their only means of distancing themselves from their former leader was to provide the following comment on the company's website:

> As HealthSouth continues its unprecedented recovery from a massive fraud that occurred during the tenure of Richard Scrushy as CEO and Chairman, it is astonishing that he would have the audacity and shamelessness to comment on the current operations or the dedication of our approximately 40,000 employees. As we have stated in the past, Scrushy will not be offered any position within the Company by this management team or this Board of Directors. Under no circumstances would we reach out to Scrushy, who by his own defense has claimed a complete lack of knowledge as to the financial workings of the Company during his tenure as CEO and Chairman, despite his claims of possessing valuable expertise.[56]

Another example is Columbia/HCA that experienced serious declines in stock prices and earnings after the revelation that it was systematically overcharging the government for Medicare services. Employees and customers also lodged complaints against the hospital chain for putting profits ahead of their interests. Employees alleged that they were forced to do jobs beyond their abilities, and many patients accused the company of charging them for services they did not need or transferring them to other facilities if questions arose about their ability to pay. Once Columbia/HCA's misconduct became public knowledge, its reputation was damaged within a few months.[57] Every day, business newspapers and magazines offer new examples of the consequences of business misconduct. It is also worth noting, however, that most of these companies have learned from their mistakes and recovered after they implemented programs to improve ethical and legal conduct. For example, Columbia/HCA, now renamed HCA—The Healthcare Company—has become a role model for organizational ethics programs in the health-care industry.

Ample evidence shows that being ethical pays off with better performance. As indicated earlier, companies that are perceived by their employees as having a high degree of honesty and integrity had a much higher average total return to shareholders than did companies perceived as having a low degree of honesty and integrity.[58] A study of the five hundred largest public corporations in the United States found that those that commit to ethical behavior or emphasize compliance with their code of conduct have better financial performance.[59] These results provide strong evidence that corporate concern for ethical conduct is becoming a part of strategic planning toward obtaining the outcome of higher profitability. Rather than being just a compliance program, ethics is becoming one of the management issues within the effort to achieve competitive advantage.

OUR FRAMEWORK FOR STUDYING BUSINESS ETHICS

We have developed a framework for this text to help you understand how people make ethical decisions and deal with ethical issues. Table 1–3 summarizes each element in the framework and describes where each topic is discussed in this book.

TABLE 1–3	Our Framework for Studying Business Ethics

Chapter	Highlights
1. The Importance of Business Ethics	• Definitions • Reasons for studying business ethics • History • Benefits of business ethics
2. Stakeholder Relationships, Social Responsibility, and Corporate Governance	• Stakeholder relationships • Stakeholder influences in social responsibility • Corporate governance
3. Emerging Business Ethics Issues	• Recognizing an ethical issue • Honesty, fairness, and integrity • Ethical issues and dilemmas in business: abusive and disruptive behavior, lying, conflicts of interest, bribery, corporate intelligence, discrimination, sexual harassment, environmental issues, fraud, insider trading, intellectual-property rights, and privacy • Determining an ethical issue in business
4. The Institutionalization of Business Ethics	• Mandatory requirements • Voluntary requirements • Core practices • Federal Sentencing Guidelines for Organizations • Sarbanes–Oxley Act
5. Understanding the Ethical Decision-Making Process	• Ethical issue intensity • Individual factors in decision making • Organizational factors in decision making • Opportunity in decision making • Business ethics evaluations and intentions • The role of leadership in a corporate culture • Leadership styles influence ethical decisions • Habits of strong ethical leaders
6. Individual Factors: Moral Philosophies and Values	• Moral philosophies, including teleological; philosophies; and cognitive moral deontological, relativist, virtue ethics, and justice philosophies • Stages of cognitive moral development
7. Organizational Factors: Corporate Culture and Relationships	• Corporate culture • Interpersonal relationships • Whistle-blowing • Opportunity and conflict
8. Developing an Effective Ethics Program	• Ethics programs • Codes of ethics • Program responsibility • Communication of ethical standards • Systems to monitor and enforce ethical standards • Continuous improvement of ethics programs
9. Implementing and Auditing Ethics	• Implementation programs • Ethics audits
10. Business Ethics in a Global Economy	• Ethical perceptions economy • Culture and cultural relations • Multinational corporations • Universal ethics • Global ethics issues

In Part One, we provide an overview of business ethics. Chapter 1 defines the term *business ethics* and explores the development and importance of this critical business area. In Chapter 2, we explore the role of various stakeholder groups in social responsibility and corporate governance.

Part Two focuses on ethical issues and the institutionalization of business ethics. In Chapter 3, we examine business issues that create ethical decision making in organizations. In Chapter 4, we look at the institutionalization of business ethics including both mandatory and voluntary societal concerns.

In Part Three, we delineate the ethical decision-making process and then look at both individual factors and organizational factors that influence decisions. Chapter 5 describes the ethical decision-making process from an organizational perspective. Chapter 6 explores individual factors that may influence ethical decisions in business, including moral philosophies and cognitive moral development. Chapter 7 focuses on the organizational dimensions including corporate culture, relationships, and conflicts.

In Part Four, we explore systems and processes associated with implementing business ethics into global strategic planning. Chapter 8 discusses the development of an effective ethics program. In Chapter 9, we examine issues related to implementing and auditing ethics programs. And finally, Chapter 10 considers ethical issues in a global context.

We hope that this framework will help you to develop a balanced understanding of the various perspectives and alternatives available to you when making ethical business decisions. Regardless of your own personal values, the more you know about how individuals make decisions, the better prepared you will be to cope with difficult ethical decisions. Such knowledge will help you improve and control the ethical decision-making environment in which you work.

It is your job to make the final decision in an ethical situation that affects you. Sometimes that decision may be right; sometimes it may be wrong. It is always easy to look back with hindsight and know what one should have done in a particular situation. At the time, however, the choices might not have been so clear. To give you practice making ethical decisions, Part Five of this book contains a number of cases. In addition, each chapter begins with a vignette, "An Ethical Dilemma," and ends with a minicase, "A Real-Life Situation," that involves ethical problems. We hope they will give you a better sense of the challenges of making ethical decisions in the real business world.

SUMMARY

This chapter provides an overview of the field of business ethics and introduces the framework for the discussion of business ethics. Business ethics comprises principles and standards that guide behavior in the world of business. Investors, employees, customers, interest groups, the legal system, and the community often determine whether a specific action is right or wrong, ethical or unethical.

Studying business ethics is important for many reasons. Recent incidents of unethical activity in business underscore the widespread need for a better understanding of the factors that contribute to ethical and unethical decisions. Individuals' personal moral philosophies and decision-making experience may not be sufficient to guide them in the business world. Studying business ethics will help you begin to identify ethical issues and recognize the approaches available to resolve them.

The study of business ethics evolved through five distinct stages. Before 1960, business ethics issues were discussed primarily from a religious perspective. The 1960s saw the emergence of many social issues involving business and the idea of social conscience as well as a rise in consumerism, which culminated with Kennedy's Consumers' Bill of Rights. Business ethics began to develop as an independent field of study in the 1970s, with academics and practitioners exploring ethical issues and attempting to understand how individuals and organizations make ethical decisions. These experts began to teach and write about the idea of corporate social responsibility, an organization's obligation to maximize its positive impact on stakeholders and to minimize its negative impact. In the 1980s, centers of business ethics provided publications, courses, conferences, and seminars, and many companies established ethics committees and social policy committees. The Defense Industry Initiative on Business Ethics and Conduct was developed to guide corporate support for ethical conduct; its principles had a major impact on corporate ethics.

However, less government regulation and an increase in businesses with international operations raised new ethical issues. In the 1990s, government continued to support self-regulation. The FSGO sets the tone for organizational ethics programs by providing incentives for companies to take action to prevent organizational misconduct. The twenty-first century ushered in a new set of ethics scandals, suggesting that many companies had not fully embraced the public's desire for higher ethical standards. The Sarbanes–Oxley Act therefore stiffened penalties for corporate fraud and established an accounting oversight board. The current trend is away from legally based ethical initiatives in organizations toward cultural initiatives that make ethics a part of core organizational values. The ethical component of a corporate culture relates to the values, beliefs, and established and enforced patterns of conduct that employees use to identify and respond to ethical issues. The term *ethical culture* describes the component of corporate culture that captures the rules and principles that an organization defines as appropriate conduct. It can be viewed as the character or decision-making process that employees use to determine whether their responses to ethical issues are right or wrong.

Research and anecdotes demonstrate that building an ethical reputation among employees, customers, and the general public provides benefits that include increased efficiency in daily operations, greater employee commitment, increased investor willingness to entrust funds, improved customer trust and satisfaction, and better financial performance. The reputation of a company has a major effect on its relationships with employees, investors, customers, and many other parties and thus has the potential to affect its bottom line.

Finally, this text introduces a framework for studying business ethics. Each chapter addresses some aspect of business ethics and decision making within a business context. The major concerns are ethical issues in business, stakeholder relationships, social responsibility and corporate governance, emerging business ethics issues, the institutionalization of business ethics, understanding the ethical decision-making process, moral philosophies and cognitive moral development, corporate culture, organizational relationships and conflicts, developing an effective ethics program, implementing and auditing the ethics program, and global business ethics.

A REAL-LIFE SITUATION*

Frank Garcia was just starting out as a salesman with Acme Corporation. Acme's corporate culture was top-down, or hierarchical. Because of the competitive nature of the medical-supplies industry, few mistakes were tolerated. Otis Hillman was a buyer for Thermocare, a national hospital chain. Frank's first meeting with Otis was a success, resulting in a $500,000 contract. This sale represented a significant increase for Acme and an additional $1000 bonus for Frank.

Some months later, Frank called on Thermocare, seeking to increase the contract by $500,000. "Otis, I think you'll need the additional inventory. It looks as if you didn't have enough at the end of last quarter," said Frank.

"You may be right. Business has picked up. Maybe it's because of your product, but then again, maybe not. It's still not clear to me whether Acme is the best for us. Speaking of which, I heard that you have season tickets to the Cubs!" replied Otis.

Frank thought for a moment and said, "Otis, I know that part of your increases are due to our quality products. How about we discuss this over a ball game?"

"Well, OK," Otis agreed.

By the seventh-inning stretch, Frank had convinced Otis that the additional inventory was needed and offered to give Thermocare a pair of season tickets. When Frank's boss, Amber, heard of the sale, she was very pleased. "Frank, this is great. We've been trying to get Thermocare's business for a long time. You seem to have connected with their buyer." As a result of the Thermocare account, Frank received an-

other large bonus check and a letter of achievement from the vice president of marketing.

Two quarters later, Frank had become one of the top producers in the division. At the beginning of the quarter, Frank had run the numbers on Thermocare's account and found that business was booming. The numbers showed that Otis's business could probably handle an additional $750,000 worth of goods without hurting return on assets. As Frank went over the figures with Otis, Otis's response was, "You know, Frank, I've really enjoyed the season tickets, but this is a big increase." As the conversation meandered, Frank soon found out that Otis and his wife had never been to Cancun, Mexico. Frank had never been in a situation like this before, so he excused himself to another room and called Amber about what he was thinking of doing.

"Are you kidding!" responded Amber. "Why are you even calling me on this? I'll find the money somewhere to pay for it."

"Is this OK with Acme?" asked Frank.

"You let me worry about that," Amber told him.

When Frank suggested that Otis and his wife be his guests in Cancun, the conversation seemed to go smoothly. In Cancun, Otis decided to purchase the additional goods, for which Frank received another bonus increase and another positive letter from headquarters.

Some time later, Amber announced to her division that they would be taking all of their best clients to Las Vegas for a thank-you party. One of those invited was Thermocare. When they arrived, Amber gave each person $500 and said, "I want you to know that Acme is very grateful for the business that you have provided us. As a result of your understanding the qualitative differences of our products, we have doubled our production facilities. This trip and everything that goes with it for the next few days is our small way of saying thank you. Every one of you has your salesperson here. If there is anything that you need, please let him or her know, and we'll try to accommodate you. Have a good time!"

That night Otis had seen Frank at dinner and suggested to him that he was interested in attending an "adult entertainment" club. When Frank came to Amber about this, she said, "Is he asking you to go with him?"

"No, Amber, not me!"

"Well, then, if he's not asking you to go, I don't understand why you're talking to me. Didn't I say we'd take care of their needs?"

"But what will Acme say if this gets out?" asked Frank.

"Don't worry; it won't," said Amber.

QUESTIONS • EXERCISES

1. What are the potential ethical issues faced by the Acme Corporation?
2. What should Acme do if there is a desire to make ethics a part of its core organizational values?
3. Identify the ethical issues of which Frank needs to be aware.
4. Discuss the advantages and disadvantages of each decision that Frank could make.

*This case is strictly hypothetical; any resemblance to real persons, companies, or situations is coincidental.

CHECK YOUR EQ

Check your EQ, or Ethics Quotient, by completing the following. Assess your performance to evaluate your overall understanding of the chapter material.

1.	Business ethics focuses mostly on personal ethical issues.	Yes	No
2.	Business ethics deals with right or wrong behavior within a particular organization.	Yes	No
3.	The 1990s could be characterized as the period when ethics programs were greatly influenced by government legislation.	Yes	No
4.	Business ethics contributes to investor loyalty.	Yes	No
5.	The trend is away from cultural or ethically based initiatives to legal initiatives in organizations.	Yes	No

ANSWERS: 1. No. Business ethics focuses on organizational concerns (legal and ethical—employees, customers, suppliers, society). 2. Yes. That stems from the basic definition. 3. Yes. The impact of the FSGO means that the 1990s are seen as the period in which business ethics were institutionalized. 4. Yes. Many studies have shown that trust and ethical conduct contribute to investor loyalty. 5. No. Many businesses are communicating their core values to their employees by creating ethics programs and appointing ethics officers to oversee them.

CHAPTER 2

Stakeholder Relationships, Social Responsibility, and Corporate Governance

CHAPTER OBJECTIVES

- To identify stakeholders' roles in business ethics
- To define social responsibility
- To examine the relationship between stakeholder orientation and social responsibility
- To delineate a stakeholder orientation in creating corporate social responsibility
- To explore the role of corporate governance in structuring ethics and social responsibility in business
- To list the steps involved in implementing a stakeholder perspective in social responsibility and business ethics

CHAPTER OUTLINE

Carla knew something was wrong when Jack got back to his desk. He had been with Aker & Aker Accounting (A&A) for seventeen years, starting there right after graduation and progressing through the ranks. Jack was a strong supporter of the company, and that was why Carla had been assigned to him. Carla had been with A&A for two years. She had graduated in the top 10 percent of her class and passed the CPA exam on the first try. She had chosen A&A over one of the "Big Five" firms because A&A was the biggest and best firm in Smallville, Ohio, where her husband, Frank, managed a locally owned machine tools company. She and Frank had just purchased a new home when things started to turn strange with Jack, her boss.

"What's the matter, Jack?" Carla asked.

"Well, you'll hear about it sooner or later. I've been denied a partner's position. Can you imagine that? I have been working sixty- and seventy-hour weeks for the last ten years, and all that management can say to me is 'not at this time,'" complained Jack.

Carla asked, "So what else did they say?"

Jack turned red and blurted out, "They said maybe in a few more years. I've done all that they've asked me to do. I've sacrificed a lot, and now they say a few more years. It's not fair."

"What are you going to do?" Carla asked.

"I don't know," Jack said. "I just don't know."

Six months later, Carla noticed that Jack was behaving oddly. He came in late and left early. One Sunday Carla went into the office for some files and found Jack copying some of the software that A&A used in auditing and consulting. A couple of weeks later, at a dinner party, Carla overheard a conversation about Jack doing consulting work for some small firms. Monday morning, she asked him if what she had heard was true.

Jack responded, "Yes, Carla, it's true. I have a few clients that I do work for on occasion."

"Don't you think there's a conflict of interest between you and A&A?" asked Carla.

"No," said Jack. "You see, these clients are not technically within the market area of A&A. Besides, I was counting on that promotion to help pay some extra bills. My oldest son decided to go to a private university, which is an extra $25,000 each year. Plus

our medical plan at A&A doesn't cover some of my medical problems. And you don't want to know the cost. The only way I can afford to pay for these things is to do some extra work on the side."

"But what if A&A finds out?" Carla asked. "Won't they terminate you?"

"I don't want to think about that. Besides, if they don't find out for another six months, I may be able to start my own company."

"How?" asked Carla.

"Don't be naive, Carla. You came in that Sunday. You know."

Carla realized that Jack had been using A&A software for his own gain. "That's stealing!" she said.

"Stealing?" Jack's voice grew calm. "Like when you use the office phones for personal long-distance calls? Like when you decided to volunteer to help out your church and copied all those things for them on the company machine? If I'm stealing, you're a thief as well. But let's not get into this discussion. I'm not hurting A&A and, who knows, maybe within the next year I'll become a partner and can quit my night job."

Carla backed off from the discussion and said nothing more. She couldn't afford to antagonize her boss and risk bad performance ratings. She and Frank had bills, too. She also knew that she wouldn't be able to get another job at the same pay if she quit. Moving to another town was not an option because of Frank's business. She had no physical evidence to take to the partners, which meant that it would be her word against Jack's, and he had seventeen years of experience with the company.

QUESTIONS • EXERCISES

1. Identify the ethical issues in this case.
2. Assume you are Carla. Discuss your options and what the consequences of each option might be.
3. Assume you are Jack. Discuss your options.
4. Discuss any additional information you feel you might need before making your decision.

*This case is strictly hypothetical; any resemblance to real persons, companies, or situations is coincidental.

Business ethics issues, conflicts, and successes revolve around relationships. Building effective relationships is considered one of the more important areas of business today. A business exists because of relationships between employees, customers, shareholders or investors, suppliers, and managers who develop strategies to attain success. In addition, an organization usually has a governing authority often called a board of directors that provides oversight and direction to make sure that the organization stays focused on objectives in an ethical, legal, and socially acceptable manner. When unethical acts are discovered in organizations, it is often found that in most instances there is knowing cooperation or compliancy that facilitates the acceptance and perpetuation of unethical conduct.[1] Therefore, relationships are not only associated with organizational success but also with organizational misconduct.

A stakeholder framework helps identify the internal stakeholders such as employees, boards of directors, and managers and external stakeholders such as customers, special-interest groups, regulators, and others who agree, collaborate, and have confrontations on ethical issues. Most ethical issues exist because of conflicts in values and belief patterns about right and wrong between and within stakeholder groups. This framework allows a firm to identify, monitor, and respond to the needs, values, and expectations of different stakeholder groups.

The formal system of accountability and control of ethical and socially responsible behavior is corporate governance. In theory, the board of directors provides oversight for all decisions and use of resources. Ethical issues relate to role of the board of directors, shareholder relationship, internal control, risk management, and executive compensation. Ethical leadership is associated with appropriate corporate governance.

In this chapter, we first focus on the concept of stakeholders and examine how a stakeholder framework can help understand organizational ethics. Then we identify stakeholders and the importance of a stakeholder orientation. Using the stakeholder framework, social responsibility is explored, including the various dimensions of social responsibility. Next, corporate governance as a dimension of social responsibility and ethical decision making is covered to provide an understanding of the importance of oversight in responding to stakeholders. Finally, we provide the steps for implementing a stakeholder perspective in creating social responsibility and ethical decisions in business.

STAKEHOLDERS DEFINE ETHICAL ISSUES IN BUSINESS

In a business context, customers, investors and shareholders, employees, suppliers, government agencies, communities, and many others who have a "stake" or claim in some aspect of a company's products, operations, markets, industry, and outcomes are known as **stakeholders.** These groups are influenced by business, but they also have the ability to influence businesses; thus, the relationship between companies and their stakeholders is a two-way street.[2]

The recent ethical/legal crisis in corporate America has demonstrated how employees and investors can suffer dire consequences as a result of unethical corporate practices. For example, with the collapse of Enron, many employees lost their jobs,

Enron retirees and those near retirement saw their pension funds essentially erased, and Enron investors lost billions of dollars after the company's stock price plummeted.[3]

On the other hand, firms such as Wal-Mart and Coca-Cola have experienced conflict with key stakeholders who have damaged their reputation and shareholder confidence. There are many potential threats to reputation. Reputation can be damaged by poor performance or ethical misconduct. Poor performance is easier to recover from than ethical misconduct. Obviously, stakeholders who are most directly affected by negative events will have a corresponding shift in their perceptions of a firm's reputation. On the other hand, even those indirectly connected to negative events can shift their reputation attributions. In many cases, those indirectly connected to the negative events may be more influenced by the news media or general public opinion than those who are directly connected to an organization.[4]

Coca-Cola continues to have many problems in stakeholder relationships; the more recent problems began with a contamination scare that had a negative effect on its European reputation. A racial discrimination lawsuit by about 2000 current and former African American employees against the company resulted in the company settling the suit by paying $193 million to the employees. Overall, it was thought that the company did not handle these crises well. In addition to reflecting poorly on Coca-Cola's reputation, these crises also had a negative impact on the firm's bottlers, distributors, and suppliers.

Coca-Cola once again ran into troubles when Matthew Whitley, a mid-level Coca-Cola executive, filed a whistle-blowing suit against the company alleging retaliation for revealing fraud in a market study performed on behalf of Burger King. To increase sales, Coca-Cola suggested that Burger King invest in and promote frozen Coca-Cola as a kid's snack. Coca-Cola exaggerated the number of frozen Cokes sold in a market test. Coca-Cola paid $21 million to Burger King to settle its disputes with the fast-food giant, $540,000 to the whistle-blower, and a $9 million pretax write-off had to be taken.[5] Coca-Cola settled a regulatory probe related to allegations of channel stuffing, and the Securities and Exchange Commission (SEC) concluded that Coke repeatedly inflated sales and misled investors by shipping extra beverage concentrate to bottlers. The SEC said Coke executives in Atlanta participated in the scheme to avoid profit shortfalls that would have rattled investors.[6] More recently, Coca-Cola bottlers who serve as the firm's wholesalers sued Coca-Cola, claiming that the plan to send the Powerade product directly to retailers such as Wal-Mart was a breach of contract.[7] Although Coca-Cola disputes or denies these allegations, the net result means that shares of Coca-Cola trade today at the same level they did nearly ten years ago while Pepsi continues to gain market share in the beverage market.

Scandals such as those faced by Coca-Cola many times will generally impact the company's reputation both from investor confidence and consumer confidence. As investor perceptions and decisions begin to take their toll, shareholder value will drop, exposing the company to consumer scrutiny that can increase the damage. Reputation is a factor in the consumers' perceptions of product attributes and corporate image features that lead to consumer willingness to purchase goods and services at profitable prices. After Radio Shack's CEO resigned for lying on his résumé, the company was so concerned about its reputation and leadership that it brought in respected interim CEO Claire Babrowski, whose leadership was key in restructuring McDonald's;

Radio Shack's stock rose 5 percent on news of her entry.[8] Some scandals may lead to boycotts and aggressive campaigns to dampen sales and earnings. Nike experienced such a backlash from its use of offshore subcontractors to manufacture its shoes and clothing. When Nike claimed no responsibility for the subcontractors' poor working conditions and extremely low wages, some consumers demanded greater accountability and responsibility by engaging in boycotts, letter-writing campaigns, and public-service announcements. Nike ultimately responded to the growing negative publicity by changing its practices and becoming a model company in managing offshore manufacturing.[9]

New reforms to improve corporate accountability and transparency also suggest that other stakeholders—including banks, attorneys, and public accounting firms—can play a major role in fostering responsible decision making.[10] Stakeholders apply their values and standards to many diverse issues—working conditions, consumer rights, environmental conservation, product safety, and proper information disclosure—that may or may not directly affect an individual stakeholder's own welfare. We can assess the level of social responsibility that an organization bears by scrutinizing its effects on the issues of concern to its stakeholders. Table 2–1 provides examples of common stakeholder issues along with indicators of businesses' impacts on those issues.[11]

Stakeholders provide resources that are more or less critical to a firm's long-term success. These resources may be both tangible and intangible. Shareholders, for example, supply capital; suppliers offer material resources or intangible knowledge; employees and managers grant expertise, leadership, and commitment; customers generate revenue and provide loyalty and positive word-of-mouth promotion; local communities provide infrastructure; and the media transmits positive corporate images. When individual stakeholders share similar expectations about desirable business conduct, they may choose to establish or join formal communities that are dedicated to better defining and advocating these values and expectations. Stakeholders' ability to withdraw—or to threaten to withdraw—these needed resources gives them power over businesses.[12]

Identifying Stakeholders

We can identify two different types of stakeholders. **Primary stakeholders** are those whose continued association is absolutely necessary for a firm's survival; these include employees, customers, investors, and shareholders, as well as the governments and communities that provide necessary infrastructure. Some firms take actions that can damage relationships with primary stakeholders. For example, General Motors diluted pensions of salaried employees and cut medical benefits to retired employees who are primary stakeholders. Figure 2–1 shows the national trend of firms, with over two hundred employees, to offer fewer health benefits for retirees, dropping from a high of around 66 percent in 1988 to around 32 percent in 2005.

Secondary stakeholders do not typically engage in transactions with a company and thus are not essential for its survival; these include the media, trade associations, and special-interest groups. The American Association of Retired People (AARP), a special-interest group, works to support retirees' rights such as health-care benefits. Both primary and secondary stakeholders embrace specific values and standards that

TABLE 2–1	Examples of Stakeholder Issues and Associated Measures of Corporate Impacts
Stakeholder Groups And Issues	**Potential Indicators Of Corporate Impact On These Issues**

Employees

1. Compensation and benefits 2. Training and development 3. Employee diversity 4. Occupational health and safety 5. Communications with management	1. Ratio of lowest wage to national legal minimum or to local cost of living 2. Changes in average years of training of employees 3. Percentages of employees from different genders and races 4. Standard injury rates and absentee rates 5. Availability of open-door policies or ombudsmen

Customers

1. Product safety and quality 2. Management of customer complaints 3. Services to disabled customers	1. Number of product recalls over time 2. Number of customer complaints and availability of procedures to answer them 3. Availability and nature of measures taken to ensure services to disabled customers

Investors

1. Transparency of shareholder communications 2. Shareholder rights	1. Availability of procedures to inform shareholders about corporate activities 2. Frequency and type of litigation involving violations of shareholder rights

Suppliers

1. Encouraging suppliers in developing countries 2. Encouraging minority suppliers	1. Prices offered to suppliers in developed countries in comparison to other suppliers 2. Percentage of minority suppliers

Community

1. Public health and safety protection 2. Conservation of energy and materials 3. Donations and support of local organizations	1. Availability of emergency-response plan 2. Data on reduction of waste produced and comparison to industry 3. Annual employee time spent in community service

Environmental Groups

1. Minimizing the use of energy 2. Minimizing emissions and waste 3. Minimizing adverse environmental effects of goods and services	1. Amount of electricity purchased; percentage of "green" electricity 2. Type, amount, and designation of waste generated 3. Percentage of product weight reclaimed after use

dictate what constitutes acceptable or unacceptable corporate behaviors. It is important for managers to recognize that while primary groups may present more day-to-day concerns, secondary groups cannot be ignored or given less consideration in the ethical decision-making process.[13]

Figure 2–2 offers a conceptualization of the relationship between businesses and stakeholders. In this **stakeholder interaction model,** there are two-way relationships between the firm and a host of stakeholders. In addition to the fundamental input of investors, employees, and suppliers, this approach recognizes other stakeholders and explicitly acknowledges the dialogue that exists between a firm's internal and external environments.

FIGURE 2-1	Declining Retiree Health Benefits

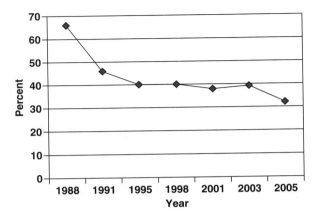

SOURCE: Kaiser/HRET; KPMG; Health Insurance Association of America. As referenced by David Wessel, Ellen E. Schultz, and Laurie McGinley, "GM's Decision to Cut Pensions Accelerates Broad Corporate Shift," *Wall Street Journal,* February 8, 2006, A1.

A Stakeholder Orientation

The degree to which a firm understands and addresses stakeholder demands can be referred to as a **stakeholder orientation.** This orientation comprises three sets of activities: (1) the organization-wide generation of data about stakeholder groups and assessment of the firm's effects on these groups, (2) the distribution of this information throughout the firm, and (3) the organization's responsiveness as a whole to this intelligence.[14]

Generating data about stakeholders begins with identifying the stakeholders that are relevant to the firm. Relevant stakeholder communities should be analyzed on the basis of the power that each enjoys as well as by the ties between them. Next, the firm should characterize the concerns about the business's conduct that each relevant stakeholder group shares. This information can be derived from formal research, including surveys, focus groups, Internet searches, or press reviews. For example, Ford Motor Company obtains input on social and environmental responsibility issues from company representatives, suppliers, customers, and community leaders. Shell has an online discussion forum where website visitors are invited to express their opinions on the company's activities and their implications. Employees and managers can also generate this information informally as they carry out their daily activities. For example, purchasing managers know about suppliers' demands, public relations executives about the media, legal counselors about the regulatory environment, financial executives about investors, sales representatives about customers, and human resources advisers about employees. Finally, the company should evaluate its impact on the issues that are important to the various stakeholders it has identified.[15]

Given the variety of the employees involved in the generation of information about stakeholders, it is essential that this intelligence be circulated throughout the firm. This requires that the firm facilitate the communication of information about the na-

| FIGURE 2–2 | Interactions Between a Company and Its Primary and Secondary Stakeholders |

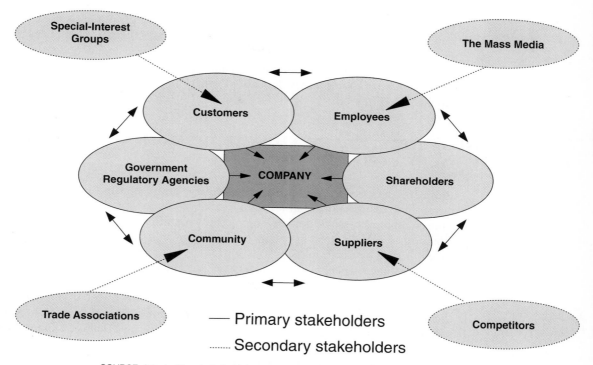

SOURCE: Adapted from Isabelle Maignan, O. C. Ferrell, and Linda Ferrell, "A Stakeholder Model for Implementing Social Responsibility in Marketing," *European Journal of Marketing* 39 (2005): 956–977. Used with permission.

ture of relevant stakeholder communities, stakeholder issues, and the current impact of the firm on these issues to all members of the organization. The dissemination of stakeholder intelligence can be organized formally through activities such as newsletters and internal information forums.[16]

A stakeholder orientation is not complete unless it includes activities that address stakeholder issues. For example Gap reported that although it is improving inspections it is still struggling to wipe out deep-seated problems such as discrimination and excessive overtime. In 2004 Gap revoked approval for seventy factories that violated its code of vendor conduct. Gap also realized that it sometimes contributes to problems by making unreasonable demands on factories; it is becoming more strict about its own deadlines to ensure that dumping rush jobs on factories does not occur.[17]

The responsiveness of the organization as a whole to stakeholder intelligence consists of the initiatives that the firm adopts to ensure that it abides by or exceeds stakeholder expectations and has a positive impact on stakeholder issues. Such activities are likely to be specific to a particular stakeholder group (for example, family-friendly work schedules) or to a particular stakeholder issue (for example, pollution-reduction programs). These responsiveness processes typically involve the participation of the concerned stakeholder groups. Kraft, for example, includes special-interest groups and university representatives in its programs to become sensitized to present and future ethical issues.

A stakeholder orientation can be viewed as a continuum in that firms are likely to adopt the concept to varying degrees. To gauge a given firm's stakeholder orientation, it is necessary to evaluate the extent to which the firm adopts behaviors that typify both the generation and dissemination of stakeholder intelligence and responsiveness to it. A given organization may generate and disseminate more intelligence about certain stakeholder communities than about others and, as a result, may respond to that intelligence differently.[18]

SOCIAL RESPONSIBILITY AND THE IMPORTANCE OF A STAKEHOLDER ORIENTATION

From the perspective of **social responsibility,** business ethics embodies standards, norms, and expectations that reflect a concern of major stakeholders, including consumers, employees, shareholders, suppliers, competitors, and the community. In other words, these stakeholders have concerns about what is fair, just, or in keeping with respect for stakeholders' rights.

Many businesspeople and scholars have questioned the role of ethics and social responsibility in business. Legal and economic responsibilities are generally accepted as the most important determinants of performance: "If this is well done," say classical theorists, "profits are maximized more or less continuously and firms carry out their major responsibilities to society."[19] Some economists believe that if companies address economic and legal issues, they are satisfying the demands of society and that trying to anticipate and meet additional needs would be almost impossible. Milton Friedman has been quoted as saying that "the basic mission of business [is] thus to produce goods and services at a profit, and in doing this, business [is] making its maximum contribution to society and, in fact, being socially responsible."[20] Even with the business ethics scandals of the twenty-first century, Friedman suggests that although those individuals guilty of wrongdoing should be held accountable, the market is a better deterrent than new laws and regulations at deterring firms from wrongdoing.[21] Thus, Friedman would diminish the role of stakeholders such as the government and employees in requiring that businesses demonstrate responsible and ethical behavior.

This Darwinian form of capitalism has been exported to many lesser and developing countries and is associated with a "Wild West" economy where anything goes in business. Friedman's capitalism is a far cry from Adam Smith's, one of the founders of capitalism. Smith created the concept of the invisible hand and spoke about self-interest; however, he went on to explain that "this common good is associated with six psychological motives and that each individual has to produce for the common good, with values such as Propriety, Prudence, Reason, Sentiment and promoting the happiness of mankind."[22] These values could be associated with the needs and concerns of stakeholders.

In the twenty-first century, Friedman's form of capitalism is being replaced by Smith's original concept of capitalism (or what is now called enlightened capitalism), a notion of capitalism that reemphasizes stakeholder concerns and issues. This shift may be occurring faster in developed countries than in those still being developed. Theodore

Levitt, a renowned business professor, once wrote that although profits are required for business just like eating is required for living, profit is not the purpose of business any more than eating is the purpose of life.[23] Norman Bowie, a well-known philosopher, extended Levitt's sentiment by noting that focusing on profit alone can create an unfavorable paradox that causes a firm to fail to achieve its objective. Bowie contends that when a business also cares about the well-being of stakeholders, it earns trust and cooperation that ultimately reduce costs and increase productivity.[24]

Relationship Between Social Responsibility and Profitability

Much evidence shows that social responsibility, including business ethics, is associated with increased profits. For example, one survey indicates that three out of four consumers refuse to buy from certain businesses, and a business's conduct was considered an important reason to avoid a business.[25] An important academic study found a direct relationship between social responsibility and profitability. The study also found that social responsibility contributes to employee commitment and customer loyalty—vital concerns of any firm trying to increase profits.[26]

It should be obvious from this discussion that ethics and social responsibility cannot be just a reactive approach to issues as they arise. Only if firms make ethical concerns a part of their foundation and incorporate ethics in their business strategy can social responsibility as a concept be embedded in daily decision making. A description of corporate ethical responsibility should include rights and duties, consequences and values, all of which refer to specific strategic decisions. The ethical component of business strategy should be capable of providing an assessment of top-management, workgroup, and individual behavior as it relates to ethical decisions. Table 2–2 lists *Fortune*'s best and worst companies in terms of social responsibility

TABLE 2–2	*Fortune*'s Best and Worst Companies for Social Responsibility
Best Companies	**Worst Companies**
United Parcel Service	Tenet Healthcare
International Paper	AK Steel Holding
Exelon	MCI
Chevron	US Airways Group
Publix Super Markets	Federal-Mogul
Weyerhaeuser	Siebel Systems
Starbucks	UTStarcom
Walt Disney	Paccar
Herman Miller	Stanley Works
Altria Group	Canadaigua Brands

SOURCE: From *Fortune*, "America's Most Admired Companies." Copyright © 2006 Time Inc. All rights reserved. March 6, 2006.

SOCIAL RESPONSIBILITY AND ETHICS

The concepts of ethics and social responsibility are often used interchangeably, although each has a distinct meaning. In Chapter 1, we defined the term *social responsibility* as an organization's obligation to maximize its positive impact on stakeholders and to minimize its negative impact. PNC Financial Services Group, for example, contributes $20 million in grants and corporate sponsorships to arts, community improvement, and educational causes. The company also supports employees with flexible work schedules and backup and holiday daycare, as well as a free daycare center for new parents. For its operations and technology center in Pittsburgh, the company built the nation's largest "green building" conforming to environmental guidelines on site planning, energy efficiency, water conservation, material conservation, and indoor environmental quality. It also built several "green" bank branches in New Jersey.[27]

Another example of a company being green is Whole Foods, which plans to become the largest buyer of wind-energy credits in North America by purchasing credits equal to 100 percent of its projected energy use.[28] General Electric also pledged to decrease pollution and double research-and-development spending on cleaner technologies.[29] Wal-Mart has also joined the growing ranks of green companies. In McKinney, Texas, and Aurora, Colorado, it has opened environmentally friendly stores, which should provide examples of the way they can work together to create stores that save energy, conserve natural resources, and reduce pollution. Wal-Mart hopes to take what it learns from the new stores and use it in all of the new stores that it builds.[30] Like Whole Foods and General Electric, many businesses have tried to determine what relationships, obligations, and duties are appropriate between the organization and various stakeholders. Social responsibility can be viewed as a contract with society, whereas business ethics involves carefully thought-out rules or heuristics of business conduct that guide decision making.

If social responsibility is considered an important corporate concern, then it does need quantitative credibility. Employee satisfaction, consumer loyalty, and other stakeholder concerns can be quantified to some extent, but some of the values and other dimensions are more qualitative. The International Organization for Standardization (ISO) has tried to establish a corporate responsibility standard, the ISO 26000; although the ISO 26000 has been demoted to a guideline rather than a standard, the discussion and debate surrounding the process is valuable. Whereas corporate responsibility needs quantitative credibility, significant aspects are more qualitative in nature: employee satisfaction, customer motivations, company values, and ethical decision-making processes, for instance. All to some extent can be broken down into quantitative data, but the essence of them cannot. However, they also shift constantly, which makes yesterday's survey an addition to today's recycle bin.[31]

Buildings are rarely considered major pollution sources. Yet 33 percent of major U.S. energy use, 33 percent of major greenhouse-gas emissions, and 30 percent of raw material use are the result of buildings.[32] Currently, there are two competitive certification groups that authorize schools, houses, and commercial buildings as green. These two rival groups, Green Globes and Leadership in Energy and Environmental Design (LEED), are vying for leadership in government adoption of environmental rules that determine whether a building can be called green. There is concern about stakeholder relationships between the two groups. Green Globes is led by a former timber-company executive and received much of its seed money from timber and wood-products companies. LEED is a nonprofit organization with less ties to business interest. Already two states, Maryland and Arkansas, have adopted Green Globes as an alternative to LEED, giving officials an alternative for government-funded construction. The Clinton Presidential Library in Little Rock as well as the 7 World Trade Center, the first tower rebuilt near Ground Zero in New York, was certified by Green Globes.[33]

There are four levels of social responsibility—economic, legal, ethical, and philanthropic—and they can be viewed as steps (see Figure 2–3).[34] At the most basic level, companies have an economic responsibility to be profitable so that they can provide a return on investment to their owners and investors, create jobs for the community, and contribute goods and services to the economy. Of course, businesses are also expected to obey all laws and regulations. Business ethics, as previously defined, comprises principles and standards that guide behavior in the world of business. Finally, philanthropic responsibility refers to activities that are not required of businesses but promote human welfare or goodwill. Ethics, then, is one dimension of social responsibility.

The term **corporate citizenship** is often used to express the extent to which businesses strategically meet the economic, legal, ethical, and philanthropic responsibilities placed on them by their various stakeholders.[35] Corporate citizenship has four interrelated dimensions: strong sustained economic performance, rigorous compliance, ethical actions beyond what the law requires, and voluntary contributions that advance the reputation and stakeholder commitment of the organization. A firm's commitment to corporate citizenship indicates a strategic focus on fulfilling the social responsibilities that its stakeholders expect of it. Corporate citizenship involves acting on the firm's commitment to the corporate citizenship philosophy and measuring the extent to which it follows through by actually implementing citizenship initiatives.

| **FIGURE 2-3** | Steps of Social Responsibility |

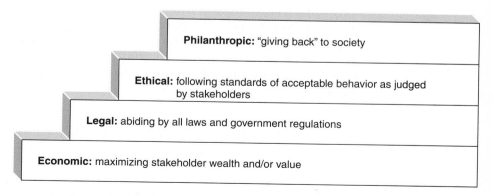

SOURCE: Adapted from Archie B. Carroll, "The Pyramid of Corporate Social Responsibility: Toward the Moral Management of Organizational Stakeholders," *Business Horizons* (July–August 1991): 42, Figure 3.

TABLE 2-3	The Top Twenty Best Corporate Citizens		
Rank	**Company**	**Rank**	**Company**
1	Green Mountain Coffee Roasters	11	Intel Corporation
2	Hewlett-Packard Company	12	Johnson & Johnson
3	Advanced Micro Devices	13	Nike
4	Motorola	14	General Mills
5	Agilent Technologies	15	Pitney Bowes
6	Timberland Company	16	Wells Fargo
7	Salesforce.com, Inc.	17	Starbucks
8	Cisco Systems, Inc.	18	Wainwright Bank and Trust
9	Dell, Inc.	19	St. Paul Travelers
10	Texas Instruments, Inc.	20	Ecolab

SOURCE: From Peter Asmus, with Sandra Waddock and Samuel Graves, "100 Best Corporate Citizens of 2005," *Business Ethics*, Spring 2005, p. 22. Reprinted with permission of Business Ethics.

Reputation is one of an organization's greatest intangible assets with tangible value. The value of a positive reputation is difficult to quantify, but it is very important. A single negative incident can influence perceptions of a corporation's image and reputation instantly and for years afterwards. Corporate reputation, image, and brands are more important than ever and are among the most critical aspects of sustaining relationships with constituents including investors, customers, financial analysts, media, and government watchdogs. It takes companies decades to build a great reputation, yet just one slip can cost a company dearly. Although an organization does not control its reputation in a direct sense, its actions, choices, behaviors, and consequences do influence the reputation that exists in perceptions of stakeholders. Companies such as Exxon Mobil, Chevron Corporation, and Royal Dutch Shell Plc. received low ratings from the public in a corporate reputation survey for what the public perceived as the "heartless" spike in prices at the pump while the companies were enjoying record profits. In the same survey, despite corporate–governance reforms and a growing commitment to ethics and social responsibility, overall reputation of American corporations continued to slip. Seventy-one percent of respondents rated American businesses' reputation as "not good" or terrible in 2005, compared to 68 percent in 2004.[36] Table 2–3 lists the top twenty best corporate citizens, according to the spring 2006 issue of *Business Ethics*.

CORPORATE GOVERNANCE PROVIDES FORMALIZED RESPONSIBILITY TO STAKEHOLDERS

Most businesses, and often courses taught in colleges of business, operate under the belief that the purpose of business is to maximize profits for shareholders. In 1919 the Michigan Supreme Court in the case of *Dodge v. Ford Motor Co.*[37] ruled that a business exists for the profit of shareholders and the board of directors should focus on that objective. On the other hand, the stakeholder model places the board of directors in the central position to balance the interests and conflicts of the various constituencies. External control of the corporation includes not only government regulation but also key stakeholders including employees, consumers, and communities to exert pressures to responsible conduct. Many of the obligations to balance stakeholder interest have been institutionalized in legislation that provides incentives for responsible conduct. The Federal Sentencing Guidelines for Organizations (FSGO) provides incentives for developing an ethical culture and efforts to prevent misconduct.

Today, the failure to balance stakeholder interests can result in a failure to maximize shareholders' wealth. Wal-Mart may be failing to maximize the growth of its market value because investors are concerned about its ability to manage stakeholder interests. Wal-Mart's shareholders have seen almost no growth over the past few years as it battles employees, communities, and special-interest groups over ethical issues. Most firms are moving more toward a balanced stakeholder model as they see that this approach will sustain the relationships necessary for long-run success.

Both directors and officers of corporations are fiduciaries for the shareholders. Fiduciaries are persons placed in positions of trust who use due care and loyalty in acting on behalf of the best interests of the organization. There is a duty of care also called a *duty of diligence* to make informed and prudent decisions.[38] Directors have a duty to avoid ethical misconduct in their director role and to provide leadership in decisions to prevent ethical misconduct in the organization.

Directors are not held responsible for negative outcomes if they are informed and diligent in their decision making. This means they have an obligation to request information, research, use accountants and attorneys, and obtain the services of ethical compliance consultants.

The duty of loyalty means that all decisions should be in the interests of the corporation and its stakeholders. Conflicts of interest exist when a director uses the position to obtain personal gain usually at the expense of the organization. For example, before the Sarbanes–Oxley Act in 2002, directors could give themselves and officers interest-free loans. Scandals at Tyco, Kmart, and WorldCom are all associated with officers receiving personal loans that damaged the corporation.

Officer compensation packages challenge directors, especially those on the board and not independent. Directors have an opportunity to vote for others' compensation in return for their own increased compensation. Opportunities to know about the investments, business ventures, and stock-market information create issues that could violate the duty of loyalty. Insider trading of a firm's stock has very specific rules, and violations can result in serious punishment. The obligations of directors and officers for legal and ethical responsibility interface and fit together based on their fiduciary relationships. Ethical values should guide decisions and buffer the possibility of illegal conduct. With increased pressure on directors to provide oversight for organizational ethics, there is a trend toward directors receiving training to increase their competency in ethics program development, as well as other areas such as accounting.

To remove the opportunity for employees to make unethical decisions, most companies have developed formal systems of accountability, oversight, and control—known as **corporate governance.** *Accountability* refers to how closely workplace decisions are aligned with a firm's stated strategic direction and its compliance with ethical and legal considerations. *Oversight* provides a system of checks and balances that limit employees' and managers' opportunities to deviate from policies and strategies and that prevent unethical and illegal activities. *Control* is the process of auditing and improving organizational decisions and actions.

A clear delineation of accountability helps employees, customers, investors, government regulators, and other stakeholders understand why and how the organization chooses and achieves its goals. Corporate governance establishes fundamental systems and processes: for preventing and detecting misconduct, for investigating and disciplining, and for recovery and continuous improvement. Effective corporate governance creates a compliance and ethics culture so that employees feel that integrity is at the core of competitiveness.[39] Even if a company has adopted a consensus approach for decision making, there should be oversight and authority for delegating tasks, making difficult and sometimes controversial decisions, balancing power throughout the firm, and maintaining ethical compliance. Governance also provides mechanisms for identifying risks and for planning for recovery when mistakes or problems occur.

The development of stakeholder orientation should interface with the corporation's governance structure. Corporate governance is also part of a firm's corporate culture that establishes the integrity of all relationships. A governance system that does not provide checks and balances creates opportunities for top managers to put their own self-interests before those of important stakeholders. Consider the accounting scandal at Adelphia Communications mentioned earlier. Founders John J. Rigas, Timothy J. Rigas, and Michael J. Rigas defrauded Adelphia's stockholders out of billions of dollars by falsifying the firm's financial reports because its corporate governance systems failed to prevent this type of fraud.[40]

Concerns about the need for greater corporate governance are not limited to the United States. Reforms in governance structures and issues are occurring all over the world.[41] In many nations, companies are being pressured to implement stronger corporate governance mechanisms by international investors, by the process of becoming privatized after years of unaccountability as state companies, or by the desire to imitate successful governance movements in the United States, Japan, and the European Union.[42]

Table 2–4 lists examples of major corporate governance issues. These issues normally involve strategic-level decisions and actions taken by boards of directors, business owners, top executives, and other managers with high levels of authority and accountability. Although these people have often been relatively free from scrutiny, changes in technology, consumer activism, government attention, recent ethical scandals, and other factors have brought new attention to such issues as transparency, executive pay, risk and control, resource accountability, strategic direction, stockholder rights, and other decisions made for the organization.

Views of Corporate Governance

To better understand the role of corporate governance in business today, it is important to consider how it relates to fundamental beliefs about the purpose of business. Some organizations take the view that as long as they are maximizing shareholder wealth and profitability, they are fulfilling their core responsibilities. Other firms, how-

TABLE 2-4	Corporate Governance Issues

Shareholder rights

Executive compensation

Composition and structure of the board of directors

Auditing and control

Risk management

CEO selection and termination decisions

Integrity of financial reporting

Stakeholder participation and input into decisions

Compliance with corporate governance reform

Role of the CEO in board decisions

Organizational ethics programs

ever, believe that a business is an important member, even citizen, of society and therefore must assume broad responsibilities that include complying with social norms and expectations. From these assumptions, we can derive two major approaches to corporate governance: the shareholder model and the stakeholder model.[43]

The **shareholder model of corporate governance** is founded in classic economic precepts, including the goal of maximizing wealth for investors and owners. For publicly traded firms, corporate governance focuses on developing and improving the formal system for maintaining performance accountability between top management and the firms' shareholders.[44] Thus, a shareholder orientation should drive a firm's decisions toward serving the best interests of investors. Underlying these decisions is a classic agency problem, where ownership (that is, investors) and control (that is, managers) are separate. Managers act as agents for investors, whose primary goal is increasing the value of the stock they own. However, investors and managers are distinct parties with unique insights, goals, and values with respect to the business. Managers, for example, may have motivations beyond stockholder value, such as market share, personal compensation, or attachment to particular products and projects. For example, former Qwest Communications International Inc. CFO Robin Szeliga pleaded guilty to one count of insider trading. She was accused of improperly selling ten thousand shares of Qwest stock, earning a net profit of $125,000, in 2001 when she knew some business units would fail to meet revenue targets and that the company had improperly used nonrecurring revenue to meet those goals. Szeliga, former CEO Joseph Nacchio, and five other former executives were accused of orchestrating a massive financial fraud that forced Qwest Communications International Inc. to restate billions of dollars in revenue. The SEC wants repayment and civil penalties from all of the accused.[45] Because of these potential differences, corporate governance mechanisms are needed to align investor and management interests. The shareholder model has been criticized for its somewhat singular purpose and focus because there are other ways of "investing" in a business. Suppliers, creditors, customers, employees, business partners, the community, and others also invest their resources into the success of the firm.[46]

The **stakeholder model of corporate governance** adopts a broader view of the purpose of business. Although a company has a responsibility for economic success and viability to satisfy its stockholders, it also must answer to other stakeholders, including employees, suppliers, government regulators, communities, and special-interest groups with which it interacts. Due to limited resources, companies must determine which of their stakeholders are primary. Once the primary groups have been identified, managers must then implement the appropriate corporate governance mechanisms to promote the development of long-term relationships.[47] This approach entails creating governance systems that consider stakeholder welfare in tandem with corporate needs and interests.

Although these two approaches seem to represent the ends of a continuum, the reality is that the shareholder model is a more restrictive precursor to the stakeholder orientation. Many businesses have evolved into the stakeholder model as a result of government initiatives, consumer activism, industry activity, and other external forces.

The Role of Boards of Directors

For public corporations, boards of directors hold the ultimate responsibility for their firms' success or failure, as well as for the ethics of their actions. This governing authority is being held responsible by the 2004 amendments to the FSGO for creating an ethical culture that provides leadership, values, and compliance. The members of a company's board of directors assume legal responsibility for the firm's resources and decisions, and they appoint its top executive officers. Board members have a fiduciary duty, meaning they have assumed a position of trust and confidence that entails certain responsibilities, including acting in the best interests of those they serve. Thus, board membership is not intended as a vehicle for personal financial gain; rather, it provides the intangible benefit of ensuring the success of both the organization and people involved in the fiduciary arrangement. The role and expectations of boards of directors assumed greater significance after the accounting scandals of the early 2000s motivated many shareholders and other stakeholders to demand greater accountability from boards.[48] For example, after $9 billion in accounting irregularities led World-Com to declare the largest ever bankruptcy, the company replaced the board members who had failed to prevent the accounting scandal. The firm also fired many managers.[49]

The traditional approach to directorship assumed that board members managed the corporation's business. Research and practical observation have shown that boards of directors rarely, if ever, perform the management function.[50] First, boards meet only a few times a year, which precludes them from managing effectively. In addition, the complexity of modern organizations mandates full attention on a daily basis. Thus, boards of directors are concerned primarily with monitoring the decisions made by executives on behalf of the company. This includes choosing top executives, assessing their performance, helping set strategic direction, and ensuring that oversight, control, and accountability mechanisms are in place. In sum, board members assume ultimate authority for their organization's effectiveness and subsequent performance.

Many CEOs have lost their jobs because the board of directors was scared. Notable examples include Michael Eisner from Disney, Carly Fiorina from Hewlett-Packard, and Scott Livengood from Krispy Kreme. The main reason for this was that the boards feared losing all of their money. This fear came from two lawsuits by share-holders who sued the directors of Enron and WorldCom over their roles in the collapse of those firms. Both settlements called for the directors to pay large sums from their own pockets.[51]

GREATER DEMANDS FOR ACCOUNTABILITY AND TRANSPARENCY Just as improved ethical decision making requires more of employees and executives, so too are boards of directors feeling greater demands for accountability and transparency. In the past, board members were often retired company executives or friends of current executives, but the trend today is toward "outside directors" who have little vested interest in the firm before assuming the director role. Inside directors are corporate officers, consultants, major shareholders, or others who benefit directly from the success of the organization. Directors today are increasingly chosen for their expertise, competence, and ability to bring diverse perspectives to strategic discussions. Outside directors are also thought to bring more independence to the monitoring function because they are not bound by past allegiances, friendships, a current role in the company, or some other issue that may create a conflict of interest.

Many of the corporate scandals uncovered in recent years might have been prevented if each of the companies' boards of directors had been better qualified, more knowledgeable, and less biased. Warren Buffett did not stand for reelection to Coca-Cola's board of directors, after serving for seventeen years. Buffett cited the need to focus his attention on Berkshire Hathaway and its subsidiaries.[52] As pointed out in an earlier example, Coca-Cola has struggled over the past ten years with involvement in ethical misconduct and high turnover of top managers. A survey by *USA Today* found that corporate boards have considerable overlap. More than one thousand corporate board members sit on four or more company boards, and of the nearly two thousand boards of directors in the United States, more than twenty-two thousand of their members are linked to boards of more than one company. For example, of the one thousand largest companies, one-fifth share at least one board member with another top one thousand firm. This overlap creates the opportunity for conflicts of interest in decision making and limits the independence of individual boards of directors. At Wal-Mart, questions have been raised by shareholders, who believe that recent reports of legal and regulatory noncompliance raise serious concerns about the adequacy of the company's controls. Such concerns involve the former Wal-Mart vice chairman Thomas Coughlin who pleaded guilty to fraud and tax charges or the charges that Wal-Mart knowingly hired contractors that furnished illegal immigrants to clean its floors. A group of institutional shareholders have called for Wal-Mart's board to form a special committee to conduct a "comprehensive review of the company's legal and regulatory controls, as well as its internal system for ensuring compliance with its own policies and standards."[53] In some cases, individuals have earned placement on multiple boards of directors because they have gained a reputation for going along with top management. This may foster a corporate culture that limits outside oversight of top managers' decisions.

Although labor and public pension-fund activities have waged hundreds of proxy battles in recent years, they rarely have much effect on the target companies. Now shareholder activists are attacking the process by which directors themselves are elected.

Shareholder resolutions at about 140 companies would require directors to gain a majority of votes cast to join the board. It is hoped that this new practice will make boards of directors more attentive.[54]

EXECUTIVE COMPENSATION   One of the biggest issues that corporate boards of directors face is **executive compensation.** In fact, most boards spend more time deciding how much to compensate top executives than they do ensuring the integrity of the company's financial reporting systems.[55] How executives are compensated for their leadership, organizational service, and performance has become a controversial topic. Indeed, 73 percent of respondents in a *BusinessWeek/*Harris poll indicated they believe that top officers of large U.S. companies receive too much compensation, while only 21 percent reported executive compensation as "just about the right amount."[56] Many executives have received large compensation and bonus packages regardless of the success of their companies. For example, Carly Fiorina, former CEO of Hewlett-Packard, received at least $14 million when she was terminated in early 2005, which represented 2.5 times her base salary and cash bonus, but not enough to require shareholder approval. However, two institutional shareholders are suing Hewlett-Packard over her severance package; they believe she received at least $21 million, more than 2.99 times her 2004 base salary and cash bonus of about $5.6 million. Stock options and other benefits raised her total exit package further to $42 million, which meant it should have received shareholder approval. It seems to be a growing trend by investors to sue over executive compensation.[57]

Many people believe that no executive is worth millions of dollars in annual salary and stock options, even if he or she has brought great financial return to investors. Their concerns often center on the relationship between the highest-paid executives and median employee wages in the company. If this ratio is perceived as too large, then critics believe that either employees are not being compensated fairly or high executive salaries represent an improper use of company resources. According to a recent report by United for a Fair Economy, the average executive now earns 431 times the average blue-collar worker. The average CEO pay is now $10.2 million, compared to worker pay that is now $27,460.[58] According to the report, if the minimum wage had risen as fast as CEO pay since 1990, the lowest paid workers in the United States would be earning $23.03 an hour today, not $5.15 an hour. Because of this enormous difference, the business press is now usually careful to support high levels of executive compensation only when it is directly linked to strong company performance.

Although the issue of executive compensation has received much attention in the media of late, some business owners have long recognized its potential ill effects. In the early twentieth century, for example, capitalist J. P. Morgan implemented a policy that limited the pay of top managers in businesses that he owned to no more than twenty times the pay of any other employee.[59]

Other people argue that because executives assume so much risk on behalf of the company, they deserve the rewards that follow from strong company performance. In addition, many executives' personal and professional lives meld to the point that they are "on call" twenty-four hours a day. Because not everyone has the skill, experience, and desire to become an executive, with the accompanying pressure and responsibility, market forces dictate a high level of compensation. When the pool of qualified individuals is limited, many corporate board members feel that offering large compensation packages is the only way to attract and retain top executives and so ensure that their firms are not left without strong leadership. In an era when top executives are increasingly willing to "jump ship" to other firms that offer higher pay, potentially lucrative stock options, bonuses, and other benefits, such thinking is not without merit.[60] The heads of America's 500 biggest companies received an aggregate 54 percent pay raise in 2005. As a group, their total compensation amounted to $5.1 billion versus $3.3 billion in fiscal 2005.[61] This means that the average salary, benefits, and options package for chief executives of major corporations in the United States in 2005 was $10.2 million.

Executive compensation is a difficult but important issue for boards of directors and other stakeholders to consider because it receives much attention in the media, sparks shareholder concern, and is hotly debated in discussions of corporate governance. One area for board members to consider is the extent to which executive compensation is linked to company performance. Plans that base compensation on the achievement of several performance goals, including profits and revenues, are intended to align the interests of owners with management. Amid rising complaints about excessive executive compensation, an increasing number of corporate boards are imposing performance targets on the stock and stock options they include in their CEOs' pay package. In 2005 thirty companies based a portion of the equity granted to their CEOs on performance targets. The expanded emphasis on performance targets is designed to keep executives from reaping rich rewards for reasons unrelated to their leadership skills. Stock options, which became a popular form of compensation in the 1990s, can gain value in a rising stock market, enabling executives to pocket windfalls even if their own companies' earnings growth is modest.[62]

Another issue is whether performance-linked compensation encourages executives to focus on short-term performance at the expense of long-term growth.[63] Shareholders today, however, may be growing more concerned about transparency than short-term performance and executive compensation. One study determined that companies that divulge more details about their corporate governance practices generate higher shareholder returns than less transparent companies.[64]

IMPLEMENTING A STAKEHOLDER PERSPECTIVE[65]

An organization that develops effective corporate governance and understands the importance of business ethics and social responsibility in achieving success should develop some processes for managing these important concerns. Although there are many different approaches, we provide some steps that have been found effective to utilize the stakeholder framework in managing responsibility and business ethics. The steps include (1) assessing the corporate culture, (2) identifying stakeholder groups, (3) identifying stakeholder issues, (4) assessing the organizational commitment to social responsibility, (5) identifying resources and determining urgency, and (6) gaining stakeholder feedback. The importance of these steps is to include feedback from relevant stakeholders in formulating organizational strategy and implementation.

Step 1: Assessing the Corporate Culture

To enhance organizational fit, a social responsibility program must align with the corporate culture of the organization. The purpose of this first step is to identify the organizational mission, values, and norms that are likely to have implications for social responsibility. In particular, relevant existing values and norms are those that specify the stakeholder groups and stakeholder issues that are deemed as most important by the organization. Very often, relevant organizational values and norms can be found in corporate documents such as the mission statement, annual reports, sales brochures, or websites. For example, Green Mountain Coffee is a pioneer in helping struggling coffee growers by paying them fair trade prices. The company also offers microloans to coffee-growing families, to underwrite business ventures that diversify agricultural economies. It has been on the *Business Ethics* "100 Best Corporate Citizens" since 2003 and climbed to the number-one position in 2006.[66]

Step 2: Identifying Stakeholder Groups

In managing this stage, it is important to recognize stakeholder needs, wants, and desires. Many important issues gain visibility because key constituencies such as consumer groups, regulators, or the media express an interest. When agreement, collaboration, or even confrontations exist on an issue, there is a need for a decision-making process. A model of collaboration to overcome the adversarial approaches to problem solving has been suggested. Managers can identify relevant stakeholders who may be affected by or may influence the development of organizational policy.

Stakeholders have some level of power over a business because they are in the position to withhold, or at least threaten to withhold, organizational resources. Stakeholders have most power when their own survival is not really affected by the success of the organization and when they have access to vital organizational resources. For example, most consumers of shoes do not need to buy Nike shoes. Therefore, if they decide to boycott Nike, they have to endure only minor inconveniences. Nevertheless, their loyalty to Nike is vital to the continued success of the sport apparel giant. The proper assessment of the power held by a given stakeholder community also requires an evaluation of the extent to which that community can collaborate with others to pressure the firm.

Step 3: Identifying Stakeholder Issues

Together, steps 1 and 2 lead to the identification of the stakeholders who are both the most powerful and legitimate. The level of power and legitimacy determines the degree of urgency in addressing their needs. Step 3 consists then in understanding the nature of the main issues of concern to these stakeholders. Conditions for collaboration exist when problems are so complex that multiple stakeholders are required to resolve the issue and the weaknesses of adversarial approaches are understood.

For example, obesity in children is becoming an issue across groups and stakeholders. In the current U.S. Congress, fifty-five introduced bills contain the word *obesity*, which is approaching the number containing *gun*.[67] According to a recent survey of readers in the *Wall Street Journal,* most people (60 percent) believed that consumers should bear the main burden of health-care costs. Only 28 percent believed the government should bear the burden, and a small 13 percent believed the employers should foot the bill for rising costs associated with obesity and other problems.[68] The United States is the most obese nation with almost 40 percent of the population obese or overweight.

Step 4: Assessing Organizational Commitment to Social Responsibility

Steps 1 through 3 consist of generating information about social responsibility among a variety of influencers in and around the organization. Step 4 brings these three first stages together to arrive at an understanding of social responsibility that specifically matches the organization of interest. This general definition will then be used to evaluate current practices and to select concrete social responsibility initiatives. Firms such as Starbucks have selected activities that address stakeholder concerns. Starbucks has formalized its initiatives in official documents such as annual reports, webpages, and company brochures. Starbucks has a website devoted to social responsibility. Starbucks is concerned with the environment and integrates policies and programs throughout all aspects of operations to minimize their environmental impact. They also have many community-building programs that help them be good neighbors and contribute positively to the communities where their partners and customers live, work, and play.[69]

Step 5: Identifying Resources and Determining Urgency

The prioritization of stakeholders and issues, along with the assessment of past performance, provides for allocating resources. Two main criteria can be considered: First is the levels of financial and organizational investments required by different actions; second is the urgency when prioritizing social responsibility challenges. When the challenge under consideration is viewed as significant and when stakeholder pressures on the issue could be expected, then the challenge can be considered as urgent. For example, Wal-Mart has been the focus of legislation in Maryland, which tried to make the retailer pay more for its employee health care. The legislation failed in its attempt to require employers with more than 10,000 workers to spend at least 8 percent of their payroll on employee health care.[70] Twenty-two other states are now considering this legislation. Wal-Mart has now offered to improve health-care benefits for its employees as a direct result of the pressure.[71]

Step 6: Gaining Stakeholder Feedback

Stakeholder feedback can be generated through a variety of means. First, stakeholders' general assessment of the firm and its practices can be obtained through satisfaction or reputation surveys. Second, gauge stakeholders' perceptions of the firm's contributions to specific issues, stakeholder-generated media such as blogs, websites, podcasts, and newsletters can be assessed. Third, more formal research may be conducted using focus groups, observation, and surveys. Websites can be both positive and negative; for example, www.wakeupwalmart.com launched by the United Food and Commercial

Workers union has over 240,000 members, and another group called Wal-Mart Watch is also gaining members. Both groups have articles and stories about the retail giant on their websites that are not flattering for Wal-Mart. The pressure has forced the retail giant to listen to its consumers and change its ways. To counter the claims by these groups, Wal-Mart launched its own site, www.walmartfacts.com, to tell its side of the story.

SUMMARY

Business ethics, issues, and conflicts revolve around relationships. Customers, investors and shareholders, employees, suppliers, government agencies, communities, and many others who have a stake, or claim, in some aspect of a company's products, operations, markets, industry, and outcomes are known as stakeholders. They are both influenced by and have the ability to affect businesses. Stakeholders provide both tangible and intangible resources that are more or less critical to a firm's long-term success, and their ability to withdraw—or to threaten to withdraw—these resources gives them power. Stakeholders define significant ethical issues in business.

Primary stakeholders are those whose continued association is absolutely necessary for a firm's survival, whereas secondary stakeholders do not typically engage in transactions with a company and thus are not essential for its survival. The stakeholder interaction model suggests that there are two-way relationships between the firm and a host of stakeholders. The degree to which a firm understands and addresses stakeholder demands can be expressed as a stakeholder orientation, which includes three sets of activities: (1) the generation of data across the firm about its stakeholder groups and the assessment of the firm's effects on these groups, (2) the distribution of this information throughout the firm, and (3) the responsiveness of every level of the firm to this intelligence. A stakeholder orientation can be viewed as a continuum in that firms are likely to adopt the concept to varying degrees.

Although the concepts of business ethics and social responsibility are often used interchangeably, the two terms have distinct meanings. Social responsibility in business refers to an organization's obligation to maximize its positive impact and minimize its negative impact on society. There are four levels of social responsibility—economic, legal, ethical, and philanthropic—and they can be viewed as a pyramid. The term *corporate citizenship* is often used to communicate the extent to which businesses strategically meet the economic, legal, ethical, and philanthropic responsibilities placed on them by their various stakeholders.

From a social responsibility perspective, business ethics embodies standards, norms, and expectations that reflect a concern of major stakeholders including consumers, employees, shareholders, suppliers, competitors, and the community. Only if firms include ethical concerns in their foundational values and incorporate ethics in their business strategy can social responsibility as a value be embedded in daily decision making.

Most businesses operate under the assumption that the main purpose of business is to maximize profits for shareholders. The stakeholders model places the board of directors in the central position to balance the interests and conflicts of the various constituencies. Both directors and officers of corporations are fiduciaries for the shareholders. Fiduciaries are persons placed in positions of trust who use due care and loyalty in acting on behalf of the best interests of the organization. There is a duty of care (also called a duty of diligence) to make informed and prudent decisions. Directors have a duty to avoid ethical misconduct in their director role and to provide leadership in decisions to prevent ethical misconduct in the organization. To remove the opportunity for employees to make unethical decisions, most companies have developed formal systems of accountability, oversight, and control—known as corporate governance. Accountability refers to how closely workplace decisions are aligned with a firm's stated strategic direction and its compliance with ethical and legal considerations. Oversight provides a system of checks and balances that limit employees' and managers' opportunities to deviate from policies and strategies and that prevent unethical and illegal activities. Control is the process of auditing and improving organizational decisions and actions.

There are two perceptions of corporate governance, which can be viewed as a continuum. The shareholder model is founded in classic economic precepts, including the maximization of wealth for investors and owners. The stakeholder model adopts a broader view of the purpose of business that includes satisfying the concerns of other stakeholders, from employees, suppliers, and government regulators to communities and special-interest groups.

Two major elements of corporate governance that relate to ethical decision making are the role of the board of directors and executive compensation. The members of a public corporation's board of directors assume legal responsibility for the firm's resources and decisions. Important issues related to corporate boards of directors include accountability, transparency, and independence. Boards of directors are also responsible for appointing and setting the compensation for top executive officers, a controversial topic. Concerns about executive pay may center on the often disproportionate relationship between the highest-paid executives and median employee wages in the company.

IMPORTANT TERMS FOR REVIEW		
stakeholder	reputation	
primary stakeholder	corporate governance	
secondary stakeholder	shareholder model of corporate governance	
stakeholder interaction model		
stakeholder orientation	stakeholder model of corporate governance	
social responsibility		
corporate citizenship	executive compensation	

A REAL-LIFE SITUATION*

Kent was getting pressure from his boss, parents, and wife about the marketing campaign for Broadway Corporation's new video game called "Lucky." He had been working for Broadway for about two years, and the Lucky game was his first big project. After Kent and his wife, Amy, had graduated from the same college, they decided to go back to their hometown of Las Cruces, New Mexico, near the Mexican border. Kent's father knew the president of Broadway, which enabled Kent to get a job in its marketing department. Broadway is a medium-size company with about five hundred employees, making it one of the largest employers in Las Cruces. Broadway develops, manufactures, and markets video arcade games.

Within the video arcade industry, competition is fierce. Games typically have a life cycle of only eighteen to twenty-four months. One of the key strategies in the industry is providing unique, visually stimulating games by using color graphics technology, fast action, and participant interaction. The target markets for Broadway's video products are children aged 5 to 12 and teenagers aged 13 to 19. Males constitute 75 percent of the market.

When Kent first started with Broadway, his task was to conduct market research on the types of games that players desired. His research showed that the market wanted more action (violence), quicker graphics, multiple levels of difficulty, and sound. Further research showed that certain tones and types of sound were more pleasing than others. As part of his research, Kent also observed people in video arcades, where he found that many became hypnotized by a game and would quickly put in quarters when told to do so. Research suggested that many target consumers exhibited the same symptoms as compulsive gamblers. Kent's research results were very well received by the company, which developed several new games using his information. The new games were instant hits with the market.

In his continuing research, Kent had found that the consumer's level of intensity increased as the game's intensity level increased. Several reports later, Kent suggested that target consumers might be willing, at strategic periods in a video game, to insert multiple coins. For example, a player who wanted to move to a higher level of difficulty would have to insert two coins; to play the final level, three coins would have to be inserted. When the idea was tested, Kent found it did increase game productivity.

Kent had also noticed that video games that gave positive reinforcements to the consumer, such as audio cues, were played much more frequently than others. He reported his findings to Brad, Broadway's president, who asked Kent to apply the information to the development of new games. Kent suggested having the machines give candy to the game players when they attained specific goals. For the teen market, the company modified the idea: The machines would give back coins at certain levels during the game. Players could then use the coins at strategic levels to play a "slot-type" chance opening of the next level. By inserting an element of chance, these games generated more coin input than output, and game productivity increased dramatically. These innovations were quite successful, giving Broadway a larger share of the market and Kent a promotion to product manager.

Kent's newest assignment was the Lucky game—a fast-action scenario in which the goal was to destroy the enemy before being destroyed. Kent expanded on the slot-type game for the older market, with two additions. First, the game employed virtual reality technology, which gives the player the sensation of actually being in the game. Second, keeping in mind that most of the teenage consumers were male, Kent incorporated a female character who, at each level, removed a piece of her clothing and taunted the player. A win at the highest level left her nude. Test market results suggested that the two additions increased profitability per game dramatically.

Several weeks later, Brad asked about the Lucky project. "I think we've got a real problem, Brad," Kent told him. "Maybe the nudity is a bad idea. Some people will be really upset about it." Brad was very displeased with Kent's response.

Word got around fast that the Lucky project had stalled. During dinner with his parents, Kent mentioned the Lucky project, and his dad said something that affected Kent. "You know, son, the Lucky project will bring in a great deal of revenue for Broadway, and jobs are at stake. Some of your coworkers are upset with your stand on this project. I'm not telling you what to do, but there's more at stake here than just a video game."

The next day Kent had a meeting with Brad about Lucky. "Well," Brad asked, "what have you decided?"

Kent answered, "I don't think we should go with the nudity idea."

Brad answered, "You know, Kent, you're right. The U.S. market just isn't ready to see full nudity as well as graphic violence in arcades in their local malls. That's why I've contacted an Internet provider who will take our game and put it on the Net as an adult product. I've also checked out the foreign markets and found that we can sell the machines to the Mexican market if we tone down the violence. The Taiwanese joint venture group has okayed the version we have now, but they would like you to develop

something that is more graphic in both areas. You see, they already have similar versions of this type of game now, and their market is ready to go to the next level. I see the Internet market as secondary because we can't get the virtual reality equipment and software into an Internet mode. Maybe when PCs get faster, we'll be able to tap into it at that level, but not now. So, Kent, do you understand what you need to be doing on Lucky?"

QUESTIONS • EXERCISES

1. What are the ethical and legal issues?
2. What are Kent's options?
3. Discuss the acceptability and commercial use of sex, violence, and gambling in the United States.
4. Are marketing sex, violence, and gambling acceptable in other countries if they fit their culture?

*This case is strictly hypothetical; any resemblance to real persons, companies, or situations is coincidental.

Check Your EQ

Check your EQ, or Ethics Quotient, by completing the following. Assess your performance to evaluate your overall understanding of the chapter material.

1. Social responsibility in business refers to maximizing the visibility of social involvement.   **Yes**   **No**
2. Stakeholders provide resources that are more or less critical to a firm's long-term success.   **Yes**   **No**
3. Three primary stakeholders are customers, special-interest groups, and the media.   **Yes**   **No**
4. The most significant influence on ethical behavior in the organization is the opportunity to engage in unethical behavior.   **Yes**   **No**
5. The stakeholder perspective is useful in managing social responsibility and business ethics.   **Yes**   **No**

ANSWERS: 1. No. Social responsibility refers to an organization's obligation to maximize its positive impact on society and minimize its negative impact. 2. Yes. These resources are both tangible and intangible. 3. No. Although customers are primary stakeholders, special-interest groups are usually considered secondary stakeholders. 4. No. Ignorant others have more impact on ethical decisions within the organization. 5. Yes. The six steps to implement this approach were provided in this chapter.

Ethical Issues and the Institutionalization of Business Ethics

CHAPTER 3

Emerging Business Ethics Issues

CHAPTER OBJECTIVES

- To define ethical issues in the context of organizational ethics

- To examine ethical issues as they relate to the basic values of honesty, fairness, and integrity

- To delineate abusive and intimidating behavior, lying, conflicts of interest, bribery, corporate intelligence, discrimination, sexual harassment, environmental issues, fraud, insider trading, intellectual-property rights, and privacy as business ethics issues

- To examine the challenge of determining an ethical issue in business

CHAPTER OUTLINE

AN ETHICAL DILEMMA*

As Lavonda sat in the Ethics Office of the vice president of Emma-Action Pharmaceuticals (EAP), she was worried. Because she was new in the company and didn't know the unwritten rules, the chain-of-command philosophy, and the employees and associates around her very well, her time in the soft leather chair of the office was very uncomfortable. Given how well things had started, it was painful for her to remember how she had gotten here.

Lavonda had been lured away from her last company because of her expertise in the pharmaceutical industry and her early success in management. Out of college just three and a half years, she had gotten out of the gate remarkably quickly. She had helpful mentors, challenging tasks that she excelled in, and came in below budget on each assignment. Lavonda was typically described as effective and efficient; in fact, at the last company, they even started to call her "E."

But the lure of a six-figure salary, the encounter with Allen (her future boss at EAP), and the chance to be close to her elderly mother made it nearly impossible for Lavonda to say no. She loved her mother and, being an only child, felt responsible for her. Her mother once said that she would prefer to take her own life rather than move to a nursing home.

In the beginning, Lavonda's immediate supervisor, Allen, had been very charming and taught her about the company, its products, the salespeople, and the politics. She knew from experience that she would have to earn the respect of the salespeople she would manage, all of whom were ten years her senior, and the fact that these men had never had a female boss was just another hurdle to overcome. Allen had helped her find a nice house in a good neighborhood, had assisted with the moving, and eventually had become more than her superior. The months slipped by, and their relationship had become "close," to the point where they began to discuss living arrangements. And then something strange happened—she heard a story about Allen and Karline.

Karline, who had come to EAP six months prior to Lavonda, worked in Human Resources, and in a few short months she had become head of the HR department at EAP amidst rumors of Allen "helping" her get the promotion. Six more months passed, and Lavonda had learned that the rumors about Karline and Allen were probably true. She heard the same type of scenario that she had experienced for herself: friend, helping with housing, possible intimacy, and so on. The rumors became so intense that Lavonda confronted Allen about them and discovered that they were true. Devastated, Lavonda ended the relationship with Allen in a heated confrontation, but it seemed as though Allen didn't understand that it was over.

Weeks went by with little contact between the two of them, and then one afternoon Allen stopped by her office. He apologized for his behavior, and Lavonda accepted his apology. But the next day he stopped by and began to touch and even grope Lavonda. She made a joke of it to defuse the situation, but several days later Allen repeated the same behavior, making several sexual remarks. He asked, "Honey, why can't it be like it was before?" and then he whispered some graphic sexual language.

Lavonda's face reddened and she said, "Allen, you are a pig. How dare you say such things to me! You've crossed the line. I've never heard such filth. Don't you ever say such things to me again, or I'll report you to Human Resources!"

Several weeks went by, and Lavonda got a phone call from Allen in which he described even more sexually suggestive things. Every few days, Allen would stop by or call and remind her of some "private" experience they had together, using vulgar sexual language. He would taunt her by saying, "Lavonda, you know you want this from me." It became almost a daily ritual. Allen never wrote any of the things down that he described to her, being sure not to leave tangible proof of his behavior, but occasionally he would grab or attempt to grab her sexually.

Eventually, Lavonda had had enough and went to the Human Resources Department to complain formally about Allen, his sexual advances, and the hostile environment that they had created. The person she met at HR was Karline. As Lavonda described the situation in detail, she finally said, "Karline, I need you to help me. What Allen is doing to me is wrong and illegal. I can't get my work done. He's undermining my position with my sales staff, he's giving me poor evaluations, and he's suggesting that I could change all that if I wanted to!"

Karline's response was, "Lavonda, I've heard what you've said, but I also have had people come to me with some very disturbing reports about you as well. For example, you and Allen were supposedly sleeping together, and he is your direct supervisor. If this was the case, then it should have been reported immediately; but it wasn't. You have no tangible evidence except for your word. Even if I believed you, the allegation that you had been sexually active with Allen can be construed as making all of what you've said mutual or consensual. If that's the case, then I would have to fire you because of the superior–employee ethics code, and a letter would go into your permanent file that would probably haunt your career for years to come. From my perspective, we can call this an informal and confidential meeting that was not to be repeated, or you can continue this formally and take your chances. It's your call, Lavonda, but you should know that I am disinclined to support your accusations."

In shock, Lavonda mumbled a thank you to Karline and left her office. The next day Allen stopped by, smiled, waved his finger at her and said, "Your next performance review is next week, and it doesn't look good. By the way, just so you know, the pharmaceutical industry is quite small, and I have friends at all the majors. Oh, I forgot to tell you how sorry I am for your mother and her cancer diagnosis. Chemo and the side effects are very draining. I'm glad that you're close by to help her through the ordeal. They say it takes months to fully recover. It would be horrible if you weren't here to help her and she had to go to a nursing home. Those places scare me."

Lavonda said, "Allen, why are you doing this to me? I'm not fond of you any more. We have no future together. Doesn't that tell you something?"

Allen smiled and said, "It tells me that you're not interested in a permanent relationship, which is good, because neither am I. And you know that if you want to be promoted or go to another company with a good recommendation, it all starts with me. Lavonda, there might be another 'solution' to your perceived problem. You know that new sales rep you just hired out of school, Soo-Chin? Well, if you could have her assigned to me and maybe 'coax her in the right way,' I know of a position in the company that would be a promotion for you and you wouldn't be around me. But everything depends upon the success of your coaxing."

So now here Lavonda was, about to meet with the vice president of ethical affairs. As she got up from the wingback leather chair, she pondered her alternatives and what had led her there. In school she had learned that each company had its own individual code of ethics, but she didn't know the reality of the code at EAP until it was too late.

QUESTIONS • EXERCISES

1. Keeping in mind the facts and timeline of this situation, discuss Lavonda's situation in terms of legal and ethical issues.
2. Discuss Lavonda's alternatives and possible professional and private outcomes for her.
3. Is Allen in violation of sexual harassment and/or sexual discrimination laws in the United States?
4. Certainly Allen has damaged Lavonda's performance level; however, discuss whether he has created a legally hostile work environment.

*This case is strictly hypothetical; any resemblance to real persons, companies, or situations is coincidental.

S takeholders' ethical concerns determine whether specific business actions and decisions are perceived as ethical or unethical. In the case of the government, community, and society, what was merely an ethical issue can soon become a legal debate and eventually law. Most ethical conflicts in which there are perceived dangers turn into litigation. Additionally, stakeholders often raise ethical issues when they exert pressure on businesses to make decisions that serve their particular agendas. For example, corporate shareholders often demand that managers make decisions that boost short-term earnings, thus maintaining or increasing the value of the shares of stock they own in that firm. Such pressure may have led managers at General Motors Corporation to overstate income by as much as $300–400 million, or approximately 50 percent of the profit it reported in one year. "It's not like that income shouldn't have been booked, it just shouldn't have been booked in all of [this year]." General Motors has denied any wrongdoing, and the Securities and Exchange Commission (SEC) is investigating General Motors and its relationship with one of its suppliers.[1]

Consumers also define the ethicality of actions relative to companies that can be in direct conflict with shareholders. For example, oil industry executives have told the U.S. Congress that legislation preventing gasoline price gouging could result in shortages and long lines, thus creating panic. Exxon Mobile's chairman and CEO has argued that higher prices would ensure less panic and that "shortage is a disaster and we don't want to go there." This initially sounds convincing, but recently Arizona's Attorney General explained that, although their gasoline comes from sources that have an adequate supply with no shortages, prices at the pumps have risen drastically. Additionally, Arizona's laws on price collusion and consumer fraud are very ineffective.[2]

People make ethical decisions only after they recognize that a particular issue or situation has an ethical component; thus, a first step toward understanding business ethics is to develop ethical-issue awareness. Ethical issues typically arise because of conflicts among individuals' personal moral philosophies and values, the values and culture of the organizations in which they work, and those of the society in which they live. The business environment presents many potential ethical conflicts. For example, a company's efforts to achieve its organizational objectives may collide with its employees' endeavors to fulfill their own personal goals. Similarly, consumers' desires for safe and quality products may conflict with a manufacturer's need to earn adequate profits. The ambition of top executives to secure sizable increases in compensation may conflict with the desires of shareholders to control costs and increase the value of the corporation. A manager's wish to hire specific employees that he or she likes may be at odds with the organization's intent to hire the best-qualified candidates, as well as with society's aim to offer equal opportunity to women and members of minority groups.

Characteristics of the job, the culture, and the organization of the society in which one does business can also create ethical issues. Gaining familiarity with the ethical issues that frequently arise in the business world will help you identify and resolve them when they occur.

In this chapter, we consider some of the ethical issues that are emerging in business today, how these issues arise from the demands of specific stakeholder groups. In the first half of the chapter, we explain certain universal ethical concepts that pervade business ethics, such as honesty, fairness, and integrity. The second half of the chapter

explores a number of emerging ethical issues, including abusive and intimidating behavior, lying, conflicts of interest, bribery, corporate intelligence, discrimination, sexual harassment, environmental issues, fraud, insider trading, intellectual-property rights,
and privacy. We also examine the challenge of determining an ethical issue in business.

RECOGNIZING AN ETHICAL ISSUE

Although we have described a number of relationships and situations that may generate ethical issues, in practice it can be difficult to recognize specific ethical issues. Failure to acknowledge such ethical issues is a great danger in any organization, particularly
if business is treated as a "game" in which ordinary rules of fairness do not apply.
Sometimes, people who take this view are willing to do things that are not only unethical but also illegal so that they can maximize their own position or boost the profits of their organization. However, just because an unsettled situation or activity is an
ethical issue does not mean the behavior is necessarily unethical. An ethical issue is
simply a situation, a problem, or even an opportunity that requires thought, discussion,
or investigation to make a decision. And because the business world is dynamic, new
ethical issues are emerging all the time. Table 3–1 defines specific ethical issues identified by employees in the National Business Ethics Survey (NBES). Two types of misconduct have been considered the leading ethical issues since 2000. Abusive or
intimidating behavior ranks as the most observed misconduct and lying to various
stakeholders is the second most observed misconduct. Conflicts of interest remain a
strong number-three ethical issue. Many of the issues discussed in this chapter are related to issues on Table 3–1.

Table 3–1 indicates the percentage of employees who observed specific types of
misconduct. Employees could select more than one form of misconduct; therefore,
each type of misconduct represents the percentage of employees who saw that particular act. Although Table 3–1 documents many types of ethical issues that exist in organizations, due to the almost infinite number of ways that misconduct can occur, it
is impossible in this chapter to list every conceivable ethical issue. Any type of manipulation, deceit, or even just the absence of transparency in decision making can create
harm to others. For example, collusion is a secret agreement between two or more
parties for a fraudulent, illegal, or deceitful purpose. "Deceitful purposes" is the relevant phrase in regards to business ethics, in that it suggests trickery, misrepresentation, or a strategy designed to lead others to believe one truth but not the entire truth.

Honesty

Honesty refers to truthfulness or trustworthiness. To be honest is to tell the truth to
the best of your knowledge without hiding anything. Confucius defined several levels
of honesty. The shallowest is called *Li*, and it relates to the superficial desires of a person. A key principle to *Li* is striving to convey feelings that outwardly are or appear to
be honest but that are ultimately driven by self-interest. The second level is *Yi*, or
righteousness, where a person does what is right based on reciprocity. The deepest
level of honesty is called *Ren*, and it is based on understanding of and empathy toward

TABLE 3-1	Specific Types of Observed Misconduct	
Abusive or intimidating behavior toward employees		21%
Lying to employees, customers, vendors, or to the public		19%
A situation that places employee interests over organizational interests		18%
Violations of safety regulations		16%
Misreporting of actual time worked		16%
E-mail and Internet abuse		13%
Discrimination on the basis of race, color, gender, age, or similar categories		12%
Stealing or theft		11%
Sexual harassment		9%
Provision of goods or services that fail to meet specifications		8%
Misuse of confidential information		7%
Alteration of documents		6%
Falsification or misrepresentation of financial records or reports		5%
Improper use of competitors' inside information		4%
Price fixing		3%
Giving or accepting bribes, kickbacks, or inappropriate gifts		3%

SOURCE: From *2005 National Business Ethics Survey: How Employees Perceive Ethics at Work,* 2005, p. 25. Copyright © 2006, Ethics Resource Center (ERC). Used with permission of the ERC, 1747 Pennsylvania Ave., N.W., Suite 400, Washington, DC 2006, www.ethics.org.

others. The Confucian version of Kant's Golden Rule is to treat inferiors as you would want superiors to treat you. As a result, virtues such as familial honor and reputation for honesty become paramount.

Issues related to honesty also arise because business is sometimes regarded as a "game" governed by its own rules rather than by those of society. Author Eric Beversluis suggests that honesty is a problem because people often reason along these lines:

1. Business relationships are a subset of human relationships that are governed by their own rules, which, in a market society, involve competition, profit maximization, and personal advancement within the organization.
2. Business can therefore be considered a game people play, comparable in certain respects to competitive sports such as basketball or boxing.
3. Ordinary rules and morality do not hold in games like basketball or boxing. (What if a basketball player did unto others as he would have them do unto him? What if a boxer decided it was wrong to try to injure another person?)
4. Logically, then, if business is a game like basketball or boxing, ordinary ethical rules do not apply.[3]

This type of reasoning leads many people to conclude that anything is acceptable in business. Indeed, several books have compared business to warfare—for example, *The Guerrilla Marketing Handbook* and *Sun Tsu: The Art of War for Managers.* The common theme in these books is that surprise attacks, guerrilla warfare, and other warlike tactics are necessary to win the battle for consumers' dollars. An example of this mentality at work is Larry Ellison, the CEO of Oracle. Ellison's warlike mentality is demonstrated by his decision to sell PeopleSoft's technology and let most of its eight thousand employees go. PeopleSoft CEO Craig Conway stated that "Ellison has followed a page straight out of Genghis Khan." Ellison has frequently recited phrases of the thirteenth century Mongol warlord such as "It's not enough that we win; everyone else must lose."[4] Recently Ellison was ordered to donate $100 million to charity and pay another $22 million to the attorneys who sued him for alleged stock-trading abuses. Ellison argues that he acted in good faith and in the best interests of Oracle and Oracle's shareholders.[5]

This business-as-war mentality may foster the idea that honesty is unnecessary in business. In addition, an intensely competitive environment creates the potential for companies to engage in questionable conduct. For example, as competition in the market for beer intensified, Miller, Coors, and Anheuser-Busch increasingly created advertising and offered products that appealed to younger consumers, even though marketing to minors under the age of 21 is illegal.

Many argue, however, that business is not a game like basketball or boxing; because people are not economically self-sufficient, they cannot withdraw from the game of business. Therefore, business ethics must not only make clear what rules apply in the "game" of business but must also develop rules appropriate to the involuntary nature of participation in it.[6]

Because of the economic motive, many in business can become confused with the opposite of honesty—dishonesty. *Dishonesty can be broadly defined as a lack of integrity, incomplete disclosure, and an unwillingness to tell the truth.* Dishonesty is also synonymous with lying, cheating, and stealing. Lying, cheating, and stealing are the actions usually associated with dishonest conduct. The causes of dishonesty are complex and relate to both individual and organizational pressures. Many employees lie to help achieve performance objectives. For example, they may be asked to lie about when a customer will receive a purchase. Lying can be segmented into (1) causing damage or harm; (2) a "white lie," which doesn't cause damage but can be called an excuse or something told to benefit someone else; and (3) statements that are obviously meant to engage or entertain with no malice. These definitions will become important to the remainder of this chapter.

Fairness

Fairness is the quality of being just, equitable, and impartial. Fairness clearly overlaps with other commonly used terms such as justice, equity, equality, and morality. There are three fundamental elements that seem to motivate people to be fair: equality, reciprocity and optimization. In business, **equality** is about how wealth or income is distributed between employees within a company, a country, or across the globe.

Reciprocity is an interchange of giving and receiving in social relationships. Reciprocity occurs when an action that has an effect upon another is reciprocated with an action that has an approximately equal effect upon the other. Reciprocity is the return of small favors that are approximately equal in value. For example, reciprocity implies that workers be compensated with wages that are approximately equal to their effort.

An ethical issue about reciprocity for business is the amount CEOs and other executives are paid in relation to their employees. Is a 431-to-1 pay ratio an example of ethical reciprocity? That is the average wage distance between a CEO and a production worker in the United States.

Optimization is the tradeoff between equity (that is, equality or fairness) and efficiency (that is, maximum productivity). Discriminating on the basis of gender, race, or religion is generally considered to be unfair because these qualities have little bearing upon a person's ability to do a job. The optimal way is to choose the employee who is the most talented, most proficient, most educated, and most able. Ideas of fairness are sometimes shaped by vested interests. One or both parties in the relationship may view an action as unfair or unethical because the outcome was less beneficial than expected.

Integrity

Integrity is one of the most important and often-cited terms regarding virtue, and it refers to being whole, sound, and in an unimpaired condition. In an organization, it means uncompromising adherence to ethical values. Integrity is connected to acting ethically; in other words, there are substantive or normative constraints on what it means to act with integrity. This usually rests on an organization's enduring values and unwillingness to deviate from standards of behavior.

At a minimum, businesses are expected to follow all applicable laws and regulations. In addition, organizations should not knowingly harm customers, clients, employees, or even other competitors through deception, misrepresentation, or coercion. Although businesspeople often act in their own economic self-interest, ethical business relations should be grounded on honesty, integrity, fairness, justice, and trust. Buyers should be able to trust sellers; lenders should be able to trust borrowers. Failure to live up to these expectations or to abide by laws and standards destroys trust and makes it difficult, if not impossible, to continue business exchanges.[7] These virtues become the glue that holds business relationships together, making everything else more effective and efficient.

ETHICAL ISSUES AND DILEMMAS IN BUSINESS

As mentioned earlier, stakeholders define a business's ethical issues. An **ethical issue** is a problem, situation, or opportunity that requires an individual, group, or organization to choose among several actions that must be evaluated as right or wrong, ethical or unethical. An **ethical dilemma** is a problem, situation, or opportunity that requires an individual, group, or organization to choose among several wrong or unethical actions. There is not simply one right or ethical choice in a dilemma, only less unethical or illegal choices as perceived by any and all stakeholders.

A constructive next step toward identifying and resolving ethical issues is to classify the issues that are relevant to most business organizations. In this section, we classify ethical issues in relation to abusive or intimidating behavior, lying, conflicts of interest, bribery, corporate intelligence, discrimination, sexual harassment, environmental issues, fraud, insider trading, intellectual-property rights, and privacy issues.

Figure 3–1 reflects the ethical issues that are most likely to have impact on shareholder value for companies over the next five years. It is interesting to note that executives feel that their companies' shareholder value will be significantly affected by job loss and offshoring jobs when outsourcing to improve efficiency. Surprisingly, the ability to exert political influence or political involvement is also a major issue.

Abusive or Intimidating Behavior

Abusive or **intimidating behavior** is the most common ethical problem for employees, but what does it mean to be abusive or intimidating? The concepts can mean anything—physical threats, false accusations, being annoying, profanity, insults, yelling,

---

FIGURE 3–1   Issues That Affect Corporate Shareholder Value

Which three issues are likely to have the most impact, positive or negative, on shareholder value for companies in your industry over the next 5 years? (Percentage of respondents selecting given issues as one of top three. All data weighted by GDP of constituent countries to adjust for differences in response rates from various regions.)

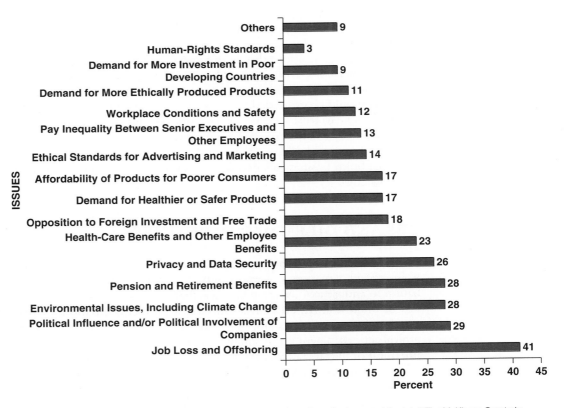

SOURCE: "The McKinsey Global Survey of Business Executives: Business and Society," *The McKinsey Quarterly: The Online Journal of McKinsey & Co.,* January 2006, http://www.mckinseyquarterly.com/article_print.aspx?L2=39&L3=0&ar=1741 (accessed March 8, 2006).

harshness, ignoring someone, and unreasonableness—and the meaning of these words can differ by person. It is important to understand that with each term there is a continuum. For example, what one person may define as yelling might be another's definition of normal speech. Civility in our society has been a concern, and the workplace is no exception. The productivity level of many organizations has been damaged by the time spent unraveling abusive relationships.

Is it abusive behavior to ask an employee to complete a project rather than be with a family member or relative in a crisis situation? What does it mean to speak profanely? Is profanity only related to specific words or other such terms that are common in today's business world? If you are using words that are normal in your language but others consider profanity, have you just insulted, abused, or disrespected them?

Within the concept of abusive behavior or intimidation, intent should be a consideration. If the employee was trying to convey a compliment, then it was probably a mistake. What if a male manager asks his female subordinate if they have a date for tonight because they are dressed so nice? Does the way (voice inflection) a word is said become important? Add to this the fact that we now live in a multicultural environment doing business and working with many different cultural groups and the businessperson soon realizes the depth of the ethical and legal issues that may arise. Finally, you have the problem of word meanings by age and within cultures. Is it ok to say "honey" to an employee, fellow employee, employee friend, your superior, and does it depend on gender or location? For example, if you were to call a friend that worked with you "honey" in southern Illinois, Arkansas, or Kentucky, do you have the same acceptability factor in northern Illinois, Michigan, or Minnesota? Does abusive behavior vary by different genders? It is possible the term *honey* could be acceptable speech in some environments, or could it be construed as being abusive or intimidating in other situations?

Bullying is associated with a hostile workplace where someone (or a group) considered a target is threatened, harassed, belittled, or verbally abused or overly criticized. Bullying may create what some may call a hostile environment, but this term is generally associated with sexual harassment. Although sexual harassment has legal recourse, bullying has little legal recourse at this time. Bullying can cause psychological damage that can result in health-endangering consequences to the target. As Table 3–2 indicates, bullying can use a mix of verbal, nonverbal, and manipulative threatening expressions to damage workplace productivity. One may wonder why workers tolerate such activities; the problem is that 81 percent of workplace bullies are supervisors. A top officer at Boeing cited an employee survey indicating that 26 percent had observed abusive or intimidating behavior by management.[8]

Bullying can also occur between companies that are in intense competition. Even respected companies such as Intel have been accused of monopolistic bullying. A competitor, Advanced Micro Devices (AMD), claimed in a lawsuit that thirty-eight companies, including Dell and Sony, were strong-arming customers into buying Intel chips rather than those marketed by AMD. The AMD lawsuit seeks billions of dollars and will take years to litigate. In many cases, the alleged misconduct can not only have monetary and legal implications but also can threaten reputation, investor confidence, and customer loyalty. A front-cover *Forbes* headline stated "Intel to AMD: Drop Dead." An example of the intense competition and Intel's ability to use its large size won it

TABLE 3-2	Actions Associated with Bullies

1. Spreading rumors to damage others

2. Blocking others' communication in the workplace

3. Flaunting status or authority to take advantage of others

4. Discrediting others' ideas and opinions

5. Use of e-mails to demean others

6. Failing to communicate or return communication

7. Insults, yelling, and shouting

8. Using terminology to discriminate by gender, race, or age

9. Using eye or body language to hurt others or their reputation

10. Taking credit for others' work or ideas

SOURCE: Cathi McMahan, "Are You A Bully?," *Inside Seven*, California Department of Transportation Newsletter, June 1999, page 6.

the high-profile Apple account, displacing IBM and Freescale. ADM said it had no opportunity to bid because Intel offered to deploy six hundred Indian engineers to help Apple software run more smoothly on Intel chips.[9]

Lying

Earlier in this chapter, we discussed the definitions of **lying** and how it relates to distorting the truth. We mentioned three types of lies, one of which is joking without malice. The other two can become very troublesome for businesses. For example, one can lie by commission or omission. *Commission lying* is creating a perception or belief by words that intentionally deceive the receiver of the message. For example, lying about being at work, expense reports, or carrying out work assignments. Commission lying also entails intentionally creating "noise" within the communication that knowingly confuses or deceives the receiver. *Noise* can be defined as technical explanations that the communicator knows the receiver does not understand. It can be the intentional use of communication forms that make it difficult for the receiver to actually hear the true message. Using legal terms or relating to unfamiliar processes and systems to explain what was done in a work situation facilitate this type of lie.

Lying by commission can be complex forms, procedures, contracts, words that are spelled the same but have different meanings, or refuting the truth with a false statement. Forms of commission lying are puffery in advertising. For example saying that a product is "homemade" when it is made in a factory is lying. "Made from scratch" in cooking technically means that all ingredients within the product were distinct and separate and have not been combined prior to the beginning of the production process. One can lie by commission by showing a picture of the product that does not reflect the actual product. This happens frequently in business. For example, a national fast-food chain came out with a new product that had lettuce in it. There are many types of lettuce and the lettuce used in the national ad campaign both in print and TV used romaine lettuce. Yet this fast-food chain does not purchase that variety; they purchase iceberg lettuce. The obvious reason for the romaine is that it is prettier or more appealing than shredded iceberg lettuce. Another example is Schick's complaint against Gillette, alleging that the latter's claims for its Mach 3 Turbo Razor as "the world's best shave" and "the best a man can get" are false and misleading.

Omission lying is intentionally not informing the channel member of any differences, problems, safety warnings, or negative issues relating to the product, service, or company that significantly affects awareness, intention, or behavior. A classic example for decades was the tobacco manufacturers that did not allow negative research to appear on cigarettes and cigars. The drug Vioxx is being questioned because the manufacturer allegedly did not inform consumers as to the degree and occurrence of side effects, one of which is death. Finally, when lying damages others, it can be the focus of a lawsuit. For example, a fifty-state class action lawsuit against Ford for failing to disclose, once it became known, the safety risk associated with driving the Ford Explorer equipped with certain Firestone tires resulted in a $51.5 million nationwide settlement.

When a lie becomes unethical in business, it is based on the context and intent to distort the truth. A lie becomes illegal if it is determined by the judgment of courts to damage others. Some businesspeople may believe that one must lie a little or that the occasional lie is sanctioned by the organization. The question you need to ask is whether lies are distorting openness and transparency and other values that are associated with ethical behavior.

Conflicts of Interest

A **conflict of interest** exists when an individual must choose whether to advance his or her own interests, those of the organization, or those of some other group. For example, former Food and Drug Administration (FDA) head Lester Crawford and his wife owned stock in companies that were regulated by the FDA while he was at the federal agency. In one case, Crawford was on a company's board of directors that directly dealt with the FDA. While he was at the FDA, records show that ethics officials were purportedly concerned with Crawford's holdings and the appearance of a conflict of interest. One ethics official wrote "need more info" and called the broker who wrote "sending more info." But no ethics officer's signature appears on any form. Soon after, Crawford announced he was leaving the FDA. People knowledgeable of the matter said that the move occurred because of stock holdings that he might have failed to fully disclose. The inspector general at the Health and Human Services investigated the circumstances surrounding his departure.[10] Because his family interests conflicted with his position at the FDA, his actions constitute a conflict of interest.

To avoid conflicts of interest, employees must be able to separate their private interests from their business dealings. Organizations must also avoid potential conflicts of interest when providing products.[11] The U.S. General Accounting Office has found conflicts of interest when the government has awarded bids on defense contracts. The conflicts of interest usually relate to hiring friends, relatives, or retired military officers to enhance the probability of getting the contract.[12]

Bribery

Bribery is the practice of offering something (usually money) in order to gain an illicit advantage. The key issue regarding whether or not something is considered bribery is determining whether the act is illicit or contrary to accepted morality or convention. Bribery therefore is defined as an unlawful act, but it can be a business ethics issue. The reason is that bribery can be defined differently in varying situations and cultural environments.

Bribery can be defined many ways. For example, there is something called active corruption or **active bribery,** meaning that the person who promises or gives the bribe commits the offense. **Passive bribery** is an offense committed by the official who receives the bribe. It is not an offense, however, if the advantage was permitted or required by the written law or regulation of the foreign public official's country, including case law.

Small **facilitation payments** made to obtain or retain business or other improper advantages do not constitute bribery payments. In some countries, such payments are made to induce public officials to perform their functions such as issuing licenses or permits. However, criminalization by other countries does not seem a practical or effective complementary action. In many developed countries, it is generally recognized that employees should not accept bribes, personal payments, gifts, or special favors from people who hope to influence the outcome of a decision. However, bribery is an accepted way of doing business in many countries. Bribes have been associated with the downfall of many managers, legislators, and government officials. One source estimates that some $80 billion is paid out worldwide in the form of bribes or some other payoff every year.[13]

When a government official accepts a bribe, it is usually from a business that seeks some favor—perhaps a chance to influence legislation that affects it. Giving bribes to legislators or public officials, then, is a business ethics issue. For example, the Bataan nuclear power plant in the Philippines was built at a cost of more than $2 billion. The contractor, Westinghouse, admitted paying $17 million in commissions to a friend of former President Marcos.[14]

Corporate Intelligence

Many issues related to corporate intelligence have surfaced in the last few years. Defined broadly, **corporate intelligence** is the collection and analysis of information on markets, technologies, customers, and competitors, as well as on socioeconomic and external political trends. There are three distinct types of intelligence models: a passive monitoring system for early warning, tactical field support, and support dedicated to top-management strategy. Today, theft of trade secrets is estimated at $100 billion. One explanation is the increase in people with intelligence gathering competence and the proliferation of advanced technology.[15]

Corporate intelligence (CI) involves an in-depth discovery of information from corporate records, court documents, regulatory filings, and press releases, as well as any other background information that can be found about a company or its executives. Corporate intelligence is a legitimate inquiry into meaningful information that can be used in staying competitive. Corporate intelligence like other areas in business can be abused if due diligence is not taken to maintain legal and ethical methods of discovery. Computers, LANs (local-area networks) and the Internet have made the theft of trade secrets very easy. Proprietary information like secret formulas, manufacturing schematics, merger or acquisition plans, and marketing strategies all have tremendous value. A lack of security and proper training allows one to use a variety of techniques to gain access to a company's vital information. Some techniques for accessing valuable corporate information include physically removing the hard drive and copying the information to another machine, hacking, dumpster diving, social engineering, bribery, and hiring away key employees.

Hacking is considered one of the top three methods for obtaining trade secrets. Currently, there are over one hundred thousand websites that offer free downloadable and customizable hacking tools that require no in-depth knowledge of protocols or Internet protocol addressing. Hacking has three categories: system, remote, and physical. **System hacking** assumes that the attacker already has access to a low-level, privileged-user account. **Remote hacking** involves attempting to penetrate remotely a system across the Internet. A remote hacker usually begins with no special privileges and tries to obtain higher level or administrative access. Several forms of this type of hacking include unexpected input, buffer overflows, default configurations, and poor system administrator practices. **Physical hacking** requires that the CI agent enter a facility personally. Once inside, he or she can find a vacant or unsecured workstation with an employee's login name and password. Next, the CI agent searches for memos or unused letterheads and inserts the documents into the corporate mail system. Or the CI agent could gain physical access to a server or telephone room, look for remote-access equipment, note any telephone numbers written on wall jacks, and place a protocol analyzer in a wiring closet to capture data, user names, and passwords.

Social engineering is another popular method of obtaining valuable corporate information. The basic goals are the same as hacking. **Social engineering** is the tricking of individuals into revealing their passwords or other valuable corporate information. Tactics include casual conversations with relatives of company executives and sending e-mail claiming to be a system administrator that asks for passwords under the guise of "important system administration work." Another common social engineering trick is **shoulder surfing,** in which someone simply looks over an employee's shoulder while he or she types in a password. **Password guessing** is another easy social engineering technique. If a person can find out personal things about someone, he or she might be able to use that information to guess a password. For example, a child's name, birthdays and anniversaries, and Social Security numbers are all common passwords and are easily guessed or figured out by someone trying to do so.

Dumpster diving is messy but very successful for acquiring trade secrets. Once trash is discarded onto a public street or alley, it is considered fair game. Trash can provide a rich source of information for any CI agent. Phone books can give a hacker names and numbers of people to target and impersonate. Organizational charts contain information about people who are in positions of authority within the organization. Memos provide small amounts of useful information and assist in the creation of authentic-looking fake memos.

Whacking is wireless hacking. To eavesdrop on wireless networks, all a CI agent needs is the right kind of radio and to be within range of a wireless transmission. Once tapped into a wireless network, an intruder can easily access anything on both the wired and wireless networks because the data sent over networks is usually unencrypted. If a company is not using wireless networking, an attacker can pose as a janitor and insert a rogue wireless access node into a supposedly secure hard-wired network.

Phone eavesdropping is yet another tool in the game of CI agent. A person with a digital recording device can monitor and record a fax line. By playing the recording back an intruder can reproduce an exact copy of a message without anyone's knowledge. Even without monitoring a fax line, a fax sent to a "communal" fax machine can be read or copied. By picking up an extension or by tapping a telephone, it is possible to record the tones that represent someone's account number and password using a tape recorder. The tape recording can then be replayed over the telephone to gain access to someone else's account.

Discrimination

Although a person's racial and sexual prejudices belong to the domain of individual ethics, racial and sexual discrimination in the workplace creates ethical issues within the business world. **Discrimination** on the basis of race, color, religion, sex, marital status, sexual orientation, public assistance status, disability, age, national origin, or veteran status are illegal in the United States. Additionally, discrimination on the basis of political opinions or affiliation with a union is defined as harassment.

A company in the United States can be sued if it (1) refuses to hire an individual, (2) maintains a system of employment that unreasonably excludes an individual from employment, (3) discharges an individual, or (4) discriminates against an individual with respect to hiring, employment terms, promotion, or privileges of employment as it relates to the definition of discrimination.

Race, gender, and age discrimination are a major source of ethical and legal debate in the workplace. Between seventy-five thousand and eighty thousand charges of discrimination are filed annually with the **Equal Employment Opportunity Commission** (EEOC).[16] Discrimination remains a significant ethical issue in business despite nearly forty years of legislation attempting to outlaw it.

Once dominated by European American men, the U.S. work force today includes significantly more women, African Americans, Hispanics, and other minorities, as well as disabled and older workers. Experts project that within the next fifty years, Hispanics will represent 24 percent of the population, and African Americans and Asian/Pacific Islanders will comprise 13 percent and 9 percent, respectively.[17] These groups have traditionally faced discrimination and higher unemployment rates and been denied opportunities to assume leadership roles in corporate America. For example, even today there are only three African Americans currently leading *Fortune* 100 companies: Richard Parsons, chairman and CEO of Time Warner Inc.; Kenneth Chenault, chairman and CEO of American Express Company; and Stanley O'Neal, chairman and CEO of Merrill Lynch. In the case of Merrill Lynch, even O'Neal is not immune to racial allegations. A complaint in federal court notes that only 2 percent of Merrill Lynch's 14,690 brokers are African American, although that percentage matches the industry standard. The ethical and potential illegal issue is Merrill Lynch's own claim of a higher, 6.5 percent, standard. George McReynolds, an African American broker for Merrill Lynch since 1983, contends that race is being used as a discrimination tool in the allocation of accounts, referrals, and leads. Although Merrill's African American broker trainee rate is approximately 7 percent, the argument is that those trainees will be discouraged to continue because of the discrimination.[18]

Another form of discrimination involves discriminating against individuals on the basis of age. The **Age Discrimination in Employment Act** specifically outlaws hiring practices that discriminate against people between the ages of 49 and 69, as well as those that require employees to retire before the age of 70. Despite this legislation, charges of age discrimination persist in the workplace. For example, the EEOC has charged Sidley Austin Brown & Wood, a Chicago-based international law firm with over fifteen hundred lawyers, with age discrimination when it selected "partners" for expulsion from the firm on account of their age. The act prohibits employers with twenty or more employees from making employment decisions, including decisions regarding the termination of employment, on the basis of age or from requiring retirement after the age of 40. EEOC trial attorney Deborah Hamilton stated that "having the power to fire an employee does not mean that a law firm or any other covered employer can do so because of the employee's age, if the employee is over 40. That is a violation of the ADEA and that the making of unlawful age-based selections for termination is precisely what EEOC is targeting in this lawsuit."[19] Sidley Austin Brown & Wood deny the charges, and at this point the case is still pending.

A survey by the American Association for Retired Persons (AARP), an advocacy organization for people ages 50 years and older, highlighted how little most companies value older workers. When the AARP mailed invitations to ten thousand companies for a chance to compete for a listing in *Modern Maturity* magazine as one of the "best employers for workers over 50," it received just fourteen applications. Given that nearly 20 percent of the nation's workers will be 55 years old or over by 2015, many companies need to change their approach toward older workers.[20]

To help build work forces that reflect their customer base, many companies have initiated **affirmative action programs,** which involve efforts to recruit, hire, train, and promote qualified individuals from groups that have traditionally been discriminated against on the basis of race, gender, or other characteristics. Such initiatives may be imposed by federal law on an employer that contracts or subcontracts for business with the federal government, as part of a settlement agreement with a state or federal agency, or by court order.[21] For example, Safeway, a chain of supermarkets, established a program to expand opportunities for women in middle- and upper-level management after settling a sex-discrimination lawsuit.[22] However, many companies voluntarily implement affirmative action plans in order to build a more diverse work force.[23] For example, a Chicago real estate developer decided to help employers identify available female workers by launching the Female Employment Initiative, an outreach program designed to create opportunities for women in the construction industry through training programs, counseling and information services, and referral listings.[24]

Although many people believe that affirmative action requires that quotas be used to govern employment decisions, it is important to note that two decades of Supreme Court rulings have made it clear that affirmative action does not permit or require quotas, reverse discrimination, or favorable treatment of unqualified women or minorities. To ensure that affirmative action programs are fair, the Supreme Court has established a number of standards to guide their implementation: (1) There must be a strong reason for developing an affirmative action program; (2) affirmative action programs must apply only to qualified candidates; and (3) affirmative action programs must be limited and temporary and therefore cannot include "rigid and inflexible quotas."[25]

Discrimination can also be an ethical issue in business when companies use race or other personal factors to discriminate against specific groups of customers. Many companies have been accused of using race to deny service or charge higher prices to certain ethnic groups. For example, four airlines have settled lawsuits alleging discrimination against perceived Arab, Middle Eastern, or Southeast Asian descent passengers. United, American, Continental, and Delta have all denied any violations but agreed to spend as much as $1.5 million to train staff on respecting civil rights.[26]

Sexual Harassment

Sexual harassment is a form of sex discrimination that violates Title VII of the Civil Rights Act of 1964. Title VII applies to employers with fifteen or more employees, including state and local governments. To understand the magnitude of this volatile issue, in one year the EEOC received 13,136 charges of sexual harassment, over 15 percent of which were filed by men. In another recent year, the EEOC resolved 13,786 sexual harassment charges and recovered $37.1 million in penalties.[27] **Sexual harassment** can be defined as any repeated, unwanted behavior of a sexual nature perpetrated upon one individual by another. It may be verbal, visual, written, or physical and can occur between people of different genders or those of the same sex. "Workplace display of sexually explicit material—photos, magazines, or posters—may constitute a hostile work environment harassment, even though the private possession, reading, and consensual sharing of such materials is protected under the Constitution."[28]

To establish sexual harassment, an employee must understand the definition of a **hostile work environment,** for which three criteria must be met: the conduct was unwelcome; the conduct was severe, pervasive, and regarded by the claimant as so hostile or offensive as to alter his or her conditions of employment; and the conduct was such that a reasonable person would find it hostile or offensive. To assert a hostile work environment, an employee need not prove that it seriously affected his or her psychological well-being nor caused an injury; the decisive issue is whether the conduct interfered with the claimant's work performance.[29]

Sexual harassment includes unwanted sexual approaches (including touching, feeling, groping) and/or repeated unpleasant, degrading, or sexist remarks directed toward an employee with the implied suggestion that the target's employment status, promotion, or favorable treatment depend on a positive response and/or cooperation. It can be regarded as a private nuisance, unfair labor practice, or, in some states, a civil wrong (tort) that may be the basis for a lawsuit against the individual who made the advances and against the employer who did not take steps to halt the harassment. The law is primarily concerned with the impact of the behavior and not the intent. An important facet of sexual harassment law is its focus on the victim's reasonable behaviors and expectations.[30] However, the definition of reasonable varies from state to state, as does the concept of expectations. In addition, an argument used by some in defense of sexual harassment is the freedom of speech granted by the First Amendment.

The key ethical issue within sexual harassment is called dual relationships or unethically intimate relationships. A **dual relationship** is defined as a personal, loving, and/or sexual relationship with someone with whom you share professional responsibilities. Potentially, **unethical dual relationships** are those where the relationship causes either a direct or indirect conflict of interest or a risk of impairment to professional judgment.[31] Another important factor in these cases is intent. If the sexual advances in any form are considered mutual, then consent is created. The problem is that, unless the employee or employer gets something in writing before the romantic action, consent can always be questioned, and when it comes to sexual harassment, the alleged perpetrator must prove mutual consent.

For example, in a case in Illinois, a professor made advances to his office assistant, repeatedly asking her "Do you love me?" and "Would you ever marry a man like me?" He would also ask her for hugs, rub her shoulders, and tickle her. The assistant was troubled by these behaviors, and although she confided her distress to the proper authorities, nothing was done until she went to another institution and filed an official complaint. The university responded by directing the professor to undergo training in proper behavior toward female students and by placing a letter in his personnel file, outlining the actions to be taken and the method for evaluating their effectiveness. In this case, the university believed that there was no duality and the EEOC awarded no monetary damages to the assistant.

Three former female employees sued Florida-based Airguide Corporation and its parent company, Pioneer Metals, Inc., for sexual harassment. The courts awarded each of the three women $1 million, but the penalties for sexual harassment do not stop there. In addition, Airguard and Pioneer Metals must conduct annual training in nineteen facilities in Florida and undergo monitoring by the EEOC for three years.[32]

To avoid sexual misconduct or harassment charges a company should, at the minimum, take the following steps:

1. *A statement of policy* naming someone in the company as ultimately responsible for preventing harassment at the company.
2. *A definition of sexual harassment* that includes unwelcome advances, requests for sexual favors, and any other verbal, visual, or physical conduct of a sexual nature; that provides examples of each; and that reminds employees that the list of examples is not all inclusive.
3. *A nonretaliation policy* that protects complainants and witnesses.
4. *Specific procedures for prevention* of such practices at early stages. However, if a company puts these procedures in writing, they are expected by law to train, measure, and ensure that the policies are being enforced.
5. *Establish, enforce, and encourage* victims of sexual harassment to report the behavior to authorized individuals.
6. *Establish a reporting procedure.*
7. *Make sure that the company has timely reporting requirements to the proper authorities.* Usually, there is a time limitation to file the complaint for a formal administrative sexual charge, ranging from six months to a year. However, the

failure to meet a shorter complaint period (for example, sixty to ninety days) so that a "rapid response" and remediation may occur and to help to ensure a harassment-free environment could be a company's defense against the charge that it was negligent.

Once these steps have been taken, a training program should identify and describe forms of sexual harassment and give examples, outline the grievance procedure, explain how to use the procedures and discuss the importance of them, discuss the penalty for violation, and train employees for the essential need of a workplace that is free from harassment, offensive conduct, or intimidation. A corporation's training program should cover such items as how to spot sexual harassment; how to investigate complaints including proper documentation; what to do about observed sexual harassment, even when no complaint has been filed; how to keep the work environment as professional and nonhostile as possible; how to teach employees that the consequences can be dismissal; and how to train management to understand follow-up procedures on incidents.

Environmental Issues

Environmental issues are becoming the significant concerns within the business community. The **Kyoto Protocol,** one example of the world's growing concern about global warming, is an international treaty on climate change committed to reducing emissions of carbon dioxide and five other greenhouse gases and to engaging in emissions trading if they maintain or increase emissions of these gases. The objective is to stabilize greenhouse-gas concentrations in the atmosphere at a level that would prevent dangerous climate changes. Some current estimates indicate that, if these objectives are not successfully and completely implemented, the predicted global temperature increase could be between 1.4°C to 5.8°C. Possible massive tidal surges and extreme weather patterns are in store for our planet in the future if countries do not restrict specific gases emanating from business activities. The United States is one of the only countries not to sign the protocol.

Water pollution results from the dumping of raw sewage and toxic chemicals into rivers and oceans, from oil and gasoline spills, and from the burial of industrial wastes in the ground where they may filter into underground water supplies. Fertilizers and pesticides used in farming and grounds maintenance also drain into water supplies with each rainfall. When these chemicals reach the oceans, they encourage the growth of algae that use up all the nearby oxygen, thus killing the sea life. According to the Environmental Protection Agency (EPA), more than a third of the nation's rivers, lakes, and coastal waters are not safe for swimming or fishing as a result of contaminated runoff.

Waste management, or the green revolution, has flourished in Europe, especially in Germany, and appears to be growing globally. One green issue is plastic; in the United States alone, 30 million plastic bottles are thrown away daily for a total of nearly 11 billion a year. Those that are recycled use large amounts of energy in the recycling process. An even bigger problem for the future is that, as the world becomes more capitalistic, more people will buy more things using plastics that are made from oil and that do not degrade easily. In the twenty-first century, businesses must devise a solution to this ethical issue.

Fraud

When an individual engages in deceptive practices to advance his or her own interests over those of his or her organization or some other group, charges of fraud may result. In general, **fraud** is any purposeful communication that deceives, manipulates, or conceals facts in order to create a false impression. Fraud is a crime and convictions may result in fines, imprisonment, or both. Fraud costs U.S. organizations more than $400 billion a year; the average company loses about 6 percent of total revenues to fraud and abuses committed by its own employees.[33] Among the most common fraudulent activities employees report about their coworkers are stealing office supplies or shoplifting, claiming to have worked extra hours, and stealing money or products.[34] Table 3–3 indicates what fraud examiners view as the biggest risk to companies. In recent years, accounting fraud has become a major ethical issue, but as we will see, fraud can also relate to marketing and consumer issues as well.

Accounting fraud usually involves a corporation's financial reports in which companies provide important information on which investors and others base decisions that may involve millions of dollars. If the documents contain inaccurate information, whether intentionally or not, then lawsuits and criminal penalties may result. Thomas H. Lee Partners, a private-equity firm that invested in Refco Inc., sued to recover $245 million in losses that it allegedly sustained because of accounting fraud. After spending $10 million and thousands of accounting hours, Thomas H. Lee Partners invested $453 million in Refco. But former CEO Phillip R. Bennett, former CEO and President Santo C. Maggio, and former President Tone Grant are alleged to have "cooked the books." Bennett was indicted by a federal grand jury on charges of hiding as much as $720 million in bad debts from auditors and investors.[35] Such scrutiny of financial reporting increased dramatically in the wake of accounting scandals in the early twenty-first century. As a result of the negative publicity surrounding the allegations of accounting fraud at a number of companies, many firms were forced to take a second look at their financial documents. More than a few chose to restate their earnings to avoid being drawn into the scandal.[36] For example, Qwest Communications, which provides local and long-distance telephone service, announced that it overstated revenue by $1.9 billion during 2000 and was forced to restate about $1.5 billion in earnings for that year.[37]

The field of accounting has changed dramatically over the last decade. The profession used to have a club-type mentality: those who became certified public accountants (CPAs) were not concerned about competition. Now CPAs advertise their

TABLE 3-3	Greatest Fraud Risk for Companies
Conflicts of interest	63%
Fraudulent financial statements	57%
Billing schemes	31%
Expense and reimbursement schemes	29%
Bribery/economic extortions	25%

SOURCE: Snapshots, "2005 Oversight Systems Report on Corporate Fraud Questionnaire of 208 Certified Fraud Examiners," *USA Today,* February 2, 2006, B1.

skills and short-term results in an environment in which competition has increased and overall billable hours have significantly decreased because of technological innovations. Additionally, accountants are now permitted to charge performance-based fees rather than hourly rates, a rule change that encouraged some large accounting firms to promote tax-avoidance strategies for high-income individuals because the firms can charge 10 to 40 percent of the amount of taxes saved.[38]

Pressures on accountants today include time, reduced fees, client requests to alter opinions concerning financial conditions or lower tax payments, and increased competition. Other issues that accountants face daily involve compliance with complex rules and regulations, data overload, contingent fees, and commissions. An accountant's life is filled with rules and data that have to be interpreted correctly, and because of such pressures and the ethical predicaments they spawn, problems within the accounting industry are on the rise.

As a result, accountants must abide by a strict code of ethics that defines their responsibilities to their clients and the public interest. The code also discusses the concepts of integrity, objectivity, independence, and due care. Despite the standards the code provides, the accounting industry has been the source of numerous fraud investigations in recent years. Congress passed the Sarbanes–Oxley Act in 2002 to address many of the issues that could create conflicts of interest for accounting firms auditing public corporations. The law generally prohibits accounting firms from providing both auditing and consulting services to the same firm. Additionally, the law specifies that corporate boards of directors must include outside directors with financial knowledge on the company's audit committee.

Marketing fraud—the process of creating, distributing, promoting, and pricing products—is another business area that generates potential ethical issues. False or misleading marketing communications can destroy customers' trust in a company. Lying, a major ethical issue involving communications, is potentially a significant problem. In both external and internal communications, it causes ethical predicaments because it destroys trust. For example, former executives of WorldCom—Bernie Ebbers, Scott Sullivan, and David Myers—were arrested and charged with concealing $3.8 billion in expenses as well as lying to investors and regulators to hide their deception.[39] As a result of their lying and fraud, Ebbers was sentenced to twenty-five years in prison, Sullivan to five years, and Myers to a year and a day—for which they must serve a minimum of 80 percent.

False or deceptive advertising is a key issue in marketing communications. One set of laws that is common to many countries are laws concerning deceptive advertising—that is, advertisements that are not clearly labeled as advertisements. For example, in the United States, Section 5 of the Federal Trade Commission (FTC) Act addresses deceptive advertising. Abuses in advertising can range from exaggerated claims and concealed facts to outright lying, although improper categorization of advertising claims is the critical point. Courts place false or misleading advertisements into three categories: puffery, implied falsity, and literal falsity. **Puffery** can be defined as exaggerated advertising, blustering, and boasting upon which no reasonable buyer would rely and is not actionable under the Lanham Act. For example, in a Lanham Act suit between two shaving products companies, the defendant advertised that the moisturizing strip on its shaving razor was "six times smoother" than its competitors' strips, while showing a man rubbing his hand down his face. The court rejected the defendant's argument that "six times smoother" implied that only the moisturizing strip on the razor's head was smoother. Instead, the court found that the "six times smoother" advertising claim implied that the consumer would receive a smoother shave from the defendant's razor as a whole, a claim that was false.[40]

Implied falsity means that the message has a tendency to mislead, confuse, or deceive the public. The advertising claims that use implied falsity are those that are literally true but imply another message that is false. In most cases, this can be done only through a time-consuming and expensive consumer survey, whose results are often inconclusive.[41]

The characterization of an advertising claim as **literally false** can be divided into two subcategories: *tests prove* (*establishment claims*), in which the advertisement cites a study or test that establishes the claim; and *bald assertions* (*nonestablishment claims*), in which the advertisement makes a claim that cannot be substantiated, as when a commercial states that a certain product is superior to any other on the market. For example, the FTC filed formal complaints against Stock Value 1 Inc. and Comstar Communications Inc. for making unsubstantiated claims that their radiation-protection patches block the electromagnetic energy emitted by cellular telephones. The FTC's complaint charged that the companies "made false statements that their products had been scientifically 'proven' and tested," when in fact that was not the case.[42]

Another form of advertising abuse involves making ambiguous statements in which the words are so weak or general that the viewer, reader, or listener must infer the advertiser's intended message. These "weasel words" are inherently vague and enable the advertiser to deny any intent to deceive. The verb *help* is a good example (as in expressions such as "helps prevent," "helps fight," "helps make you feel").[43] Consumers may view such advertisements as unethical because they fail to communicate all the information needed to make a good purchasing decision or because they deceive the consumer outright.

Labeling issues are even murkier. For example, Netgear Inc. agreed to settle a class-action suit that claimed it exaggerated the data-transfer speeds of its wireless equipment. As part of the settlement, the company must pay $700,000 in legal fees, give a 15 percent discount to members of the class action, donate $25,000 of product to charity, and include disclaimers about the data-transfer speed of its products.[44]

Slamming, or changing a customer's phone service without authorization, is another important issue involving labeling that is specific to the telephone industry. AT&T sued Business Discount Plan (BDP), accusing it of using fraud and deception to routinely "slam" customers to its telecommunication service by suggesting that they were affiliated with AT&T. As part of the settlement, BDP had to send letters to consumers telling them that BDP was not affiliated with AT&T.[45] Such misleading behavior creates ethical issues because the communicated messages do not include all the information that consumers need to make good purchasing decisions, frustrating and angering customers who feel that they have been deceived. In addition, they damage the seller's credibility and reputation.

Advertising and direct sales communication can also mislead by concealing the facts within the message. For instance, a salesperson anxious to sell a medical insurance policy might list a large number of illnesses covered by the policy but fail to mention that it does not cover some commonly covered illnesses. Indeed, the fastest-growing area of fraudulent activity is in direct marketing, which employs the telephone and impersonal media to communicate information to customers, who then purchase products via mail, telephone, or the Internet.

Consumer Fraud

Consumer fraud is when consumers attempt to deceive businesses for their own gain. In 2005 the FTC estimated that 25 million consumers had engaged in consumer fraud.[46] Shoplifting, for example, accounts for nearly 32 percent of the losses of the 118 largest U.S. retail chains, although this figure is still far outweighed by the nearly 49 percent of losses perpetrated by store employees, according to the National Retail Security Survey. Together with vendor fraud and administrative error, these losses cost U.S. retailers more than $31 billion annually.[47]

Consumers engage in many other forms of fraud against businesses, including price-tag switching, item switching, lying to obtain age-related and other discounts, and taking advantage of generous return policies by returning used items, especially clothing that has been worn (with the price tags still attached). Such behavior by consumers affects retail stores as well as other consumers who, for example, may unwittingly purchase new clothing that has actually been worn.[48]

Consumer fraud involves intentional deception to derive an unfair economic advantage by an individual or group over an organization. Examples of fraudulent activities include shoplifting, collusion or duplicity, and guile. *Collusion* typically involves an employee who assists the consumer in fraud. For example, a cashier may not ring up all merchandise or may give an unwarranted discount. *Duplicity* may involve a consumer staging an accident in a grocery store and then seeking damages against the store for its lack of attention to safety. A consumer may purchase, wear, and then return an item of clothing for a full refund. In other situations, the consumer may ask for a refund by claiming a defect. *Guile* is associated with a person who is crafty or understands right/wrong behavior but uses tricks to obtain an unfair advantage. The advantage is unfair because the person has the intent to go against the right behavior or end. Although some of these acts warrant legal prosecution, they can be very difficult to prove, and many companies are reluctant to accuse patrons of a crime when there is no way to verify it. Businesses that operate with the "customer is always right" philosophy have found that some consumers will take advantage of this promise and have therefore modified return policies to curb unfair use.

Insider Trading

An insider is any officer, director, or owner of 10 percent or more of a class of a company's securities. There are two types of **insider trading:** illegal and legal. *Illegal insider trading* is the buying or selling of stocks by insiders who possess material that is still not public. The act, which puts insiders in breach of their fiduciary duty, can be committed by anyone who has access to nonpublic material, such as brokers, family, friends, and employees. In addition, someone caught "tipping" an outsider with material nonpublic information can also be found liable. To determine if an insider gave a tip illegally, the SEC uses the *Dirks test,* which states that if a tipster breaches his or her trust with the company and understands that this was a breach, he or she is liable for insider trading.

Legal insider trading involves legally buying and selling stock in an insider's own company, but not all the time. Insiders are required to report their insider transactions within two business days of the date the transaction occurred. For example, if an insider sold ten thousand shares on Monday, June 12, he or she would have to report this change to the SEC by Wednesday, June 14. To deter insider trading, insiders are prevented from buying and selling their company stock within a six-month period; therefore, insiders buy stock when they feel the company will perform well over the long-term.

An example of insider trading occurred at Charter One Bank, where federal prosecutors accused an insider of failing to report several of her transactions. Wang, the insider, and her husband, Liu, invested personal funds in a hedge fund operated by a former coworker. After learning that Citizens Corporation coworkers were performing due diligence on a Charter One Bank, Wang passed on her insider information to the manager of a hedge fund, who then purchased a large quantity of Charter One stock. On the following day, when Citizens announced the Charter One acquisition, the hedge fund yielded a profit of about $700,000. As a result of their actions, the players in this scandal each face a maximum sentence of ten years in prison and a $1 million fine.[49]

Intellectual-Property Rights

Intellectual-property rights involve the legal protection of intellectual properties such as music, books, and movies. Laws such as the Copyright Act of 1976, the Digital Millennium Copyright Act, and the Digital Theft Deterrence and Copyright Damages Improvement Act of 1999 were designed to protect the creators of intellectual property. However, with the advance of technology, ethical issues still abound for websites. For example, until it was sued for copyright infringement, Napster.com allowed individuals to download copyrighted music for personal use without providing compensation to the artists.

A decision by the Federal Copyright Office (FCO) helped lay the groundwork for intellectual property rules in a digital world. The FCO decided to make it illegal for Web users to hack through barriers that copyright holders erect around material released online, allowing only two exceptions. The first exception was for software that blocks users from finding obscene or controversial material on the Web, and the second was for people who want to bypass malfunctioning security features of software or other copyrighted goods they have purchased. This decision reflects the fact that copyright owners are typically being favored in digital copyright issues.[50] There have been many lawsuits related to this issue, and some have had costly results. MP3.com paid Universal Music Group $53.4 million to end its dispute with major record labels over copyright infringement.[51]

Privacy Issues

Consumer advocates continue to warn consumers about new threats to their privacy especially within the health-care and Internet industries.[52] As the number of people using the Internet increases, the areas of concern related to its use increase as well.[53]

Some **privacy issues** that must be addressed by businesses include the monitoring of employees' use of available technology and consumer privacy. Current research suggests that, even if businesses use price discounts or personalized services, consumers remain suspicious. However, certain materialistic consumers are still willing to provide personal information, despite the potential risks.[54]

A challenge for companies today is meeting their business needs while protecting employees' desires for privacy. There are few legal protections of an employee's right to privacy, which allows businesses a great deal of flexibility in establishing policies regarding employees' privacy while they are on company property and using company equipment. The increased use of electronic communications in the workplace and technological advances that permit employee monitoring and surveillance have provided companies with new opportunities to obtain data about employees. From computer monitoring and telephone taping to video surveillance and GPS satellite tracking, employers are using technology to manage their productivity and protect their resources.

To motivate employee compliance, over 25 percent of 596 companies have fired workers for misusing the Internet, 6 percent have fired employees for misusing office telephones, 76 percent monitor their workers' website connections, and 65 percent use software to block connections to inappropriate websites. In addition, 36 percent of those employers track content, keystrokes, and time spent at keyboards and store the data in order to review it later. Employers are also notifying employees when they are being watched; of the organizations monitoring employees, 80 percent informed their workers.[55]

Because of the increased legal and regulatory investigations, employers have established policies governing personal e-mail use, personal Internet use, personal instant messenger use, personal blogs, and operation of personal websites on company time. Companies are also concerned about inappropriate telephone use, such as 1-900 lines or personal long-distance calls. Hence, some businesses routinely track phone numbers and, in selected job categories, record and review all employees' phone calls. More than half of the companies surveyed use video monitoring to counter theft, violence, and sabotage. The use of video surveillance to track employees' on-the-job performance has also increased, although companies that videotape workers usually notify them of the practice.

Concerns about employee privacy extend to Europe as well. In Finland an executive vice president and several employees of Sonera Corporation were arrested as part of an investigation into whether the wireless telecommunications company violated the privacy of its workers by monitoring their call records, a serious offense in Finland. The investigation was launched after a local newspaper reported that Sonera was tracing employees' phone calls in order to identify who may have leaked information about the company to the media. The company denied the accusations.[56]

Clearly conveying the organization's policy on workplace privacy should reduce the opportunity for employee lawsuits and the resulting costs of such actions. However, if a company fails to monitor employees' use of e-mail and the Internet, the costs can be huge. For example, Chevron Corporation agreed to pay $2.2 million to employees who claimed that unmonitored sexually harassing e-mail created a threatening environment for them.[57] Instituting practices that show respect for employee privacy but do not abdicate the employer's responsibility should help create a climate of trust that promotes opportunities for resolving employee–employer disputes without lawsuits.

Electronic monitoring allows a company to determine whether productivity is being reduced because employees are spending too much time on personal Web activities. Knowing this can then enable the company to take steps to remedy the situation. Internet filtering companies such as Cyber Patrol, Surfcontrol, Surfwatch, and Web-Sense provide products that block employee access to websites deemed distracting or objectionable. WebSense launched AfterWork.com, a personal homepage for each employee at a company that allows employees to visit nonwork-related websites during breaks and lunch, as well as before and after work hours.[58] One survey about this subject found that 58 percent of employees considered using company resources for personal Web surfing to be an "extremely serious" or "very serious" business ethics violation.[59]

There are two dimensions to consumer privacy: consumer awareness of information collection and a growing lack of consumer control over how companies use the personal information that they collect. For example, many are not aware that Google Inc. reserves the right to track every time you click on a link from one of its searches.[60] Online purchases and even random Web surfing can be tracked without a consumer's knowledge. A survey by the Progress and Freedom Foundation found that 96 percent of popular commercial websites collect personally identifying information from visitors.[61]

For example, the FTC asked a federal judge to shut down Odysseus Marketing Inc. on the grounds that it secretly installed spyware that could not be removed by the consumers whose computers it infected. The company offered a free software package to make peer-to-peer file sharing anonymous, but consumers ended up downloading a program called Clientman, a spyware program that altered search results, disseminated pop-up ads, and installed third-party ads without notice to consumers. The company denies any wrongdoing.[62]

A U.S. Department of Commerce study on e-commerce and privacy found that 81 percent of Internet users and 79 percent of consumers who buy products and services over the Web were concerned about online threats to privacy.[63] Another survey found that 38 percent of respondents felt that it is never ethical to track customers' Web activities, and 64 percent said that they do not trust websites that do.[64] These concerns have led some companies to cut back on the amount of information they collect: Of the sites surveyed by the Progress and Freedom Foundation, 84 percent indicated that they are collecting less data than before.[65] However, in a random survey of 1006 consumers on consumer fraud and privacy, only 13 percent believed that the problem of payment fraud would improve over the next six months, while 55 percent believed that it would worsen. In addition, nearly 35 percent expressed a low level of confidence in their ability to avoid becoming a victim of credit or debit card fraud.[66]

Companies are also working to find ways to improve consumers' trust in their websites. For example, an increasing number of websites display an online seal from BBBOnline, available only to sites that subscribe to certain standards. A similar seal is available through TRUSTe, a nonprofit global initiative that certifies those websites that adhere to its principles. (Visit e-businessethics.com for more on Internet privacy.)

THE CHALLENGE OF DETERMINING AN ETHICAL ISSUE IN BUSINESS

Most ethical issues will become visible through stakeholder concerns about an event, activity, or the results of a business decision. The mass media, special-interest groups, and individuals, through the use of blogs, podcasts, or other individual-generated media, often generate discussion about the ethicalness of a decision. Another way to determine whether a specific behavior or situation has an ethical component is to ask other individuals in the business how they feel about it and whether they view it as ethically challenging. Trade associations and business self-regulatory groups such as the Better Business Bureau often provide direction for companies in defining ethical issues. Finally, it is important to determine whether the organization has adopted specific policies on the activity. An activity approved of by most members of an organization, if it is also customary in the industry, is probably ethical. An issue, activity, or situation that can withstand open discussion between many stakeholders, both inside and outside the organization, probably does not pose ethical problems.

Figure 3–2 identifies the frequency of misconduct observed by employees in the Ethics Resource Center Survey. Over half (52 percent) of the national sample of employees observed some type of misconduct. Figure 3–2 provides a view of how many different forms of misconduct

However, over time, problems can become ethical issues as a result of changing societal values. For instance, for decades Kraft Foods Inc. has been a staple in almost every home in the United States, with products such as Kraft Macaroni and Cheese, Chips Ahoy! cookies, Lunchables, Kool-Aid, Fruity Pebbles, and Oreos. Nothing was said about such foods until 2004. However, a problem was perceived first by parents, then schools, and then politicians who became aware that the United States has the most obese people in the world, with approximately 40 percent of the population overweight.

The fact is that since 1980 the rate of obesity in children (ages 6 to 11) has more than doubled, and it has tripled in adolescents. Children who are 10 years of age weigh ten pounds more than they did in the 1960s. As a result, Congress has proposed legislation relative to obesity and concerning the advertising of unhealthy food products to children. Kraft realized that they now have an ethical situation regarding the advertising of such items as hotdogs, cookies, and cereals with high-sugar levels. Some consumer groups might now perceive Kraft's $90 million annual advertising budget, which was primarily directed at children, as unethical. Because ignoring the situation could be potentially disastrous, Kraft instead devised a compromise: It would stop advertising some of its products to children under 12 years of age and instead market healthier foods. As a result of government recommendations, Kraft executives have continually revised their advertising guidelines regarding children and the advertisement of products containing large amounts of sugar, fat, and calories, knowing that their decisions would probably negatively affect their bottom line.[67]

| FIGURE 3-2 | Observed Frequency of Specific Misconduct by Employees |

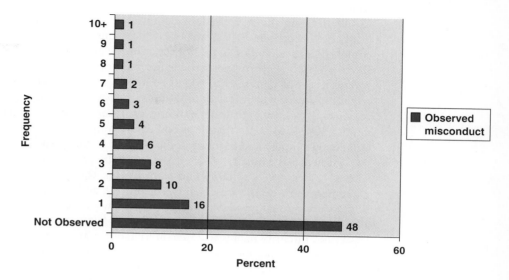

SOURCE: From *2005 National Business Ethics Survey: How Employees Perceive Ethics at Work,* 2005, p. 25. Copyright © 2006, Ethics Resource Center (ERC). Used with permission of the ERC, 1747 Pennsylvania Ave., N.W., Suite 400, Washington, DC 2006, www.ethics.org.

Once stakeholders trigger ethical-issue awareness and individuals openly discuss it and ask for guidance and the opinions of others, one enters the ethical decision-making process, which we examine in Chapter 5.

SUMMARY

Customers, investors and shareholders, employees, suppliers, government agencies, communities, and many others who have a "stake" or claim in some aspect of a company's products, operations, markets, industry, and outcomes are known as stakeholders. They are both influenced by and have the ability to affect businesses. Stakeholders provide both tangible and intangible resources that are more or less critical to a firm's long-term success, and their ability to withdraw—or to threaten to withdraw—these resources gives them power.

Primary stakeholders are those whose continued association is absolutely necessary for a firm's survival, whereas secondary stakeholders do not typically engage in transactions with a company and thus are not essential for its survival. The stakeholder interaction model suggests that there are two-way relationships between the firm and a host of stakeholders. The degree to which a firm understands and addresses stakeholder demands can be expressed as a stakeholder orientation, which includes generation of data across the firm about its stakeholder groups and the assessment of the firm's effects on these groups, (2) the distribution of this information throughout the firm, and (3) the responsiveness of every level of the firm to this intelligence. A stakeholder orientation can be viewed as a continuum in that firms are likely to adopt the concept to varying degrees.

Underlying the stakeholder orientation are universal moral constants that businesspeople accept and that, without which, business becomes more difficult to accomplish. These constants are honesty, fairness, and integrity. To be honest is to tell the truth to the best of your knowledge and not to hide anything. Confucius defined several levels of honesty: *Li,* which relates to the superficial desires of a person; *Yi* (righteousness), which relates to doing right based on reciprocity; and *Ren,* which is based on empathy and understanding of others. The Confucian version of Kant's Golden Rule is to treat inferiors as you would want superiors to treat you. Virtues such as a family's honor and reputation for honesty become paramount.

Fairness is the quality of being just, equitable, and impartial, and it overlaps terms such as *justice, equity, equality,* and *morality.* The three fundamental elements that motivate people to be fair are equality, reciprocity, and optimization. Equality relates to how wealth is distributed between employees, within a company or a country, or globally; reciprocity relates to the return of small favors that are approximately equal in value; and integrity relates to a person's character and is made up of two basic parts: a formal relation that one has to oneself and a person's set of terminal, or enduring, values from which he or she does not deviate.

An ethical issue is a problem, situation, or opportunity that requires an individual, group, or organization to choose among several actions that must be evaluated as right or wrong, ethical or unethical, but an ethical dilemma has no right or ethical choice.

Bribery is the practice of offering something (usually money) in order to gain an illicit advantage. A conflict of interest is when an individual must choose whether to advance his or her own interests, those of the organization, or those of some other group. Corporate intelligence is the collection and analysis of information on markets, technologies, customers, and competitors, as well as on socioeconomic and external political trends. There are three intelligence models: passive, tactical, and top-management. The tools of corporate intelligence are many. One tool is hacking, which has three categories: system, remote, and physical; another is social engineering in which someone is tricked into revealing valuable corporate information; and other techniques include dumpster diving, whacking, and phone eavesdropping.

Another ethical/legal issue is discrimination, which is illegal in the United States when it occurs on the basis of race, color, religion, sex, marital status, sexual orientation, public-assistance status, disability, age, national origin, or veteran status. Additionally, discrimination on the basis of political opinions or affiliation with a union is defined as harassment. Sexual harassment is a form of sex discrimination. To help build work forces that reflect their customer base, many companies have initiated affirmative action programs. Environmental issues such as air, water, and waste are becoming an ethical concern within business. In general, fraud is any purposeful communication that deceives, manipulates, or conceals facts in order to create a false impression. There are several types of fraud: accounting, marketing, and consumer.

An insider is any officer, director, or owner of 10 percent or more of a class of a company's securities. There are two types of insider trading: legal and illegal. Intellectual-property rights involve the legal protection of intellectual properties such as music, books, and movies. Consumer advocates continue to warn consumers about new threats to their privacy.

IMPORTANT TERMS FOR REVIEW

honesty
fairness
equality
reciprocity
optimization
integrity
ethical issue
ethical dilemma
abusive/intimidating behavior
lying
conflict of interest
bribery
active bribery
passive bribery
facilitation payment
corporate intelligence
hacking
system hacking
remote hacking
physical hacking
social engineering
shoulder surfing
password guessing
dumpster diving
whacking

phone eavesdropping
discrimination
Equal Employment Opportunity
    Commission
Age Discrimination in Employment Act
affirmative action program
sexual harassment
hostile work environment
dual relationship
unethical dual relationship
environmental issue
Kyoto Protocol
water pollution
fraud
accounting fraud
marketing fraud
puffery
implied falsity
literally false
labeling issue
slamming
consumer fraud
insider trading
intellectual-property right
privacy issue

Joseph Freberg had been with Alcon for eighteen months. He had begun his career right out of college with a firm in the Southeast called Cala Industrial, which specialized in air compressors. Because of his work with Cala, he had been lured away to Alcon, in Omaha, as a sales manager. Joseph's first six months had been hard. Working with salespeople older than he, trying to get a handle on his people's sales territories, and settling into the corporate culture of a new firm took sixteen-hour days, six days a week. During those six months, he also bought a house, and his fiancé, Ellen, furnished it. Ellen had stepped right in and decided almost everything, from the color of the rugs to the style of the curtains.

Ellen had taken a brokerage job with Trout Brothers and seemed to be working even more hours than Joseph. But the long days were paying off. Ellen was now starting to handle some large accounts and was being noticed by the "right" crowd in the wealthier Omaha areas.

Costs for the new home had exceeded their anticipated spending limit, and the plans for their wedding seemed to be getting larger and larger. In addition, Ellen was commuting from her apartment to the new home and then to her job, and the commute killed her car. As a result, she decided to lease something that exuded success.

"Ellen, don't you think a Mercedes is a little out of our range? What are the payments?" inquired Joseph.

"Don't worry, darling. When my clients see me in this—as well as when we start entertaining at the new house once we're married—the payments on the car will seem small compared with the money I'll be making," Ellen mused as she ran her fingers through Joseph's hair and gave him a peck on the cheek.

By the time of the wedding and honeymoon, Joseph and Ellen's bank statement looked like a bullfighter's cape—red. "Don't worry, Joseph, everything will turn out okay. You've got a good job. I've

got a good job. We're young and have drive. Things will straighten out after a while," said Ellen as she eyed a Rolex in a store window.

After the wedding, things did settle down—to a hectic pace, given their two careers and their two sets of parents two thousand miles in either direction. Joseph had realized that Alcon was a paternal type of organization, with good benefits and tremendous growth potential. He had identified whom to be friends with and whom to stay away from in the company. His salespeople seemed to tolerate him, sometimes calling him "Little Joe" or "Joey" because of his age, and his salespeople were producing—slowly climbing up the sales ladder to the number-one spot in the company.

While doing some regular checkup work on sales personnel, Joseph found out that Carl had been giving kickbacks to some of his buyers. Carl's sales volume accounted for a substantial amount of the company's existing clientele sales, and he had been a trainer for the company for several years. Carl also happened to be the vice president's son-in-law. Joseph started to check on the other reps more closely and discovered that, although Carl seemed to be the biggest offender, three of his ten people were doing the same thing. The next day, Joseph looked up Alcon's policy handbook and found this statement: "Our company stands for doing the right thing at all times and giving our customers the best product for the best prices." There was no specific mention of kickbacks, but everyone knew that kickbacks ultimately reduce fair competition, which eventually leads to reduced quality and increased prices for customers.

By talking to a few of the old-timers at Alcon, Joseph learned that there had been sporadic enforcement of the "no kickback" policy. It seemed that when times were good it became unacceptable and when times were bad it slipped into the acceptable range. And then there was his boss, Kathryn, the vice president. Joseph knew that Kathryn had a tendency to shoot the bearer of bad news. He remembered a story that he had heard about a sales manager coming in to see Kathryn to explain an error in a bid that one of his salespeople had made. Kathryn called in the entire sales staff and fired the salesman on the spot. Then, smiling, she told the sales manager: "This was your second mistake, so I hope that you can get a good recommendation from personnel. You have two weeks to find employment elsewhere." From then on, the office staff had a nickname for Kathryn—Jaws.

Trying to solve the problem that he was facing, Joseph broached the subject of kickbacks at his monthly meeting with Carl. Carl responded, "You've been in this business long enough to know that this happens all the time. I see nothing wrong with this practice if it increases sales. Besides, I take the money out of my commission. You know that right now I'm trying to pay off some big medical bills. I've also gotten tacit clearance from above, but I wouldn't mention that if I were you." Joseph knew that the chain-of-command structure in the company made it very dangerous to go directly to a vice president with this type of information.

As Joseph was pondering whether to do nothing, bring the matter into the open and state that it was wrong and that such practices were against policy, or talk to Kathryn about the situation, his cell phone rang. It was Ellen. "Honey, guess what just happened. Kathryn, your boss, has decided to use me as her new broker. Isn't that fantastic!"

What should Joseph do?

QUESTIONS • EXERCISES

1. What are Joseph's ethical problems?
2. Assume that you are Joseph and discuss your options.
3. What other information do you feel you need before making your decision?
4. Discuss in which business areas the ethical problems lie.

*This case is strictly hypothetical; any resemblance to real persons, companies, or situations is coincidental.

Check Your EQ

Check your EQ, or Ethics Quotient, by completing the following. Assess your performance to evaluate your overall understanding of the chapter material.

1.	Business can be considered a game people play like basketball or boxing.	Yes	No
2.	Key ethical issues in an organization relate to fraud, discrimination, honesty and fairness, conflicts of interest, and technology.	Yes	No
3.	Over half of a national sample of employees observe some type of misconduct.	Yes	No
4.	Fraud occurs when a false impression exists, which conceals facts.	Yes	No
5.	The most observed form of misconduct is fraud.	Yes	No

ANSWERS: 1. No. People are not economically self-sufficient and cannot withdraw from the game of business. 2. Yes. See pages 64–82 regarding these key ethical issues and their implications for the organization. 3. Yes. Figure 3-2 indicates observed misconduct by employees. 4. No. Fraud must be purposeful, rather than accidental, and exists when deception and manipulation of facts are concealed to create a false impression that causes harm. 5. No. The most observed form of misconduct in Table 3-1 is abusive or intimidating behavior toward employees.

CHAPTER 4

The Institutionalization of Business Ethics

CHAPTER OBJECTIVES

- To distinguish between the voluntary and mandated boundaries of ethical conduct

- To provide specific mandated requirements for legal compliance in specific subject matter areas related to competition, consumers, safety, and the environment

- To specifically address the requirements of the Sarbanes–Oxley legislation and implementation by the Securities and Exchange Commission

- To provide an overview of regulatory efforts to provide incentives for ethical behavior

- To provide an overview of the Federal Sentencing Guidelines for Organizations recommendations and incentives for developing an ethical corporate culture

- To provide an overview of voluntary boundaries and the relationship to social responsibility

CHAPTER OUTLINE

Myron had just graduated from West Coast University with both chemistry–pharmacy and business degrees and was excited to work for Producto International (PI). He loved having the opportunity to discover medicinal products around the world. His wife, Quan, was also enthusiastic about her job as an import–export agent for a subsidiary of PI.

Producto International was the industry leader, with headquarters in Paris. Worldwide, hundreds of small firms were competing with PI; however, only six had equivalent magnitude. These six had cornered 75 percent of world sales. So many interrelationships had developed that competition had become "managed." However, this did not constitute any illegal form of monopolistic behavior as defined by the European Union.

Myron's first assignment was in India and concerned exporting betel nuts to South and perhaps North America. It is estimated that more than 20 million people chew betel nuts in India alone. The betel nut is one of the world's most popular plants, and its leaf is used as a paper for rolling tobacco. The betel nut is also mashed or powdered with other ingredients and rolled up in a leaf and sold as candy. Myron quickly found that regular use of the betel nut will, in time, stain the mouth, gums, and teeth a deep red, which in Asia is a positive quality. As Myron was learning more about the betel nut, he came across the following report from the People's Republic of China: "Studies show that the chewing of the spiced betel nut can lead to oral cancer. According to research, 88 percent of China's oral cancer patients are betel nut chewers. Also, people who chew betel nuts and smoke are ninety times more likely to develop oral cancer than nonusers." Myron found that the betel nut primarily affects the central nervous system. It increases respiration while decreasing the workload on the heart (a mild high). Myron also found that demand for it was starting to emerge in the United States as well as in other developed countries.

While Myron was working on the betel nut, David, Myron's boss, also wanted him to work on introducing khat (pronounced "cot") into Asia. Khat is a natural stimulant from a plant grown in East Africa and southern Arabia. Fresh khat leaves, which are typically chewed like tobacco, produce a mild cocaine- or amphetamine-like euphoria. However, its effect is much less intense than that produced by either of those substances, with no reports of a rush sensation or paranoia, for example. Chewing khat produces a strong aroma and generates intense thirst. Casual users claim that khat lifts spirits, sharpens thinking, and, when its effects wear off, generates mild lapses into depression similar to those observed among cocaine users. The body appears to have a physical intolerance to khat due in part to limitations in how much can be ingested by chewing. As a result, reports suggest that there are no physical symptoms accompanying withdrawal. Advocates of khat use claim that it eases symptoms of diabetes, asthma, and disorders of the stomach and the intestinal tract. Opponents claim that khat damages health, suppresses appetite, and prevents sleep. In the United States, khat has been classified as a schedule IV substance by the Drug Enforcement Agency (DEA): freshly picked khat leaves (that is, within forty-eight hours of harvest) are classified as a schedule I narcotic, the most restrictive category used by the DEA.

After doing his research, Myron delivered his report to David and said, "I really think that, given the right marketing to some of the big pharmaceutical companies, we should have two huge revenue makers."

"That's great, Myron, but the pharmaceutical market is only secondary to our primary market—the two billion consumers to whom we can introduce these products."

"What do you mean, David?" Myron asked.

"I mean these products are grown legally around the world, and the countries that we are targeting have no restrictions on these substances," David explained. "Why not tailor the delivery of the product by country? For example, we find out which flavors people want the betel nut in, in North and South America or the Middle East. The packaging will have to change by country as well as branding. Pricing strategies will need to be developed relative to our branding decisions, and of course quantity usages will have to be calculated. For example, single, multiple, supervalue sizes, and the like need to be explored. The same can be done for khat. Because of your research and your business background, I'm putting you on the marketing team for both. Of course, this means that you're going to have to be promoted and at least for a while live in Hong Kong. I know Quan will be excited. In fact, I told her the news this morning that she would be working on the same project in Hong Kong. Producto International tries to be sensitive to the dual-career family problems that can occur. Plus you'll be closer to relatives. I told Quan that with living allowances and all of the other things that go with international placement, you two should almost triple your salaries! You don't have to thank me, Myron. You've worked hard on these projects, and now you deserve to have some of the benefits."

Myron went back to his office to think about his and Quan's future. He had heard of another employee who had rejected a similar offer, and that person's career had languished at PI. Eventually, that individual left the industry, never to be heard from again.

QUESTIONS • EXERCISES

1. Identify the social responsibility issues in this scenario.
2. Discuss the advantages and disadvantages of each decision that Myron could make.
3. Discuss the issue of marketing products that are legal but have addictive properties associated with them.

*This case is strictly hypothetical; any resemblance to real persons, companies, or situations is coincidental.

To understand the institutionalization of business ethics it is important to understand the voluntary and legally mandated dimensions of organizational practices. In addition, there are core practices sometimes called best practices that most responsible firms—trying to achieve acceptable conduct—embrace and implement. The effective organizational practice of business ethics requires all three dimensions to be integrated into an ethics and compliance program. This creates an ethical culture that can effectively manage the risks of misconduct. Institutionalization relates to legal and societal forces that provide both rewards and punishment to organizations based on the stakeholder evaluations of specific conduct. Institutionalization in business ethics relates to established laws, customs, and expected organizational programs that are considered normative in establishing reputation. Institutions provide requirements, structure, and societal expectations to reward and sanction ethical decision making.

MANAGING ETHICAL RISK THROUGH MANDATED AND VOLUNTARY PROGRAMS

Table 4–1 provides an overview of the three dimensions of institutionalization. **Voluntary practices** include the beliefs, values, and voluntary contractual obligations. All businesses engage in some level of commitment to voluntary activities to benefit both internal and external stakeholders. For example, Starbucks provides health benefits to

TABLE 4–1	Voluntary Boundary, Core Practices, and Mandated Boundaries of Ethical Decisions
Voluntary boundary	A management-initiated boundary of conduct (beliefs, values, voluntary policies, and voluntary contractual obligations)
Core practice	A highly appropriate and common practice that helps ensure compliance with legal requirements, industry self-regulation, and societal expectations
Mandated boundary	An externally imposed boundary of conduct (laws, rules, regulations, and other requirements)

SOURCE: Adapted from the "Open Compliance Ethics Group (OCEG) Foundation Guidelines," v1.0, Steering Committee Update, December 2005, Phoenix, AZ.

part-time employees. Under pressure from many states to require Wal-Mart to increase health care for employees, it developed voluntary contractual commitments to increase health-care benefits to part-time workers. Most firms engage in **philanthropy**—giving back to communities and causes.

Core practices are documented best practices, often encouraged by legal and regulatory forces as well as industry trade associations. The **Better Business Bureau** is a leading self-regulatory body that provides directions for managing customer disputes and reviews advertising cases. These practices are appropriate and common practices that help ensure compliance with legal requirements and societal expectations. Although these practices are not enforced, there are consequences for not engaging in these practices when there is misconduct. For example, the Federal Sentencing Guidelines for Organizations (FSGO) suggest that the governing authority (board of directors) be responsible for and assess an organization's ethical and compliance activities. There is no required reporting of investigations by government regulatory bodies, but there are incentives to the firm that effectively implement this recommendation. If misconduct occurs, there may be opportunities to avoid serious punishment. On the other hand, if there has been no effort by the board to oversee ethics and compliance, this could increase and compound the level of punishment. In this way, the government in institutionalizing core practices provides organizations the opportunity to take their own approach and only taking action if there are violations. **Mandated boundaries** are the externally imposed boundaries of conduct, such as laws, rules, regulations, and other requirements.

There is a need to maintain the values, ethical culture, and expectations for appropriate conduct in an organization. This is achieved through compliance, corporate governance, risk management, and voluntary activities. The development of these drivers of an ethical culture has been institutionally supported by government initiatives and the demands of stakeholders. The compliance element represents areas that must conform to existing legal and regulatory requirements. Established laws and regulatory decisions leave limited flexibility to organizations in adhering to these standards. Corporate governance (as discussed in Chapter 2) is structured by a governing authority providing oversight as well as checks and balances to make sure that the organization meets its goals and objectives for ethical performance. Risk management analyzes the probability or chance that misconduct could occur based on the nature of

FIGURE 4–1   Elements That Create an Ethical Culture

SOURCE: Based on the principles and framework of the "Open Compliance Ethics Group (OCEG) Foundation Guidelines," v1.0, Steering Committee Update, December 2005, Phoenix, AZ. Copyright © O.C. Ferrell 2007.

the business and the exposure to risky events. Voluntary activities often represent the values and responsibilities that firms accept in contributing to society.

Figure 4–1 depicts how these various elements of ethical culture shape the character of an organization. Corporate culture is created by corporate vision, values, principles, and rules. Vision and values provide aspirational guidance, whereas rules encourage mandatory compliance in activities. Principles provide a guiding sense of the right conduct in varying situations and dilemmas. Corporate governance, risk management, compliance, and voluntary activities, relate to formal structures in organizations that help shape and maintain the corporate culture.

In this chapter, we examine the boundaries of ethical conduct and focus on the voluntary, core practices, and mandated requirements for legal compliance—three important areas in developing an ethical culture. In particular, we concentrate on compliance in specific areas related to competition, consumers, safety, and the environment. We also consider the requirements of the Sarbanes–Oxley legislation and its implementation by the Securities and Exchange Commission (SEC) and how its implementation has affected companies. We also provide an overview of the FSGO for organizations and give recommendations and incentives for developing an ethical corporate culture. The FSGO, the Sarbanes–Oxley Act, industry trade associations, and societal expectations support core practices. Finally, we examine philanthropic contributions and how strategic philanthropy can be an important core competency to manage stakeholder relationships.

MANDATED REQUIREMENTS FOR LEGAL COMPLIANCE

Laws and regulations are established by governments to set minimum standards for responsible behavior—society's codification of what is right and wrong. Laws regulating business conduct are passed because certain stakeholders believe that business cannot be trusted to do what is right in certain areas, such as consumer safety and environmental protection. Because public policy is dynamic and often changes in response to business abuses and consumer demands for safety and equality, many laws have been passed to resolve specific problems and issues. But the opinions of society, as expressed in legislation, can change over time, and different courts or state legislatures may take diverging views. For example, the thrust of most business legislation can be summed up as follows: Any practice is permitted that does not substantially lessen or reduce competition or harm consumers or society. Courts differ, however, in their interpretations of what constitutes a "substantial" reduction of competition. Laws can help businesspeople determine what society believes at a certain time, but what is legally wrong today may be perceived as acceptable tomorrow, and vice versa. For example, KPMG settled with federal prosecutors for a sum of $456 million for selling dodgy tax shelters to customers between 1996 and 2002.[1] Still, personal views on legal issues may vary tremendously. Instructions to employees to "just obey the law" are meaningless without effective training and experience in dealing with specific legal risk areas.

Laws are categorized as either civil or criminal. **Civil law** defines the rights and duties of individuals and organizations (including businesses). **Criminal law** not only prohibits specific actions—such as fraud, theft, or securities trading violations—but also imposes fines or imprisonment as punishment for breaking the law. The primary difference between criminal and civil law is that the state or nation enforces criminal laws, whereas individuals (generally, in court) enforce civil laws. Criminal and civil laws are derived from four sources: the U.S. Constitution (constitutional law), precedents established by judges (common law), federal and state laws or statutes (statutory law), and federal and state administrative agencies (administrative law). Federal administrative agencies established by Congress control and influence business by enforcing laws and regulations to encourage competition and to protect consumers, workers, and the environment. State laws and regulatory agencies also exist to achieve these objectives. Marsh and McLennan were charged with bid rigging and breach of duty by the New York attorney general Eliot Spitzer; they settled the case for $859 million.[2]

The primary method of resolving conflicts and serious business ethics disputes is through lawsuits in which one individual or organization uses civil laws to take another individual or organization to court. To avoid lawsuits and to maintain the standards necessary to reduce risk and create an ethical culture, it is necessary to have both legal and organizational standards enforced. When violations of organizational standards

| **FIGURE 4–2** | Violations of Standards, Law, or Both by Employees |

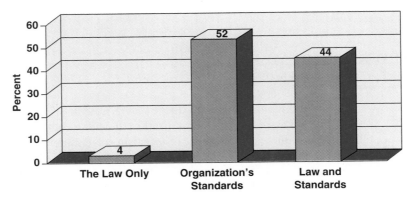

SOURCE: National Business Ethics Survey, *How Employees View Ethics in Their Organizations 1994–2005* (Washington, DC: Ethics Resource Center, 2005), 24.

occur, the National Business Ethics Survey (NBES) notes that three categories of misconduct are reported (Figure 4–2). Of those employees who reported that they had observed misconduct (without further classification of specific behaviors, constituting 26 percent of respondents), 4 percent observed a violation of only the law, not organizational standards, 52 percent observing misconduct considered the act to be a violation of their organization's standards, and 44 percent observed misconduct that they thought violated both the law and their organization's standards of conduct.

The role of laws is not so much to distinguish what is ethical or unethical as to determine the appropriateness of specific activities or situations. In other words, laws establish the basic ground rules for responsible business activities. Most of the laws and regulations that govern business activities fall into one of five groups: (1) regulation of competition, (2) protection of consumers, (3) promotion of equity and safety, (4) protection of the natural environment, and (5) incentives to encourage organizational compliance programs to deter misconduct, which we examine later.

Laws Regulating Competition

The issues surrounding the impact of competition on business's social responsibility arise from the rivalry among businesses for customers and profits. When businesses compete unfairly, legal and social responsibility issues can result. Intense competition sometimes makes managers feel that their company's very survival is threatened. In these situations, managers may begin to see unacceptable alternatives as acceptable, and they may begin engaging in questionable practices to ensure the survival of their organizations. For example, Aventis SA and Andrx Corporation agreed to pay $80 million to settle charges that Aventis had paid Andrx nearly $100 million not to market a cheaper, generic version of Cardizem CD, a blood-pressure medication. Although both companies denied conspiring to manipulate the supply of the drug, pharmaceutical wholesalers also sued them over the same practice. Aventis claimed the agreement was necessary to protect its patent.[3] Because medications are necessary to so many people, ethical and social issues arise when a lower-price drug that should be available is not.

Size frequently gives some companies an advantage over others. For example, large firms can often generate economies of scale (for example, by forcing their suppliers to lower their prices) that allow them to put smaller firms out of business. Consequently, small companies and even whole communities may resist the efforts of firms like Wal-Mart, Home Depot, and Best Buy to open stores in their vicinity. These firms' sheer size enables them to operate at such low costs that small, local firms often cannot compete. In Austin, Texas, for example, many consumers threatened to boycott a new development that would have featured a Borders Books and Music superstore because it would have competed with popular locally owned book and music stores across the street from the new development.[4] Borders eventually withdrew from the project, citing "economic reasons."

Some companies' competitive strategies may focus on weakening or destroying a competitor, which can harm competition and ultimately reduce consumer choice. For example, Clear Channel Communications, which owns more than 10 percent of the nation's radio stations, was summoned before a U.S. Senate hearing to answer charges that it was using unfair competitive tactics. Small radio station owners and musicians charged that Clear Channel forces musicians to offer "payola" to promoters to get their songs played on the company's stations. They also charged that Clear Channel's ownership of so many stations in certain large markets represents a monopoly that limits consumer access to new music. Other critics accused the conglomerate of "blackballing" artists and promoters who refuse to use Clear Channel stations to promote their songs and concerts. Musician Don Henley argued that the firm's domination of the airwaves in some large cities had transformed the radio dial from a place where consumers had great choice in music to one where "everyone gets the same McDonald's hamburger." The Senate was considering whether to allow the modification of current regulations on the number of stations that one company can own in certain markets and strengthen punishment for anticompetitive tactics in radio and television. Despite the issues raised during the hearing, the Federal Communications Commission (FCC) further relaxed regulations to permit companies to operate even more media outlets within a single market.[5]

Other examples of anticompetitive strategies include sustained price cuts, discriminatory pricing, and price wars. The primary objective of U.S. antitrust laws is to distinguish competitive strategies that enhance consumer welfare from those that reduce it. The difficulty of this task lies in determining whether the intent of a company's pricing policy is to weaken or even destroy a competitor.[6] For example, concerns about anticompetitive behavior emerged in the software industry when the Department of Justice investigated Microsoft. Ken Wasch, president of the Software Publishers Association, stated that "justice clearly recognizes that the restoration of a level playing field in the computer software and technology industries is critical for ensuring consumer choice and ongoing innovation."[7] Microsoft's competitors complained that the company's practice of bundling its Internet Explorer Web browser into its Windows operating system stifled consumers' choice as to which Internet browser they would use. They also claimed that Microsoft's virtual monopoly on the market for operating system software reduced consumer choice and stifled innovation in the software industry.[8] After a year-long process, Microsoft settled the charges with the Justice Department and nine states. The company later settled a suit brought by the state of California, agreeing to repay consumers $1 billion in the form of vouchers.[9]

Intense competition may also lead companies to resort to corporate espionage. According to the CSI/FBI Computer Crime and Security survey, theft of proprietary information cost the 639 companies that responded almost $31 billion. Total losses for all companies and all types of categories were in excess of $130 billion. The top four categories for losses were viruses, unauthorized access, theft of proprietary information, and denial of service attacks.[10] *Fortune* 1000 companies lose an estimated $100 billion annually from the theft of corporate trade secrets, although determining an accurate amount is difficult because most companies do not report such losses for fear that the publicity will harm their stock price or encourage further break-ins. Espionage may be carried out by outsiders or by employees—executives, programmers, network or computer auditors, engineers, or janitors who have legitimate reasons to access facilities, data, computers or networks. They may use a variety of techniques for obtaining valuable information such as dumpster diving, whacking, and hacking as discussed in Chapter 3.

Laws have been passed to prevent the establishment of monopolies, inequitable pricing practices, and other practices that reduce or restrict competition among businesses. These laws are sometimes called **procompetitive legislation** because they were enacted to encourage competition and prevent activities that restrain trade (Table 4–2). The Sherman Antitrust Act of 1890, for example, prohibits organizations from holding monopolies in their industry, and the Robinson–Patman Act of 1936 bans price discrimination between retailers and wholesalers.

In law, however, there are always exceptions. Under the McCarran–Ferguson Act of 1944, for example, Congress exempted the insurance industry from the Sherman Antitrust Act and other antitrust laws. Insurance companies were allowed to join together and set insurance premiums at specific industry-wide levels. However, this legal "permission" could still be viewed as irresponsible and unethical if it neutralizes competition and if prices no longer reflect the true costs of insurance protection. This illustrates the point that what is legal is not always considered ethical by some interest groups.

Laws Protecting Consumers

Laws that protect consumers require businesses to provide accurate information about products and services and to follow safety standards (Table 4–3). The first **consumer protection law** was passed in 1906, partly in response to a novel by Upton Sinclair. *The Jungle* describes, among other things, the atrocities and unsanitary conditions of the meatpacking industry in turn-of-the-century Chicago. The outraged public response to this book and other exposés of the industry resulted in the passage of the Pure Food and Drug Act. Likewise, Ralph Nader had a tremendous impact on consumer protection laws with his book *Unsafe at Any Speed*. His critique and attack of General Motors' Corvair had far-reaching effects on autos and other consumer products. Other consumer protection laws emerged from similar processes.

TABLE 4-2	Laws Regulating Competition
Sherman Antitrust Act, 1890	Prohibits monopolies.
Clayton Act, 1914	Prohibits price discrimination, exclusive dealing, and other efforts to restrict competition.
Federal Trade Commission Act, 1914	Created the Federal Trade Commission (FTC) to help enforce antitrust laws.
Robinson–Patman Act, 1936	Bans price discrimination between retailers and wholesalers.
Wheeler–Lea Act, 1938	Prohibits unfair and deceptive acts regardless of whether competition is injured.
McCarran–Ferguson Act, 1944	Exempts the insurance industry from antitrust laws.
Lanham Act, 1946	Protects and regulates brand names, brand marks, trade names, and trademarks.
Celler–Kefauver Act, 1950	Prohibits one corporation from controlling another where the effect is to lessen competition.
Consumer Goods Pricing Act, 1975	Prohibits price maintenance agreements among manufacturers and resellers in interstate commerce.
FTC Improvement Act, 1975	Gives the FTC more power to prohibit unfair industry practices.
Antitrust Improvements Act, 1976	Strengthens earlier antitrust laws—Justice Department has more investigative authority.
Trademark Counterfeiting Act, 1980	Provides penalties for individuals dealing in counterfeit goods.
Trademark Law Revision Act, 1988	Amends the Lanham Act to allow brands not yet introduced to be protected through patent and trademark registration.
Federal Trademark Dilution Act, 1995	Gives trademark owners the right to protect trademarks and requires them to relinquish those that match or parallel existing trademarks.
Digital Millenium Copyright Act, 1998	Refines copyright laws to protect digital versions of copyrighted materials, including music and movies.

In recent years, large groups of people with specific vulnerabilities have been granted special levels of legal protection relative to the general population. For example, the legal status of children and the elderly, defined according to age-related criteria, has received greater attention. American society has responded to research and documentation showing that young consumers and senior citizens encounter difficulties in the acquisition, consumption, and disposition of products. Special legal protection provided to vulnerable consumers is considered to be in the public interest.[11] For example, the Children's Online Privacy Protection Act (COPPA) requires commercial Internet sites to carry privacy policy statements, obtain parental consent before soliciting information from children under the age of 13, and provide an opportunity to remove any information provided by children using such sites. As a result, Zeeks.com, a children's website, discontinued its chat area, free e-mail system, and other features because the cost of obtaining parents' permission was prohibitive.[12] Critics of COPPA argue that children age 13 and older should not be treated as adults on the Web. In a study of children ages 10 to 17, nearly half indicated that they would give their name, address, and other demographic information in exchange for a gift worth $100 or more. In addition, about half of the teens surveyed would provide information on family cars and their parents' favorite stores in exchange for a free gift. More than 20 percent would reveal their parents' number of sick days, alcohol consumption, weekend hobbies, church attendance—and whether they speed when driving.[13]

TABLE 4-3	Laws Protecting Consumers
Pure Food and Drug Act, 1906	Prohibits adulteration and mislabeling of foods and drugs sold in interstate commerce.
Wool Products Labeling Act, 1939	Prohibits mislabeling of wool products.
Fur Products Labeling Act, 1951	Requires proper identification of the fur content of all products.
Federal Hazardous Substances Labeling Act, 1960	Controls the labeling of hazardous substances for household use.
Truth in Lending Act, 1968	Requires full disclosure of credit terms to purchasers.
Consumer Product Safety Act, 1972	Created the Consumer Product Safety Commission to establish safety standards and regulations for consumer products.
Fair Credit Billing Act, 1974	Requires accurate, up-to-date consumer credit records.
Magnuson–Moss Warranty Act, 1975	Established standards for consumer product warranties.
Energy Policy and Conservation Act, 1975	Requires auto dealers to have "gas mileage guides" in their showrooms.
Consumer Goods Pricing Act, 1975	Prohibits price maintenance agreements.
Consumer Leasing Act, 1976	Requires accurate disclosure of leasing terms to consumers.
Fair Debt Collection Practices Act, 1978	Defines permissible debt collection practices.
Toy Safety Act, 1984	Gives the government the power to recall dangerous toys quickly.
Nutritional Labeling and Education Act, 1990	Prohibits exaggerated health claims and requires all processed foods to have labels showing nutritional information.
Telephone Consumer Protection Act, 1991	Establishes procedures for avoiding unwanted telephone solicitations.
Children's Online Privacy Protection Act, 1998	Requires the FTC to formulate rules for collecting online information from children under age thirteen.
Do Not Call Implementation Act, 2003	Directs the FCC and the FTC to coordinate so that their rules are consistent regarding telemarketing call practices including the Do Not Call Registry and other lists, as well as call abandonment.

The role of the FTC's Bureau of Consumer Protection is to protect consumers against unfair, deceptive, or fraudulent practices. The bureau, which enforces a variety of consumer protection laws, is divided into five divisions. The Division of Enforcement monitors compliance with and investigates violations of laws, including unfulfilled holiday delivery promises by online shopping sites, employment opportunities fraud, scholarship scams, misleading advertising for health-care products, and more.

Laws Promoting Equity and Safety

Laws promoting equity in the workplace were passed during the 1960s and 1970s to protect the rights of minorities, women, older persons, and persons with disabilities; other legislation has sought to protect the safety of all workers (Table 4–4). Of these laws, probably the most important to business is Title VII of the Civil Rights Act, originally passed in 1964 and amended several times since. Title VII specifically prohibits discrimination in employment on the basis of race, sex, religion, color, or national origin. The Civil Rights Act also created the Equal Employment Opportunity Commission (EEOC) to help enforce the provisions of Title VII. Among other things, the EEOC helps businesses design affirmative action programs. These programs aim to increase job oppor-

TABLE 4-4	Laws Promoting Equity and Safety
Equal Pay Act of 1963	Prohibits discrimination in pay on the basis of sex.
Equal Pay Act of 1963 (amended)	Prohibits sex-based discrimination in the rate of pay to men and women working in the same or similar jobs.
Title VII of the Civil Rights Act of 1964 (amended in 1972)	Prohibits discrimination in employment on the basis of race, color, sex, religion, or national origin.
Age Discrimination in Employment Act, 1967	Prohibits discrimination in employment against persons between the ages of 40 and 70.
Occupational Safety and Health Act, 1970	Designed to ensure healthful and safe working conditions for all employees.
Title IX of Education Amendments of 1972	Prohibits discrimination based on sex in education programs or activities that receive federal financial assistance.
Vocational Rehabilitation Act, 1973	Prohibits discrimination in employment because of physical or mental handicaps.
Vietnam Era Veterans Readjustment Act, 1974	Prohibits discrimination against disabled veterans and Vietnam War veterans.
Pension Reform Act, 1974	Designed to prevent abuses in employee retirement, profit-sharing, thrift, and savings plans.
Equal Credit Opportunity Act, 1974	Prohibits discrimination in credit on the basis of sex or marital status.
Age Discrimination Act, 1975	Prohibits discrimination on age in federally assisted programs.
Pregnancy Discrimination Act, 1978	Prohibits discrimination on the basis of pregnancy, childbirth, or related medical conditions.
Immigration Reform and Control Act, 1986	Prohibits employers from knowingly hiring a person who is an unauthorized alien.
Americans with Disabilities Act, 1990	Prohibits discrimination against people with disabilities and requires that they be given the same opportunities as people without disabilities.
Civil Rights Act of 1991	Provides monetary damages in cases of intentional employment discrimination.

tunities for women and minorities by analyzing the present pool of employees, identifying areas where women and minorities are underrepresented, and establishing specific hiring and promotion goals, along with target dates for meeting those goals.

Other legislation addresses more specific employment practices. The Equal Pay Act of 1963 mandates that women and men who do equal work must receive equal pay. Wage differences are allowed only if they can be attributed to seniority, performance, or qualifications. The Americans with Disabilities Act of 1990 prohibits discrimination against people with disabilities. Despite these laws, inequities in the workplace still exist. According to a report from the Bureau of Labor Statistics, women earn, on average, 67 cents for every dollar earned by men. The disparity in wages is even higher for African American, Hispanic, and older women.[14]

Congress has also passed laws that seek to improve safety in the workplace. By far the most significant of these is the Occupational Safety and Health Act of 1970, which mandates that employers provide safe and healthy working conditions for all workers. The **Occupational Safety and Health Administration** (OSHA), which enforces the act, makes regular surprise inspections to ensure that businesses maintain safe working environments.

Even with the passage and enforcement of safety laws, many employees still work in unhealthy or dangerous environments. Safety experts suspect that companies underreport industrial accidents to avoid state and federal inspection and regulation. The current emphasis on increased productivity has been cited as the main reason for the growing number of such accidents. Competitive pressures are also believed to lie behind the increases in manufacturing injuries. Greater turnover in organizations due to downsizing means that employees may have more responsibilities and less experience in their current positions, thus increasing the potential for accidents. They may also be required to work longer hours, perhaps in violation of the law. Wal-Mart, for example, was found guilty of illegally requiring some employees to work unpaid overtime in Oregon stores. More than four hundred employees sued the discount retailer because they say they were reprimanded for claiming overtime hours and felt pressured to comply with managers' requests to clean stores "off the clock." They also claim that the company deleted some of their hours from time-keeping records.[15] In a class-action lawsuit that claimed Wal-Mart routinely denied workers meal breaks, the company was ordered to pay $172 million to more than 100,000 California employees. California has a law, which requires a thirty-minute meal break within the first five hours of a shift or an extra hour's pay. The employees also alleged that they were denied rest breaks and that Wal-Mart managers deliberately altered timecards to keep people from earning overtime. Another similar case in New Mexico and Colorado ended with Wal-Mart paying over $50 million to sixty-seven thousand workers. There are still more than forty unresolved cases involving wage and hour disputes against Wal-Mart.[16]

Laws Protecting the Environment

Environmental protection laws have been enacted largely in response to concerns over business's impact on the environment, which began to emerge in the 1960s. Many people have questioned the cost–benefit analyses often used in making business decisions. Such analyses try to take into account all factors in a situation, represent them with dollar figures, calculate the costs and benefits of the proposed action, and determine whether an action's benefits outweigh its costs. The problem, however, is that it is difficult to arrive at an accurate monetary valuation of environmental damage or physical pain and injury. In addition, people outside the business world often perceive such analyses as inhumane.

The **Environmental Protection Agency** (EPA) was created in 1970 to coordinate environmental agencies involved in enforcing the nation's environmental laws. The major area of environmental concern relates to air, water, and land pollution. Large corporations are being encouraged to establish pollution-control mechanisms and other policies favorable to the environment. Otherwise, these companies could deplete resources and damage the health and welfare of society by focusing only on their own economic interests. For example, 3M voluntarily stopped making Scotchguard, a successful product for forty years with $300 million in sales, after tests showed that it did not decompose in the environment.[17]

Increases in toxic waste in the air and water, as well as noise pollution, have prompted the passage of a number of laws (Table 4–5). Many environmental protection laws have resulted in the elimination or modification of goods and services. For instance, leaded gasoline was phased out during the 1990s by the EPA because catalytic converters, which reduce pollution caused by automobile emissions and are required by law on most vehicles, do not work properly with leaded gasoline.

TABLE 4-5	Laws Protecting the Environment
Clean Air Act, 1970	Established air-quality standards; requires approved state plans for implementation of the standards.
National Environmental Policy Act, 1970	Established broad policy goals for all federal agencies; created the Council on Environmental Quality as a monitoring agency.
Coastal Zone Management Act, 1972	Provides financial resources to the states to protect coastal zones from overpopulation.
Federal Water Pollution Control Act, 1972	Designed to prevent, reduce, or eliminate water pollution.
Endangered Species Act, 1973	Provides a program for the conservation of threatened and endangered plants and animals and the habitats in which they are found.
Noise Pollution Control Act, 1972	Designed to control the noise emission of certain manufactured items.
Federal Insecticide, Fungicide and Rodenticide Act, 1972	Provides federal control of pesticide distribution, sale, and use.
Safe Drinking Water Act, 1974	Established to protect the quality of drinking water in the United States; focused on all waters actually or potentially designed for drinking use, whether from above ground or underground sources; established safe standards of purity and required all owners or operators of public water systems to comply with primary (health-related) standards.
Toxic Substances Control Act, 1976	Requires testing and restricts use of certain chemical substances, to protect human health and the environment.
Resource Conservation and Recovery Act, 1976	Gives the EPA authority to control hazardous waste from the "cradle to grave"; includes the generation, transportation, treatment, storage, and disposal of hazardous waste, as well as a framework for the management of nonhazardous waste.
Comprehensive Environmental Response, Compensation, and Liability Act, 1980	Created a tax on chemical and petroleum industries and provides broad federal authority to respond directly to releases or threatened releases of hazardous substances that may endanger public health or the environment.
Emergency Planning and Community Right-to-Know Act, 1986	The national legislation on community safety, designed to help local communities protect public health, safety, and the environment from chemical hazards.
Oil Pollution Act, 1990	Streamlined and strengthened the EPA's ability to prevent and respond to catastrophic oil spills; a trust fund financed by a tax on oil is available to clean up spills when the responsible party is incapable or unwilling to do so.
Pollution Prevention Act, 1990	Focuses industry, government, and public attention on reducing the amount of pollution through cost-effective changes in production, operation, and raw materials use.
Food Quality Protection Act, 1996	Amended the Federal Insecticide, Fungicide and Rodenticide Act and the Federal Food Drug and Cosmetic Act; the requirements included a new safety standard—reasonable certainty of no harm—that must be applied to all pesticides used on foods.

The harmful effects of toxic waste on water life and on leisure industries such as resorts and fishing have raised concerns about proper disposal of these wastes. Few disposal sites meet EPA standards, so businesses must decide what to do with their waste until disposal sites become available. Some firms have solved this problem by illegal or unethical measures: dumping toxic wastes along highways, improperly burying drums containing toxic chemicals, and discarding hazardous waste at sea. For example, a five-year investigation found that ships owned by Royal Caribbean Cruises Ltd.

used "secret bypass pipes" to dump waste oil and hazardous materials overboard, often at night. Justice Department officials accused the company of dumping to save the expense of properly disposing waste at the same time that the cruise line was promoting itself as environmentally friendly. The company ultimately pleaded guilty to twenty-one felony counts, paid $27 million in fines, spent as much as $90,000 per vessel to install new oily water–treatment systems and placed an environmental officer on board each vessel.[18] Congress regularly evaluates legislation to increase the penalties for disposing of toxic wastes in this way. Disposal issues remain controversial because, although everyone acknowledges that the wastes must go somewhere, no community wants them dumped in its own backyard.

One solid-waste problem is the result of rapid innovations in computer hardware, which render machines obsolete after just eighteen months. Today 350 million computers have reached obsolescence, and at least 55 million are expected to end up in landfills.[19] Computers contain such toxic substances as lead, mercury, and polyvinyl chloride, which can leach into the soil and contaminate groundwater when disposed of improperly. Dell Computer has come under increasing criticism from environmental groups for failing to adopt a leadership role in reducing the use of toxic materials in the manufacture of computers and in recycling used computers parts. The company has also encountered criticism for using prison labor to handle the recycling it does do. Several states are considering legislation that would require computers to be recycled at the same levels as in Europe.[20]

THE SARBANES–OXLEY ACT

In 2002, largely in response to widespread corporate accounting scandals, Congress passed the Sarbanes–Oxley Act to establish a system of federal oversight of corporate accounting practices. In addition to making fraudulent financial reporting a criminal offense and strengthening penalties for corporate fraud, the law requires corporations to establish codes of ethics for financial reporting and to develop greater transparency in financial reporting to investors and other stakeholders.[21]

Supported by both Republicans and Democrats, the Sarbanes–Oxley Act was enacted to restore stakeholder confidence after accounting fraud at Enron, WorldCom, and hundreds of other companies resulted in investors and employees losing much of their savings. During the resulting investigations, the public learned that hundreds of corporations had not reported their financial results accurately. Many stakeholders came to believe that accounting firms, lawyers, top executives, and boards of directors had developed a culture of deception to ensure investor approval and gain competitive advantage. Many boards failed to provide appropriate oversight of the decisions of their companies' top officers. At Adelphia Communications, for example, the Rigas family amassed $3.1 billion in off-balance-sheet loans backed by the company. Dennis Kozlowski, CEO of Tyco, was accused of improperly using corporate funds for personal use as well as fraudulent accounting practices.[22] At Kmart, CEO Charles Conaway allegedly hired unqualified executives and consultants for excessive fees. Kmart's board also approved $24 million in loans to various executives, just a month before the retailer filed for Chapter 11 bankruptcy protection. Conaway and the other executives have since left the company or were fired. Loans of this type are now illegal under the Sarbanes–Oxley Act.[23]

As a result of public outrage over the accounting scandals, the Sarbanes–Oxley Act garnered nearly unanimous support not only in Congress but also by government regulatory agencies, the president, and the general public. When President George W. Bush signed the Sarbanes–Oxley Act into law, he emphasized the need for new standards of ethical behavior in business, particularly among the top managers and boards of directors responsible for overseeing business decisions and activities.

At the heart of the Sarbanes–Oxley Act is the **Public Company Accounting Oversight Board,** which monitors accounting firms that audit public corporations and establishes standards and rules for auditors in accounting firms. The law gave the board investigatory and disciplinary power over auditors and securities analysts who issue reports about corporate performance and health. The law attempts to eliminate conflicts of interest by prohibiting accounting firms from providing both auditing and consulting services to the same client companies without special permission from the client firm's audit committee; it also places limits on the length of time lead auditors can serve a particular client. Table 4–6 summarizes the significant provisions of the new law.

TABLE 4–6	Major Provisions of the Sarbanes–Oxley Act

1. Requires the establishment of a Public Company Accounting Oversight Board in charge of regulations administered by the SEC.

2. Requires CEOs and CFOs to certify that their companies' financial statements are true and without misleading statements.

3. Requires that corporate board of directors' audit committees consist of independent members who have no material interests in the company.

4. Prohibits corporations from making or offering loans to officers and board members.

5. Requires codes of ethics for senior financial officers; code must be registered with the SEC.

6. Prohibits accounting firms from providing both auditing and consulting services to the same client without the approval of the client firm's audit committee.

7. Requires company attorneys to report wrongdoing to top managers and, if necessary, to the board of directors; if managers and directors fail to respond to reports of wrongdoing, the attorney should stop representing the company.

8. Mandates "whistle-blower protection" for persons who disclose wrongdoing to authorities.

9. Requires financial securities analysts to certify that their recommendations are based on objective reports.

10. Requires mutual fund managers to disclose how they vote shareholder proxies, giving investors information about how their shares influence decisions.

11. Establishes a ten-year penalty for mail/wire fraud.

12. Prohibits the two senior auditors from working on a corporation's account for more than five years; other auditors are prohibited from working on an account for more than seven years. In other words, accounting firms must rotate individual auditors from one account to another from time to time.

TABLE 4-7	Benefits of the Sarbanes–Oxley Act

1. Greater accountability of top managers and boards of directors to employees, investors, communities, and society
2. Renewed investor confidence
3. Clear explanations by CEOs as to why their compensation package is in the best interest of the company; the loss of some traditional senior-management perks such as company loans; greater disclosures by executives about their own stock trades
4. Greater protection of employee retirement plans
5. Improved information from stock analysts and rating agencies
6. Greater penalties for and accountability of senior managers, auditors, and board members

The Sarbanes–Oxley Act requires corporations to take greater responsibility for their decisions and to provide leadership based on ethical principles. For instance, the law requires top managers to certify that their firms' financial reports are complete and accurate, making CEOs and CFOs personally accountable for the credibility and accuracy of their companies' financial statements. Similar provisions are required of corporate boards of directors, especially audit committees, and senior financial officers are now subject to a code of ethics that addresses their specific areas of risk. Additionally, the law modifies the attorney–client relationship to require lawyers to report wrongdoing to top managers and/or the board of directors. It also provides protection for "whistle-blowing" employees who might report illegal activity to authorities. These provisions provide internal controls to make managers aware of and responsible for legal and ethical problems. Table 4–7 summarizes the benefits of the legislation.

On the other hand, the Sarbanes–Oxley Act has raised a number of concerns. The complex law may impose burdensome requirements on executives; the rules and regulations already run to thousands of pages. Some people also believe that the law will not be sufficient to stop those executives who want to lie, steal, manipulate, or deceive. They believe that a deep commitment to managerial integrity, rather than additional rules and regulations, are the key to solving the current crisis in business.[24] Additionally, the new act has caused many firms to restate their financial reports to avoid penalties. Big public companies spent thousands of hours and an average of $4.4 million each last year to make sure that someone was looking over the shoulder of key accounting personnel at every step of every business process, according to Financial Executives International. Section 404 is a core provision of the 2002 corporate reform law. The number of companies that disclosed serious chinks in their internal accounting controls jumped to more than 586 in 2005 compared to 313 for 2004.[25]

Public Company Accounting Oversight Board

The Sarbanes–Oxley Act establishes an oversight board to oversee the audit of public companies in order to protect the interests of investors and further the public interest in the preparation of informative, accurate, and independent audit reports for companies. Their duties include (1) registration of public accounting firms, (2) establishment of auditing, quality control, ethics, independence and other standards relating to preparation of audit reports, (3) inspection of accounting firms, (4) investigations, disciplinary proceedings, and imposition of sanctions, and (5) enforcement of compliance with accounting rules of the board, professional standards, and securities laws relating to the preparation and issuance of audit reports and obligations and liabilities of accountants.

The board reports to the SEC on an annual basis that includes any new established rules and any final disciplinary rulings. The board works with designated professional groups of accountants and other standard-setting advisory groups in establishing auditing, quality control, ethics, and independence rules.

Conflicts of Interest: Auditor and Analyst Independence

The Sarbanes–Oxley Act also seeks to eliminate conflicts of interest among auditors, security analysts, brokers, and dealers and the public companies they serve in order to ensure enhanced financial disclosures of public companies' true condition. To accomplish auditor independence, Section 201 of the act no longer allows registered public accounting firms to provide both nonaudit and audit services to a public company. National securities exchanges and registered securities associations have already adopted similar conflict-of-interest rules for security analysts, brokers, and dealers, who recommend equities in research reports. The face of Wall Street is experiencing major changes. In early 2003, ten of the nation's largest securities firms agreed to pay a record $1.4 billion to settle government charges involving abuse of investors during the stock market bubble of the late 1990s. Wall Street firms routinely issued overly optimistic stock research to investors in order to gain favor with corporate clients and win their lucrative investment–banking business.

Enhanced Financial Disclosures

With independence, the Sarbanes–Oxley Act is better able to ensure compliance with the enhanced financial disclosures of public companies' true condition. For example, registered public accounting firms are now required to identify all material correcting adjustments to reflect accurate financial statements. Also, all material off-balance-sheet transactions and other relationships with unconsolidated entities that affect current or future financial conditions of a public company must be disclosed in each annual and quarterly financial report. In addition, public companies must also report "on a rapid and current basis" material changes in the financial condition or operations.

Whistle-Blower Protection

Employees of public companies and accounting firms, in general, are also accountable to report unethical behavior. The Sarbanes–Oxley Act intends to motivate employees through whistle-blower protection that would prohibit the employer from taking certain actions against employees who lawfully disclose private employer information to, among others, parties in a judicial proceeding involving a fraud claim.

Whistle-blowers are also granted a remedy of special damages and attorney's fees. Two years after the act, the SEC received approximately forty thousand whistle-blowing reports per month, compared with sixty-four hundred per month in 2001.[26] With only eleven thousand publicly-traded companies in the United States, it seems that even though 75 percent of the whistle-blowing reports have no validity, there are still more whistle-blowing reports every month than the number of companies listed.[27]

Also, any act of retaliation that harms informants, including interference with the lawful employment or livelihood of any person, for providing to a law enforcement officer any truthful information relating to the commission or possible commission of any federal offense, will be fined and/or imprisoned for ten years. (Whistle-blowers are discussed in more detail in Chapter 8.)

Corporate and Criminal Fraud Accountability

Title VIII of the Sarbanes–Oxley Act, Corporate and Criminal Fraud Accountability, makes the knowing destruction or creation of documents to "impede, obstruct or influence" any existing or contemplated federal investigation a felony. The White-Collar Crime Penalty Enhancements Act of 2002 increased the maximum penalty for mail and wire fraud from five to ten years in prison. It also makes record tampering or otherwise impeding with any official proceeding a crime. If necessary, the SEC could freeze extraordinary payments to directors, officers, partners, controlling persons, and agents of employees. The U.S. Sentencing Commission reviews sentencing guidelines for securities and accounting fraud.

The act may not prevent future Enron-type businesses from occurring. However, the act's uniqueness from past legislation is its perspective to mandate accountability from the many players in the "game of business," creating more explicit rules in playing fair. The act creates a foundation to strongly discourage wrongdoing and sets ethical standards of what's expected of American business.

Cost of Compliance

The national cost of compliance of the Sarbanes–Oxley Act is estimated at $1 million per $1 billion in revenues.[28] For many companies, this means the cost of compliance is in excess of $10 million annually.[29] The average total cost for only the first year of Section 404 compliance is $4.36 million. These costs come from internal costs, external costs, and auditor fees. In a survey by Financial Executives International, nearly all the respondents (94 percent) said that the costs of compliance exceeded the benefits.[30] This act has increased external auditing costs for mid- to large-size companies between 52 and 81 percent. The section that has caused the most cost for companies has been compliance with Section 404. Section 404 has three central issues: It requires that (1) management create reliable internal financial controls, (2) that management attest to the reliability of those controls and the accuracy of financial statements that result from those controls, and (3) an independent auditor to further attest to the statements made by management. Section 404 requires companies to document both the results of financial transactions and the processes they have used to generate them. A company may have thousands of processes that may work, but they have never been written down. Writing down the processes is time consuming and costly.[31] Many companies such as Eastman Kodak and Toys "Я" Us have reported "material weaknesses" in their 2004 internal financial controls. Also, because the cost of compliance is so high for many small companies, some publicly traded companies are even considering delisting themselves from the U.S. Stock Exchange. Companies based outside the United States have also been weighing the costs of compliance versus the savings of deregistration. Sweden-based Electrolux was among the first to delist from NASDAQ after the Sarbanes–Oxley Act was passed. Many new non-U.S. companies may be avoiding the U.S. market altogether. New listings with the SEC from companies outside the United States have dropped to almost zero since the act passed in 2002.[32]

However, there are some cases where companies are benefiting from the act's implementation. Apart from the obvious increase in books and materials to help people comply with the act, there is also a growing business for people teaching and implementing ethics programs and hot lines for organizations. Companies such as EthicsPoint and LRN have grown rapidly as companies rush to learn ethics virtually overnight; as they do, a vast new industry of consultants and suppliers has emerged.[33] Other benefits and savings have come in the form of increased efficiency as companies such as Pitney Bowes Inc. find that they can meld various units such as combining four accounts-receivable offices into one, saving more than $500,000 a year. At Genentech Inc., simply having detailed reports on financial controls sped up installation, by several months, of a new computer system that consolidates financial data, which meant that they were running months ahead of schedule. The new system allows managers to analyze data from customers rather than just collecting it. Cisco spent $50 million and two hundred and forty thousand hours on its first-year audit of internal controls. The mind-numbing effort revealed opportunities to streamline steps for ordering products and services, making it easier for customers to do business with Cisco. It forced them to make sure that sales and support were integrated when a customer called, resulting in one-stop shopping for their customers. Other companies have been able to streamline steps for ordering products and services, making it easier for customers to do business with them.[34]

LAWS THAT ENCOURAGE ETHICAL CONDUCT

Violations of the law usually begin when businesspeople stretch the limits of ethical standards, as defined by company or industry codes of conduct, and then choose to engage in schemes that knowingly or unwittingly violate the law. In recent years, new laws and regulations have been passed to discourage such decisions—and to foster programs designed to improve business ethics and social responsibility (Table 4–8). The most important of these are the FSGO and the Sarbanes–Oxley Act. One of the goals of both acts is to require employees to report observed misconduct. The development of reporting systems has advanced with most companies having some method for employees to report observed misconduct. Figure 4–3 provides changes in reporting observed misconduct between 2000 and 2005.

TABLE 4–8	Institutionalization of Ethics Through Laws

1991	*Organizational Sentencing Guidelines created.* These guidelines, added to the FSGO, created organizational responsibility for employee conduct. Sentences and fines are lessened for organizations with ethics programs. Firms that fail to take due diligence actions to prevent misconduct are given stricter sentences or fines.
2002	*Sarbanes–Oxley Act passed.* Companies now must create an independent board audit committee, a code of conduct and ethics policies, whistle-blower hot lines, and annual reports on effectiveness of financial reporting systems. CEOs and CFOs must sign off on the accuracy of financial statements. The act directs that Organizational Sentencing Guidelines be reviewed and amended. Penalties: up to $5 million and twenty years in prison.
2004	*Organizational Sentencing Guidelines stiffened.* In accord with the Sarbanes–Oxley Act, guidelines are revised so that organizations are held to a stiffer definition of an effective ethics program in order to receive lenient treatment for offenses. Directors and executives must assume responsibility for such programs, identify areas of risk, train officials in ethics, create an ethics hot line, designate an individual to oversee ethics, and give that person sufficient authority and resources to do the job. Companies must also create a corporate culture that encourages ethics.

SOURCE: Adapted from James C. Hyatt, "Birth of the Ethics Industry," *Business Ethics,* Summer 2005, p. 27. Reprinted with permission of Business Ethics.

FEDERAL SENTENCING GUIDELINES FOR ORGANIZATIONS

As mentioned in Chapter 1, Congress passed the FSGO in 1991 to create an incentive for organizations to develop and implement programs designed to foster ethical and legal compliance. These guidelines, which were developed by the U.S. Sentencing Commission, apply to all felonies and class A misdemeanors committed by employees in association with their work. As an incentive, organizations that have demonstrated due diligence in developing effective compliance programs that dis-

FIGURE 4–3	Reported Misconduct by Employees

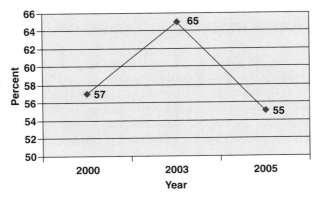

SOURCE: National Business Ethics Survey, *How Employees View Ethics in Their Organizations 1994–2005* (Washington, DC: Ethics Resource Center, 2005), 17.

courage unethical and illegal conduct may be subject to reduced organizational penalties if an employee commits a crime.[35] Overall, the government philosophy is that legal violations can be prevented through organizational values and a commitment to ethical conduct.

The commission delineated seven steps that companies must implement to demonstrate due diligence:

1. A firm must develop and disseminate a code of conduct that communicates required standards and identifies key risk areas for the organization.
2. High-ranking personnel in the organization who are known to abide by the legal and ethical standards of the industry (such as an ethics officer, vice president of human resources, general counsel, and so forth) must have oversight over the program.
3. No one with a known propensity to engage in misconduct should be put in a position of authority.
4. A communications system for disseminating standards and procedures (ethics training) must also be put into place.
5. Organizational communications should include a way for employees to report misconduct without fearing retaliation, such as an anonymous toll-free hot line or an ombudsman. Monitoring and auditing systems designed to detect misconduct are also required.
6. If misconduct is detected, then the firm must take appropriate and fair disciplinary action. Individuals both directly and indirectly responsible for the offense should be disciplined. In addition, the sanctions should be appropriate for the offense.
7. After misconduct has been discovered, the organization must take steps to prevent similar offenses in the future. This usually involves making modifications to the ethical compliance program, additional employee training, and issuing communications about specific types of conduct.

The government expects these seven steps for compliance programs to undergo continuous improvement and refinement.[36]

These steps are based on the commission's determination to emphasize compliance programs and to provide guidance for both organizations and courts regarding program effectiveness. Organizations have flexibility about the type of program they develop; the seven steps are not a checklist requiring that legal procedures be followed to gain certification of an effective program. Organizations implement the guidelines through effective core practices that are appropriate for their firms. The program must be capable of reducing the opportunity that employees have to engage in misconduct.

A 2005 Supreme Court decision held that the sentences for violations of law were not mandatory but should serve only as recommendations for judges to use in their decisions. Some legal and business experts believe that this decision might weaken the implementation of the FSGO, but as shown in Table 4–9, most sentences have remained in the same range as before the Supreme Court decision. The guidelines remain an important consideration in developing an effective ethics and compliance program.

A 2004 amendment to the FSGO requires that a business's governing authority be well informed about its ethics program with respect to content, implementation, and

TABLE 4-9	Recent Changes in Organizational Sentencing

After the U.S. Supreme Court ruled that exact sentences were not mandatory and gave judges more latitude in 2005, most judges continued to use sentences within the range of the sentencing guidelines.

62%	Sentences within the range of the sentencing guidelines; compares with 68% in previous four years, when guidelines were mandatory
24%	Sentences cut below the guidelines at the government's request; unchanged from previous four years
7.8%	Sentences cut at least in part as a result of the Court's decision

SOURCE: U.S. Sentencing Commission Special Post-Booker Coding Project, as referenced in *Forbes,* January 30, 2006, 48.

effectiveness. This places the responsibility squarely on the shoulders of the firm's leadership, usually the board of directors. The board must ensure that there is a high-ranking manager accountable for the day-to-day operational oversight of the ethics program. The board must provide for adequate authority, resources, and access to the board or an appropriate subcommittee of the board. The board must ensure that there are confidential mechanisms available so that the organization's employees and agents may report or seek guidance about potential or actual misconduct without fear of retaliation. Finally, the board is required to oversee the discovery of risks and to design, implement, and modify approaches to deal with those risks. Figure 4–4 provides an overview from NBES about how well prepared employees are to respond to various ethical and legal risk. Over three-quarters of employees who encounter risk feel adequately prepared to respond. If board members do not understand the nature, purpose, and methods available to implement an ethics program, the firm is at risk of inadequate oversight in the event of ethical misconduct that escalates into a scandal.[37]

The Department of Justice, through the Thompson Memo (Larry Thompson, deputy attorney general, 2003 memo to U.S. Attorneys), advanced general principles

FIGURE 4-4	Employees Preparation to Respond to Risk

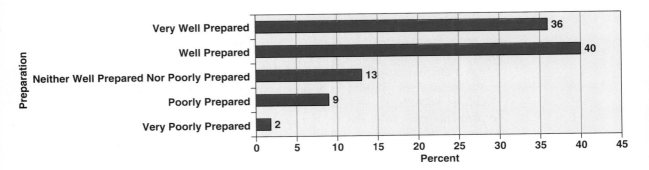

SOURCE: National Business Ethics Survey, *How Employees View Ethics in Their Organizations 1994–2005* (Washington, DC: Ethics Resource Center, 2005), 39.

to consider in cases involving corporate wrongdoing. This memo makes it clear that ethics and compliance programs are important to detect types of misconduct most likely to occur in a particular corporation's line of business. Without an effective ethics and compliance program to detect ethical and legal lapses, the firm should not be treated leniently. Also, the prosecutor generally has wide latitude in determining when, whom, and whether to prosecute violations of federal law. U.S. Attorneys are directed that charging for even minor misconduct may be appropriate when the wrongdoing was pervasive by a large number of employees in a particular role—for example, sales staff, procurement officers—or was condoned by upper management. Without an effective program to identify an isolated rogue employee involved in misconduct, serious consequences can be associated with regulatory issues, enforcement, and sentencing.[38] Therefore, there is general agreement both from laws and administrative policy that an effective ethics and compliance program is necessary to prevent conduct and reduce the legal consequences.

HIGHLY APPROPRIATE CORE PRACTICES

The FSGO and the Sarbanes–Oxley Act provide incentives for developing core practices that help ensure ethical and legal compliance. Core practices move the emphasis from a focus on individuals' moral capability to developing structurally sound organization core practices and developing structural integrity for both financial performance and nonfinancial performance. Although the Sarbanes–Oxley Act provides standards for financial performance, most ethical issues relate to nonfinancial issues such as marketing, human resource management, and customer relationships. Abusive behavior, lying, and conflict of interest are still the top three ethical issues.

The Integrity Institute has developed an integrated model to standardize the measurement of nonfinancial performance. Methodologies have been developed to assess communications, compensation, social responsibility, corporate culture, leadership, risk, and stakeholder perceptions, as well as more subjective aspects of earnings, corporate governance, technology, and other important nonfinancial areas. The model exists to establish a standard that can predict sustainability and success of an organization. The Integrity Institute uses the measurement to an established standard as the basis of certification of integrity.[39]

The majority of executives and board members want to measure nonfinancial performance, but no standards currently exist. The Open Compliance Ethics Group (OCEG.org) has developed benchmarking studies available to organizations to conduct self-assessments to develop ethics program elements. Developing organizational systems and processes is a requirement of the regulatory environment, but organizations are given considerable freedom in developing ethics and compliance programs. Core practices do exist and can be identified in every industry. Trade associations self-regulatory groups and research studies often provide insights about the expected best core practices. The most important is for each firm to assess its legal and ethical risk areas and then develop structures to prevent, detect, and quickly correct any misconduct.

TABLE 4–10	Key Findings from 2005 Open Compliance Ethics Group Benchmarking Survey
Crisis Can Help the Cause	Companies that have experienced reputation damage in the past see themselves as much further along in terms of program maturity and in relation to their peers—both today and in the future.
Pay Now or Pay Later	Companies that have experienced reputation damage invest *three* times more than their nondamaged peers in specific compliance and ethics processes.
Preference for Proactive and Values-Based Programs	Compliance and ethics programs are becoming more proactive and values based, allowing companies to prevent ethical and compliance violations before they become a crisis.
Proactive Skills Training May Need More Emphasis	To reach the objective of more proactive programs, companies must provide training to the people who are accountable for the compliance and ethics program—training that focuses on more proactive disciplines.
Set/Align Objectives for More Benefit	Companies that set explicit objectives for their compliance and ethics programs rate the benefits of their programs more highly and ascribe them more than companies that do not set explicit objectives.
Integrate/Cooperate for More Benefit	Additional benefits and performance can be realized when an organization integrates the compliance and ethics program with other aspects of the enterprise and when the program has a good working relationship with other business functions/processes.
Experience	Of the companies in this study, 54% have implemented a compliance and ethics program relatively recently (within the last five years). *Zero* companies in this study with a program in place for ten years or more experienced highly visible reputation damage in the last five years, a testament to the important impact these programs can have over time.

SOURCE: Open Compliance Ethics Group 2005 Benchmarking Study Key Findings, http://www.oceg.org/benchmarking.asp (accessed January 12, 2006). Reprinted with permission.

Consider McDonald's approach to answering critics about nutritional guidance. It announced a move to provide nutritional information on its product packaging worldwide. Nutrient information will be featured on its packaging across 20,000 of its 31,561 restaurants around the world. Mike Roberts, the president and chief operating officer for McDonald's, said, "There is nothing more important to McDonald's than building customer trust and loyalty around the world. We know how important transparency is, which is what this initiative is all about." McDonald's also introduced a "Balanced Lifestyles" initiative for kids, which involved offering healthier menu options, promoting physical activity, and providing more nutritional information to its customers about its products. In 2004 it withdrew its supersize meals after a damaging portrayal of the company in the film *Super Size Me*. The product sizes available at McDonald's are small, medium, and large, but upgrading to a bigger-portion size remains cheap.[40]

Table 4–10 provides some general findings from the 2005 OCEG benchmarking survey that provides insights on effective core practices.

Philanthropic Contributions

Philanthropic issues are another dimension of voluntary social responsibility and relate to business's contributions to stakeholders. Philanthropy provides four major benefits to society:

1. Philanthropy improves the quality of life and helps make communities places where people want to do business, raise families, and enjoy life. Thus, improving the quality of life in a community makes it easier to attract and retain employees and customers.
2. Philanthropy reduces government involvement by providing assistance to stakeholders.
3. Philanthropy develops employee leadership skills. Many firms, for example, use campaigns by the United Way and other community service organizations as leadership- and skill-building exercises for their employees.
4. Philanthropy helps create an ethical culture and the values that can act as a buffer to organizational misconduct.[41]

The most common way that businesses demonstrate philanthropy is through donations to local and national charitable organizations. Corporations gave more than $12 billion to environmental and social causes in 2004.[42] Wells Fargo & Company, for example, contributed $93 million to fifteen thousand different organizations. It helped finance the construction of single-family homes on or near Native American reservations in seven states, bringing private mortgage capital to those historically denied access.[43] Indeed, many companies have become concerned about the quality of education in the United States after realizing that the current pool of prospective employees lacks many basic work skills. Recognizing that today's students are tomorrow's employees and customers, firms such as Kroger, Campbell Soup Company, Eastman Kodak, American Express, Apple Computer, Xerox, and Coca-Cola have donated money, equipment, and employee time to help improve schools in their communities and throughout the nation.

Wal-Mart donated more than $200 million in 2005 to help charities and organizations throughout the United States. More than 90 percent of the contributions were directed at the local level. The Chronicle of Philanthropy recognized Wal-Mart as the largest corporate cash contributor in America. They helped more than one hundred thousand charitable organizations around the country and gave back $547,945 each day. The money supported a variety of causes such as child development, education, the environment, and disaster relief. Wal-Mart feels that they can make the greatest impact on communities by supporting issues and causes that are important to their customers and associates in their own neighborhoods. Wal-Mart relies on their own associates to know which organizations are the most important to their hometowns, and they empower them to determine how money will be spent in their communities. Wal-Mart supports charities such as the American Cancer Society and The Salvation Army, as well as helping out soldiers wounded in Iraq and donating more than $2.5 million to tsunami relief efforts. After Hurricane Katrina, Wal-Mart donated more than $17 million in cash to help the victims of the hurricane, as well as donating much needed supplies right after the disaster. By supporting communities at the local level, it encourages customer loyalty and goodwill.[44]

Strategic Philanthropy

Tying philanthropic giving to overall strategy and objectives is also known as strategic philanthropy. **Strategic philanthropy** is the synergistic and mutually beneficial use of an organization's core competencies and resources to deal with key stakeholders so as to bring about organizational and societal benefits. For example, last year Bisto, a staple of Britain's meal tables since 1908 with its instant gravy, launched a new marketing campaign. The focus was on families trying to eat one meal together a week. Bisto called it "ahh nights" based on its long time marketing slogan of "ahh . . . Bisto." Families eat fewer and fewer meals together; this has been identified by social policy experts as playing a key role in a wide range of social problems such as teenage drug abuse, sexual promiscuity, teenage pregnancy, crime, antisocial behavior, truancy, and poor academic performance. Bisto used the new marketing slogan to extol the virtues of eating together as a family while explicitly recognizing the challenges of doing this in the modern world. It used a website www.aahnight.co.uk to make it easy for families to have a meal together at least once a week. It used three steps: (1) Download a contract that families can sign and stick on the refrigerator; (2) invite the family or friends by e-mail; (3) make a delicious meal with recipes provided using—you guessed it—Bisto.[45]

Founder's Week, McDonald's annual celebration of company founder Ray Kroc's birthday, focuses on giving back to local communities. Last year, McDonald's employees nationwide participated in twenty-five thousand hours of community service, including tutoring children, painting classrooms, planting trees and shrubs, constructing homes with Habitat for Humanity, and assisting families and children at Ronald McDonald Houses across the country.[46]

Home Depot directs much of the money it spends on philanthropy to affordable housing, at-risk youth, the environment, and disaster recovery. Through Team Depot, an organized volunteer force of Home Depot, more than 6 million hours of volunteer community service is contributed annually. Together with Habitat for Humanity, Home Depot and its associates have built more than 150 affordable homes across the country. Home Depot has been supporting Habitat for Humanity since 1989 with donations and volunteers to build affordable housing for people in need of adequate shelter, and in Canada, Home Depot donates its unsold merchandise to Habitat to Humanity.[47] Through its partnership with "Rebuilding Together with Christmas in April," they have helped renovate more than twenty thousand homes in over 230 communities nationwide.[48]

SUMMARY

To understand the institutionalization of business ethics, it is important to understand the voluntary and legally mandated dimensions of organizational practices. Core practices are documented best practices, often encouraged by legal and regulatory forces as well as industry trade associations. The effective organizational practice of business ethics requires all three dimensions to be integrated into an ethics and compliance program. This creates an ethical culture that can effectively manage the risks of misconduct. Institutionalization in business ethics relates to established laws, customs, and expected organizational programs that are considered normative in establishing reputation. Institutions provide requirements, structure, and societal expectations to reward and sanction ethical decision making. In this way, society is institutionalizing core practices and provides organizations the opportunity to take their own approach, only taking action if there are violations.

Laws and regulations are established by governments to set minimum standards for responsible behavior—society's codification of what is right and wrong. Civil and criminal laws regulating business conduct are passed because society—including consumers, interest groups, competitors, and legislators—believes that business must comply with society's standards. Such laws regulate competition, protect consumers, promote safety and equity in the workplace, protect the environment, and provide incentives for preventing misconduct.

In 2002, largely in response to widespread corporate accounting scandals, Congress passed the Sarbanes–Oxley Act to establish a system of federal oversight of corporate accounting practices. In addition to making fraudulent financial reporting a criminal offense and strengthening penalties for corporate fraud, the law requires corporations to establish codes of ethics for financial reporting and to develop greater transparency in financial reporting to investors and other stakeholders. The Sarbanes–Oxley Act requires corporations to take greater responsibility for their decisions and to provide leadership based on ethical principles. For instance, the law requires top managers to certify that their firms' financial reports are complete and accurate, making CEOs and CFOs personally accountable for the credibility and accuracy of their companies' financial statements. The act establishes an oversight board to oversee the audit of public companies in order to protect the interests of investors and further the public interest in the preparation of informative, accurate, and independent audit reports for companies.

Congress passed the Federal Sentencing Guidelines for Organizations (FSGO) in 1991 to create an incentive for organizations to develop and implement programs designed to foster ethical and legal compliance. These guidelines, which were developed by the U.S. Sentencing Commission, apply to all felonies and class A misdemeanors committed by employees in association with their work. As an incentive, organizations that have demonstrated due diligence in developing effective compliance programs that discourage unethical and illegal conduct may be subject to reduced organizational penalties if an employee commits a crime.[49] Overall, the government philosophy is that legal violations can be prevented through organizational values and a commitment to ethical conduct. A 2004 amendment to the FSGO requires that a business's governing authority be well informed about its ethics program with respect to content, implementation, and effectiveness. This places the responsibility squarely on the shoulders of the firm's leadership, usually the board of directors. The board must ensure that there is a high-ranking manager accountable for the day-to-day operational oversight of the ethics program. The board must provide for adequate authority, resources, and access to the board or an appropriate subcommittee of the board. The board must ensure that there are confidential mechanisms available so that the organization's employees and agents may report or seek guidance about potential or actual misconduct without fear of retaliation.

The FSGO and the Sarbanes–Oxley Act provide incentives for developing core practices that help ensure ethical and legal compliance. Core practices move the emphasis from a focus on the individual's moral capability to developing structurally sound organization core practices and develop structural integrity for both financial performance and nonfinancial performance. The Integrity Institute has developed an integrated model to standardize the measurement of nonfinancial performance.

Methodologies have been developed to assess communications, compensation, social responsibility, corporate culture, leadership, risk, and stakeholder perceptions, as well as more subjective aspects of earnings, corporate governance, technology, and other important non-financial areas.

Philanthropic issues touch on businesses' social responsibility insofar as businesses contribute to the local community and to society. Philanthropy provides four major benefits to society: improving the quality of life, reducing government involvement, developing staff leadership skills, and building staff morale. Companies contribute significant amounts of money to education, the arts, environmental causes, and the disadvantaged by supporting local and national charitable organizations. Strategic philanthropy involves linking core business competencies to societal and community needs.

IMPORTANT TERMS FOR REVIEW	voluntary practice
	philanthropy
	core practices
	Better Business Bureau
	mandated boundary
	civil law
	criminal law
	procompetitive legislation
		consumer protection law
		Occupational Safety and Health
		    Administration
		Environmental Protection Agency
		Public Company Accounting Oversight
		    Board
		strategic philanthropy

A REAL-LIFE SITUATION*

Albert Chen was sweating profusely in his Jaguar on the expressway as he thought about his options and the fact that Christmas and the Chinese New Year were at hand. He and his wife, Mary, who were on their way to meet Albert's parents at New York's John F. Kennedy Airport, seemed to be looking up from an abyss, with no daylight to be seen. Several visits and phone calls from various people had engulfed both him and Mary.

He had graduated with honors in finance and had married Mary in his senior year. They had both obtained prestigious brokerage jobs in the New York area, and both had been working killer hours to develop their accounts. Listening to other brokers, both had learned that there were some added expenses to their professions. For example, they were told that brokers need to "look" and "act" successful. So Albert and Mary bought the appropriate clothes and

cars, joined the right clubs, and ate at the right restaurants with the right people. They also took the advice of others, which was to identify the "players" of large corporations at parties and take mental notes. "You'd be surprised at what information you hear with a little alcohol in these people," said one broker. Both started using this strategy, and five months later their clients began to see significant profits in their portfolios.

Their good luck even came from strange places. For example, Albert had an uncle whose work as a janitor gave him access to many law offices that had information on a number of companies, especially those about to file for bankruptcy. Mary and Albert were able to use information provided by this uncle to benefit their clients' portfolios. The uncle even had some of his friends use Albert. To Albert's surprise, his uncle's friends often had nest eggs in excess of $200,000. Because some of these friends were quite elderly, Albert was given permission to buy and sell nonrisky stocks at will.

Because both of them were earning good salaries, the Chens soon managed to invest in the market themselves, and their investments included stock in the company for which Mary's father worked. After eighteen months, Albert decided to jump ship and start working for Jarvis, Sunni, Lamar & Morten (JSL&M). JSL&M's reputation was that of a fast mover in the business. "We go up to the line and then measure how wide the line is so that we know how far we can go into it," was a common remark at the brokerage firm.

About six months ago, Mary's father, who was with a major health-care company, commented that the management team was running the company into the ground. "If only someone could buy the company and put in a good management team," he mused. After the conversation, Mary investigated the company and discovered that the stock was grossly undervalued. She made a few phone calls and found a company that was interested in doing a hostile takeover. Mary also learned from her father that if a new management were acceptable to the union, the union would do everything in its power to oust the old management—by striking, if necessary—and welcome the new one. As things started to materialize, Mary told several of her best clients, who in turn did very well on the stock. This increased her status in the firm, which kept drawing bigger clients.

Albert soon became a player in initial public stock offerings (IPOs) of new companies. Occasionally, when Albert saw a very hot IPO, he would talk to some of his best venture-capital friends, who then bought the IPOs and gained some very good returns. This strategy helped attract some larger players in the market. By this point in his young career, Albert had made a great many friends.

One of those friends was Barry, who worked on the stock floor. As they were talking, Barry mentioned that if Albert wanted to, he, as a favor, when placing orders to buy shares, would occasionally put Albert's or Mary's trade before the client order.

The first sign of trouble came when Mary told Albert about what was happening at her office. "I'm getting e-mail from some of the brokers with off-color jokes and even some nude photos of women and men. I just don't care for it."

"So what are you doing about it?" Albert asked.

"Well, I've just started not even opening my messages if they come from these people," Mary replied.

"What about messages that request that you send them on? What do you do with those?" queried Albert.

"I just e-mail them along without looking at them," was her response.

"This isn't good, Mary. A couple of analysts were just fired for doing that at a big firm last week," said Albert.

Several weeks later the people who were sending Mary the obnoxious messages were fired. Mary was also asked to see the head of her division. When she came to his office, he said, "Please shut the door, Mary. I have some bad news. I know that you weren't involved with what was happening with the e-mail scandal; however, you did forward messages that contained such material. As a result, I have no alternative but to give you your two weeks' notice. I know this is unfair, but I have my orders. Because of this mess, the SEC wants to check all your trades for the last eight months. It seems to be a formality, but it will take time, and as you well know, the chances of going to another firm with that hanging over your head are slim. I'm sorry that it's only two months until the holidays." That night Mary fell into a depression.

To exacerbate the situation, Albert's parents were flying in from the People's Republic of China. They were not happy with Albert's marriage to a white woman, but they had consoled themselves that Mary had a good job. They had also said that if things should go badly for them in New York, they could always come to the parents' retirement home in Taiwan. However, the idea of leaving the United States, attempting to learn Mandarin, and raising children in an unfamiliar culture did not appeal to Mary.

Albert was also having some problems. Because their income was cut in half, Albert tried to make up for the loss by trading in some high-risk markets, such as commodities and precious metals. However, many of these investments turned sour, and he found himself buying and selling more and more to pull his own portfolio, as well as those of his clients, into the black. He was getting worried because some of his uncle's friends' portfolios were losing significant value. Other matters, however, were causing him even more anxiety. The previous week, Barry had called him, asking for some inside information on several companies that he was working with for an IPO. Albert knew that this could be construed as insider information and had said no.

Today, Barry called again and said, "Look, Al, I've been doing you favors for a while. I need to score big because of the holidays. You probably don't know, but what I've been doing for you could be construed as spinning, which is not looked upon favorably. I'm not asking for the IPO information—I'm demanding it. Is that clear enough for you, Al? E-mail it over by tomorrow morning." Then Barry hung up.

An hour later Albert's supervisor came in and said, "Al, I need a favor from you. I want you to buy some stock for a few friends and me. When it goes to $112, I want you to sell it. We'll pay the taxes and give you a little bonus for Christmas as well. I want you to buy tomorrow as soon as the market opens. Here are the account numbers for the transaction. I must run. See you tomorrow."

QUESTIONS • EXERCISES

1. Identify the ethical and legal issues of which Albert needs to be aware.
2. Discuss the advantages and disadvantages of each decision that Albert could make and has made.
3. Identify the pressures that have brought about these issues.

*This case is strictly hypothetical; any resemblance to real persons, companies, or situations is coincidental.

Check Your EQ

Check your EQ, or Ethics Quotient, by completing the following. Assess your performance to evaluate your overall understanding of the chapter material.

	Yes	No
1. Voluntary practices include documented best practices.	Yes	No
2. The primary method for resolving business ethics disputes is through the criminal court system.	Yes	No
3. The FSGO provides an incentive for organizations to conscientiously develop and implement ethics programs.	Yes	No
4. The Sarbanes–Oxley Act encourages CEOs and CFOs to report their financial statements accurately.	Yes	No
5. Strategic philanthropy represents a new direction in corporate giving that maximizes the benefit to societal or community needs and relates to business objectives.	Yes	No

ANSWERS: 1. No. Core practices are documented best practices. 2. No. Lawsuits and civil litigation are the primary way in which business ethics disputes are resolved. 3. Yes. Well-designed ethics and compliance programs can minimize legal liability when organizational misconduct is detected. 4. No. The Sarbanes–Oxley Act *requires* CEOs and CFOs to accurately report their financial statements to a federal oversight committee; they must sign the document and are held personally liable for any inaccuracies. 5. Yes. Strategic philanthropy helps both society and the organization.

The Decision-Making Process

CHAPTER 5

Ethical Decision Making and Ethical Leadership

CHAPTER OBJECTIVES

- To provide a comprehensive framework for ethical decision making in business
- To examine the intensity of ethical issues as an important element influencing the ethical decision-making process
- To introduce individual factors that may influence ethical decision making in business
- To introduce organizational factors that may influence ethical decision making in business
- To explore the role of opportunity in ethical decision making in business
- To explain how knowledge about the ethical decision-making framework can be used to improve ethical leadership
- To provide leadership styles and habits that promote an ethical culture

CHAPTER OUTLINE

Bill Church was in a bind. A recent graduate of a prestigious business school, he had taken a job in the auditing division of Greenspan & Company, a fast-growing leader in the accounting industry. Greenspan relocated Bill, his wife, and their 1-year-old daughter from the Midwest to the East Coast. On arriving, they bought their first home and a second car. Bill was told that the company had big plans for him. Thus, he did not worry about being financially overextended.

Several months into the job, Bill found that he was working late into the night to complete his auditing assignments. He realized that the company did not want its clients billed for excessive hours and that he needed to become more efficient if he wanted to move up in the company. He asked one of his friends, Ann, how she managed to be so efficient in auditing client records.

Ann quietly explained: "Bill, there are times when being efficient isn't enough. You need to do what is required to get ahead. The partners just want results—they don't care how you get them."

"I don't understand," said Bill.

"Look," Ann explained, "I had the same problem you have a few years ago, but Mr. Reed [the manager of the auditing department] explained that everyone 'eats time' so that the group shows top results and looks good. And when the group looks good, everyone in it looks good. No one cares if a little time gets lost in the shuffle."

Bill realized that "eating time" meant not reporting all the hours required to complete a project. He also remembered one of Reed's classic catch phrases, "results, results, results." He thanked Ann for her input and went back to work. Bill thought of going over Reed's head and asking for advice from the division manager, but he had met her only once and did not know anything about her.

QUESTIONS • EXERCISES

1. What should Bill do?
2. Describe the process through which Bill might attempt to resolve his dilemma.
3. Consider the impact of this company's approach on young accountants. How could working long hours be an ethical problem?

*This case is strictly hypothetical; any resemblance to real persons, companies, or situations is coincidental.

To improve ethical decision making in business, one must first understand how individuals make ethical decisions in an organizational environment. Too often it is assumed that individuals in organizations make ethical decisions in the same way that they make ethical decisions at home, in their family, or in their personal lives. Within the context of an organizational work group, however, few individuals have the freedom to decide ethical issues independent of organizational pressures.

This chapter summarizes our current knowledge of ethical decision making in business and provides insights into ethical decision making in organizations. Although it is impossible to describe exactly how any one individual or work group might make ethical decisions, we can offer generalizations about average or typical behavior patterns within organizations. These generalizations are based on many studies and at least six ethical decision models that have been widely accepted by academics and practitioners.[1] Based on these models, we present a framework for understanding ethical decision making in the context of business organizations. In addition to business, this framework integrates concepts from philosophy, psychology, and sociology, and organizational behavior.

A FRAMEWORK FOR ETHICAL DECISION MAKING IN BUSINESS

As Figure 5–1 shows, our model of the ethical decision-making process in business includes ethical-issue intensity, individual factors, and organizational factors such as corporate culture and opportunity. All of these interrelated factors influence the evaluations of and intentions behind the decisions that produce ethical or unethical behavior.

Ethical-Issue Intensity

The first step in ethical decision making is to recognize that an ethical issue requires an individual or work group to choose among several actions that various stakeholders inside or outside the firm will ultimately evaluate as right or wrong. The intensity of an ethical issue relates to its perceived importance to the decision maker.[2] **Ethical-issue intensity,** then, can be defined as the relevance or importance of an ethical issue in the eyes of the individual, work group, and/or organization. It is personal and temporal in character to accommodate values, beliefs, needs, perceptions, the special characteristics of the situation, and the personal pressures prevailing at a particular place and time.[3] Senior employees and those with administrative authority contribute significantly to intensity because they typically dictate an organization's stance on ethical issues. In fact, under current law, managers can be held liable for the unethical and illegal

---

FIGURE 5–1   Framework for Understanding Ethical Decision Making in Business

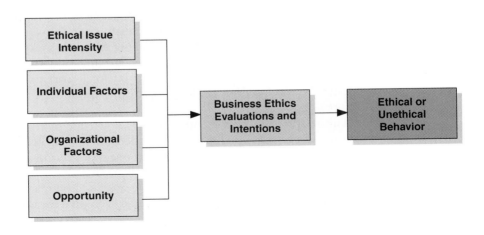

actions of subordinates. In the United States, the Federal Sentencing Guidelines for Organizations have a liability formula that judges those who are in positions of authority in regards to their action or inaction regarding the unethical and illegal activities of those around them. For example, many of the Enron employees and managers who were aware of the firm's use of off-balance-sheet partnerships—which turned out to be the major cause of the energy firm's collapse—were advised that these partnerships were legal, so they did not perceive them as an ethical issue. Although such partnerships were in fact legal at that time, the way that some Enron officials designed them and the methods they used to provide collateral (that is, Enron stock) created a scheme that brought about the collapse of the company.[4] Thus, ethical-issue intensity involves individuals' cognitive state of concern about an issue, whether or not they have knowledge that an issue is unethical, which indicates their involvement in making choices.

Ethical-issue intensity reflects the ethical sensitivity of the individual or work group that faces the ethical decision-making process. Research suggests that individuals are subject to six "spheres of influence" when confronted with ethical choices—the workplace, family, religion, legal system, community, and profession—and that the level of importance of each of these influences will vary depending on how important the decision maker perceives the issue to be.[5] Additionally, the individual's sense of the situation's moral intensity increases the individual's perceptiveness regarding ethical problems, which in turn reduces his or her intention to act unethically.[6] **Moral intensity** relates to a person's perception of social pressure and the harm the decision will have on others.[7] All other factors in Figure 5–1, including individual factors, organizational factors, and intentions, determine why different individuals perceive ethical issues differently. Unless individuals in an organization share common concerns about ethical issues, the stage is set for ethical conflict. The perception of ethical-issue intensity can be influenced by management's use of rewards and punishments, corporate policies, and corporate values to sensitize employees. In other words, managers can affect the degree to which employees perceive the importance of an ethical issue through positive and/or negative incentives.[8]

For some employees, ethical issues may not reach the critical awareness level if managers fail to identify and educate employees about specific problem areas. Organizations that consist of employees with diverse values and backgrounds must train them in the way the firm wants specific ethical issues handled. Identifying the ethical issues that employees might encounter is a significant step toward developing their ability to make ethical decisions. Many ethical issues are identified by industry groups or through general information available to a firm. Companies must assess areas of ethical and legal risk that are in reality ethical issues. Issues that are communicated as being high in ethical importance could trigger increases in employees' ethical-issue intensity. The perceived importance of an ethical issue has been found to have a strong influence on both employees' ethical judgment and their behavioral intention. In other words, the more likely individuals are to perceive an ethical issue as important, the less likely they are to engage in questionable or unethical behavior.[9] Therefore, ethical-issue intensity should be considered a key factor in the ethical decision-making process.

Individual Factors

When people need to resolve ethical issues in their daily lives, they often base their decisions on their own values and principles of right or wrong. They generally learn these values and principles through the socialization process with family members, social groups, and religion and in their formal education. The actions of specific individuals in scandal-plagued companies such as Enron, WorldCom, Halliburton, Qwest, Arthur Andersen, and Adelphia often raise questions about those individuals' personal character and integrity. They appear to operate in their own self-interest or in total disregard of the law and interests of society. At Adelphia Communications, for example, the Rigas family members who founded the firm had forgotten about general societal values. As a result, U.S. Attorney General Alberto Gonzales stated:

> As many of you know, on July 8, 2004, Adelphia's founder, Chairman and CEO, John J. Rigas, and his son, CFO Timothy J. Rigas, were convicted on conspiracy, securities fraud and bank fraud charges . . . . John and Timothy Rigas each face up to 215 years in prison for their actions.
>
> The Justice Department has reached an agreement with John Rigas that obligates all members of the Rigas family to forfeit to the United States in excess of 95 percent of all the family's assets. These assets include privately owned cable systems worth between 700 and 900 million dollars; all Adelphia securities owned by the Rigas family and its affiliated entities, valued at approximately 567 million dollars; and real estate holdings valued at approximately ten million dollars. In total, this represents the largest forfeiture ever made by individuals in a corporate fraud matter.
>
> Second, today I am announcing the creation of the Adelphia Victim Compensation Fund to compensate the victims who lost money as the result of fraud at Adelphia. Under the terms of a second agreement reached in this matter, Adelphia Corporation will not be prosecuted for the actions of its executives but will incur two obligations: To continue to cooperate with the government—and to contribute 715 million dollars to this new fund.[10]

In the workplace, personal ethical issues typically involve honesty, conflicts of interest, discrimination, nepotism, and theft of organizational resources. For example, many individuals make personal phone calls on company time. Most employees limit personal calls to a few minutes, and most companies probably overlook these as reasonable. Some employees, however, make personal calls in excess of thirty minutes, which companies are likely to view as an excessive use of company time for personal reasons. The decision to use company time to make a personal phone call is an example of a personal ethical decision. It illustrates the fine line between what may be acceptable or unacceptable in a business environment. It also reflects how well an individual will assume responsibilities in the work environment. Often this decision will depend on company policy and the corporate environment.

The way the public perceives individual ethics generally varies according to the profession in question. Telemarketers, car salespersons, advertising practitioners, stockbrokers, and real estate brokers are often perceived as having the lowest ethics. Research regarding individual factors that affect ethical awareness, judgment, intent, and behavior include gender, education, work experience, nationality, age, and locus of control.

Extensive research has been done regarding the link between gender and ethical decision making. The research shows that in many aspects there are no differences between men and women, but when differences are found, women are generally more ethical than men.[11] By "more ethical," we mean that women seem to be more sensitive to ethical scenarios and less tolerant of unethical actions. As more and more women work in managerial positions, these findings may become increasingly significant.

Education, the number of years spent in pursuit of academic knowledge, is also a significant factor in the ethical decision-making process. The important thing to remember about education is that it does not reflect experience. Work experience is defined as the number of years within a specific job, occupation, and/or industry. Generally, the more education or work experience that one has, the better he or she is at ethical decision making. The type of education has little or no effect on ethics. For example, it doesn't matter if you are a business student or a liberal arts student—you're pretty much the same in terms of ethical decision making. Lest you assume that the higher the education level the less likely one is to commit unethical acts, Seton Hall University has created Halls of Shame. There's Kozlowski Hall, named after Tyco's ex-CEO Dennis Kozlowski, who looted more than $600 million from shareholders. Near the library there is a green area named after Frank Walsh Jr., a former Tyco board member being sued by the company for breach of fiduciary responsibility for receiving a $20 million bonus from Kozlowski without the board's approval. Next to the library is the recreation center named for First Jersey Securities founder Robert Brennan, who was convicted of bankruptcy fraud and money laundering. Current research, however, does show that students are less ethical than businesspeople, which is likely because businesspeople have been exposed to more ethically challenging situations than students.[12]

Nationality is the legal relationship between a person and the country in which he/she is born. Within the twenty-first century, nationality is being redefined by such things as the European Union (EU). When European students are asked their nationality, they are less likely to state where they were born than where they currently live. The same thing is happening in the United States, as someone born in Florida who lives in New York might consider him- or herself to be a New Yorker. Research about nationality and ethics appears to be significant in that it affects ethical decision making; however, the true effect is somewhat hard to interpret.[13] Because of cultural differences, it is impossible to state, for example, whether Belgians are more ethical than Nigerians. The fact is that the concept of nationality is in flux. The reality of today is that multinational companies look for businesspeople who can make decisions regardless of nationality. Perhaps in twenty years, nationality will no longer be an issue in that the multinational's culture will replace the national status, a fact that can be seen in the number of young people in the European Union who are less likely to align themselves with a country and more open to the multinational EU concept.

Age is another individual factor that has been researched within business ethics. Several decades ago, we believed that age was positively correlated with ethical decision making. In other words, the older you are, the more ethical you are. However, recent research suggests that there is probably a more complex relationship between ethics and age. As a result, we can no longer say "the older, the wiser."[14]

Locus of control relates to individual differences in relation to a generalized belief about how one is affected by internal versus external events or reinforcements. In other words, the concept relates to where people view themselves in relation to power. Those who believe in **external control** (that is, externals) see themselves as going with the flow because that's all they can do. They believe that the events in their lives are due to uncontrollable forces. They consider what they want to achieve depends on luck, chance, and powerful people in their company. In addition, they believe that the probability of being able to control their lives by their own actions and efforts is low. Conversely, those who believe in **internal control** (that is, internals) believe that they control the events in their lives by their own effort and skill, viewing themselves as masters of their destinies and trusting in their capacity to influence their environment.

Current research suggests that we still can't be sure how significant locus of control is in terms of ethical decision making. One study that found a relationship between locus of control and ethical decision making concluded that internals were positively related whereas externals were negative.[15] In other words, those who believe that their fate is in the hands of others were more ethical than those who believed that they formed their own destiny.

Organizational Factors

Although people can and do make individual ethical choices in business situations, no one operates in a vacuum. Indeed, research has established that in the workplace the organization's values often have greater influence on decisions than a person's own values.[16] Ethical choices in business are most often made jointly, in work groups and committees, or in conversations and discussions with coworkers. Employees approach ethical issues on the basis of what they have learned not only from their own backgrounds but also from others in the organization. The outcome of this learning process depends on the strength of each person's personal values, the opportunities he or she has to behave unethically, and the exposure he or she has to others who behave ethically or unethically. Although people outside the organization, such as family members and friends, also influence decision makers, an organization's culture and structure operate through the relationships of its members to influence their ethical decisions.

A **corporate culture** can be defined as a set of values, beliefs, goals, norms, and ways of solving problems that members (employees) of an organization share. As time passes, stakeholders come to view the company or organization as a living organism, with a mind and will of its own. The Walt Disney Company, for example, requires all new employees to take a course in the traditions and history of Disneyland and Walt Disney, including the ethical dimensions of the company. The corporate culture at American Express Company stresses that employees help customers out of difficult situations whenever possible. This attitude is reinforced through numerous company legends of employees who have gone above and beyond the call of duty to help customers. This strong tradition of customer loyalty thus might encourage an American Express employee to take unorthodox steps to help a customer who encounters a problem while traveling overseas. Employees learn that they can take some risks in helping customers. Saturn is a division of General Motors, but it has developed its own corporate culture, including values related to product quality, customer service, and fairness in pricing. Such strong traditions and values have become a driving force in many companies, including McDonald's, IBM, Procter & Gamble, Southwest Airlines, and Hershey Foods.

An important component of corporate, or organizational, culture is the company's ethical culture. Whereas corporate culture involves values and rules that prescribe a wide range of behavior for organizational members, the **ethical culture** reflects whether the firm also has an ethical conscience. Ethical culture is a function of many factors, including corporate policies on ethics, top management's leadership on ethical issues, the influence of coworkers, and the opportunity for unethical behavior. Within the organization as a whole, subclimates can develop within individual departments or work groups, but they are influenced by the strength of the firm's overall ethical culture, as well as the function of the department and the stakeholders it serves.[17]

The more ethical employees perceive an organization's culture to be, the less likely they are to make unethical decisions. Corporate culture and ethical culture are closely associated with the idea that significant others within the organization help determine ethical decisions within that organization. Research also indicates that the ethical values embodied in an organization's culture are positively related to employees' commitment to the firm and their sense that they fit into the company. These findings suggest that companies should develop and promote ethical values to enhance employees' experiences in the workplace.[18]

Those who have influence in a work group, including peers, managers, coworkers, and subordinates, are referred to as **significant others.** They help workers on a daily basis with unfamiliar tasks and provide advice and information in both formal and informal ways. Coworkers, for instance, can offer help in the comments they make in discussions over lunch or when the boss is away. Likewise, a manager may provide directives about certain types of activities that employees perform on the job. Indeed, an employee's supervisor can play a central role in helping employees develop and fit in socially in the workplace.[19] Numerous studies conducted over the years confirm that significant others within an organization may have more impact on a worker's decisions on a daily basis than any other factor.[20]

Obedience to authority is another aspect of the influence that significant others can exercise. Obedience to authority helps to explain why many employees resolve business ethics issues by simply following the directives of a superior. In organizations that emphasize respect for superiors, for example, employees may feel that they are expected to carry out orders by a supervisor even if those orders are contrary to the employees' sense of right and wrong. Later, if the employee's decision is judged to have been wrong, he or she is likely to say, "I was only carrying out orders" or "My boss told me to do it this way." In addition, the type of industry and the size of organization have also been researched and found to be relevant factors; the bigger the company, the more unethical it has the potential to become.[21]

Opportunity

Opportunity describes the conditions in an organization that limit or permit ethical or unethical behavior. Opportunity results from conditions that either provide rewards, whether internal or external, or fail to erect barriers against unethical behavior.

Examples of internal rewards include feelings of goodness and personal worth generated by performing altruistic acts. External rewards refer to what an individual expects to receive from others in the social environment. Rewards are external to the individual to the degree that they bring social approval, status, and esteem.

An example of a condition that fails to erect barriers against unethical behavior is a company policy that does not punish employees who accept large gifts from clients. The absence of punishment essentially provides an opportunity for unethical behavior because it allows individuals to engage in such behavior without fear of consequences. The prospect of a reward for unethical behavior can also create an opportunity for questionable decisions. For example, a salesperson who is given public recognition and a large bonus for making a valuable sale that he or she obtained through unethical tactics will probably be motivated to use such tactics in the future, even if such behavior goes against the salesperson's personal value system. If 10 percent of employees report observing others at the workplace abusing drugs or alcohol, then the opportunity to engage in these activities exists if there is a failure to report and respond to this conduct.[22]

Opportunity relates to individuals' **immediate job context**—where they work, whom they work with, and the nature of the work. The immediate job context includes the motivational "carrots and sticks" that superiors use to influence employee behavior. Pay raises, bonuses, and public recognition act as carrots, or positive reinforcements, whereas demotions, firings, reprimands, and pay penalties act as sticks, the negative reinforcements. A survey by Vault.com indicates that 67 percent of employees take office supplies for personal use. As Figure 5–2 shows, many employees pilfer office-supply rooms for matters unrelated to the job. It is possible that the opportunity is provided, and in some cases, there are no concerns if employees take pens, Post-its, envelopes, notepads, and paper. Respondents to the Vault survey indicate that

---

| **FIGURE 5–2** | Items That Employees Pilfer in the Workplace |

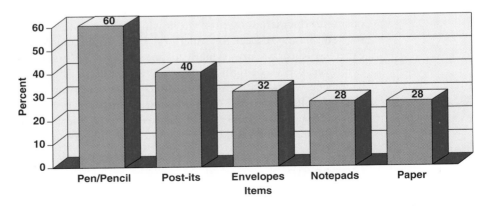

SOURCE: "Top Items Employees Pilfer." The most popular items that employees take from office-supply rooms for matters unrelated to the job. Vault's office survey of 1152 respondents. In Snapshots, *USA Today,* March 29, 2006, B1.

25 percent felt that no one cared if they took office supplies, 34 percent said that they never got caught, and 1 percent said that they were caught and got in trouble.[23] If there is no policy against this practice, one concern is that employees will not learn where to draw the line and will get into the habit of taking even more expensive items for personal use.

The opportunity that employees have for unethical behavior in an organization can be eliminated through formal codes, policies, and rules that are adequately enforced by management. For example, financial companies—such as banks, savings and loan associations, and securities companies—have developed elaborate sets of rules and procedures to avoid the opportunity for individual employees to manipulate or take advantage of their trusted position. In banks, one such rule requires most employees to take a vacation and stay out of the bank a certain number of days every year so that they cannot be physically present to cover up embezzlement or other diversion of funds. This rule prevents the opportunity for inappropriate conduct. Often opportunity can arise from someone whose job is to create opportunity for others. Barbara Toffler, an ethics consultant and professor, learned firsthand how difficult it can be to follow one's own moral compass when she worked as a consultant at Arthur Andersen creating ethics programs for Andersen clients (the firm itself had no internal ethics program). After charging a client $1 million for developing an ethics program that should have cost $500,000, the praise Toffler earned from Andersen "was the only day in four years that I felt truly valued by Arthur Andersen." Despite her expertise, she learned that "unethical or illegal behavior happens when decent people are put under the unbearable pressure to do their jobs and meet ambitious goals without the resources to get the job done right."[24]

Opportunity also comes from knowledge. Major misconduct observed among employees in the workplace include lying to employees, customers, vendors, or the public or withholding needed information from them.[25] A person who has an information base, expertise, or information about competition has the opportunity to exploit this knowledge. An individual can be a source of information because he or she is familiar with the organization. Individuals who have been employed by one organization for many years become "gatekeepers" of its culture and often have the opportunity to make decisions related to unwritten traditions and rules. They help socialize newer employees to abide by the rules and norms of the company's internal and external ways of doing business, as well as understanding when the opportunity exists to cross the line. They may function as mentors or supervise managers in training. Like drill sergeants in the army, these trainers mold the new recruits into what the company wants. This can contribute to either ethical or unethical conduct.

The opportunity for unethical behavior cannot be eliminated without aggressive enforcement of codes and rules. A national jewelry store–chain president explained to us how he dealt with a jewelry buyer in one of his stores who had taken a bribe from a supplier. There was an explicit company policy against taking incentive payments in order to deal with a specific supplier. When the president of the firm learned that one of his buyers had taken a bribe, he immediately traveled to that buyer's office and terminated his employment. He then traveled to the supplier (manufacturer) selling jewelry to his stores and terminated his relationship with the firm. The message was clear: Taking a bribe is unacceptable for the store's buyers, and salespeople from supplying companies could cost their firm significant sales by offering bribes. This type of policy enforcement illustrates how the opportunity to commit unethical acts can be eliminated.

Business Ethics Evaluations and Intentions

Ethical dilemmas involve problem-solving situations in which decision rules are often vague or in conflict. The results of an ethical decision are often uncertain; no one can always tell us whether we have made the right decision. There are no magic formulas, nor is there computer software that ethical dilemmas can be plugged into for a solution. Even if they mean well, most businesspeople will make ethical mistakes. Thus, there is no substitute for critical thinking and the ability to take responsibility for our own decisions.

An individual's intentions and the final decision regarding what action he or she will take are the last steps in the ethical decision-making process. When the individual's intentions and behavior are inconsistent with his or her ethical judgment, the person may feel guilty. For example, when an advertising account executive is asked by her client to create an advertisement that she perceives as misleading, she has two alternatives: to comply or to refuse. If she refuses, she stands to lose business from that client and possibly her job. Other factors—such as pressure from the client, the need to keep her job to pay her debts and living expenses, and the possibility of a raise if she develops the advertisement successfully—may influence her resolution of this ethical dilemma. Because of these other factors, she may decide to act unethically and develop the advertisement even though she believes it to be inaccurate. Because her actions are inconsistent with her ethical judgment, she will probably feel guilty about her decision.

Guilt or an uneasiness is the first sign that an unethical decision has occurred. The next step is changing one's behavior to reduce such feelings. This change can reflect a person's values shifting to fit the decision or the person changing his or her decision type the next time a similar situation occurs. Finally, one can eliminate some of the situational factors by quitting. For those who begin the value shift, the following are the usual justifications that will reduce and finally eliminate guilt:

1. I need the paycheck and can't afford to quit right now.
2. Those around me are doing it so why shouldn't I? They believe it's okay.
3. If I hadn't have done this, I may not be able to get a good reference from my boss or company when I leave.
4. This is not such a big deal, given the potential benefits.
5. Business is business with a different set of rules.
6. If not me, someone else would do it and get rewarded.

The road to success depends on how the businessperson defines *success*. The success concept drives intentions and behavior in business either implicitly or explicitly. Money, security, family, power, wealth, and personal or group gratification are all types of success measures that people use. The list described is not comprehensive, and in the next chapter, you will understand more about how success can be defined. Another concept that affects behavior is the probability of rewards and punishments. That too will be explained further in Chapter 6.

USING THE ETHICAL DECISION-MAKING FRAMEWORK TO IMPROVE ETHICAL DECISIONS

The ethical decision-making framework presented in this chapter cannot tell you if a business decision is ethical or unethical. It bears repeating that it is impossible to tell you what is right or wrong; instead, we are attempting to prepare you to make informed ethical decisions. Although this chapter does not moralize by telling you what to do in a specific situation, it does provide an overview of typical decision-making processes and factors that influence ethical decisions. The framework is not a guide for how to make decisions but is intended to provide you with insights and knowledge about typical ethical decision-making processes in business organizations.

Because it is impossible to agree on normative judgments about what is ethical, business ethics scholars developing descriptive models have instead focused on regularities in decision making and the various phenomena that interact in a dynamic environment to produce predictable behavioral patterns. Furthermore, it is unlikely that an organization's ethical problems will be solved strictly by having a thorough knowledge about how ethical decisions are made. By its very nature, business ethics involves value judgments and collective agreement about acceptable patterns of behavior.

We propose that gaining an understanding of typical ethical decision making in business organizations will reveal several ways that such decision making could be improved. With more knowledge about how the decision process works, you will be better prepared to analyze critical ethical dilemmas and to provide ethical leadership regardless of your role in the organization. One important conclusion that should be taken from our framework is that ethical decision making within an organization does not rely strictly on the personal values and morals of individuals. Organizations take on a culture of their own, which, when combined with corporate governance mechanisms, have a significant influence on business ethics.

THE ROLE OF LEADERSHIP IN A CORPORATE CULTURE

Top managers provide a blueprint for what a firm's corporate culture should be.[26] If these leaders fail to express desired behaviors and goals, a corporate culture will evolve on its own but will still reflect the goals and values of the company. **Leadership,** the ability or authority to guide and direct others toward achievement of a goal, has a significant impact on ethical decision making because leaders have the power to motivate others and enforce the organization's rules and policies as well as their own viewpoints. Leaders are key to influencing an organization's corporate culture and ethical posture. However, one poll found that less than half (47 percent) of employees in large (twenty-five hundred employees or more) organizations think that their senior leadership is highly ethical.[27]

Although we often think of CEOs and other top managers as the most important leaders in an organization, the corporate governance reforms discussed in Chapter 4 make it clear that a firm's board of directors is also an important leadership component.

TABLE 5–1	The Role of Leadership in Developing an Ethics Program

1. Conduct a rigorous self-assessment of the firm's values and its existing ethics and compliance program.
2. Maintain commitment from top managers.
3. Publish, post, and make codes of ethics available and understandable.
4. Communicate ethical standards through multiple channels (for example, paper documents and webpages).
5. Provide timely training to reinforce knowledge.
6. Provide confidential resources to whom employees can go for advice or to report their concerns.
7. Ensure consistent implementation.
8. Respond and enforce consistently, promptly, and fairly
9. Monitor and assess using appropriate methods.
10. Revise and reform to ensure continuous improvement.

SOURCE: Adapted from Jane E. Dubinsky, "Business Ethics: A Set of Practical Tools," *Internal Auditing,* July/August 2002.

Indeed, directors have a legal obligation to manage companies "for the best interests of the corporation." To determine what is in the best interest of the firm, directors can consider the effects that a decision may have on not only shareholders and employees but also other important stakeholders.[28] Therefore, when we discuss leadership, we include the corporate directors as well as top executives.

In the long run, if stakeholders are not reasonably satisfied with a company's leader, he or she will not retain a leadership position. A leader must have not only his or her followers' respect but also provide a standard of ethical conduct to them. Sunbeam, for example, fired CEO Al Dunlap after the Securities and Exchange Commission (SEC) initiated an investigation into whether the firm had fraudulently manipulated its financial reports (see Case 8). Dunlap, nicknamed "Chainsaw Al" for his track record of aggressive downsizing, wrote a book entitled *Mean Business,* which took a somewhat questionable approach to achieving organizational profitability.[29] He ultimately paid $500,000 to settle the SEC's charges that he had defrauded investors by inflating the small-appliance maker's sales. He also paid $15 million to shareholders who filed a class-action suit on similar charges.[30] Table 5–1 summarizes the steps executives should take to demonstrate that they understand the importance of ethics in doing business.

LEADERSHIP STYLES INFLUENCE ETHICAL DECISIONS

Leadership styles influence many aspects of organizational behavior, including employees' acceptance of and adherence to organizational norms and values. Styles that focus on building strong organizational values among employees contribute to shared standards of conduct. They also influence the organization's transmittal and monitoring of values, norms, and codes of ethics.[31] In short, the leadership style of an organization influences how its employees act. For example, the management philosophy of Mike Armstrong, former CEO of AT&T, is characterized by the observations of its labs chief, David Nagel: "Most bosses hate conflict. Mike is delighted when he sees us getting at each other." Armstrong has been characterized as scary, demanding, a taskmaster, and a maniac—in an affectionate way. The fast-paced, intensely competitive telecommunications industry requires a "nontraditional" leadership style to achieve success.[32] Studying a firm's leadership styles and attitudes can also help pinpoint where future ethical issues may arise. Even for actions that may be against the law, employees often look to their organizational leaders to determine how to resolve the issue.

Although we often think of CEOs and other top managers as the most important leaders in an organization, a firm's board of directors is also a required leadership and an oversight component. The ethical leadership concept is not only for CEOs, boards of directors, and managers but can also be fellow employees. Ethical leadership by the CEO requires an understanding of the firm's vision and values, as well as the challenges of responsibility and the risk in achieving organizational objectives. Lapses in ethical leadership do occur even in people who possess strong ethical character, especially if they view the organization's ethical culture as being outside the realm of decision making that exists in the home, family, and community. This phenomenon has been observed in countless cases of so-called good community citizens engaging in unethical business activities. For example, Robin Szeliga, former CFO of Qwest, who pleaded guilty for insider trading, was an excellent community leader, even serving on a college-of-business advisory board.

Ethical leaders need both knowledge and experience to make decisions. Strong ethical leaders must have the right kind of moral integrity. Such integrity must be transparent or, in other words, do in private as if it were always public. This type of integrity relates to values and is discussed in later chapters. They must be proactive and be ready to leave the organization if its corporate governance system makes it impossible to make the right choice. Such right choices are complex by definition. The ethical leader must choose a balance of all involved today as well as in the future. Such a person must be concerned with shareholders as well as the lowest-paid employee. Experience shows that no leader can always be right or judged ethical by stakeholders in every case. The acknowledgment of this may be perceived as a weakness, but in reality it supports integrity and increases the debate exchange of views on ethics and openness.

Six leadership styles that are based on emotional intelligence—the ability to manage ourselves and our relationships effectively—have been identified by Daniel Goleman.[33]

1. The coercive leader demands instantaneous obedience and focuses on achievement, initiative, and self-control. Although this style can be very effective during times of crisis or during a turnaround, it otherwise creates a negative climate for organizational performance.
2. The authoritative leader—considered to be one of the most effective styles—inspires employees to follow a vision, facilitates change, and creates a strongly positive performance climate.

3. The affiliative leader values people, their emotions, and their needs and relies on friendship and trust to promote flexibility, innovation, and risk taking.
4. The democratic leader relies on participation and teamwork to reach collaborative decisions. This style focuses on communication and creates a positive climate for achieving results.
5. The pacesetting leader can create a negative climate because of the high standards that he or she sets. This style works best for attaining quick results from highly motivated individuals who value achievement and take the initiative.
6. The coaching leader builds a positive climate by developing skills to foster long-term success, delegates responsibility, and is skillful in issuing challenging assignments.

The most successful leaders do not rely on one style but alter their techniques based on the characteristics of the situation. Different styles can be effective in developing an ethical culture depending on the leader's assessment of risks and desire to achieve a positive climate for organizational performance.

Another way to consider leadership styles is to classify them as transactional or transformational. **Transactional leaders** attempt to create employee satisfaction through negotiating, or "bartering," for desired behaviors or levels of performance. **Transformational leaders** strive to raise employees' level of commitment and to foster trust and motivation.[34] Both transformational and transactional leaders can positively influence the corporate culture.

Transformational leaders communicate a sense of mission, stimulate new ways of thinking, and enhance as well as generate new learning experiences. They consider employee needs and aspirations in conjunction with organizational needs. They also build commitment and respect for values that provide agreement on how to deal with ethical issues.

Thus, transformational leaders strive to promote activities and behavior through a shared vision and common learning experience. As a result, they have a stronger influence on coworker support for ethical decisions and building an ethical culture than do transactional leaders. Transformational ethical leadership is best suited for organizations that have higher levels of ethical commitment among employees and strong stakeholder support for an ethical culture. A number of industry trade associations—including the American Institute of Certified Public Accountants, Defense Industry Initiative on Business Ethics and Conduct, Ethics and Compliance Officer Association, and Mortgage Bankers Association of America—are helping companies provide transformational leadership.[35]

In contrast, transactional leaders focus on ensuring that required conduct and procedures are implemented. Their negotiations to achieve desired outcomes result in a dynamic relationship with subordinates in which reactions, conflict, and crisis influence the relationship more than ethical concerns. Transactional leaders produce employees who achieve a negotiated level of performance, including compliance with ethical and legal standards. As long as employees and leaders both find this exchange mutually rewarding, the relationship is likely to be successful. However, transactional leadership is best suited for rapidly changing situations, including those that require responses to ethical problems or issues. When Michael Capellas took over as CEO and chairman of WorldCom, he used transactional leadership to change the firm's culture and ethical conduct after an accounting scandal had forced the company into bankruptcy proceedings. Capellas sought to restore WorldCom's credibility in the marketplace by bringing in a new board of directors, creating a corporate ethics office, enhancing the code of ethics, and launching new employee financial-reporting and ethics-training initiatives.[36]

HABITS OF STRONG ETHICAL LEADERS

Archie Carroll, University of Georgia business professor, crafted "7 Habits of Highly Moral Leaders" based on the idea of Stephen Covey's *The 7 Habits of Highly Effective People*.[37] We have adapted Carroll's "7 Habits of Highly Moral Leaders"[38] to create our own "Seven Habits of Strong Ethical Leaders" (Table 5–2). In particular, we believe that ethical leadership is based on holistic thinking that embraces the complex and challenging issues that companies face on a daily basis. Ethical leaders need both knowledge and experience to make the right decision. Strong ethical leaders have both the courage and the most complete information to make decisions that will be the best in the long run. Strong ethical leaders must stick to their principles and, if necessary, be ready to leave the organization if its corporate governance system is so flawed that it is impossible to make the right choice.

Founders of many corporations—such as Sam Walton, Bill Gates, Milton Hershey, Martha Stewart, Michael Dell, and Steve Jobs, as well as Ben Cohen and Jerry Greenfield—left their ethical stamp on their companies. Their conduct set the tone, making them role models for desired conduct in the early growth of their respective corporations. In the case of Milton Hershey, his legacy endures, and Hershey Foods continues to be a role model for ethical corporate culture. In the case of Sam Walton, Wal-Mart embarked on a course of rapid growth after his death and became involved in numerous conflicts with various stakeholder groups, especially employees, regulators, competitors and communities. Despite the ethical foundation left by Sam Walton,

TABLE 5–2 Seven Habits of Strong Ethical Leaders
1. Ethical leaders have strong personal character.
2. Ethical leaders have a passion to do right.
3. Ethical leaders are proactive.
4. Ethical leaders consider stakeholders' interests.
5. Ethical leaders are role models for the organization's values.
6. Ethical leaders are transparent and actively involved in organizational decision making.
7. Ethical leaders are competent managers who take a holistic view of the firm's ethical culture.

Wal-Mart, as well as most large corporations, deals with hundreds of reported ethical lapses every month.[39] (See Case 1.)

Ethical Leaders Have Strong Personal Character

There is general agreement that ethical leadership is highly unlikely without a strong personal character. The question is how to teach or develop a moral person in a corporate environment. Thomas I. White, a leading authority on character development, believes the focus should be on "ethical reasoning" rather than on being a "moral person." According to White, the ability to resolve the complex ethical dilemmas encountered in a corporate culture requires intellectual skills.[40] For example, when Lawrence S. Benjamin took over as president of U.S. Food Service after a major ethical disaster, he initiated an ethics and compliance program to promote transparency and to teach employees how to make difficult ethical choices. A fundamental problem in traditional character development is that specific values and virtues are used to teach a belief or philosophy. This approach may be inappropriate for a business environment where cultural diversity and privacy must be respected. On the other hand, teaching individuals who want to do the right thing regarding corporate values and ethical codes, and equipping them with the intellectual skills to address the complexities of ethical issues, is the correct approach.

Ethical Leaders Have a Passion to Do Right

The passion to do right is "the glue that holds ethical concepts together." Some leaders develop this trait early in life, whereas others develop it over time through experience, reason, or spiritual growth. They often cite familiar arguments for doing right—to keep society from disintegrating, to alleviate human suffering, to advance human prosperity, to resolve conflicts of interest fairly and logically, to praise the good and punish the guilty, or just because something "is the right thing to do."[41] Having a passion to do right indicates a personal characteristic of not only recognizing the importance of ethical behavior but also the willingness to face challenges and make tough choices. Consider the crisis faced by Harry Kraemer, the CEO of Baxter International, after fifty-three dialysis patients died during treatment. "We have this situation. The financial people will assess the potential financial impact. The legal people will do the same. But at the end of the day, if we think it's a problem that a Baxter product was involved in the deaths of 53 people, then those other issues become pretty easy. If we don't do the right thing, then we won't be around to address those other issues."[42]

Ethical Leaders Are Proactive

Ethical leaders do not hang around waiting for ethical problems to arise. They anticipate, plan, and act proactively to avoid potential ethical crises.[43] One way to be proactive is to take a leadership role in developing effective programs that provide employees with guidance and support for making more ethical choices even in the face of considerable pressure to do otherwise. Ethical leaders who are proactive understand social needs and apply or even develop "the best practices" of ethical leadership that exist in their industry. PepsiCo has made diversity a high priority to make its work force better reflect its customer demographics and to channel those diverse perspectives into innovative marketing and products, like Mountain Dew Code Red. To enforce the importance of that goal, CEO Steve Reinemund made eight members of his senior-management team executive sponsors, each for a specific group of employees: African Americans, Latinos, women, women of color, white males, the disabled, gays and lesbians, and the transgendered. Reinemund expects each executive to understand his or her group members' unique needs, discover new talent, and personally mentor at least three people from within the group. Reinemund's directive exemplifies the proactive approach that PepsiCo has adopted toward diversity in recent years and illustrates why the company was recently named the best workplace for Latinos and African Americans.[44]

Ethical Leaders Consider Stakeholders' Interests

Ethical leaders consider the interests of and implications for all stakeholders, not just those that have an economic impact on the firm. This requires acknowledging and monitoring the concerns of all legitimate stakeholders, actively communicating and cooperating with them, employing processes that are respectful of them, recognizing interdependencies among them, avoiding activities that would harm their human rights, and recognizing the potential conflicts between leaders' "own role as corporate stakeholders and their legal and moral responsibilities for the interests of other stakeholders."[45]

Ethical leaders have the responsibility to balance stakeholder interests to ensure that the organization maximizes its role as a responsible corporate citizen. Wal-Mart, for example, opened a 206,000-square-foot "green" store in McKinney, Texas, that features a 120-foot-tall wind turbine to generate electricity, a rain water–harvesting pond that provides 95 percent of the water needed for irrigation, and many other environmentally friendly and energy-saving features. One such effort is reclaiming used motor oil from the auto center to help heat the building. Long criticized by environmentalists, consumer activists, and neighborhood groups, Wal-Mart says the new store is evidence that the retail giant is listening to stakeholders' desires for it to support sustainability, be more economical, and be more environmentally responsible. Although the store is a prototype, the store manager says many of its features may one day be standard in all new Wal-Mart stores.[46]

Ethical Leaders Are Role Models for the Organization's Values

If leaders do not actively serve as role models for the organization's core values, then those values become nothing more than lip service. According to behavioral scientist Brent Smith, as role models, leaders are the primary influence on individual ethical behavior. Leaders whose decisions and actions are contrary to the firm's values send a signal that the firm's values are trivial or irrelevant.[47] Firms such as Enron and WorldCom articulated core values that were only used as window dressing. On the other hand, when leaders model the firm's core values at every turn, the results can be powerful.

Consider New Belgium Brewing Company, the third-largest craft brewer in the United States. Early in the firm's history, founders Jeff Lebesch and Kim Jordan wrestled with defining New Belgium's core purpose above and beyond profitability (see Case 18). The values they developed (see Table 5–3) have changed little over the years despite mostly double-digit growth. Indeed, those values dictated a more controlled pace of growth to ensure quality, even when so-called experts believed the firm could have grown much faster. Those values were also behind the company's state-of-the-art, wind-powered brew house with numerous award-winning environmentally friendly and waste-minimizing features. They are also behind the firm's generous donations to many charitable causes and event sponsorships. New Belgium also gives employees a piece of the company (and a fat-tire bicycle) after one year's tenure. The owners believe that employee ownership and open-book management policy translate into a community of trust and mutual responsibility. This proactive approach and devotion to core values have helped New Belgium gain a cultlike customer base, devoted employee-owners, and numerous awards for environmental stewardship, ethics, entrepreneurship and beer making.[48]

Ethical Leaders Are Transparent and Actively Involved in Organizational Decision Making

Being transparent fosters openness, freedom to express ideas, and the ability to question conduct, and it encourages stakeholders to learn about and comment on what a firm is doing. Transparent leaders will not be effective unless they are per-

TABLE 5–3	New Belgium Brewing Company's Core Values

- Producing world-class beers
- Promoting beer culture and the responsible enjoyment of beer
- Seeking continuous, innovative quality and efficiency improvements
- Transcending customers' expectations
- Practicing environmental stewardship: minimizing resource consumption, maximizing energy efficiency, and recycling
- Kindling social, environmental, and cultural change as a business role model
- Cultivating potential through learning, participative management, and the pursuit of opportunities
- Balancing the myriad needs of the company, staff and their families
- Committing ourselves to authentic relationships, communications and promises
- Having fun

sonally involved in the key decisions that have ethical ramifications. Transformational leaders are collaborative, which opens the door for transparency through interpersonal exchange. Earlier we said that transformational leaders instill commitment and respect for values that provide guidance on how to deal with ethical issues. Herb Baum, former CEO of the Dial Corporation, says, "In today's business environment, if you're a leader—or want to be—and you aren't contributing to a values based business culture that encourages your entire organization to operate with integrity, your company is as vulnerable as a baby chick in a pit of rattlesnakes." Baum's three remarkably simple principles of transparency are (1) tell the whole truth, (2) build a values-based culture, and (3) hire "people people."[49]

Ethical Leaders Are Competent Managers Who Take a Holistic View of the Firm's Ethical Culture

Ethical leaders can see a holistic view of their organization and therefore view ethics as a strategic component of decision making, much like marketing, information systems, production, and so on. When Charles O. Prince took over as chairman of Citigroup, Inc., he sought to not only placate regulators and other stakeholders but also reshape the troubled company from the inside out. He viewed Citigroup not just as a profit-seeking business but also as a "quasi-public institution." Prince instituted numerous internal controls, slashed costs, and slowed the huge company's pace of expansion, and he spent a major portion of his time addressing issues related to the company's culture and values. Although his inward focus and management style resulted in the exodus of a number of executives and the first earnings drop in years, Prince says, "You can never sacrifice your long-term growth, your long-term reputation, to the short term."[50] The challenges of being an effective leader is illustrated in Table 5–4 that most senior executives believe that it is much more challenging to be a leader in today's business environment compared to five years ago. Leadership continues to be one of the most important drivers of ethical conduct in organizations.

TABLE 5–4	Leadership Is More Challenging in Today's Business Environment

Do you think it is more or less challenging to be a company leader in today's business environment compared with five years ago?

• More challenging	89%
• No change	9%
• Less challenging	1%
• Don't know	1%

SOURCE: Robert Half Management Resources poll of 150 senior executives at companies with revenue of $1 billion to $40 billion. In *USA Today,* March 6, 2006, B1.

SUMMARY

The key components of the ethical decision-making framework include ethical-issue intensity, individual factors, organizational factors, and opportunity. These factors are interrelated and influence business ethics evaluations and intentions, which result in ethical or unethical behavior.

The first step in ethical decision making is to recognize that an ethical issue requires that an individual or work group choose among several actions that will ultimately be evaluated as ethical or unethical by various stakeholders. Ethical-issue intensity is the perceived relevance or importance of an ethical issue to the individual or work group. It reflects the ethical sensitivity of the individual or work group that triggers the ethical decision process. Other factors in our ethical decision-making framework influence this sensitivity, thus determining why different individuals often perceive ethical issues differently.

Individual factors such as gender, education, nationality, age, and locus of control can affect the ethical decision-making process, with some factors being more important than others. Organizational factors such as an organization's values often have greater influence on an individual's decisions than that person's own values. In addition, decisions in business are most often made jointly, in work groups and committees, or in conversations and discussions with coworkers. Corporate cultures and structures operate through the individual relationships of the organization's members to influence those members' ethical decisions. A corporate culture can be defined as a set of values, beliefs, goals, norms, and ways of solving problems that members (employees) of an organization share. Corporate culture involves norms that prescribe a wide range of behavior for the organization's members. The ethical culture of an organization indicates whether it has an ethical conscience. Significant others—including peers, managers, coworkers, and subordinates—who influence the work group have more daily impact on an employee's decisions than any other factor in the decision-making framework. Obedience to authority may explain why many business ethics issues are resolved simply by following the directives of a superior.

Ethical opportunity results from conditions that either provide rewards, whether internal or external, or limit barriers to ethical or unethical behavior. Included in opportunity is a person's immediate job context, which includes the motivational techniques superiors use to influence employee behavior. The opportunity employees have for unethical behavior in an organization can be eliminated through formal codes, policies, and rules that are adequately enforced by management.

The ethical decision-making framework is not a guide for making decisions. It is intended to provide insights and knowledge about typical ethical decision-making processes in business organizations. Ethical decision making within organizations does not rely strictly on the personal values and morals of employees. Organizations have a culture of their own, which when combined with corporate governance mechanisms, may significantly influence business ethics.

Leadership styles and habits promote an organizational ethical climate. Leadership styles include coercive, authoritative, affiliative, democratic, and coaching elements. Transactional leaders negotiate or barter with employees. Transformational leaders strive for a shared vision and common learning experience. Strong ethical leaders have a strong personal character, have a passion to do the right thing, are proactive, focus on stakeholders' interests, are role models for the organization's values, make transparent decisions, and take a holistic view of the firm's ethical culture.

IMPORTANT TERMS FOR REVIEW		
ethical-issue intensity		ethical culture
moral intensity		significant other
education		obedience to authority
nationality		opportunity
locus of control		immediate job context
external control		leadership
internal control		transactional leader
corporate culture		transformational leader

A REAL-LIFE SITUATION*

Peter had been a human resource (HR) manager for eighteen years and vice president for two more years for Zyedego Corporation, a small company in New Orleans. In the last decade, there have been many changes to what can be asked to a potential/actual employee and what constitutes fair and equitable treatment. Frankly, the situation Peter was in was partly his own fault.

The first issue began with a hurricane. After Hurricane Katrina, Zyedego employees had been working around the clock to get the company up and running. The company had been calling all former employees (if they could locate them) to rehire them. Gwyn, one of Peter's HR managers, was planning on rehiring Dana Gonzales but found out that Dana was pregnant. Because of the "rough" condition of the workplace, Gwyn was concerned for Dana's safety. Gwyn feels that if Dana is rehired, her hourly wages should be decreased by 25 percent because, as she said, "the entire group had exceeded their budget." Gwyn had asked some difficult questions, and Dana stated that if not rehired she would go to a competitor and expected the company to pay severance of two weeks' wages. In addition, Gwyn is concerned that Dana may not really be a U.S. citizen because some of her documents appear to be ques-

tionable and possibly fake. The flooding destroyed the original documents, and although Gwyn has requested new documents, Dana has been slow in providing them.

Another issue is the hiring of truck drivers. Zyedego hires many truck drivers and routinely requests driving records as part of the preemployment process. Several of the potential new hires have past DWI records, but in all cases, it was over five years ago. All have stated that they would never do it again, have maintained a clean record for at least five years, and understand the consequences of another infraction. Gwyn has been hiring some drivers with infractions, including DWI, to secure the number of drivers needed for the company. Gwyn is beginning to wonder if she is creating a potential risk for the company if any of these drivers are involved in an accident that relates to a repeat violation. From Peter, Gwyn needs guidance related to continuing these hiring practices.

If it were only these issues, Peter would not be so concerned, but he is. The problem really started when Peter was still an HR manager, and it revolves around one "family." Guy Martin started working for Zyedego twenty years ago. He was married, with two children, and had a mortgage. The family has had its ups and downs. On several occasions, Guy separated from his wife, and last year they divorced.

But six months later, they remarried one another. When Guy was hired, Peter had made sure that Guy's son who had asthma would be covered instead of being listed as a preexisting condition. Peter also helped out the family several times when money was tight and provided Guy with overtime work.

"I know how it is, Guy, to have kids and a stay-at-home wife. It can be really hard to make ends meet, but in the long run, your children have a better chance of turning out ok."

"I know what you mean, Pete. If Martha had been working, I'm afraid the boys would have gotten into real trouble. But she was always there, making sure that homework was done, meals prepared, and just all the things a mother has to do to keep a house going."

"You know, Guy," said Peter, "we in HR calculated that a mother at home is equal to about $80,000 to $100,000 a year."

"Wow!" said Guy. "I'm glad Martha hasn't heard she's worth that much. She'll want a pay increase."

Pete said, "Don't worry about overtime. When you need it, it will always be there for you."

But tragedy struck the Martins when Guy was killed in the hurricane. He had gone to the Zyedego warehouses to help evacuate machinery and products when a gust of wind tore off the roof and the levee broke with massive flooding. Police and rescue workers hunted for his body, but it was never found. It was a strong possibility that he could have been taken away by the floodwaters that were infested with alligators and venomous snakes. Because Martha, Guy's wife, was a stay-at-home mother, their only income had been from Zyedego. Death benefits from his retirement program only provide 50 percent benefits for a surviving spouse. Also, because the body had not been found, there was the legal question of death. Usually, it takes seven years before one can claim any type of insurance or death-benefit payments, as well as medical insurance, for the family. Even with Social Security benefits, Martha would probably lose the house and could be forced to seek employment.

Zyedego has been sustaining substantial losses since the hurricane. Insurance companies were extremely slow concerning payments to all the small businesses, arguing about wind versus water damage. Impeding the process of obtaining benefits was the lack of many documents destroyed in the storm.

The storm really began for Peter late last week when he met with the insurance company about medical reimbursements, death benefits, and the pension plans. Darrell Lambert was the chief adjuster for Zyedego's insurance and pension provider.

"Here's another case that we will not cover," said Darrell as he flipped the file to Peter. "We can't help the Martins for a variety of reasons. First, there's no body. No body, no payment until after a judge declares him legally dead. That will take at least a year. While that is being settled, Mrs. Martin and her family will not be eligible for medical coverage unless Zyedego is going to pay their amount. Finally, and I know this may sound heartless, but Mrs. Martin will only get a maximum of half of Mr. Martin's pension."

"But he was killed on the job!" exclaimed Peter.

"Did you require him to work that day? Did he punch in or out? Is there any record that he was called in from Zyedego to help? The answer is no to all of the above. He helped because he felt obligated to Zyedego. But I am not Zyedego, and I do not have any obligation to the Martins," Darrell said with a smile.

"Peter," exclaimed Darrell, "I know that Zyedego is under intense financial pressure, but we are too. You have approximately one hundred families that we will have to pay something to. You and I can spend the next twelve months going over every case, bit by bit, item by item, but if that's what you want, Zyedego will go into bankruptcy. We don't want that to happen. But we also are not going to pay for everything that you claim you are due. Our lawyers will stall the system until you go broke, and your one hundred families will get nothing. Well, maybe something in five to seven years. What I am proposing is a way for you to stay in business and for my company to reduce its financial payouts. Remember, we have hundreds of small businesses like you to deal with."

Darrell then calmly said, "My proposal is that you look over these files and reduce your total reimbursements to us by 40 percent. To help you out, I'll start with this case [Martin's]. You decide whether we pay out 40 percent or nothing. Tomorrow at 9:00 A.M., I want you to have twenty-five cases, including this one, pared down by forty percent. If not, well, I'm sure my superiors have informed your superiors about this arrangement by now. You should be getting a call within the hour. So, I'll see you here at 9:00," and Darrell walked out the door.

Several hours later, Peter received a phone call from upper management about the deal he was to implement to save the company.

QUESTIONS • EXERCISES

1. What are the legal and ethical risks associated with the decision about hiring truck drivers at Zyedego?
2. What should Peter recommend to Gwyn about Dana's case?
3. Do you think Peter is too emotionally attached to the Martin case to make an objective decision?

*This case is strictly hypothetical; any resemblance to real persons, companies, or situations is coincidental.

Check Your EQ

Check your EQ, or Ethics Quotient, by completing the following. Assess your performance to evaluate your overall understanding of the chapter material.

1.	The first step in ethical decision making is to understand the individual factors that influence the process.	**Yes**	**No**
2.	Opportunity describes the conditions within an organization that limit or permit ethical or unethical behavior.	**Yes**	**No**
3.	Transactional leaders negotiate compliance and ethics.	**Yes**	**No**
4.	The most significant influence on ethical behavior in the organization is the opportunity to engage in (un)ethical behavior.	**Yes**	**No**
5.	Obedience to authority relates to the influence of corporate culture.	**Yes**	**No**

ANSWERS 1. No. The first step is to become more aware that an ethical issue exists and to consider its relevance to the individual or work group. 2. Yes. Opportunity results from conditions that provide rewards or fail to erect barriers against unethical behavior. 3. Yes. Transactional leaders barter or negotiate with employees. 4. No. Significant others have more impact on ethical decisions within an organization. 5. No. Obedience to authority relates to the influence of significant others and supervisors.

CHAPTER 6

Individual Factors: Moral Philosophies and Values

CHAPTER OBJECTIVES

- To understand how moral philosophies and values influence individual and group ethical decision making in business

- To compare and contrast the teleological, deontological, virtue, and justice perspectives of moral philosophy

- To discuss the impact of philosophies on business ethics

- To recognize the stages of cognitive moral development and its shortcomings

- To introduce white-collar crime as it relates to moral philosophies, values, and corporate culture

CHAPTER OUTLINE

Moral Philosophy Defined

Moral Philosophies

    Goodness—Instrumental and Intrinsic

    Teleology

    Deontology

    Relativist Perspective

    Virtue Ethics

    Justice

Applying Moral Philosophy to Ethical Decision Making

Cognitive Moral Development

White-Collar Crime

The Role of Individual Factors in Business Ethics

One of the problems that Lael Matthews has had to deal with in trying to climb the corporate ladder is the "glass ceiling" faced by minorities and women. In her current position, she must decide which of three managers to promote, a decision that, as her superior has informed her, could have serious repercussions for her future. These people are the candidates.

Liz is a 34-year-old African American, divorced with one child, who graduated in the lower half of her college class at Northwest State. She has been with the company for four years and in the industry for eight years, with mediocre performance ratings but a high-energy level. She has had, however, some difficulties in managing her staff. In addition, her child has had various medical problems, and so higher pay would be helpful. If promoted, Liz would be the first African American female manager at this level. Although Lael has known Liz only a short time, they seem to have hit it off; in fact, Lael once baby-sat Liz's daughter, Janeen, in an emergency. The downside to promoting Liz, though, might be a perception that Lael is playing favorites.

Roy is a white 57-year-old, married with three children, who graduated from a private university in the top half of his class. Roy has been with the company for twenty years and in the industry for thirty, and he has always been a steady performer, with mostly average ratings. The reason why Roy had been passed over before was his refusal to relocate, but that is no longer a problem. Roy's energy level is average to low; however, he has produced many of the company's top sales performers in the past. This promotion would be his last before retirement, and many in the company feel that he has earned it. In fact, one senior manager stopped Lael in the hall and said, "You know, Lael, Roy has been with us for a long time. He has done many good things for the company, sacrificing not only himself but also his family. I really hope that you can see your way to promoting him. It would be a favor to me that I wouldn't forget."

Quang Yeh, a single, 27-year-old Asian American, graduated from State University in the top 3 percent of her class and has been with the company for three years. She is known for putting in sixty-hour weeks and for her meticulous management style, which has generated some criticism from her sales staff. The last area that she managed showed record increases, despite the loss of some older accounts that for some reason did not like dealing with Quang. Moreover, Quang sued her previous employer for discrimination and won. A comment that Lael had heard from that company was that Quang was intense and that nothing would stop her from reaching her goals. As Lael was going over some of her notes, another upper-management individual came to her office and said, "You know, Lael, Quang is engaged to my son. I've looked over her personnel files, and she looks very good. She looks like a rising star, which would indicate that she should be promoted as quickly as possible. I realize that you're not in my division, but the way people get transferred, you never know. I would really like to see Quang get this promotion."

As she was considering the choices, Lael's immediate supervisor came to her to talk about Liz. "You know, Lael, Liz is one of a very few people in the company who is both an African American woman and qualified for this position. I've been going over the company's hiring and promotion figures, and it would be very advantageous for me personally and for the company to promote her. I've also spoken to public relations, and they believe that this would be a tremendous boost for the company."

As Lael pondered her decision, she mentally went through each candidate's records and found that each had advantages and disadvantages. While she was considering her problem, the phone rang. It was Liz, sounding frantic. "Lael, I'm sorry to disturb you at this late hour, but I need you to come to the hospital. Janeen has been in an accident, and I don't know who to turn to." When Lael got to the hospital, she found that Janeen's injuries were fairly serious and that Liz would have to miss some work to help with the recuperation process. Lael also realized that this accident would create a financial problem for Liz, which a promotion could help solve.

The next day seemed very long and was punctuated by the announcement that Roy's son was getting married to the vice president's daughter. The wedding would be in June, and it sounded as though it would be a company affair. By 4:30 that afternoon, Lael had gone through four aspirins and two antacids. Her decision was due in two days. What should she do?

QUESTIONS • EXERCISES

1. Discuss the advantages and disadvantages of each candidate.

2. What are the ethical and legal considerations for Lael?
3. Identify the pressures that have made her promotion decision an ethical and legal issue.
4. Discuss the implications of each decision that Lael could make.

*This case is strictly hypothetical; any resemblance to real persons, companies, or situations is coincidental.

Most discussions of business ethics address the role of the individual in ethical decision making. The ethical decision-making model that was described in Chapter 5 placed the individual moral perspectives as a central component in making an ethical decision. In this chapter, we provide a detailed description and analysis of how individuals' background and philosophies influence their decisions. It is important to determine when one action is right and when another is viewed as wrong, and individual moral philosophies are often used to justify decisions or explain actions. To understand how people make ethical decisions, it is useful to have a grasp of the major types of moral philosophies. In this chapter, a discussion of the stages of cognitive development as it relates to these moral philosophies and its shortcomings is addressed. Finally, we examine white-collar crime as it relates to moral philosophies and values.

MORAL PHILOSOPHY DEFINED

When people talk about philosophy, they usually mean the general system of values by which they live. **Moral philosophy,** on the other hand, refers in particular to the specific principles or rules that people use to decide what is right or wrong. For example, a production manager may be guided by a general philosophy of management that emphasizes encouraging workers to know as much as possible about the product that they are manufacturing. However, his moral philosophy comes into play when he must make decisions such as whether to notify employees in advance of upcoming layoffs. Although workers would prefer advance warning, giving it might adversely affect the quality and quantity of production. Such decisions require a person to evaluate the "rightness," or morality, of choices in terms of his or her own principles and values.

Moral philosophies present guidelines for "determining how conflicts in human interests are to be settled and for optimizing mutual benefit of people living together in groups," guiding businesspeople as they formulate business strategies and resolve specific ethical issues.[1] However, there is no single moral philosophy that everyone accepts. Some managers, for example, view profit as the ultimate goal of an enterprise and therefore may not be concerned about the impact of their firms' decisions on society. As we have seen, the economist Milton Friedman supports this viewpoint, contending that the market will reward or punish companies for unethical conduct without the need for government regulation.[2] The emergence of this Friedman-type capitalism as the dominant and most widely accepted economic system has created market-driven societies around the world. However, economic systems not only allocate resources and products within a society but also affect individuals and society as a whole. Thus, the success of an economic system depends both on its philosophical framework and on the individuals within the system who maintain moral philosophies that bring people together in a cooperative, efficient, and productive marketplace. Going back to Aristotle, there is a long Western tradition of questioning whether a market economy and individual moral behavior are compatible. In reality, individuals in today's society exist within the framework of social, political, and economic institutions.

People who face ethical issues often base their decisions on their own values and principles of right or wrong, most of which are learned through the socialization process with the help of family members, social groups, church, and formal education. Individual factors that influence decision making include personal moral philosophies. Ethical dilemmas arise in problem-solving situations in which the rules governing decision making are often vague or in conflict. In real-life situations, there is no substitute for an individual's own critical thinking and ability to accept responsibility for his or her decision.

Moral philosophies are ideal moral perspectives that provide individuals with abstract principles for guiding their social existence. For example, individuals' decisions to recycle waste or to purchase or sell recycled or recyclable products are influenced by moral philosophies and attitudes toward recycling.[3] Thus, it is often difficult to implement an individual moral philosophy within the complex environment of a business organization. On the other hand, the functioning of our economic system depends on individuals coming together and sharing philosophies that create the moral values, trust, and expectations that allow the system to work. Most employees within a business organization do not think about what particular moral philosophy they are using when they are confronted with an ethical issue. Individuals learn decision-making approaches or philosophies through their cultural and social development.

Many theories associated with moral philosophies refer to a value orientation and such things as economics, idealism, and relativism. The concept of the **economic value orientation** is associated with values that can be quantified by monetary means; thus, according to this theory, if an act produces more value than its effort, then it should be accepted as ethical. **Idealism,** on the other hand, is a moral philosophy that places special value on ideas and ideals as products of the mind, in comparison with the world's view. The term refers to efforts to account for all objects in nature and experience and assign to such representations a higher order of existence. Studies have found that there is a positive correlation between idealistic thinking and ethical decision making. **Realism** is the view that an external world exists independent of our perception of it. Realists work under the assumption that humankind is not inherently benevolent and kind but instead is inherently self-centered and competitive. According to realists, each person is always ultimately guided by his or her own self-interest. Research shows a negative correlation between realistic thinking and ethical decision making. Thus, the belief that all actions are ultimately self-motivated leads to a tendency toward negative ethical decision making.

MORAL PHILOSOPHIES

There are many moral philosophies, but because a detailed study of all moral philosophies is beyond the scope of this book, we limit our discussion to those that are most applicable to the study of business ethics. Our approach focuses on the most basic concepts needed to help you understand the ethical decision-making process in business. We do not prescribe the use of any particular moral philosophy, for there is no one "correct" way to resolve ethical issues in business.

To help you understand how the moral philosophies discussed in this chapter may be applied in decision making, we use a hypothetical situation as an illustration. Suppose that Sam Colt, a sales representative, is preparing a sales presentation for his firm Midwest Hardware, which manufactures nuts and bolts. Sam hopes to obtain a large sale from a construction firm that is building a bridge across the Mississippi River near St. Louis. The bolts manufactured by Midwest Hardware have a 3 percent defect rate, which, although acceptable in the industry, makes them unsuitable for use in certain types of projects, such as those that may be subject to sudden, severe stress. The new bridge will be located near the New Madrid Fault line, the source of the United States' greatest earthquake in 1811. The epicenter of that earthquake, which caused extensive damage and altered the flow of the Mississippi, is less than two hundred miles from the new bridge site. Earthquake experts believe there is a 50 percent chance that an earthquake with a magnitude greater than 7 on the Richter scale will occur somewhere along the New Madrid Fault by the year 2015. Bridge construction in the area is not regulated by earthquake codes, however. If Sam wins the sale, he will earn a commission of $25,000 on top of his regular salary. But if he tells the contractor about the defect rate, Midwest may lose the sale to a competitor that markets bolts with a lower defect rate. Thus, Sam's ethical issue is whether to point out to the bridge contractor that, in the event of an earthquake, some Midwest bolts could fail, possibly resulting in the collapse of the bridge.

We will come back to this illustration as we discuss particular moral philosophies, asking how Sam Colt might use each philosophy to resolve his ethical issue. We don't judge the quality of Sam's decision, nor do we advocate any one moral philosophy; in fact, this illustration and Sam's decision rationales are necessarily simplistic as well as hypothetical. In reality, the decision maker would probably have many more factors to consider in making his or her choice and thus might reach a different decision. With that note of caution, we introduce the concept of goodness and several types of moral philosophy: teleology, deontology, the relativist perspective, virtue ethics, and justice theories (Table 6–1).

Goodness—Instrumental and Intrinsic

To appreciate moral philosophy, one must understand the differing perspectives of goodness. Are there clearly defined goods and bads, and if so, what is the relationship between the ends and the means of bringing them about? Is there some intrinsic way of determining if the ends can be identified independently as good or bad? Aristotle, for example, argued that happiness is an intrinsically good end—in other words, its goodness is natural and universal, without relativity. On the other hand, the philoso-

TABLE 6-1	A Comparison of the Philosophies Used in Business Decisions
Teleology	Stipulates that acts are morally right or acceptable if they produce some desired result, such as realization of self-interest or utility.
Egoism	Defines right or acceptable actions as those that maximize a particular person's self-interest as defined by the individual.
Utilitarianism	Defines right or acceptable actions as those that maximize total utility, or the greatest good for the greatest number of people.
Deontology	Focuses on the preservation of individual rights and on the intentions associated with a particular behavior rather than on its consequences.
Relativist	Evaluates ethicalness subjectively on the basis of individual and group experiences.
Virtue ethics	Assumes that what is moral in a given situation is not only what conventional morality requires but also what the mature person with a "good" moral character would deem appropriate.
Justice	Evaluates ethicalness on the basis of fairness: distributive, procedural, and interactional.

pher Immanuel Kant emphasized means and motivations to argue that goodwill, seriously applied toward accomplishment, is the only thing good in itself.

Two basic concepts of goodness are monism and pluralism. **Monists** believe that only one thing is intrinsically good, and the pluralists believe that two or more things are intrinsically good. Monists are often exemplified by **hedonism**—that one's pleasure is the ultimate intrinsic good or that the moral end, or goodness, is the greatest balance of pleasure over pain. Hedonism defines right or acceptable behavior as that which maximizes personal pleasure. Moral philosophers describe those who believe that more pleasure is better as **quantitative hedonists** and those who believe that it is possible to get too much of a good thing (such as pleasure) as **qualitative hedonists.**

Pluralists, often referred to as nonhedonists, take the opposite position that no *one* thing is intrinsically good. For example, a pluralist might view other ultimate goods as beauty, aesthetic experience, knowledge, and personal affection. Plato argued that the good life is a mixture of (1) moderation and fitness, (2) proportion and beauty, (3) intelligence and wisdom, (4) sciences and arts, and (5) pure pleasures of the soul.

Although all pluralists are nonhedonists, it is important to note that all monists are not necessarily hedonists. An individual can believe in a single intrinsic good other than pleasure; Machiavelli and Nietzsche, for example, each held power to be the sole good, and Kant's belief in the single virtue of goodwill classifies him as a monistic nonhedonist.

A more modern view is expressed in the instrumentalist position. Sometimes called pragmatists, **instrumentalists** reject the idea that (1) ends can be separated from the means that produce them and (2) ends, purposes, or outcomes are intrinsically good in and of themselves. The philosopher John Dewey argued that the ends–means perspective is a relative distinction, that the difference between ends and means is no difference at all but merely a matter of the individual's perspective; thus, almost any action can be an end or a means. Dewey gives the example that people eat in order to be able to work, and they work in order to eat. From a practical standpoint, an end is only a remote means, and a means is but a series of acts viewed from an earlier stage. From this it follows that there is no such thing as a single, universal end.

So how does this discussion equate to business? Isn't business about shareholder wealth and the wealth of executives? To measure success in business is to measure monetary wealth . . . right? To answer this question, let's go back to 1923 when a meeting was held at the Edgewater Beach Hotel in Chicago. Attending this meeting were nine of the richest men in the world: (1) Charles Schwab, president of the world's largest independent steel company; (2) Samuel Insull, president of the world's largest utility company; (3) Howard Hopson, president of the world's largest gas firm; (4) Arthur Cutten, the greatest wheat speculator; (5) Richard Whitney, president of the New York Stock Exchange; (6) Albert Fall, member of the president's cabinet; (7) Leon Frazier, president of the Bank of International Settlements; (8) Jessie Livermore, the greatest speculator in the stock market; and (9) Ivar Kreuger, head of the company with the most widely distributed securities in the world. Twenty-five years later, (1) Charles Schwab had died having lived on borrowed money for the last five years of his life, (2) Samuel Insull had died a penniless fugitive, (3) Howard Hopson had gone insane, (4) Arthur Cutten had died bankrupt, (5) Richard Whitney had spent time in prison, (6) Albert Fall had been pardoned from prison so that he could die at home, and (7) Leon Fraizer, (8) Jessie Livermore, and (9) Ivar Kreuger had committed suicide. Measured by wealth and power, these men had achieved success, at least temporarily. So this begs the question of whether money guarantees happiness; in other words, do the ends always justify the means?

A discussion of moral value often revolves around the nature of goodness—instrumental or intrinsic. Theories of moral obligation, by contrast, change the question to "What makes a given action right or obligatory?" **Goodness theories** typically focus on the *end result* of actions and the goodness or happiness created by them, whereas **obligation theories** emphasize the *means* and *motives* by which actions are justified. These obligation theories are teleology and deontology, respectively.

Teleology

Teleology (from the Greek word for "end" or "purpose") refers to moral philosophies in which an act is considered morally right or acceptable if it produces some desired result such as pleasure, knowledge, career growth, the realization of self-interest, utility, wealth, or even fame. In other words, teleological philosophies assess the moral worth of a behavior by looking at its consequences, and thus moral philosophers today often refer to these theories as **consequentialist.** Two important teleological philosophies that often guide decision making in individual business decisions are egoism and utilitarianism.

Egoism defines right or acceptable behavior in terms of its consequences for the individual. Egoists believe that they should make decisions that maximize their own self-interest, which is defined differently by each individual. Depending on the egoist, self-interest may be construed as physical well-being, power, pleasure, fame, a satisfying career, a good family life, wealth, or something else. In an ethical decision-making situation, an egoist will probably choose the alternative that contributes most to his or her self-interest. The egoist's creed can be generally stated as "Do the act that promotes the greatest good for oneself." Many believe that egoistic people and companies are inherently unethical, are short-term oriented, and will take advantage of any opportunity. For example, some telemarketers demonstrate this negative tendency when they prey on elderly consumers who may be vulnerable because of loneliness or fear of losing their financial independence. Thousands of senior citizens fall victim to fraudulent telemarketers every year, in many cases losing all of their savings and sometimes their homes.

However, there is also **enlightened egoism.** Enlightened egoists take a long-range perspective and allow for the well-being of others although their own self-interest remains paramount. Enlightened egoists may, for example, abide by professional codes of ethics, control pollution, avoid cheating on taxes, help create jobs, and support community projects. Yet they do so not because these actions benefit others but because they help achieve some ultimate goal for the egoist, such as advancement within the firm. An enlightened egoist might call management's attention to a coworker who is making false accounting reports but only to safeguard the company's reputation and thus the egoist's own job security. In addition, some enlightened egoists may become whistle-blowers and report misconduct to a government regulatory agency to keep their job and receive a reward for exposing misconduct. When businesses donate money, resources, or time to specific causes and institutions, their motives may not be purely altruistic either. For example, International Business Machines (IBM) has a policy of donating or reducing the cost of computers to educational institutions; in exchange, the company receives tax breaks for donations of equipment, which reduces the cost of its philanthropy. In addition, IBM hopes to build future sales by placing its products on campuses. When students enter the work force, they may request the IBM products with which they have become familiar. Although the company's actions benefit society in general, in the long run they also benefit IBM.

Let's return to the hypothetical case of Sam Colt, who must decide whether to warn the bridge contractor that 3 percent of Midwest Hardware's bolts are likely to be defective. If he is an egoist, he will probably choose the alternative that maximizes his own self-interest. If he defines self-interest in terms of personal wealth, his personal moral philosophy may lead him to value a $25,000 commission more than a chance to reduce the risk of a bridge collapse. As a result, an egoist might well resolve this ethical dilemma by keeping quiet about the bolts' defect rate, hoping to win the sale and the $25,000 commission, rationalizing that there is a slim chance of an earthquake, that bolts would not be a factor in a major earthquake, and that, even if they were, no one would be able to prove that defective bolts caused the bridge to collapse.

Like egoism, **utilitarianism** is concerned with consequences, but the utilitarian seeks the greatest good for the greatest number of people. Utilitarians believe that they should make decisions that result in the greatest total *utility,* that achieve the greatest benefit for all those affected by a decision.

Utilitarian decision making relies on a systematic comparison of the costs and benefits to all affected parties. Using such a cost–benefit analysis, a utilitarian decision maker calculates the utility of the consequences of all possible alternatives and then selects the one that results in the greatest benefit. For example, the U.S. Supreme Court has ruled that supervisors are responsible for the sexual misconduct of employees, even if the employers knew nothing about the behavior, establishing a strict standard for harassment on the job. One of the justices indicated in the ruling that the employer's burden to prevent harassment is "one of the costs of doing business."[4] Apparently, the Court has decided that the greatest utility to society will result from forcing businesses to prevent harassment.

In evaluating an action's consequences, some utilitarians consider the effects on animals as well as on human beings. This perspective is especially significant in the controversy surrounding the use of animals for research purposes by cosmetics and pharmaceutical companies. Animal rights groups have protested that such testing is unethical because it harms and even kills the animals, depriving them of their rights. Researchers for pharmaceutical and cosmetics manufacturers, however, defend animal testing on utilitarian grounds. The consequences of the research (such as new or improved drugs to treat disease, or safer cosmetics) create more benefit for society, they argue, than would be achieved by halting the research and preserving the animals' rights. Nonetheless, many cosmetics firms have responded to the controversy by agreeing to stop animal research.

Now suppose that Sam Colt, the bolt salesperson, is a utilitarian. Before making his decision, he would conduct a cost–benefit analysis to assess which alternative would create the greatest utility. On one hand, building the bridge would improve roadways and allow more people to cross the Mississippi River to reach jobs in St. Louis. The project would create hundreds of jobs, enhance the local economy, and unite communities on both sides of the river. Additionally, it would increase the revenues of Midwest Hardware, allowing the firm to invest more in research to lower the defect rate of bolts it produced in the future. On the other hand, a bridge collapse could kill or injure as many as one hundred people. But the bolts have only a 3 percent defect rate, there is only a 50 percent probability of an earthquake *somewhere* along the fault line, and there might be only a few cars on the bridge at the time of a disaster.

After analyzing the costs and benefits of the situation, Sam might rationalize that building the bridge with his company's bolts would create more utility (jobs, unity, economic growth, and company growth) than would result from telling the bridge contractor that the bolts might fail in an earthquake. If so, a utilitarian would probably not alert the bridge contractor to the defect rate of the bolts.

Utilitarians use various criteria to judge the morality of an action. Some utilitarian philosophers have argued that general rules should be followed to decide which action is best.[5] These **rule utilitarians** determine behavior on the basis of principles, or rules, designed to promote the greatest utility rather than on an examination of each particular situation. One such rule might be "Bribery is wrong." If people felt free to offer bribes whenever they might be useful, the world would become chaotic; therefore, a rule prohibiting bribery would increase utility. A rule utilitarian would not bribe an official, even to preserve workers' jobs, but would adhere strictly to the rule. Rule utilitarians do not automatically accept conventional moral rules, however; thus, if they determined that an alternative rule would promote greater utility, they would advocate changing it.

Other utilitarian philosophers have argued that the rightness of each individual action must be evaluated to determine whether it produces the greatest utility for the greatest number of people.[6] These **act utilitarians** examine a specific action itself, rather than the general rules governing it, to assess whether it will result in the greatest utility. Rules such as "Bribery is wrong" serve only as general guidelines for act utilitarians. They would likely agree that bribery is generally wrong, not because there is anything inherently wrong with bribery, but because the total amount of utility decreases when one person's interests are placed ahead of those of society.[7] In a particular case, however, an act utilitarian might argue that bribery is acceptable.

For example, a sales manager might believe that his or her firm will not win a construction contract unless a local government official gets a bribe; moreover, if the firm does not obtain the contract, it will have to lay off one hundred workers. The manager might therefore argue that bribery is justified because saving a hundred jobs creates more utility than obeying a law. Another example may be found in the actions of John Rigas, the billionaire founder of Adelphia Communications. In his hometown, Rigas was viewed as a hero because he helped fund everything from hospitals to roads and gave loans to local people in need. In one instance, he flew a resident's daughter who was dying of cancer from Pennsylvania to Denver to see a faith healer. However, Rigas drove Adelphia—and himself—into bankruptcy because of questionable accounting practices and the improper use of $3 billion in company funds for loans to himself and family members. When these actions became public, Adelphia's stock plummeted to 13 cents a share from a high of $86.56.[8] In 2005 Rigas was sentenced to fifteen years in prison; he is 80 years old and has bladder cancer. Timothy Rigas, the company's former CFO, was sentenced to twenty years in prison. As of this writing, both he and his father are free on bail pending their appeals.

Deontology

Deontology (from the Greek word for "ethics") refers to moral philosophies that focus on the rights of individuals and on the intentions associated with a particular behavior rather than on its consequences. Fundamental to deontological theory is the idea that equal respect must be given to all persons. Unlike utilitarians, deontologists argue that there are some things that we should *not* do, even to maximize utility. For example, deontologists would consider it wrong to kill an innocent person or commit a serious injustice against a person, no matter how much greater social utility might result from doing so, because such an action would infringe on that person's rights as an individual. The utilitarian, however, might consider as acceptable an action that resulted in a person's death if that action created some greater benefit. Deontological philosophies regard certain behaviors as inherently right, and the determination of this rightness focuses on the individual actor, not society. Thus, these perspectives are sometimes referred to as **nonconsequentialist,** an ethics based on *respect for persons*.

Contemporary deontology has been greatly influenced by the German philosopher Immanuel Kant, who developed the so-called categorical imperative: "Act as if the maxim of thy action were to become by thy will a universal law of nature."[9] Simply put, if you feel comfortable allowing everyone in the world to see you commit an act and if your rationale for acting in a particular manner is suitable to become a universal principle guiding behavior, then committing that act is ethical. For example, if a person borrows money, promising to return it but with no intention of keeping that promise, he or she cannot "universalize" that act. If everyone were to borrow money without the intention of returning it, no one would take such promises seriously, and all lending would cease.[10] Therefore, the rationale for the action would not be a suitable universal principle, and the act could not be considered ethical.

The term *nature* is crucial for deontologists. In general, deontologists regard the nature of moral principles as permanent and stable, and they believe that compliance with these principles defines ethicalness. Deontologists believe that individuals have certain absolute rights:

◆ Freedom of conscience
◆ Freedom of consent
◆ Freedom of privacy
◆ Freedom of speech
◆ Due process[11]

To decide whether a behavior is ethical, deontologists look for conformity to moral principles. For example, if a manufacturing worker becomes ill or dies as a result of conditions in the workplace, a deontologist might argue that the company must modify its production processes to correct the condition, no matter what the cost—even if it means bankrupting the company and thus causing all workers to lose their jobs. In contrast, a utilitarian would analyze all the costs and benefits of modifying production processes and make a decision on that basis. This example is greatly oversimplified, of course, but it helps clarify the difference between teleology and deontology. In short, teleological philosophies consider the *ends* associated with an action whereas deontological philosophies consider the *means*.

Returning again to our bolt salesman, let's consider a deontological Sam Colt. He would probably feel obliged to tell the bridge contractor about the defect rate because of the potential loss of life that might result from an earthquake-caused bridge collapse. Even though constructing the bridge would benefit residents and earn the salesman a substantial commission, the failure of the bolts during an earthquake would infringe on the rights of any person crossing the bridge at the time of the collapse. Thus, the deontological Colt would likely inform the bridge contractor of the defect rate and point out the earthquake risk, even though, by doing so, he would probably lose the sale.

As with utilitarians, deontologists may be divided into those who focus on moral rules and those who focus on the nature of the acts themselves. **Rule deontologists** believe that conformity to general moral principles determines ethicalness. Deontological philosophies use reason and logic to formulate rules for behavior. Examples include Kant's categorical imperative and the Golden Rule of the Judeo-Christian tradition: Do unto others as you would have them do unto you. Such rules, or principles, guiding ethical behavior override the imperatives that emerge from a specific context. One could argue that Jeffery Wigand—who exposed the underside of the tobacco industry when he blew the whistle on his employer, Brown & Williamson Tobacco—was such a rule deontologist. Although it cost him both financially and socially, Wigand testified to Congress about the realities of marketing cigarettes and their effects on society.[12]

Rule deontology is determined by the relationship between the basic rights of the individual and a set of rules governing conduct. For example, a video store owner accused of distributing obscene materials could argue from a rule deontological perspective that the basic right to freedom of speech overrides the other indecency or pornography aspects of his business. Indeed, the free-speech argument has held up in many courts. Kant and rule deontologists would support a process of discovery to identify the moral issues relevant to a firm's mission and objectives. Then, they would follow a process of justifying that mission or those objectives based on rules.[13]

Act deontologists, in contrast, hold that actions are the proper basis on which to judge morality or ethicalness. Act deontology requires that a person use equity, fairness, and impartiality when making and enforcing decisions.[14] For act deontologists, as for act utilitarians, rules serve only as guidelines, with past experiences weighing more heavily than rules upon the decision-making process. In effect, act deontologists suggest that people simply *know* that certain acts are right or wrong, regardless of the consequences or any appeal to deontological rules. In addition, act deontologists regard the particular act or moment in time as taking precedence over any rule. For example, many people view data collection by Internet sites as a violation of personal privacy in itself. Regardless of any website's stated rules or policies, many Internet users want to be left alone unless they provide permission to be tracked while online.[15] Current research suggests that rule and act deontological principles play a larger role in a person's decision than teleological philosophies.[16]

As we have seen, ethical issues can be evaluated from many different perspectives. Each type of philosophy discussed here would have a distinct basis for deciding whether a particular action is right or wrong. Adherents of different personal moral philosophies may disagree in their evaluations of a given action, yet all are behaving ethically *according to their own standards.* All would agree that there is no one "right" way to make ethical decisions and no best moral philosophy except their own. The relativist perspective may be helpful in understanding how people make such decisions in practice.

Relativist Perspective

From the **relativist perspective,** definitions of ethical behavior are derived subjectively from the experiences of individuals and groups. Relativists use themselves or the people around them as their basis for defining ethical standards, and the various forms of relativism include descriptive, metaethical, or normative.[17] **Descriptive relativism** relates to observing cultures. We may observe that different cultures exhibit different norms, customs, and values and, in so doing, arrive at a factual description of a culture. These observations say nothing about the higher questions of ethical justification, however. At this point metaethical relativism comes into play.

Metaethical relativists understand that people naturally see situations from their own perspectives and argue that, as a result, there is no objective way of resolving ethical disputes between value systems and individuals. Simply put, one culture's moral philosophy cannot logically be preferred to another because there exists no meaningful basis for comparison. Because ethical rules are relative to a specific culture, the values and behaviors of people in one culture need not influence the behaviors of people in another culture.[18] At the individual level of reasoning, we have **normative relativism.** Normative relativists assume that one person's opinion is as good as another's.[19]

Basic relativism acknowledges that we live in a society in which people have many different views and bases from which to justify decisions as right or wrong. The relativist looks to the interacting groups and tries to determine probable solutions based on group consensus. When formulating business strategies and plans, for example, a relativist would try to anticipate the conflicts that might arise between the different philosophies held by members of the organization, its suppliers, its customers, and the community at large.

The relativist observes the actions of members of an involved group and attempts to determine that group's consensus on a given behavior. A positive consensus, for example, would signify that the group considers the action to be right or ethical. However, such judgments may not remain valid forever. As circumstances evolve or the makeup of the group changes, a formerly accepted behavior may come to be viewed as wrong or unethical, or vice versa. Within the accounting profession, for example, it was traditionally considered unethical to advertise. However, advertising has been gaining acceptance among accountants. This shift in ethical views may have come about as a result of the steady increase in the number of accountants, which has led to greater competition. Moreover, the federal government investigated the restrictions that accounting groups placed on their members and concluded that they inhibited free competition. Consequently, an informal consensus has emerged in the accounting industry that advertising is now acceptable. A problem with relativism is that it places too much emphasis on peoples' differences while ignoring their basic similarities. Similarities within different people and cultures—such as beliefs against incest, murder, and theft or promoting reciprocity and respect for the elderly—are hard to argue away and hard to explain from the relativist perspective.

In the case of the Midwest Hardware salesperson, if he were a relativist, he would attempt to determine the group consensus before deciding whether to tell his prospective customer about the bolts' defect rate. The relativist Sam Colt would look at both his own company's policy and at the general industry practice. He might also informally survey his colleagues and superiors as well as consulting industry trade journals and codes of ethics. Such investigations would help him determine the group consensus, which should reflect a variety of moral philosophies. If he learns that general company policy, as well as industry practice, is to discuss defect rates with those customers for whom faulty bolts may cause serious problems, he may infer that there is a consensus on the matter. As a relativist, he would probably then inform the bridge contractor that some of the bolts may fail, perhaps leading to a bridge collapse in the event of an earthquake. Conversely, if Sam determines that the normal practice in his company and the industry is to not inform customers about defect rates, he would probably not raise the subject with the bridge contractor.

Empirical research into the general concept of relativism suggests that it is negatively related to a person's ethical sensitivity to issues. Thus, if someone scores high on relativism, he or she will probably be less likely to detect or be sensitive to issues that are defined by others as having an ethical component.[20]

Virtue Ethics

A moral virtue represents an acquired disposition that is valued as a part of an individual's character. As an individual develops socially, he or she may become disposed to behave in the same way (in terms of reasons, feelings, and desires) as what he considers to be moral.[21] A person who has the character trait of honesty will be disposed to tell the truth because it is considered to be right and comfortable. This individual will always try to tell the truth because of its importance in human communication. A virtue is considered praiseworthy because it is an achievement that an individual develops through practice and commitment.[22]

This philosophy is called **virtue ethics,** and it posits that what is moral in a given situation is not only what conventional morality or moral rules (current societal definitions) require but also what the mature person with a "good" moral character would deem appropriate.

Proponents of virtue ethics frequently discuss lists of basic goods and virtues, which are generally presented as positive and useful mental habits or cultivated character traits. Aristotle named, among others, standards of loyalty, courage, wit, community, and judgment as the "excellences" that society requires. While listing the important virtues is a popular theoretical task, the philosopher Dewey cautions that virtues should not be looked at separately. The pluralism of virtues gives the businessperson a positive character and constitutes the very best idea of integrity of character. The virtue ethics approach to business can be summarized as follows:

1. Individual virtue and integrity count, but good corporate ethics programs encourage individual virtue and integrity.
2. By the employee's role in the community (organization), these virtues associated with appropriate conduct form a good person.
3. The ultimate purpose is to serve society's demands and the public good and to be rewarded in one's career.
4. The well-being of the community goes together with individual excellence because of the social consciousness and public spirit of every individual.[23]

The difference between deontology, teleology, and virtue ethics is that the first two are applied *deductively* to problems whereas virtue ethics is applied *inductively.* Virtue ethics assumes that what current societal moral rules require may indeed be the moral minimum for the beginning of virtue. The viability of our political, social, and economic systems depends on the presence of certain virtues among the citizenry that are vital for the proper functioning of a market economy.[24]

Indeed, virtue theory could be thought of as a dynamic theory of how to conduct business activities. The virtue ethicist believes that to have a successful market economy, society must be capable of carving out sanctuaries such as family, school, church, and community, where virtues can be nurtured. These virtues, including truth, trust, tolerance, and restraint, can play a role in the functioning of an individualistic, contractual economy and create obligations that make social cooperation possible. The operation of a market economy based on virtues provides a traditional existence where individuals in the economic system have powerful inducements to conform to prevailing standards of behavior. Some philosophers think that virtues may be weakened by the operation of the market, but virtue ethicists believe that institutions and society must maintain a balance and constantly add to their stock of virtues.[25] Some of the virtues that could drive a market economy are listed in Table 6–2; the list, although not comprehensive, provides examples of the types of virtues that support the business environment.

The elements of virtue that are important to business transactions have been defined as trust, self-control, empathy, fairness, and truthfulness. Attributes in contrast to virtue would include lying, cheating, fraud, and corruption. In their broadest sense, these concepts appear to be accepted within all cultures. The problem of virtue ethics

TABLE 6–2	Virtues That Support Business Transactions

Trust: The predisposition to place confidence in the behavior of others while taking the risk that the expected behavior will not be performed	Trust eliminates the need for and associated cost of monitoring compliance with agreements, contracts, and reciprocal agreements. There is the expectation that a promise or agreement can be relied on.
Self-control: The disposition to pass up an immediate advantage or gratification. It indicates the ability to avoid exploiting a known opportunity for self-interest	The tradeoff is between short-term self-interest and long-term benefits.
Empathy: The ability to share the feelings or emotions of others	Empathy promotes civility because success in the market depends on the courteous treatment of people who have the option of going to competitors. The ability to anticipate needs and satisfy customers and employees contributes to a firm's economic success.
Fairness: The disposition to deal equitably with the perceived injustices of others	Fairness often relates to doing the right thing with respect to small matters in order to cultivate a long-term business relationship.
Truthfulness: The disposition to provide the facts or correct information as known to the individual	Telling the truth involves avoiding deception and contributes to trust in business relationships.
Learning: The disposition to constantly acquire knowledge internal and external to the firm, whether of an industry, culture, or other societies	Learning involves gaining knowledge to make better, more informed decisions.
Gratitude: A sign of maturity that is the beginning of civility and decency	Gratitude is the recognition that people do not succeed alone.
Civility: The disposition or essence of courtesy, politeness, respect, and consideration for others	Civility relates to the process of doing business in a culturally correct way, thus decreasing communication errors and increasing trust.
Moral leadership: Strength of character, peace of mind, heart, and happiness in life	Moral leadership is a trait of those leaders who follow a consistent pattern of behavior based on virtues.

SOURCE: Adapted from Ian Maitland, "Virtuous Markets: The Market as School of the Virtues," *Business Ethics Quarterly* (January 1997): 97; and Gordon B. Hinckley, *Standing for Something: 10 Neglected Virtues That Will Heal Our Hearts and Homes* (New York: Three Rivers Press, 2001).

comes in its implementation within and between cultures, as those who practice virtue ethics go beyond social norms. For example, if a company tacitly approves of corruption, the employee who adheres to the virtues of trust and truthfulness would consider it wrong to sell unneeded repair parts despite the organization's approval of such acts. Some employees might view this truthful employee as highly ethical but, in order to rationalize their own behavior, judge his or her ethics as going beyond what is required by their job or society. They might argue that virtue is an unattainable goal and thus one should not be obliged to live up to its standards. However, to those who espouse virtue ethics, this relativistic argument is meaningless because they believe in the universal reality of the elements of virtue.

If our salesman Sam Colt were a virtue ethicist, he would consider the elements of virtue and then tell the prospective customer about the defect rate and about his concerns regarding the building of the bridge. He would not resort to puffery to explain the product or its risks and, indeed, might suggest alternative products or companies that would lower the probability of the bridge collapsing.

Justice

Justice as it is applied in business ethics involves evaluations of fairness or the disposition to deal with perceived injustices of others. Justice is fair treatment and due reward in accordance with ethical or legal standards. In business, this means that the decision rules used by an individual to determine the justice of a situation could be based on the perceived rights of individuals and on the intentions of the people involved in a given business interaction. For that reason, justice is more likely to be based on deontological moral philosophies than on teleological or utilitarian philosophies. In other words, justice deals more with the issue of what individuals feel they are due based on their rights and performance in the workplace. For example, the U.S. Equal Employment Opportunity Commission exists to help employees who suspect they have been unjustly discriminated against in the workplace.

Three types of justice provide a framework for evaluating the fairness of different situations (Table 6–3). **Distributive justice** is based on the evaluation of the outcomes or results of the business relationship. If some employees feel that they are paid less than their coworkers for the same work, then they have concerns about distributive justice. Distributive justice is difficult to develop when one member of the business exchange intends to take advantage of the relationship. A boss who forces his employees to do more work so that he can take more time off would be seen as unjust because he is taking advantage of his position to redistribute the workers under him. Situations such as this cause an imbalance in distributive justice.

Procedural justice is based on the processes and activities that produce the outcome or results. Evaluations of performance that are not consistently developed and applied can lead to problems with procedural justice. For instance, employees' concerns about inequitable compensation would relate to their perception that the processes of fairness or justice in their company were inconsistent. A climate that emphasizes procedural justice is expected to positively influence employees' attitudes and behaviors toward work-group cohesion. The visibility of supervisors and the work group's perceptions of its own cohesiveness are products of a climate of procedural justice.[26] When there is strong employee support for decisions, decision makers, organizations, and outcomes, procedural justice is less important to the individual. In contrast, when employees' support for decisions, decision makers, organizations, or outcomes is not very

---

TABLE 6–3   Types of Justice

Justice Type	Evaluations of Fairness
Distributive justice: Based on the evaluation of outcomes or results of the business relationship	Benefits derived Equity in rewards
Procedural justice: Based on the processes and activities that produce the outcome or results	Decision-making process Level of access, openness, and participation
Interactional justice: Based on an evaluation of the communication process used in the business relationship	Accuracy of information Truthfulness, respect, and courtesy in the process

strong, then procedural justice becomes more important.[27] For example, Wainwright Bank and Trust Corporation in Boston has made a commitment to promoting justice to all stakeholders by providing a "sense of inclusion and diversity that extends from the boardroom to the mail room."[28] The bank, in other words, uses methods of procedural justice to establish positive stakeholder relationships by promoting understanding and inclusion in the decision-making process.

Interactional justice is based on evaluating the communication processes used in the business relationship. Because interactional justice is linked to fairness in communication, it often involves the individual's relationship with the business organization through the accuracy of the information the organization provides. Employees can also be guilty in interactional justice disputes. For example, many employees admit that they stay home when they are not really sick if they feel they can get away with it. Such workplace absenteeism costs businesses millions of dollars each year. Being untruthful about the reasons for missing work is an example of an interactional justice issue.

All three types of justice—distributive, procedural, and interactional—could be used to evaluate a single business situation and the fairness of the organization involved. In the example of Sam Colt, Sam's decision to implement a justice perspective would be identical to using a deontological moral philosophy. That is, he would feel obligated to tell all affected parties about the bolt defect rate and the possible consequences of it. In general, justice evaluations result in restitution seeking, relationship building, and evaluations of fairness in business relationships.

APPLYING MORAL PHILOSOPHY TO ETHICAL DECISION MAKING

Strong evidence shows that individuals use different moral philosophies depending on whether they are making a personal decision outside the work environment or making a work-related decision on the job.[29] Two possible reasons may explain this. First, in the business arena, some goals and pressures for success differ from the goals and pressures in a person's life outside of work. As a result, an employee might view a specific action as "good" in the business sector but "unacceptable" in the nonwork environment. The second reason people change moral philosophies could be the corporate culture where they work. When a child enters school, for example, he or she learns certain rules such as raising your hand to speak or asking permission to use the restroom. So it is with a new employee. Rules, personalities, and historical precedence exert pressure on the employee to conform to the new firm's culture. As this occurs, the individual's moral philosophy may change to be compatible with the work environment. The employee may alter some or all of the values within his or her moral philosophy as he or she shifts into the firm's different moral philosophy.

Obviously, the concept of a moral philosophy is inexact. For that reason, moral philosophies must be assessed on a continuum rather than as static entities. Simply put, when examining moral philosophies, we must remember that each philosophy states an ideal perspective and that most individuals seem to shift to other moral philosophies in their individual interpretation of and experiencing of ethical dilemmas. In other words, implementing moral philosophies from an individual perspective is not an exact science. It requires individuals to apply their own accepted value systems to real-world situations. Individuals make judgments about what they believe to be right or wrong, but in their business lives they make decisions that may be based not only on perceived right or wrong but also on producing the greatest benefits with the least harm. Such decisions should respect fundamental moral rights as well as perspectives on fairness, justice, and the common good, but these issues become complicated in the real world.

The virtue approach to business ethics, as discussed earlier, assumes that there are certain ideals and values that everyone should strive for in order to achieve the maximum welfare and happiness of society.[30] Aspects of these ideals and values are expressed through individuals' specific moral philosophies. Every day in the workplace, employees must decide what is right or wrong and act accordingly. At the same time, as a member of a larger organization, an employee cannot simply enforce his or her own personal perspective, especially if he or she adheres narrowly to a single moral philosophy. Because individuals cannot control most of the decisions in their work environment, though they are always responsible for their own actions, they rarely have the power (especially in entry-level and middle-management positions) to impose their own personal moral perspective on others. In fact, the idea that a new employee has the freedom to make independent decisions on a variety of job responsibilities is not realistic.

Sometimes a company makes decisions that could be questionable according to individual customers' values and moral philosophies. For example, a brewery or a distributor of sexually explicit movies could be considered unethical to some stakeholders based on a personal perspective. A company's core values will determine how decisions that bring moral philosophies into conflict are made. Most businesses have developed a mission statement, a corporate culture, and a set of core values that express how they want to relate to their stakeholders, including customers, employees, the legal system, and society. It is usually impossible to please all stakeholders.

Problems arise when employees encounter ethical situations that they cannot resolve. Sometimes gaining a better understanding of the basic premise of their decision rationale can help them choose the "right" solution. For instance, to decide whether they should offer bribes to customers to secure a large contract, salespeople need to understand their own personal moral philosophies as well as their firm's core values. If complying with company policy or legal requirements is an important motivation to the individual, he or she is less likely to offer a bribe. On the other hand, if the salesperson's ultimate goal is a "successful" career and if offering a bribe seems likely to result in a promotion, then bribery might not be inconsistent with that person's moral philosophy of acceptable business behavior. Even though bribery is illegal under U.S. law, the employee may rationalize that bribery is necessary "because everyone else does it."

COGNITIVE MORAL DEVELOPMENT

Many people believe that individuals advance through stages of moral development as their knowledge and socialization continue over time. In this section, we examine a model that describes this cognitive moral development process—that is, the stages through which people may progress in their development of moral thought. Many models, developed to explain, predict, and control individuals' ethical behavior within business organizations, have proposed that cognitive moral processing is an element in ethical decision making. Cognitive moral processing is based on a body of literature in psychology that focuses on studying children and their cognitive development.[31] Psychologist Lawrence Kohlberg adapted Piaget's theory and developed the six-stage model of cognitive development, which, although not specifically designed for business contexts, provides an interesting perspective on the question of moral philosophy in business. According to **Kohlberg's model of cognitive moral development,** people make different decisions in similar ethical situations because they are in different stages of six cognitive moral development stages:

1. *The stage of punishment and obedience.* An individual in Kohlberg's first stage defines *right* as literal obedience to rules and authority. A person in this stage will respond to rules and labels of "good" and "bad" in terms of the physical power of those who determine such rules. Right and wrong are not associated with any higher order or philosophy but rather with a person who has power. Stage 1 is usually associated with small children, but signs of stage 1 development are also evident in adult behavior. For example, some companies forbid their buyers to accept gifts from salespeople. A buyer in stage 1 might justify a refusal to accept gifts from salespeople by referring to the company's rule that defines accepting gifts as an unethical practice, or the buyer may accept the gift if he or she believes that there is no chance of being caught and punished.

2. *The stage of individual instrumental purpose and exchange.* An individual in stage 2 defines *right* as that which serves his or her own needs. In this stage, the individual no longer makes moral decisions solely on the basis of specific rules or authority figures; he or she now evaluates behavior on the basis of its fairness to him or her. For example, a sales representative in stage 2 doing business for the first time in a foreign country may be expected by custom to give customers "gifts." Although gift giving may be against company policy in the United States, the salesperson may decide that certain company rules designed for operating in the United States do not apply overseas. In the culture of some foreign countries, gifts may be considered part of a person's pay. So, in this instance, not giving a gift might put the salesperson at a disadvantage. Some refer to stage 2 as the stage of reciprocity because, from a practical standpoint, ethical decisions are based on an agreement that "you scratch my back and I'll scratch yours" instead of on principles of loyalty, gratitude, or justice.

3. *The stage of mutual interpersonal expectations, relationships, and conformity.* An individual in stage 3 emphasizes others rather than him- or herself. Although ethical motivation is still derived from obedience to rules, the individual considers the well-being of others. A production manager in this stage might obey upper management's order to speed up an assembly line if he or she believed that this would generate more profit for the company and thus save employee jobs. This manager not only considers his or her own well-being in deciding to follow the order but also tries to put him- or herself in upper management's and fellow employees' shoes. Thus, stage 3 differs from stage 2 in that fairness to others is one of the individual's ethical motives.

4. *The stage of social system and conscience maintenance.* An individual in stage 4 determines what is right by considering his or her duty to society, not just to other

specific people. Duty, respect for authority, and maintaining the social order become the focal points. For example, some managers consider it a duty to society to protect privacy and therefore refrain from monitoring employee conversations.

5. *The stage of prior rights, social contract, or utility.* In stage 5, an individual is concerned with upholding the basic rights, values, and legal contracts of society. Individuals in this stage feel a sense of obligation or commitment, a "social contract," to other groups and recognize that in some cases legal and moral points of view may conflict. To reduce such conflict, stage 5 individuals base their decisions on a rational calculation of overall utilities. The president of a firm may decide to establish an ethics program because it will provide a buffer against legal problems and the firm will be perceived as a responsible contributor to society.

6. *The stage of universal ethical principles.* A person in this stage believes that right is determined by universal ethical principles that everyone should follow. Stage 6 individuals believe that there are inalienable rights, which are universal in nature and consequence. These rights, laws, or social agreements are valid, not because of a particular society's laws or customs, but because they rest on the premise of universality. Justice and equality are examples of principles that are deemed universal in nature. A person in this stage may be more concerned with social ethical issues and thus not rely on the business organization for ethical direction. For example, a businessperson at this stage might argue for discontinuing a product that has caused death and injury because the inalienable right to life makes killing wrong, regardless of the reason. Therefore, company profits would not be a justification for the continued sale of the product.[32]

Kohlberg's six stages can be reduced to three different levels of ethical concern. At the first level, a person is concerned with his or her own immediate interests and with external rewards and punishments. At the second level, an individual equates *right* with conformity to the expectations of good behavior of the larger society or some significant reference group. Finally, at the third, or "principled," level, an individual sees beyond the norms, laws, and authority of groups or individuals. Employees at this level make ethical decisions regardless of negative external pressures. However, research has shown that most workers' abilities to identify and resolve moral dilemmas do not reside at this third level and that their motives are often a mixture of selflessness, self-interest, and selfishness.

Kohlberg suggests that people continue to change their decision-making priorities after their formative years, and as a result of time, education, and experience, they may change their values and ethical behavior. In the context of business, an individual's moral development can be influenced by corporate culture, especially ethics training. Ethics training and education have been shown to improve managers' cognitive development scores.[33] Because of corporate reform, most employees in *Fortune* 1000 companies today receive some type of ethics training.

Some feel that experience in resolving moral conflicts accelerates an individual's progress in moral development. A manager who relies on a specific set of values or rules may eventually come across a situation in which the rules do not apply. For example, suppose Sarah is a manager whose policy is to fire any employee whose productivity declines for four consecutive months. Sarah has an employee, George, whose productivity has suffered because of depression, but George's coworkers tell Sarah that George will recover and soon be a top performer again. Because of the circumstances and the perceived value of the employee, Sarah may bend the rule and keep George. Managers in the highest stages of the moral development process seem to be more democratic than autocratic, more likely to consider the ethical views of the other people involved in an ethical decision-making situation.

Once thought to be critical, the theory of cognitive moral development and the empirical research for the last ten years has been mixed, suggesting both a positive and negative relationship between it and ethical decision making. The consensus appears to be that cognitive moral development is difficult at best to measure and connect with ethical decision making.[34]

WHITE-COLLAR CRIME

The terms *crime* and *criminal* normally conjures up thoughts of rape, arson, armed robbery, or murder. The news constantly reports on the damages that occur as a result of these types of crimes. But, although the devastation caused by these "crimes of the street" is more appealing to the evening news, it is no less destructive than the crimes perpetrated every year by seemingly nonviolent white-collar criminals. Referred to as **white-collar crimes** (WCCs), these "crimes of the suite" do more damage in monetary and emotional loss in one year than the crimes of the street over several years combined.[35]

WCC creates victims by establishing trust and respectability. WCCs are often considered to be different than crimes of the street. It is interesting to note in Figure 6–1 that deceptive pricing, unnecessary repairs, and credit card fraud are the three victim categories that were found in the national public household survey of consumers reporting over their lifetime. The victims of WCC are often trusting consumers who be-

---

FIGURE 6–1   Individual Victimization Trends (Lifetime Consumer Experiences)

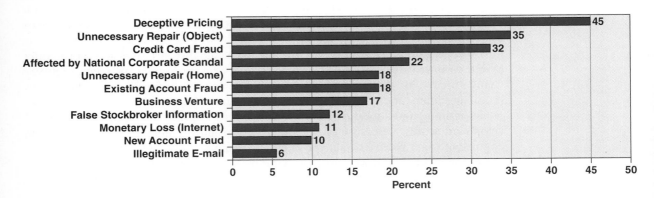

SOURCE: "The 2005 National Public Survey on White Collar Crime," National White Collar Crime Center, http://www.nw3c.org/research/national_public_survey.cfm (accessed March 9, 2006).

lieve that businesses are legitimate. Unfortunately, senior citizens and other disadvantaged consumers fall prey to WCC perpetrators. In the White Collar Crime Center's survey nearly one in two households was victimized by WCC in 2005, and well over half of the individuals surveyed had been victimized by WCC over their lifetimes. WCC cost the United States more than $300 billion annually.[36]

From various proposed definitions of WCC, the following appears to be inclusive of the main criminology literature yet parsimonious and exacting enough to be understood:

> An individual or group committing an illegal act in relation to his/her employment, who is highly educated (college), in a position of power, trust, respectability and responsibility, within a profit/nonprofit business or government organization and who abuses the trust and authority normally associated with the position for personal and/or organizational gains.

The presence of technology also seems to be giving a whole new generation of criminals the opportunity to score big. WCCs that previously originated at the top of organizations are now able to be committed at lower levels. Because of these advanced technology systems and corporate culture's increased reliance on them, anyone with the ability to hack into a system now can access the highly sensitive information necessary to commit WCC.

A classic example of WCC is Barry Minkow, an entrepreneur who borrowed $1500 to form a carpet-cleaning company called ZZZZ Best (pronounced Zee-Best). Carpet cleaning is a largely unregulated industry with a history of questionable practices, from deceptive advertising to "bait and switch" telephone solicitations—a process through which service people, upon arriving at the customer's house, can double or triple a low-priced contract by talking customers into costly extra services after entering their homes. Minkow decided to make ZZZZ Best a public corporation, but the Securities and Exchange Commission (SEC) requires substantial documentation in order to solicit stock.

Minkow used a technique called a "shell route" in which he merged his company with Morningstar Industries, an inactive Utah mineral exploration firm. He then acquired Morningstar's public-owned shares in exchange for stock in the newly formed corporation, thus getting around the SEC documentation. With 76 percent of the outstanding shares in his name, he was now worth $12 million on paper. In less than a year, ZZZZ Best stock was selling for $18 a share, and the company's book value (total shares multiplied by price per share) was $210 million. Minkow was now worth $109 million on paper. That same year, Minkow met with the Wall Street firm of Drexel, Burnham, Lambert, whose junk bond department raised $80 million via junk bonds for ZZZZ Best to buy out KeyServ, a Philadelphia-based cleaning service that operated in forty-three major markets under contract to Sears, Roebuck and Company. In less than three years, Minkow's paper worth was over $200 million. But then the FBI discovered what Minkow had been up to and he was charged with and convicted of fifty-seven counts of bank, stock, and mail fraud; money laundering; racketeering; conspiracy; and tax evasion. Minkow was sentenced to twenty-five years in prison.

The focus of criminology is often the behavior of the individual and discovery of the reasons why people commit such crimes. Advocates of the organizational deviance perspective argue that a corporation is a living, breathing organism that can collectively become deviant; that companies have a life of their own, separate and distinct from biological persons; that the ultimate "actors" in an organization are individuals; and that the corporate culture of the company transcends the individuals who occupy these positions. With time, patterns of activities become institutionalized within the organization that live on after those who established them have left the firm.[37]

Another common cause of WCC is peer influence, the result of an individual's circle of acquaintances within an organization, with their accompanying views and behaviors. Employees, at least in part, self-select the people with whom they associate within an organization. For companies with a high number of ethical employees, there is a higher probability that a fence sitter (the 40 percent of businesspeople who could be persuaded to be ethical or unethical) will go along with their coworkers.

Finally, there is an argument to be made that some businesspeople may have personalities that are inherently criminal.[38] Personality tests have been used to predict behavior in individuals working within an organization, but such tests presuppose that values and philosophies are constant; thus, they seem to be ineffective as an approach to understanding the subtleties of white-collar criminals.[39] We also know that businesspeople and companies must make a profit on revenue to exist, slanting their orientation toward teleology and making them increasingly likely to commit white-collar crimes. The answer to the increase in WCC is not easy to pinpoint because many variables cause good people to make bad decisions.

As Figure 6–2 shows, the National White Collar Crime Center survey indicates that over half the respondents disagree that the government is devoting enough resources to combat WCC. The current focus of the Federal Sentencing Guidelines for Organizations is that all organizations should develop effective ethics and compliance programs to prevent WCC.

FIGURE 6–2   Does the Government Devote Enough Resources to Combat White-Collar Crime?

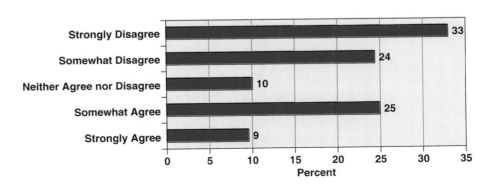

SOURCE: "The 2005 National Public Survey on White Collar Crime," National White Collar Crime Center, http://www.nw3c.org/research/national_public_survey.cfm (accessed March 9, 2006).

THE ROLE OF INDIVIDUAL FACTORS IN BUSINESS ETHICS

Of course, not everyone agrees on what the role of traditional moral philosophies in ethical decision making in an organization is. Some types such as Machiavellianism, which comes from the writing of Machiavelli, an Italian political theorist, have been found to influence ethical decisions. *The Prince* (a letter that Machiavelli wrote from exile to an Italian prince) argues against the relevance of morality in political affairs and holds that craft and deceit are justified in pursuing and maintaining political power. Machiavelli is famous for the idea that, for a leader, it is better to be feared than to be loved, and this type of thinking abounds within *The Prince* because Machiavelli presents basically a guidebook for obtaining and maintaining power without the need for morality. Most business managers do not embrace this extreme philosophy, and most managers cannot communicate the exact moral philosophy that they use to make ethical decisions.

According to ethics consultant David Gebler, "Most unethical behavior is not done for personal gain, it's done to meet performance goals."[40] Unfortunately, many people believe that individual moral philosophies are the main driver of ethical behavior in business. This belief can be a stumbling block in assessing ethical risk and preventing misconduct in an organizational context. The moral values learned within the family and through religion and education are key factors that do influence decision making, but as indicated in the models in Chapter 5, it is only one major factor. The fact that many companies and business schools focus on personal character or moral development in their training programs as the main consideration reinforces the idea that employees can control the work environment. Although a personal moral compass is important, it is not sufficient to prevent ethical misconduct in an organizational context. The rewards for meeting performance goals and the corporate culture, especially for coworkers and managers, have been found to be the most important drivers of ethical decision making.[41]

Strong abilities in ethical reasoning will probably lead to more ethical business decisions in the future than trying to provide detached character education for each employee.[42] Equipping employees with intellectual skills that will allow them to understand and resolve complex ethical dilemmas that they encounter in complex corporate cultures will help them make the right decisions. This approach will hopefully keep them from being carried along by peer pressure and lulled by unethical managers to engage in misconduct.[43] The West Point model for character development focuses on the fact that competence and character must be developed simultaneously. This model assumes that ethical reasoning has to be approached in the context of a specific profession. The military has been effective in teaching skills and developing principles and values that can be used in most situations that a soldier will encounter. In a similar manner, accountants, managers, or marketers need to develop ethical reasoning in the context of their jobs.

SUMMARY

Moral philosophy refers to the set of principles, or rules, that people use to decide what is right or wrong. These principles, rules, or philosophies present guidelines for resolving conflicts and for optimizing the mutual benefit of people living in groups.

Businesspeople are somewhat guided by moral philosophies as they formulate business strategies and resolve specific ethical issues.

Teleological, or consequentialist, philosophies stipulate that acts are morally right or acceptable if they produce some desired result, such as realization of self-interest or utility. Egoism defines right or acceptable behavior in terms of the consequences for the individual. In an ethical decision-making situation, the egoist will choose the alternative that contributes most to his or her own self-interest. Egoism can be further classified into hedonism and enlightened egoism. Utilitarianism is concerned with maximizing total utility, or providing the greatest benefit for the greatest number of people. In making ethical decisions, utilitarians often conduct a cost-benefit analysis, which considers the costs and benefits to all affected parties. Rule utilitarians determine behavior on the basis of rules designed to promote the greatest utility rather than by examining particular situations. Act utilitarians examine the action itself, rather than the rules governing the action, to determine whether it will result in the greatest utility.

Deontological, or nonconsequentialist, philosophies focus on the rights of individuals and on the intentions behind an individual's particular behavior rather than on its consequences. In general, deontologists regard the nature of moral principles as permanent and stable, and they believe that compliance with these principles defines ethicalness. Deontologists believe that individuals have certain absolute rights that must be respected. Rule deontologists believe that conformity to general moral principles determines ethicalness. Act deontologists hold that actions are the proper basis on which to judge morality or ethicalness and that rules serve only as guidelines.

According to the relativist perspective, definitions of ethical behavior are derived subjectively from the experiences of individuals and groups. The relativist observes behavior within a relevant group and attempts to determine what consensus group members have reached on the issue in question.

Virtue ethics posits that what is moral in a given situation is not only what is required by conventional morality or current social definitions, however justified, but also what a person with a "good" moral character would deem appropriate. Those who profess virtue ethics do not believe that the end justifies the means in any situation.

Ideas of justice as applied in business relate to evaluations of fairness. Justice relates to the fair treatment and due reward in accordance with ethical or legal standards. Distributive justice is based on the evaluation of the outcome or results of a business relationship. Procedural justice is based on the processes and activities that produce the outcomes or results. Interactional justice is based on an evaluation of the communication process in business.

The concept of a moral philosophy is not exact; moral philosophies can only be assessed on a continuum. Individuals use different moral philosophies depending on whether they are making a personal or a workplace decision.

According to Kohlberg's model of cognitive moral development, individuals make different decisions in similar ethical situations because they are in different stages of moral development. In Kohlberg's model, people progress through six stages of moral development: (1) punishment and obedience; (2) individual instrumental purpose and exchange; (3) mutual interpersonal expectations, relationships, and conformity; (4) social system and conscience maintenance; (5) prior rights, social contract, or utility;

and (6) universal ethical principles. Kohlberg's six stages can be further reduced to three levels of ethical concern: immediate self-interest, social expectations, and general ethical principles. Cognitive moral development may not explain as much as was once believed.

White-collar crime can be defined as an individual committing an illegal act in relation to his or her employment, who is highly educated; in a position of power, trust, respectability and responsibility; and abuses the trust and authority normally associated with the position for personal and/or organizational gains. Some reasons why white-collar crime is not being heavily researched is that it doesn't come to mind when people think of crime, the offender (or organization) is in a position of trust and respectability, criminology or criminal justice systems look at white-collar crime differently, and many researchers have not moved past the definitional issues. The increase in technology use seems to be increasing the opportunity to commit white-collar crime with less risk.

Individual factors such as religion, moral intensity, and a person's professional affiliations can affect a person's values and decision-making process. Other factors such as ethical awareness, biases, conflict, personality type, and intelligence have been studied, but no definitive conclusions can be made at this time about their relationship to ethical behavior. One thing we do know is that moral philosophies, values, and business are more complex than merely giving people honesty tests or value profiles that are not business oriented. Paper-and-pencil techniques do not yield accurate profiles for companies.

IMPORTANT TERMS FOR REVIEW

moral philosophy	act utilitarian
economic value orientation	deontology
idealism	nonconsequentialist
realism	rule deontologist
monist	act deontologist
hedonism	relativist perspective
quantitative hedonist	descriptive relativism
qualitative hedonist	metaethical relativist
pluralist	normative relativism
instrumentalist	virtue ethics
goodness theory	justice
obligation theory	distributive justice
teleology	procedural justice
consequentialism	interactional justice
egoism	Kohlberg's model of cognitive moral
enlightened egoism	development
utilitarianism	white-collar crime
rule utilitarian	

A REAL-LIFE SITUATION*

Twenty-eight-year-old Elaine Hunt, who is married and has one child, has been with United Banc Corporation (UBC) for several years. During that time, she has seen it grow from a relatively small-size to a medium-size company with domestic and international customers. Elaine's husband, Dennis, has been involved in the import–export business.

The situation that precipitated their current problem began six months ago. Elaine had just been promoted to senior financial manager, which put her in charge of ten branch-office loan managers, each of whom had five loan officers who reported to him or her. For the most part, the branch loan officers would go through the numbers of their loan people, as well as sign off on loans under $250,000. However, recently this limit had been increased to $500,000. For any loan over this amount and up to $40 million, Elaine had to sign off. For larger loans, a vice president would have to be involved.

Recently, Graphco Inc. requested a $10 million loan, which Elaine had been hesitant to approve. Graphco was a subsidiary of a tobacco firm embroiled in litigation concerning the promotion of its products to children. When reviewing the numbers, Elaine could not find any glaring problems, yet she had decided against the loan even when Graphco had offered to pay an additional interest point. Some at UBC applauded her moral stance while others did not, arguing that it was not a good financial business decision. The next prospective loan was for a Canadian company that was exporting cigars from Cuba. Elaine cited the U.S. policy against Cuba as the reason for not approving that loan. "The Helms-Burton Amendment gives us clear guidance as to what we shouldn't be doing with Cuba," she said to others in the company, even though the loan was to a Canadian firm. The third loan application she was unwilling to approve had come from Electrode International, which sought $50 million. The numbers had been marginal, but the sticking point for Elaine was Electrode's unusually high profits during the last two years. During dinner with Dennis, she had learned about a meeting in Zurich during which Electrode and others had allegedly fixed the prices on their products. Because only a handful of companies manufactured these particular products, the price increases were very successful. When Elaine suggested denying the loan on the basis of this information, she was overruled. At the same time, a company in Brazil was asking for an agricultural loan to harvest parts of the rain forest. The Brazilian company was willing to pay almost 2 points over the going rate for a $40 million loan. Because of her stand on environmental issues, Elaine rejected this application as well. The company obtained the loan from one of UBC's competitors.

Recently, Elaine's husband's decision making had fallen short of his superior's expectations. First, there was the problem of an American firm wanting to export nicotine and caffeine patches to Southeast Asia. With new research showing that both these drugs to be more problematic than previously thought, the manufacturing firm had decided to attempt a rapid-penetration marketing strategy—that is, to price the products very low or at cost in order to gain market share and then over time slightly increase the margin. With 2 billion potential customers, a 1-cent markup could result in millions of dollars in profits. Dennis had rejected the deal, and the firm had gone to another company. One person in Dennis's division had said, "Do you realize that you had the perfect product—one that was low cost and both physically and psychologically addictive? You could have serviced that one account for years and would have had enough for early retirement. Are you nuts for turning it down?!"

Soon afterward, an area financial bank manager wanted Elaine to sign off on a revolving loan for ABCO. ABCO's debt/equity ratio had increased significantly and did not conform to company regulations. However, Elaine was the one who had written the standards for UBC. Some in the company felt that Elaine was not quite up with the times. For example, several very good bank staff members had left in the past year because they found her regulations too provincial for the emerging global marketplace. As Elaine reviewed ABCO's credit report, she found many danger signals; however, the loan was relatively large, $30 million, and the company had been in a credit sales slump. As she questioned ABCO, Elaine learned that the loan was to develop a new business venture within the People's Republic of China, which rumor had it was also working with the Democratic People's Republic of Korea. The biotech venture was for fetal tissue research and harvesting. Recently, attention had focused on the economic benefits of such tissue in helping a host of ailments. Anticipated global market sales for such products were being estimated at $10 billion for the next decade. ABCO was also willing to go almost 2 points above the standard interest equation for such a revolving loan. Elaine realized that if she signed off on this sale, it would signal an end to her standards. However, if she did not and ABCO went to another company for the loan and paid off the debt, she would have made a gross error, and everyone in the company would know it.

As Elaine was wrestling with this problem, Dennis's commissions began to slip, putting a crimp in their cash-flow projections. If things did not turn around quickly for him, they would lose their new home, fall behind in other payments, and reduce the number of educational options for their child. Elaine had also had a frank discussion with senior management about her loan standards as well as her stand on tobacco, which had lost UBC precious income. The response was, "Elaine, we applaud your moral outrage about such products, but your morals are negatively impacting the bottom line. We can't have that all the time."

QUESTIONS • EXERCISES

1. Discuss the advantages and disadvantages of each decision that Elaine has made.
2. What are the ethical and legal considerations facing Elaine, Dennis, and UBC?
3. Discuss the moral philosophies that may be relevant to this situation.
4. Discuss the implications of each decision that Elaine could make.

*This case is strictly hypothetical; any resemblance to real persons, companies, or situations is coincidental.

Check Your EQ

Check your EQ, or Ethics Quotient, by completing the following. Assess your performance to evaluate your overall understanding of the chapter material.

1. Teleology defines right or acceptable behavior in terms of consequences for the individual. **Yes** **No**
2. A relativist looks at an ethical situation and considers the individuals and groups involved. **Yes** **No**
3. A utilitarian is most concerned with the bottom-line benefits. **Yes** **No**
4. Act deontology requires that a person use equity, fairness, and impartiality in making decisions and evaluating actions. **Yes** **No**
5. Virtues that support business transactions include trust, fairness, truthfulness, competitiveness, and focus. **Yes** **No**

ANSWERS: 1. No. That's egoism. 2. Yes. Relativists look at themselves and those around them to determine ethical standards. 3. Yes. Utilitarians look for the greatest good for the greatest number of people and use a cost–benefit approach. 4. Yes. The rules serve only as guidelines, and past experience weighs more heavily than the rules. 5. No. The characteristics include trust, self-control, empathy, fairness, and truthfulness—not competitiveness and focus.

CHAPTER 7

Organizational Factors: The Role of Ethical Culture and Relationships

CHAPTER OBJECTIVES

- To examine the influence of corporate culture on business ethics

- To determine how leadership, power, and motivation relate to ethical decision making in organizations

- To assess organizational structure and its relationship to business ethics

- To explore how the work group influences ethical decisions

- To discuss the relationship between individual and group ethical decision making

CHAPTER OUTLINE

AN ETHICAL DILEMMA*

Dawn Prarie had been with PCA Health Care Hospitals for three years and had been promoted to marketing director in the Miami area. She had a staff of ten and a fairly healthy budget. Dawn's job was to attract more patients into the HMO while helping keep costs down. At a meeting with Dawn, Nancy Belle, the vice president, had explained the ramifications of the Balanced Budget Act and how it was affecting all HMOs. "Being here in Miami does not help our division," she told Dawn. "Because of this Balanced Budget Act, we have been losing money on many of our elderly patients. For example, we used to receive $600 or more a month, per patient, from Medicare, but now our minimum reimbursement is just $367 a month! I need solutions, and that's where you come in. By the end of the month, I want a list of things that will help us show a profit. Anything less than a positive balance sheet will be unacceptable."

It was obvious that Nancy was serious about cutting costs and increasing revenues within the elderly market. That's why Dawn had been promoted to marketing director. The first thing Dawn did after the meeting with Nancy was to fire four key people. She then gave their duties to six who were at lower salaries and put the hospital staff on notice that changes would be occurring at the hospital over the next several months. In about three weeks, Dawn presented Nancy with an extensive list of ideas. It included these suggestions:

1. Trimming some prescription drug benefits
2. Reducing redundant tests for terminal patients
3. Hiring physician assistants to see patients but billing patients at the physician rate
4. Allowing physicians to buy shares in PCA, thus providing an incentive for bringing in more patients
5. Sterilizing and reusing cardiac catheters
6. Instituting a one-vendor policy on hospital products to gain quantity discounts
7. Prescreening "insurance" patients for probability of payment

Dawn's assistants felt that some of the hospital staff could be more aggressive in the marketing area. They urged using more promotional materials, offering incentives for physicians who suggested PCA or required their patients to be hospitalized, and prescreening potential clients into categories. "You see," said Ron, one of Dawn's staff, "we feel that there are four types of elderly patients. There are the healthy elderly, whose life expectancies are ten or more years. There are the fragile elderly, with life expectancies of two to seven years. Then there are the demented and dying elderly, who usually have one to three years. Finally, we have the high-cost or uninsured elderly. Patients who are designated healthy would get the most care, including mammograms, prostate-cancer screening, and cholesterol checks. Patients in the other categories would get less."

As she implemented some of the recommendations on Dawn's list, Nancy also launched an aggressive plan to destabilize the nurses' union. As a result, many nurses began a work slowdown and were filing internal petitions to upper management. Headquarters told Nancy to give the nurses and other hospital staff as much overtime as they wanted but not to hire anyone new. One floor manager suggested splitting up the staff into work teams, with built-in incentives for those who worked smarter and/or faster. Nancy approved the plan, and in three months productivity jumped 50 percent, with many of the hospital workers making more money. The downside for Nancy was an increase in worker-related accidents.

When Dawn toured the hospital around this time, she found that some of the most productive workers were using substandard procedures and poorly made products. One nurse said, "Yes, the surgical gloves are somewhat of a problem, but we were told that the quality met the minimum requirements and so we have to use them." Dawn brought this to Nancy's attention, whereupon Nancy drafted the following memo:

ATTENTION HOSPITAL STAFF

It has come to management's attention that minor injuries to staff and patients are on the rise.

Please review the Occupational Safety and Health Administration guidelines, as well as the standard procedures handbook, to make sure you are in compliance. I also want to thank all those teams that have been keeping costs down. We have finally gone into the plus side as far as profitability. Hang on and we'll be able to stabilize the hospital to make it a better place to care for patients and to work.

At Nancy's latest meeting with Dawn, she told Dawn, "We've decided on your staff's segmentation strategy for the elderly market. We want you to develop a questionnaire to prescreen incoming HMO patients, as well as existing clients, into one of the four categories so that we can tag their charts and alert the HMO physicians to the new protocols. Also, because the recommendations that we've put into practice have worked so well, we've decided to use the rest of your suggestions. The implementation

phase will start next month. I want you, Dawn, to be the lead person in developing a long-term strategy to break the unions in the hospital. Do whatever it takes. We just need to do more with less. I'm firm on this—so you're either on board or you're not. Which is it going to be?"

QUESTIONS • EXERCISES

1. Discuss PCA Health Care Hospitals' corporate culture and its ethical implications.
2. What factors are affecting Dawn's options?
3. Discuss the issue of for-profit versus nonprofit health-care facilities.
4. If you were Dawn, what information would you like to have to make your decisions?

*This case is strictly hypothetical; any resemblance to real persons, companies, or situations is coincidental.

Organizations are much more than structures in which we work. Although they are not alive, we attribute human characteristics to them. When times are good, we say the company is "well"; when times are not so good, we may try to "save" the company. Understandably, people have feelings toward the place that provides them with income and benefits; challenge, satisfaction, self-esteem, and often lifelong friendships. In fact, excluding the time spent sleeping, we spend almost 50 percent of our lives in this second home with our second "family." It is important, then, to examine how the culture and structure of these organizations influence the ethical decisions made within them.

In the ethical decision-making framework described in Chapter 5, we introduced the idea that organizational factors such as corporate culture and interpersonal relationships influence the ethical decision-making process. In this chapter, we take a closer look at corporate culture and the way a company's values and traditions can affect employees' ethical behavior. We also discuss the role of leadership in influencing ethical behavior within the organization. Next we describe two organizational structures and examine how they may influence ethical decisions. Then we consider the impact of groups within organizations. Finally, we examine the implications of organizational relationships for ethical decisions.

THE ROLE OF CORPORATE CULTURE IN ETHICAL DECISION MAKING

Chapter 5 defined the term *corporate culture* as a set of values, beliefs, goals, norms, and ways of solving problems shared by the members (employees) of an organization of any size (for profit or nonprofit). A founder and his or her values and expectations can create corporate culture, as in the case of McDonald's. The fast-food giant's support of and reputation for quality, service, cleanliness, and value derive from founder Ray Kroc. However, McDonald's faces problems with customer satisfaction. Over 10 percent of McDonald's customers are dissatisfied with their visit and share their complaint with the restaurant. The top-five customer complaints at McDonald's include (1) rude employees, (2) being out of Happy Meal toys, (3) slow service, (4) missing product/wrong order, and (5) unclean restaurants.[1] Corporate culture includes the behavioral patterns, concepts, values, ceremonies, and rituals that take place in the organization.[2] It gives the members of the organization meaning as well as the internal rules of behavior.[3] When these values, beliefs, customs, rules, and ceremonies are accepted, shared, and circulated throughout the organization, they represent its culture. All organizations, not just corporations, have some sort of culture, and thus we use the terms *organizational culture* and *corporate culture* interchangeably.

Although corporate culture is a broad and widely used concept, the term has a multitude of definitions, none of which has achieved universal acceptance. These range from highly specific to generically broad. For example, *culture* has been defined as "the way we do things around here,"[4] "the collective programming of the mind,"[5] and "the social fiber that holds the organization together."[6] Culture is also viewed as "the shared beliefs top managers in a company have about how they should manage themselves and other employees, and how they should conduct their business(es)."[7] Mutual of Omaha defines corporate culture as the "personality of the organization, the shared beliefs that determine how its people behave and solve business problems."[8] Mutual of Omaha executives believe that its corporate culture provides the foundation for the company's work and objectives, and the company has adopted a set of core values called "Values for Success" (Table 7–1). The company believes that these values form the foundation for a corporate culture that will help the organization realize its vision and achieve its goals.

A company's history and unwritten rules are a part of its culture. Thus, for many years, IBM salespeople adhered to a series of unwritten standards for dealing with clients. The history or stories passed down from generation to generation within an organization are like the traditions that are propagated within society. Henry Ford, the founder of Ford Motor Company, left a legacy that emphasized the importance of the individual employee and the natural environment. Just as Henry Ford pioneered the then-unheard-of high wage of $5 a day in the early years of the twentieth century, current chairman William Clay Ford, Jr., continues to affirm that employees represent the only sustainable advantage of a company. William Ford has maintained his grandfather's legacy by taking a leadership role in improving vehicle fuel efficiency while reducing emissions. Ford faces many financial challenges and plans to cut its capacity by 26 percent by 2008. In addition, Ford will reduce their hourly labor force by thirty thousand over the next several years. William Ford is committed to successfully restructuring Ford to more successfully compete in the future.[9]

Some cultures are so strong that to outsiders they come to represent the character of the entire organization. For example, Levi Strauss, Ben & Jerry's Homemade (the ice cream company), and Hershey Foods are widely perceived as casual organizations with strong ethical cultures, whereas Lockheed Martin, Procter & Gamble, and Texas

TABLE 7-1	Mutual of Omaha's "Values for Success"

Openness and Trust—We encourage an open sharing of ideas and information, displaying a fundamental respect for each other as well as our cultural diversity.

Teamwork (Win/Win)—We work together to find solutions that carry positive results for others as well as ourselves, creating an environment that brings out the best in everyone.

Accountability/Ownership—We take ownership and accept accountability for achieving end results, and empower team members to do the same.

Sense of Urgency—We set priorities and handle all tasks and assignments in a timely manner.

Honesty and Integrity—We are honest and ethical with others, maintaining the highest standards of personal and professional conduct.

Customer-Focus—We never lose sight of our customers, and constantly challenge ourselves to meet their requirements even better.

Innovation and Risk—We question "the old way of doing things" and take prudent risks that can lead to innovative performance and process improvements.

Caring/Attentive (Be Here Now)—We take time to clear our minds to focus on the present moment, listening to our teammates and customers, and caring enough to hear their concerns.

Leadership—We provide direction, purpose, support, encouragement, and recognition to achieve our vision, meet our objectives and our values.

Personal and Professional Growth—We challenge ourselves and look for ways to be even more effective as a team and as individuals.

SOURCE: "Transforming Our Culture: The Values for Success," Mutual of Omaha, www.careerlink.org/emp/mut/corp.htm (accessed March 30, 2006). Reprinted with permission.

Instruments are perceived as more formal, ethical ones. The culture of an organization may be explicitly articulated or left unspoken.

Explicit statements of values, beliefs, and customs usually come from upper management. Memos, written codes of conduct, handbooks, manuals, forms, and ceremonies are all formal expressions of an organization's culture. Many of these statements can be found on company websites, like Mutual of Omaha's "Values for Success."

Corporate culture is often expressed informally—for example, through comments, both direct and indirect, that communicate the wishes of management. In some companies, shared values are expressed through informal dress codes, working late, and participation in extracurricular activities. Corporate culture can even be expressed through gestures, looks, labels, promotions, programs, and legends (or the lack of these). Southwest Airlines is involved with more than thirty thousand students nationwide as part of their "Adopt-a-Pilot" educational program. The program encourages students to research careers, set personal goals, and realize the importance of succeeding in school. During the four-week mentorship program, pilots volunteer their time and correspond with their student, mentor while on the road, and speak in their classes.[10] This program reinforces Southwest's commitment to its communities and caring organizational culture. The press generated by community involvement reinforces organizational values and priorities.

The "tone at the top" is often cited as a determining factor in creating a high-integrity organization. Employees were asked, in a KPMG Forensic Integrity Survey

| **FIGURE 7–1** | Perceived Tone and Culture, Tone at the Top, and Perceptions of the CEO and Other Senior Executives |

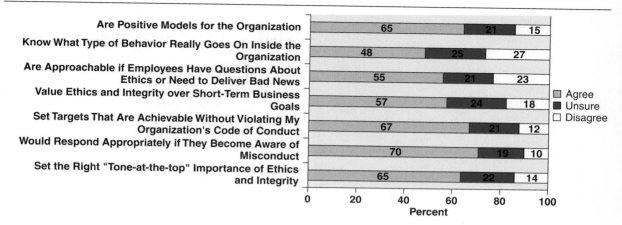

SOURCE: "KPMG Forensic Integrity Survey 2005–2006,"
http://www.kpmginsiders.com/display_analysis.asp?cs_id=148597 (accessed March 9, 2006).

(Figure 7–1) whether their CEO and other senior executives exhibited characteristics attributable to personal integrity and ethical leadership. Nearly two-thirds of employees believed that their leaders served as positive role models for their organizations. However, roughly half suggested a lack of confidence (based on "unsure" and "disagree" responses) that their CEOs knew about behaviors further down in the organization. Nearly half suggested a lack of confidence that their leaders would be approachable if employees had ethics concerns, and 70 percent agreed that their CEOs would respond appropriately to matters brought to their attention. Overall, nearly two-thirds of employees agreed their leaders set the right tone at the top, leaving one-third unsure or in disagreement.

Ethical Framework and Audit for Corporate Culture

Corporate culture has been conceptualized in many ways. Authors N. K. Sethia and Mary Ann Von Glinow have proposed two basic dimensions to describe an organization's culture: (1) concern for people—the organization's efforts to care for its employees' well-being; and (2) concern for performance—the organization's efforts to focus on output and employee productivity. A two-by-two matrix represents the four general types of organizational cultures (Figure 7–2).[11]

As Figure 7–2 shows, the four organizational cultures can be classified as apathetic, caring, exacting, and integrative. The *apathetic culture* shows minimal concern for either people or performance. In this culture, individuals focus on their own self-interests. Apathetic tendencies can occur in almost any organization. Steel companies

| FIGURE 7–2 | A Framework of Organizational Culture Typologies |

SOURCE: From *Gaining Control of the Corporate Culture*, by N.K. Sethia and M.A. Von Glinow, 1985, Jossey-Bass, Inc. Reprinted with permission of John Wiley & Sons, Inc.

and airlines were among the first to freeze employee pensions to keep their businesses operating, now *Fortune* 500 companies such as Sears, IBM, and Verizon are engaging in the same behaviors. Workers can still keep their pensions, but the payout will not be based on their final, higher paying salary years. A study by Hewitt Associates found that 21 percent of the nation's companies plan to freeze employee benefits at their current levels, and 17 percent will omit them completely for new employees.[12] Sweeping changes in corporate America are impacting employee compensation and retirement plans. Simple gestures of appreciation, such as anniversary watches, rings, dinners, or birthday cards for family members, are being dropped. Many companies view long-serving employees as deadwood and do not take into account past performance. This attitude demonstrates the companies' apathetic culture.

The *caring culture* exhibits high concern for people but minimal concern for performance issues. From an ethical standpoint, the caring culture seems to be very appealing. Southwest Airlines, for example, has a long-standing reputation of concern for its employees. CEO Herb Kelleher is the purveyor of wit, wisdom, and continuity in Southwest's culture. Employees "love the company" because they believe it cares for and is concerned about them. Employee loyalty and commitment at Southwest are very high. Kelleher has been known to go into the cargo hold of a plane attired in a dress and feather boa to assist employees with baggage. Southwest feels that if employees are well cared for, then customers will be taken care of and the competition will be surpassed. Customers must indeed feel that they are being taken care of because Southwest received the fewest customer complaints since 1987, as reported in the Department of Transportation's *Air Travel Consumer Report*. Southwest also ranked first in customer satisfaction.[13]

In contrast, the *exacting culture* shows little concern for people but a high concern for performance; it focuses on the interests of the organization. United Parcel Service (UPS) has always been very exacting. It knows precisely how many workers it needs to deliver its 14.8 million packages a day. To combat the uncaring, unsympathetic attitude of many of its managers, UPS developed a community service program for its employees. Global Volunteer Week gives UPS employees around the world the opportunity to help paint schools, renovate shelters, and assist with many other needed projects within their communities. In 2005 more than twenty thousand employees participated in at least one activity over the "seven days of service." UPS was also named in *Fortune* magazine as "America's Most Admired Company" in its industry.[14]

The *integrative culture* combines high concern for people and for performance. An organization becomes integrative when superiors recognize that employees are more than interchangeable parts—that employees have an ineffable quality that helps the firm meet its performance criteria. Many companies, such as U.S. Foodservice, have such a culture. U.S. Foodservice is the number-two food service distributor, behind Sysco, serving over two hundred and fifty thousand customers, including restaurants, hotels, schools, and other institutions. The company was involved in improper revenue recognition resulting in an $800 million revenue overstatement. Today, U.S. Foodservice operates a comprehensive ethics and compliance program including training videos featuring Ben Stein (actor and comedian) and the company's president and CEO Lawrence Benjamin.[15]

Companies can classify their corporate culture and identify its specific values, norms, beliefs, and customs by conducting a cultural audit. A *cultural audit* is an assessment of the organization's values. It is usually conducted by outside consultants but may be performed internally as well. Table 7–2 illustrates some of the issues that an ethics

TABLE 7–2	Ethics Related Actions Among Levels of Employees
Statement Describing Ethics Related Actions	**Percentage of Employees Strongly Agreeing or Agreeing (2005)**
Top management provides information	80
Top management keeps commitments	81
Top management communicates ethics	89
Top management sets a good example of ethics	87
Middle management keeps commitments	85
Middle management communicates ethics	89
Middle management sets good example of ethics	89
Supervisor sets good example of ethics	91
Supervisor keeps commitments	88
Supervisor talks about ethics	90
Supervisor supports standards	93
Coworkers consider ethics in decisions	91
Coworkers support standards	94
Coworkers set good example of ethics	92
Coworkers talk about ethics	80

SOURCE: From *2005 National Business Ethics Survey: How Employees Perceive Ethics at Work*, p. 20. Copyright © 2006, Ethics Resource Center (ERC). Used with permission of the ERC, 1747 Pennsylvania Ave., N.W., Suite 400, Washington, DC 2006, www.ethics.org.

audit of a corporate culture should address. The table identifies components of an organizational ethical culture, with the percentage of those employees who strongly agreed or agreed that the specific action was being displayed in their organizations. There has been little change since 2000–2005 in the figures. These issues can help identify a corporate culture that creates ethical conflict.

Ethics as a Component of Corporate Culture

As indicated in the framework presented in Chapter 5, ethical culture, the ethical component of corporate culture, is a significant factor in ethical decision making. If a firm's culture encourages or rewards unethical behavior, its employees may well act unethically. If the culture dictates hiring people who have specific, similar values and if those values are perceived as unethical by society, society will view the organization and its members as unethical. Such a pattern often occurs in certain areas of marketing. For instance, salespeople may be seen as unethical because they sometimes use aggressive selling tactics to get customers to buy things they do not need or want. If a company's primary objective is to make as much profit as possible, through whatever means, its culture may foster behavior that conflicts with stakeholders' ethical values. For example, Boeing general counsel, Doug Bain, noted in an annual leadership meeting that Boeing operated with a culture of winning at any cost. He continued noting that fifteen company vice presidents have been removed for a variety of ethical lapses. Boeing is under investigation by the Justice Department and could face heavy fines.[16] The interests of diverse Boeing stakeholders (shareholders, suppliers, and employees) may have been ignored in their efforts to boost profits.

On the other hand, if the organization values ethical behaviors, it will reward them. At Microsoft, for example, the mission is to "help people and businesses throughout the world realize their potential." The company values passion for customers, for partners, and for technology.[17] This strong corporate culture may help explain the company's reputation for corporate citizenship, which is reflected in its position on such lists as *Fortune*'s "America's Most Admired Companies" ranking number ten overall."[18]

An organization's failure to monitor or manage its culture may foster questionable behavior. In a patent infringement case brought against Gateway in Utah, a federal judge reprimanded the company for destroying or losing evidence in "bad faith." A former IBM engineer brought the suit against Gateway, indicating that they infringed upon his patents for addressing defects in floppy-disk drives. The engineer also added that Gateway lost or destroyed documents that would have helped prove his case. Attempts to cover up wrongdoing by destroying documents should not be tolerated.[19]

Management's sense of the organization's culture may be quite different from the values and ethical beliefs that are actually guiding the firm's employees. Table 7–3 provides an example of a corporate culture ethics audit. Companies interested in assessing their culture can use this tool and benchmark against previous years' results to measure for organizational improvements. Ethical issues may arise because of conflicts between the cultural values perceived by management and those actually at work in the organization. For example, managers may believe that the culture encourages respect for peers and subordinates. On the basis of the rewards or sanctions associated with var-

TABLE 7–3	Corporate Culture Ethics Audit

Answer Yes or No to each of the following questions.*

Yes	No	Has the founder or top management of the company left an ethical legacy to the organization?
Yes	No	Does the company have methods for detecting ethical concerns within the organization and outside it?
Yes	No	Is there a shared value system and understanding of what constitutes appropriate behavior within the organization?
Yes	No	Are stories and myths embedded in daily conversations about appropriate ethical conduct when confronting ethical situations?
Yes	No	Are codes of ethics or ethical policies communicated to employees?
Yes	No	Are there ethical rules or procedures in training manuals or other company publications?
Yes	No	Are there penalties that are publicly discussed for ethical transgressions?
Yes	No	Are there rewards for good ethical decisions even if they don't always result in a profit?
Yes	No	Does the company recognize the importance of creating a culture that is concerned about people and their self-development as members of the business?
Yes	No	Does the company have a value system of fair play and honesty toward customers?
Yes	No	Do employees treat each other with respect, honesty, and fairness?
Yes	No	Do employees spend their time working in a cohesive way on what is valued by the organization?
Yes	No	Are there ethically based beliefs and values about how to succeed in the company?
Yes	No	Are there heroes or stars in the organization who communicate a common understanding about what positive ethical values are important?
Yes	No	Are there day-to-day rituals or behavior patterns that create direction and prevent confusion or mixed signals on ethics matters?
Yes	No	Is the firm more focused on the long run than on the short run?
Yes	No	Are employees satisfied or happy, and is employee turnover low?
Yes	No	Do the dress, speech, and physical work setting prevent an environment of fragmentation or inconsistency about what is right?
Yes	No	Are emotional outbursts about role conflict and ambiguity very rare?
Yes	No	Has discrimination and/or sexual harassment been eliminated?
Yes	No	Is there an absence of open hostility and severe conflict?
Yes	No	Do people act on the job in a way that is consistent with what they say is ethical?
Yes	No	Is the firm more externally focused on customers, the environment, and the welfare of society than on its own profits?
Yes	No	Is there open communication between superiors and subordinates on ethical dilemmas?
Yes	No	Have employees ever received advice on how to improve ethical behavior or been disciplined for committing unethical acts?

*Add the number of Yes answers. The greater the number of Yes answers, the less ethical conflict is likely in your organization.

ious behaviors, however, the firm's employees may believe that the company encourages competition among organizational members. A competitive orientation may result in a less ethical corporate culture. On the other hand, employees appreciate working in an environment that is designed to enhance workplace experiences through goals that encompass more than just maximizing profits.[20] Thus, it is very important for top managers to determine what the organization's culture is and to monitor its values, traditions, and beliefs to ensure that they represent the desired culture. However, the rewards and punishments imposed by an organization need to be consistent with the actual corporate culture. As two business ethics experts have observed, "Employees will value and use as guidelines those activities for which they will be rewarded. When a behavior that is rewarded comes into conflict with an unstated and unmonitored ethical value, usually the rewarded behavior wins out."[21]

Differential Association

Differential association refers to the idea that people learn ethical or unethical behavior while interacting with others who are part of their role-sets or belong to other intimate personal groups.[22] The learning process is more likely to result in unethical behavior if the individual associates primarily with persons who behave unethically. Associating with others who are unethical, combined with the opportunity to act unethically, is a major influence on ethical decision making, as described in the decision-making framework in Chapter 5.[23]

Consider two cashiers working different shifts at the same supermarket. Kevin, who works in the evenings, has seen his cashier friends take money from the bag containing the soft-drink machine change, which is collected every afternoon but not counted until closing time. Although Kevin personally believes that stealing is wrong, he has often heard his friends rationalize that the company owes them free beverages while they work. During his break one evening, Kevin discovers that he has no money to buy a soda. Because he has seen his friends take money from the bag and has heard them justify the practice, Kevin does not feel guilty about taking four quarters. However, Sally, who works the day shift, has never seen her friends take money from the bag. When she discovers that she does not have enough money to purchase a beverage for her break, it does not occur to her to take money from the change bag. Instead, she borrows from a friend. Although both Sally and Kevin view stealing as wrong, Kevin has associated with others who say the practice is justified. When the opportunity arose, Kevin used his friends' rationalization to justify his theft.

A variety of studies have supported the notion that such differential association influences ethical decision making. In particular, superiors have a strong influence on the ethics of their subordinates. Consider the actions of Mark Hernandez, who worked at NASA's Michoud Assembly Facility applying insulating foam to the space shuttles' external fuel tanks. Within a few weeks on the job, coworkers taught him to repair scratches in the insulation without reporting the repairs. Supervisors encouraged the workers not to bother filling out the required paperwork on the repairs so they could meet the space shuttle program's tight production schedules. After the shuttle *Columbia* broke up on reentry, killing all seven astronauts on board, investigators focused on whether a piece of foam falling off a fuel tank during liftoff may have irreparably damaged the shuttle. The final determination of the cause of the disaster may require years of investigation.[24]

Several research studies have found that employees, especially young managers, tend to go along with their superiors' moral judgments to demonstrate loyalty.[25] Hopefully, we have made it clear that *how* people typically make ethical decisions is not necessarily the way they *should* make ethical decisions. But we believe that you will be able to improve your own ethical decision making once you understand the potential influence of your interaction with others in your intimate work groups.

Whistle-Blowing

Interpersonal conflict ensues when employees think they know the right course of action in a situation, yet their work group or company promotes or requires a different, unethical decision. In such cases, employees may choose to follow their own values and refuse to participate in the unethical or illegal conduct. If they conclude that they cannot discuss what they are doing or what should be done with their coworkers or immediate supervisors, these employees may go outside the organization to publicize and correct the unethical situation.

Whistle-blowing means exposing an employer's wrongdoing to outsiders (external to the company) such as the media or government regulatory agencies. The term *whistle-blowing* is also used for internal reporting of misconduct to management, especially through anonymous reporting mechanisms, often called hot lines. The Sarbanes–Oxley Act and the Federal Sentencing Guidelines for Organizations (FSGO) has institutionalized internal whistle-blowing to encourage discovery of internal misconduct.

Whistle-blowers have provided pivotal evidence documenting corporate malfeasance at a number of companies. The importance of their role was highlighted when *Time* magazine named three whistle-blowers a few years ago as "Persons of the Year": Sherron Watkins of Enron, Cynthia Cooper of WorldCom, and Coleen Rowley of the FBI. Watkins, an Enron vice president, warned Kenneth Lay, the firm's CEO, that the company was using improper accounting procedures. "I am incredibly nervous that we will implode in a wave of accounting scandals," she told him, and the energy firm did exactly that within a few short months. Lay seemed skeptical of her concerns because of approval of Arthur Andersen, their external auditor, and Vinson and Elkins (their law firm). Lay turned over the case to their law and accounting firms for investigation, an activity that Watkins referred to as "whitewash" with these firms reviewing their own work. Soon after, Watkins became an external whistle-blower testifying before Congress that Enron had concealed billions of dollars in debt through a complex scheme of off-balance-sheet partnerships.[26]

Historically, the fortunes of external whistle-blowers have not been as positive: Most were labeled traitors, and many lost their jobs. Even Watkins was a potential candidate for firing as the Enron investigation unfolded with law firms assessing the implications of terminating her in light of her ethical and legal concerns about Enron.[27]

A study of three hundred whistle-blowers by researchers at the University of Pennsylvania found that 69 percent lost their jobs or were forced to retire after exposing their companies' misdeeds.[28] For example, the whistle-blower who exposed Wal-Mart chairman Thomas Coughlin of defrauding the company was terminated about a week after Coughlin resigned. Jared Bowen, a former vice president for Wal-Mart Stores, Inc., claims that he was terminated for his exposure of Coughlin, in violation of a provision of the Sarbanes–Oxley Act protecting whistle-blowers.[29] If an employee provides information to the government about their company's wrongdoing, under the Federal False Claims Act, the whistle-blower is known as a *qui tam relator*. Upon investigation

TABLE 7-4	Questions to Ask Before Engaging in External Whistle-Blowing

1. Have I exhausted internal anonymous reporting opportunities within the organization?
2. Have I examined company policies and codes that outline acceptable behavior and violations of standards?
3. Is this a personal issue that should be resolved through other means?
4. Can I manage the stress that may evolve from exposing potential wrongdoing in the organization?
5. Can I deal with the consequences of resolving an ethical or legal conflict within the organization?

by the U.S. Department of Justice, the whistle-blower can receive between 15 and 25 percent of the recovered funds, depending upon how instrumental their claims were in holding the firm accountable for their wrongdoing.[30] Although most whistle-blowers do not receive positive recognition for pointing out corporate misconduct, some have turned to the courts and obtained substantial settlements. Table 7–4 provides a checklist of questions an employee should ask before blowing the whistle externally. Figure 7–3 shows that nearly one in four employees experience retaliation after reporting misconduct. Nearly half of all employees who report misconduct received positive feedback for having done so.

If whistle-blowers present an accurate picture of organizational misconduct, they should not fear for their jobs. Indeed, the Sarbanes–Oxley Act makes it illegal to "discharge, demote, suspend, threaten, harass, or in any manner discriminate against" a whistle-blower and sets penalties of up to ten years in jail for executives who retaliate against whistle-blowers. The law also requires publicly traded companies to implement an anonymous reporting mechanism that allows employees to question actions that they

FIGURE 7-3	Outcome for Internal Whistle-Blowers Reporting Misconduct

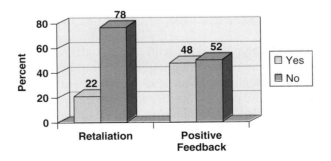

SOURCE: National Business Ethics Survey, *How Employees View Ethics in Their Organizations 1994–2005* (Washington, DC: Ethics Resource Center, 2005), 32.

| FIGURE 7-4 | Reasons Why Employees Do Not Report Observed Misconduct |

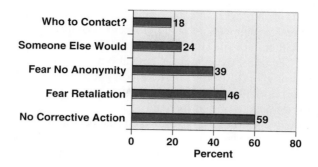

SOURCE: National Business Ethics Survey, *How Employees View Ethics in Their Organizations 1994–2005* (Washington, DC: Ethics Resource Center, 2005), 29.

believe may indicate fraud or other misconduct.[31] Additionally, the FSGO provides rewards for companies that systematically detect and address unethical or illegal activities.

Some U.S. companies are setting up computer systems that encourage internal whistle-blowing. With over fifty-five hundred employees, Marvin Windows (one of the world's largest custom manufacturer of wood windows and doors) is concerned about employees feeling comfortable reporting violations of safety conditions, bad management, fraud, or theft. The system is anonymous and allows for reporting in native-country languages. This system is used to alert management to potential problems in the organization and facilitate an investigation.[32]

Even before the passage of the Sarbanes–Oxley Act, an increasing number of companies were setting up anonymous reporting services, normally toll-free numbers, through which employees can report suspected violations or seek input on how to proceed when encountering ambiguous situations. These internal reporting services are perceived to be most effective when they are managed by an outside organization that specializes in maintaining ethics hot lines.

Figure 7–4 indicates the reasons why employees do not report misconduct in the organization. The extent to which employees feel there will be no corrective action or there will be retaliation are leading factors influencing their decisions not to report observed misconduct.

LEADERS INFLUENCE CORPORATE CULTURE

Organizational leaders use their power and influence to shape corporate culture. *Power* refers to the influence that leaders and managers have over the behavior and decisions of subordinates. An individual has power over others when his or her presence causes them to behave differently. Exerting power is one way to influence the ethical decision-making framework described in Chapter 5 (especially significant others and opportunity).

The status and power of leaders is directly related to the amount of pressure that they can exert on employees to conform to their expectations. A superior in an authority position can put strong pressure on employees to comply, even when their personal ethical values conflict with the superior's wishes. For example, a manager might say to a subordinate, "I want the confidential data about our competitor's sales on my desk by Monday morning, and I don't care how you get it." A subordinate who values his or her job or who does not realize the ethical questions involved may feel pressure to do something unethical to obtain the data.

There are five power bases from which one person may influence another: (1) reward power, (2) coercive power, (3) legitimate power, (4) expert power, and (5) referent power.[33] These five bases of power can be used to motivate individuals either ethically or unethically.

REWARD POWER   **Reward power** refers to a person's ability to influence the behavior of others by offering them something desirable. Typical rewards might be money, status, or promotion. Consider, for example, a retail salesperson who has two watches (a Timex and a Casio) for sale. Let's assume that the Timex is of higher quality than the Casio but is priced about the same. In the absence of any form of reward power, the salesperson would logically attempt to sell the Timex watch. However, if Casio gave him an extra 10 percent commission, he would probably focus his efforts on selling the Casio watch. This "carrot dangling" and incentives have been shown to be very effective in getting people to change their behavior in the long run. In the short run, however, it is not as effective as coercive power.

COERCIVE POWER   **Coercive power** is essentially the opposite of reward power. Instead of rewarding a person for doing something, coercive power penalizes actions or behavior. As an example, suppose a valuable client asks an industrial salesperson for a bribe and insinuates that he will take his business elsewhere if his demands are not met. Although the salesperson believes bribery is unethical, her boss has told her that she must keep the client happy or lose her chance at promotion. The boss is imposing a negative sanction if certain actions are not performed. Every year 20 percent of Enron's workforce was asked to leave as they were ranked as "needs improvement" or other issues were noted. Employees, not wanting to fall into the bottom 20 percent went along with the corporate culture, which might include complacency toward corruption.[34]

Coercive power relies on fear to change behavior. For this reason, it has been found to be more effective in changing behavior in the short run than in the long run. Coercion is often employed in situations where there is an extreme imbalance in power. However, people who are continually subjected to coercion may seek a counterbalance by aligning themselves with other, more powerful persons or by simply leaving the organization. In firms that use coercive power, relationships usually break down in the long run. Power is an ethical issue not only for individuals but also for work groups that establish policy for large corporations.

LEGITIMATE POWER   **Legitimate power** stems from the belief that a certain person has the right to exert influence and that certain others have an obligation to accept it. The titles and positions of authority that organizations bestow on individuals appeal to this traditional view of power. Many people readily acquiesce to those who wield legitimate power, sometimes committing acts that are contrary to their beliefs and values. Betty Vinson, an accountant at WorldCom, objected to her supervisor's requests to produce improper accounting entries in an effort to conceal WorldCom's deteriorating financial condition. She finally gave in to their requests, being told this was the only way to save the company. She and other WorldCom accountants eventually plead guilty to conspiracy and fraud charges. She was sentenced to five months in prison and five months of house arrest.[35]

Such staunch loyalty to authority figures can also be seen in corporations that have strong charismatic leaders and centralized structures. In business, if a superior tells an employee to increase sales "no matter what it takes" and that employee has a strong affiliation to legitimate power, the employee may try anything to fulfill that order.

EXPERT POWER   **Expert power** is derived from a person's knowledge (or the perception that the person possesses knowledge). Expert power usually stems from a superior's credibility with subordinates. Credibility, and thus expert power, is positively related to the number of years that a person has worked in a firm or industry, the person's education, or the honors that he or she has received for performance. Others who perceive a person to be an expert on a specific topic can also confer expert power on him or her. A relatively low-level secretary may have expert power because he or she knows specific details about how the business operates and can even make suggestions on how to inflate revenue through expense reimbursements.

Expert power may cause ethical problems when it is used to manipulate others or to gain an unfair advantage. Physicians, lawyers, or consultants can take unfair advantage of unknowing clients, for example. Accounting firms may gain extra income by ignoring concerns about the accuracy of financial data that they are provided in an audit.

REFERENT POWER   **Referent power** may exist when one person perceives that his or her goals or objectives are similar to another's. The second person may attempt to influence the first to take actions that will lead both to achieve their objectives. Because they share the same objective, the person influenced by the other will perceive the other's use of referent power as beneficial. For this power relationship to be effective, however, some sort of empathy must exist between the individuals. Identification with others helps boost the decision maker's confidence when making a decision, thus increasing his or her referent power.

Consider the following situation: Lisa Jones, a manager in the accounting department of a manufacturing firm, has asked Michael Wong, a salesperson, to speed up the delivery of sales contracts, which usually take about one month to process after a deal is reached. Michael protests that he is not to blame for the slow process. Rather than threaten to slow delivery of Michael's commission checks (coercive power), Lisa makes use of referent power. She invites Michael to lunch, and they discuss some of their work concerns, including the problem of slow-moving documentation. They agree that if document processing cannot be speeded up, both will be hurt. Lisa then suggests that Michael start faxing contracts instead of mailing them. He agrees to give it a try, and within several weeks the contracts are moving faster. Lisa's job is made easier, and Michael gets his commission checks a little sooner.

The five bases of power are not mutually exclusive. People typically use several power bases to effect change in others. Although power in itself is neither ethical nor unethical, its use can raise ethical issues. Sometimes a leader uses power to manipulate a situation or a person's values in a way that creates a conflict with the person's value structure. For example, a manager who forces an employee to choose between staying home with his sick child and keeping his job is using coercive power, which creates a direct conflict with the employee's values.

MOTIVATING ETHICAL BEHAVIOR

A leader's ability to motivate subordinates plays a key role in maintaining an ethical organization. **Motivation** is a force within the individual that focuses his or her behavior toward achieving a goal. To create motivation, an organization offers incentives to encourage employees to work toward organizational objectives. Understanding motivation is important to the effective management of people, and it also helps explain their ethical behavior. For example, a person who aspires to higher positions in an organization may sabotage a coworker's project so as to make that person look bad. This unethical behavior is directly related to the first employee's ambition (motivation) to rise in the organization.

As businesspeople move into middle management and beyond, higher-order needs (social, esteem, and recognition) tend to become more important than lower-order needs (salary, safety, and job security).[36] Research has shown that an individual's career stage, age, organization size, and geographic location affect the relative priority that he or she gives to satisfying respect, self-esteem, and basic physiological needs.

From an ethics perspective, needs or goals may change as a person progresses through the ranks of the company. This shift may cause or help solve problems depending on that person's current ethical status relative to the company or society. For example, junior executives might inflate purchase or sales orders, overbill time worked on projects, or accept cash gratuities if they are worried about providing for their families' basic physical necessities. As they continue up the ladder and are able to fulfill these needs, such concerns may become less important. Consequently, these managers may go back to obeying company policy or culture and be more concerned with internal recognition and achievement than their families' physical needs.

An individual's hierarchy of needs may influence his or her motivation and ethical behavior. After basic needs such as food, working conditions (existence needs), and survival are satisfied, relatedness needs and growth needs become important. **Relatedness needs** are satisfied by social and interpersonal relationships, and **growth needs** are satisfied by creative or productive activities.[37] Consider what happens when a new employee, Jill Taylor, joins a company. At first Jill is concerned about working conditions, pay, and security (existence needs). After some time on the job, she feels she has satisfied these needs and begins to focus on developing good interpersonal relations with coworkers. When these relatedness needs have been satisfied, Jill wants to advance to a more challenging job. However, she learns that a higher-level job would require her to travel a lot. She greatly values her family life and feels that travel and nights away from home would not be good for her. She decides, therefore, not to work toward a promotion (resulting in a "need frustration"). Instead, she decides to focus on furthering good interpersonal relations with her coworkers. This is termed *frustration-regression* because, to reduce her anxiety, Jill is now focusing on an area (interpersonal relations) not related to her main problem: the need for a more challenging job. In this example, Jill's need for promotion has been modified by her values. To feel productive, she attempts to fill her needs by going back to an earlier stage in her hierarchy of needs. Whatever her present job is, Jill would continue to emphasize high performance in it. But this regression creates frustration that may lead Jill to seek other employment.

Examining the role that motivation plays in ethics offers a way to relate business ethics to the broader social context in which workers live and the deeper moral assumptions on which society depends. Workers are individuals and they will be motivated by a variety of personal interests. Although we keep emphasizing that managers are positioned to exert pressure and force individuals' compliance on ethically related issues, we also acknowledge that an individual's personal ethics and needs will significantly affect his or her ethical decisions.

ORGANIZATIONAL STRUCTURE AND BUSINESS ETHICS

An organization's structure is important to the study of business ethics because the various roles and job descriptions that comprise that structure may create opportunities for unethical behavior.[38] The structure of organizations can be described in many ways. For simplicity's sake, we discuss two broad categories of organizational structures—centralized and decentralized. Note that these are not mutually exclusive structures; in the real world, organizational structures exist on a continuum. Table 7–5 compares some strengths and weaknesses of centralized and decentralized structures.

In a **centralized organization,** decision-making authority is concentrated in the hands of top-level managers, and little authority is delegated to lower levels. Responsibility, both internal and external, rests with top-level managers. This structure is especially suited for organizations that make high-risk decisions and whose lower-level managers are not highly skilled in decision making. It is also suitable for organizations in which production processes are routine and efficiency is of primary importance. These organizations are usually extremely bureaucratic, and the division of labor is typically very well defined. Each worker knows his or her job and what is specifically expected, and each has a clear understanding of how to carry out assigned tasks. Centralized organizations stress formal rules, policies, and procedures, backed up with elaborate control systems. Their codes of ethics may specify the techniques to be used for decision making. General Motors, the Internal Revenue Service, and the U.S. Army are examples of centralized organizations.

| TABLE 7–5 | Structural Comparison of Organizational Types | |

	Emphasis	
Characteristic	**Decentralized**	**Centralized**
Hierarchy of authority	Decentralized	Centralized
Flexibility	High	Low
Adaptability	High	Low
Problem recognition	High	Low
Implementation	Low	High
Dealing with changes in environmental complexity	Good	Poor
Rules and procedures	Few and informal	Many and formal
Division of labor	Ambiguous	Clear-cut
Span of control	Few employees	Many employees
Use of managerial techniques	Minimal	Extensive
Coordination and control	Informal and personal	Formal and impersonal

Because of their top-down approach and the distance between employee and de-cision maker, centralized organizational structures can lead to unethical acts. If the centralized organization is very bureaucratic, some employees may behave according to "the letter of the law" rather than the spirit. For example, a centralized organiza-tion can have a policy about bribes that does not include wording about donating to a client's favorite charity before or after a sale. Such donations or gifts can, in some cases, be construed as a tacit bribe because the employee buyer could be swayed by the do-nation, or gift, to act in a less than favorable way or not to act in the best interests of his or her firm.

Other ethical concerns may arise in centralized structures because they typically have very little upward communication. Top-level managers may not be aware of prob-lems and unethical activity. Some companies' use of sweatshop labor may be one man-ifestation of this lack of upward communication. Sweatshops produce products such as garments by employing laborers, sometimes forced immigrant labor, who often work twelve- to sixteen-hour shifts for little or no pay. Many illegal immigrants in Eu-rope become indentured slaves or earn little more than the food they eat. By out-sourcing production to such sweatshops, small- and mid-size suppliers are able to offer products to retailers that beat or match the lowest global market prices. Many of these products end up in leading retailers' stores because their suppliers' top managers claim they were not aware of how their products were made.[39]

Another ethical issue that may arise in centralized organizations is blame shifting, or scapegoating. People may try to transfer blame for their actions to others who are not responsible. The specialization and significant division of labor in centralized or-ganizations can also create ethical problems. Employees may not understand how their actions can affect the overall organization because they work on one piece of a much larger puzzle. This lack of connectedness can lead employees to engage in unethical behavior because they fail to understand the overall ramifications of their behavior.

In a **decentralized organization,** decision-making authority is delegated as far down the chain of command as possible. Such organizations have relatively few formal rules, and coordination and control are usually informal and personal. They focus instead on increasing the flow of information. As a result, one of the main strengths of decentralized organizations is their adaptability and early recognition of external change. With greater flexibility, managers can react quickly to changes in their ethical environment. A parallel weakness of decentralized organizations is the difficulty that they have in responding quickly to changes in policy and procedures established by top management. In addition, independent profit centers within a decentralized organization may deviate from organizational objectives. Other decentralized firms may look no further than the local community for their ethical standards. For example, if a firm that produces toxic wastes leaves decisions on disposal to lower-level operating units, the managers of those units may feel that they have solved their waste-disposal problem as long as they find a way to dump wastes outside their immediate community. Table 7–6 gives examples of centralized versus decentralized organizations and describes their corporate culture.

Due to the strict formalization and implementation of ethics policies and procedures in centralized organizations, they tend to be more ethical in their practices than decentralized organizations. Centralized organizations may also exert more influence on their employees because they have a central core of policies and codes of ethical conduct. Decentralized organizations give employees extensive decision-making autonomy because management empowers the employees. However, it is also true that decentralized organizations may be able to avoid ethical dilemmas by tailoring their decisions to the specific situations, laws, and values of a particular community. If widely shared values are in place in decentralized organizations, there may be no need for excessive compliance programs. However, different units in the company may evolve diverse value systems and approaches to ethical decision making. For example, a high-tech defense firm like Lockheed Martin, which employs more than two hundred thousand people, might have to cope with many different decisions on the same ethical issue if it did not have a centralized ethics program. Boeing has become more centralized since the entrance of CEO W. James McNerney, Jr., and exit of previous CEO

TABLE 7–6	Examples of Centralized and Decentralized Corporate Cultures	
Company	**Organizational Culture**	**Characterized by**
Nike	Decentralized	Creativity, freedom, informality
Southwest Airlines	Decentralized	Fun, teamwork orientation, loyalty
General Motors	Centralized	Unions, adherence to task assignments, structured
Microsoft	Decentralized	Creative, investigative, fast paced
Procter & Gamble	Centralized	Experienced, dependable, a rich history and tradition of products, powerful

Harry Stonecipher who carried on a relationship with a female vice president of the company, resulting in his exit. Boeing had gone through several years of ethics and legal difficulties including the jailing of the former CFO for illegal job negotiations with Pentagon officials, indictment of a manager for stealing twenty-five thousand pages of proprietary documents, abuse of attorney–client privilege to cover up internal studies showing pay inequities, and other scandals.[40]

Unethical behavior is possible in either centralized or decentralized structures when specific corporate cultures permit or encourage workers to deviate from accepted standards or ignore corporate legal and ethical responsibilities. Centralized firms may have a more difficult time uprooting unethical activity than decentralized organizations. The latter may have a more fluid history in which changes affect only a small portion of the company. Often, when a centralized firm uncovers unethical activity and it appears to be pervasive, the leadership is removed so that the old unethical culture can be uprooted and replaced with a more ethical one. For example, Mitsubishi Motors suggested significant management changes after it was discovered that a cover-up of auto defects had been going on for more than two decades.

Some centralized organizations are seeking to restructure to become more decentralized, flexible, and adaptive to the needs of employees and customers. In other cases, entire industries are being impacted by a trend of decentralization. For example, many software companies, such as Citrix Systems, can cut their employee costs by decentralizing and operating development centers in Florida, Washington, and California.[41] Decentralized decisions about ethics and social responsibility allow regional or local operators to set policy and establish conduct requirements.

GROUP DIMENSIONS OF CORPORATE STRUCTURE AND CULTURE

When discussing corporate culture, we tend to focus on the organization as a whole. But corporate values, beliefs, patterns, and rules are often expressed through smaller groups within the organization. Moreover, individual groups within organizations often adopt their own rules and values.

Types of Groups

Two main categories of groups affect ethical behavior in business. A **formal group** is defined as an assembly of individuals that has an organized structure accepted explicitly by the group. An **informal group** is defined as two or more individuals with a common interest but without an explicit organizational structure.

FORMAL GROUPS Formal groups can be divided into committees and work groups and teams.

Committees A *committee* is a formal group of individuals assigned to a specific task. Often a single manager could not complete the task, or management may believe that a committee can better represent different constituencies and improve the coordination and implementation of decisions. Committees may meet regularly to review performance, develop plans, or make decisions. Most formal committees in organizations operate on an ongoing basis, but their membership may change over time. A committee is an excellent example of a situation in which coworkers and significant others within the organization can influence ethical decisions. Committee decisions are to some extent legitimized because of agreement or majority rule. In this respect, minority views on issues such as ethics can be pushed aside through the majority's authority. Committees bring diverse personal moral values into the ethical decision-making process, which may expand the number of alternatives considered.

The main disadvantage of committees is that they typically take longer to reach a decision than an individual would. Committee decisions are also generally more conservative than those made by individuals and may be based on unnecessary compromise rather than on identifying the best alternative. Also inherent in the committee structure is a lack of individual responsibility. Because of the diverse composition of the group, members may not be committed or willing to assume responsibility for the group decision. Groupthink may emerge and the majority can explain ethical considerations away.

Although many organizations have financial, diversity, personnel, or social responsibility committees, only a very few organizations have committees that are devoted exclusively to ethics. An ethics committee might raise ethical concerns, resolve ethical dilemmas in the organization, and create or update the company's code of ethics. Motorola, for example, maintains a Business Ethics Compliance Committee, which interprets, classifies, communicates, and enforces the company's code and ethics initiatives. An ethics committee can gather information on functional areas of the business and examine manufacturing practices, personnel policies, dealings with suppliers, financial reporting, and sales techniques to find out whether the company's practices are ethical. Though much of a corporation's culture operates informally, an ethics committee would be a highly formalized approach for dealing with ethical issues.

Ethics committees can be misused if they are established for the purpose of legitimizing management's ethical standards on some issue. For example, ethics committees may be quickly assembled for political purposes—that is, to make a symbolic decision on some event that has occurred within the company. If the CEO or manager in charge selects committee members who will produce a predetermined outcome, the ethics committee may not help the organization resolve its ethical issues in the long run. For example, organizations have been known to quickly assemble an ethics committee to fire someone for a minor infraction because they wanted him or her out of the organization and needed an excuse for termination.

Ethics committee members may also fail to understand their role or function. If they attempt to apply their own personal ethics to complex business issues, resolving ethical issues may be difficult. Because most people's personal ethical perspectives differ, the committee may experience conflict. Even if the committee members reach a consensus, they may enforce their personal beliefs rather than the organization's standards on certain ethical issues.

Ethics committees should be organized around professional, business-related issues that occur internally. In general, the ethics committee should formulate policy, develop ethical standards, and then assess the organization's compliance with these requirements. Ethics committees should be aware of their industries' codes of ethics, community standards, and the organizational culture in which they work. Although ethics committees do not always succeed, they can provide one of the best organizational approaches to resolving internal ethical issues fairly. As one of many examples in the corporate world, Sunstrand Corporation, a *Fortune* 500 company, has established employee-managed ethics committees at each of its facilities to stimulate employees' "ownership" of their ethical conduct and to distribute accountability throughout the organization.

Work Groups and Teams   *Work groups* are used to subdivide duties within specific functional areas of a company. For example, on an automotive assembly line, one work group might install the seats and interior design elements of the vehicle while another group installs all the dashboard instruments. This enables production supervisors to specialize in a specific area and provide expert advice to work groups.

Whereas work groups operate within a single functional area, *teams* bring together the functional expertise of employees from several different areas of the organization—for example, finance, marketing, and production—on a single project, such as developing a new product. Many manufacturing firms, including General Motors, Westinghouse, and Procter & Gamble, are using the team concept to improve participative management. Ethical conflicts may arise because team members come from different functional areas. Each member of the team has a particular role to play and has probably had limited interaction with other members of the team. Members may have encountered different ethical issues in their own functional areas and may therefore bring different viewpoints when the team faces an ethical issue. For example, a production quality-control employee might believe that side-impact air bags should be standard equipment on all automobiles for safety reasons. A marketing member of the team may reply that the cost of adding the air bags would force the company to raise prices beyond the reach of some consumers. The production employee might then argue that it is unethical for an automobile maker to fail to include a safety feature that could save hundreds of lives. Such conflicts often occur when members of different organizational groups must interact. However, airing viewpoints representative of all the functional areas helps provide more options from which to choose.

Work groups and teams provide the organizational structure for group decision making. One of the reasons why individuals cannot implement their personal ethical beliefs in organizations is that so many decisions are reached collectively by work groups. However, those who have legitimate power are in a position to influence ethics-related activities. The work group and team often sanction certain activities as ethical or define others as unethical.

INFORMAL GROUPS   In addition to the groups that businesses formally organize and recognize—such as committees, work groups, and teams—most organizations have a number of informal groups. These groups are usually composed of individuals, often from the same department, who have similar interests and band together for companionship or for purposes that may or may not be relevant to the goals of the organization. For example, four or five people who have similar tastes in outdoor activities and music may discuss their interests while working, and they may meet outside work for dinner, concerts, sports events, or other activities. Other informal groups may evolve to form a union, improve working conditions or benefits, get a manager fired, or protest work practices that they view as unfair. Informal groups may generate disagreement and conflict, or they may enhance morale and job satisfaction.

Informal groups help develop informal channels of communication, sometimes called the "grapevine," which are important in every organization. Informal communication flows up, down, diagonally, and horizontally, not necessarily following the communication lines on a company's organization chart. Information passed along the grapevine may relate to the job, the organization, or an ethical issue, or it may simply be gossip and rumors. The grapevine can act as an early warning system for employees. If employees learn informally that their company may be sold or that a particular action will be condemned as unethical by top management or the community, they have time to think about what they will do. Because gossip is not uncommon in an organization, the information passed along the grapevine is not always accurate. Managers who understand how the grapevine works can use it to reinforce acceptable values and beliefs.

The grapevine is also an important source of information for individuals to assess ethical behavior within their organization. One way an employee can determine acceptable behavior is to ask friends and peers in informal groups about the consequences of certain actions such as lying to a customer about a product-safety issue. The corporate culture may provide employees with a general understanding of the patterns and rules that govern behavior, but informal groups make this culture come alive and provide direction for employees' daily choices. For example, if a new employee learns anecdotally through the grapevine that the organization does not punish ethical violations, he or she may seize the next opportunity for unethical behavior if it accomplishes the organization's objectives. There is a general tendency to discipline top sales performers more leniently than poor sales performers for engaging in identical forms of unethical selling behavior. A superior sales record appears to induce more lenient forms of discipline, despite organizational policies that state otherwise.[42] In this case, the grapevine has clearly communicated that the organization rewards those who break the ethical rules to achieve desirable objectives.

Group Norms

Group norms are standards of behavior that groups expect of their members. Just as corporate culture establishes behavior guidelines for an organization's members, so group norms help define acceptable and unacceptable behavior within a group. In particular, group norms define the limit allowed on deviations from group expectations.

Most work organizations, for example, develop norms that govern groups' rates of production and communication with management as well as providing a general understanding of behavior considered right or wrong, ethical or unethical, within the group. For example, an employee who reports to a supervisor that a coworker has covered up a serious production error may be punished by other group members for this breach of confidence. Other members of the group may glare at the informant, who has violated a group norm, and refuse to talk to or sit by him or her.

Norms have the power to enforce a strong degree of conformity among group members. At the same time, norms define the different roles for various positions within the organization. Thus, a low-ranking member of a group may be expected to carry out an unpleasant task such as accepting responsibility for someone else's ethical mistake. Abusive behavior toward new or lower-ranking employees could be a norm in an informal group.

Sometimes group norms conflict with the values and rules prescribed by the organization's culture. For example, the organization may have policies about the personal use of computers during work hours and may use rewards and punishments to encourage this culture. In a particular informal group, however, norms may encourage using computers for personal use during work hours and avoiding management's attention. Issues of equity may arise in this situation if other groups believe they are unfairly forced to follow policies that are not enforced. These other employees may complain to management or to the offending group. If they believe management is not taking corrective action, they, too, may use computers for personal use, thus hurting the whole organization's productivity. For this reason, management must carefully monitor not only the corporate culture but also the norms of all the various groups within the organization. Sanctions may be necessary to bring in line a group whose norms deviate sharply from the overall culture.

VARIATION IN EMPLOYEE CONDUCT

Although the corporation is required to take responsibility for conducting its business ethically, a substantial amount of research indicates that significant differences exist in the values and philosophies that influence how the individuals that comprise corporations make ethical decisions.[43] In other words, because people are culturally diverse and have different values, they interpret situations differently and will vary in the ethical decisions they make on the same ethical issue.

Table 7–7 shows that approximately 10 percent of employees take advantage of situations to further their own personal interests. These individuals are more likely to manipulate, cheat, or be self-serving when the benefits gained from doing so are greater than the penalties for the misconduct. Such employees may choose to take office sup-

TABLE 7-7	Variation in Employee Conduct*		
10%	**40%**	**40%**	**10%**
Follow their own values and beliefs; believe that their values are superior to those of others in the company.	Always try to follow company policies.	Go along with the work group.	Take advantage of situations if the penalty is less than the benefit and the risk of being caught is low.

*These percentages are based on a number of studies in the popular press and data gathered by the authors. These percentages are not exact and represent a general typology that may vary by organization.

SOURCE: From John Fraedrich and O.C. Ferrell, "Cognitive Consistency of Marketing Managers in Ethical Situations," *Journal of the Academy of Marketing Science*, Summer 1992, Vol. 20, pp. 243–252. Copyright © 1992 by Sage Publications, Inc. Reprinted by permission of Sage Publications, Inc.

plies from work for personal use if the only penalty they may suffer if caught is having to pay for the supplies. The lower the risk of being caught, the higher is the likelihood that the 10 percent most likely to take advantage will be involved in unethical activities.

Another 40 percent of workers go along with the work group on most matters. These employees are most concerned about the social implications of their actions and want to fit into the organization. Although they have their own personal opinions, they are easily influenced by what people around them are doing. These individuals may know that using office supplies for personal use is improper, yet they view it as acceptable because their coworkers do so. These employees rationalize their action by saying that the use of office supplies is one of the benefits of working at their particular business and it must be acceptable because the company does not enforce a policy precluding the behavior. Coupled with this philosophy is the belief that no one will get into trouble for doing what everybody else is doing, for there is safety in numbers.

About 40 percent of a company's employees, as shown in Table 7–7, always try to follow company policies and rules. These workers not only have a strong grasp of their corporate culture's definition of acceptable behavior but also attempt to comply with codes of ethics, ethics training, and other communications about appropriate conduct. If the company has a policy prohibiting taking office supplies from work, these employees probably would observe it. However, they likely would not speak out about the 40 percent who choose to go along with the work group, for these employees prefer to focus on their jobs and steer clear of any organizational misconduct. If the company fails to communicate standards of appropriate behavior, members of this group will devise their own.

The final 10 percent of employees try to maintain formal ethical standards that focus on rights, duties, and rules. They embrace values that assert certain inalienable rights and actions, which they perceive to be always ethically correct. In general, members of this group believe that their values are right and superior to the values of others in the company, or even to the company's value system, when an ethical conflict arises. These individuals have a tendency to report the misconduct of others or to speak out when they view activities within the company as unethical. Consequently, members of this group would probably report colleagues who take office supplies.

The significance of this variation in the way individuals behave ethically is simply this: Employees use different approaches when making ethical decisions. Because of the probability that a large percentage of any work group will either take advantage of a situation or at least go along with the work group, it is vital that companies provide communication and control mechanisms to maintain an ethical culture. Companies that fail to monitor activities and enforce ethics policies provide a low-risk environment for those employees who are inclined to take advantage of situations to accomplish their personal, and sometimes unethical, objectives.

Good business practice and concern for the law requires organizations to recognize this variation in employees' desire to be ethical. The percentages cited in Table 7–7 are only estimates, and the actual percentages of each type of employee may vary widely across organizations based on individuals and corporate culture. The specific percentages are less important than the fact that our research has identified these variations as existing within most organizations. Organizations should focus particular attention

TABLE 7–8	Penalties for Convictions of Organizational Wrongdoing
Executive/Company	**Trial Outcome**
Franklin Brown, former general counsel, Rite Aid	Convicted and sentenced to 10 years in prison.
Bernard Ebbers, former chairman and CEO, WorldCom	Convicted and sentenced to 25 years to life in prison.
Dennis Kozlowski, former CEO, Tyco	Mistrial in first trial; in second, convicted and sentenced to 8⅓ years to 25 years in prison.
Jamie Olis, former vice president of finance, Dynegy	Convicted and sentenced to 24 years in prison without the chance of parole; the sentence was tossed out on appeal.
Frank Quattrone, former investment banker, CSFB	Convicted in second trial, but conviction overturned due to error in jury instructions.
John Rigas, founder, Adelphia	Convicted and sentenced to 15 years in prison.
Richard Scrushy, founder, HealthSouth	Acquitted by the Justice Department but found guilty by an Alabama jury; awaits sentencing.
Theodore Sihpol, broker, Bank of America	Acquitted on twenty-nine of thirty-three criminal counts; no retrial on remaining counts.
Martha Stewart, founder, Martha Stewart Living Omnimedia	Convicted and sentenced to 5 months in prison and 5 months of home confinement.

SOURCE: From *Wall Street Journal Online*, "White-Collar Defendants: Take the Stand, or Not?," April 2, 2006. Copyright © 2006 by Dow Jones & Company, Inc. Reproduced with permission of Dow Jones & Company, Inc. via Copyright Clearance Center. http://online.wsj.com (accessed April 6, 2006).

on managers who oversee the day-to-day operations of employees within the company. They should also provide training and communication to ensure that the business operates ethically, that it does not become the victim of fraud or theft, and that employees, customers, and other stakeholders are not abused through the misconduct of people who have a pattern of unethical behavior.

As we have seen throughout this book, many examples can be cited of employees and managers who have no concern for ethical conduct but are nonetheless hired and placed in positions of trust. Some corporations continue to support executives who ignore environmental concerns, poor working conditions, or defective products, or who engage in accounting fraud. Executives who can get results, regardless of the consequences, are often admired and lauded, especially in the business press. When their unethical or even illegal actions become public knowledge, however, they risk more than the loss of their positions. Table 7–8 summarizes the penalties that corporate executives have experienced over the past several years.

CAN PEOPLE CONTROL THEIR OWN ACTIONS WITHIN A CORPORATE CULTURE?

Many people find it hard to believe that an organization's culture can exert so strong an influence on individuals' behavior within the organization. In our society, we want to believe that individuals control their own destiny. A popular way of viewing business ethics is therefore to see it as a reflection of the alternative moral philosophies that individuals use to resolve their personal moral dilemmas. As this chapter has shown, however, ethical decisions within organizations are often made by committees and formal and informal groups, not by individuals. Decisions related to financial reporting, advertising, product design, sales practices, and pollution-control issues are often beyond the influence of individuals alone. In addition, these decisions are frequently based on business rather than personal goals.

Most new employees in highly bureaucratic organizations have almost no input into the basic operating rules and procedures for getting things done. Along with learning sales tactics and accounting procedures, employees may be taught to ignore a design flaw in a product that could be dangerous to users. Although many personal ethics issues may seem straightforward and easy to resolve, individuals entering business will usually need several years of experience within a specific industry to understand how to resolve ethical close calls. For example, what constitutes misleading advertising? When Corvette introduced the new C-6 design, they wanted to reach a younger demographic. They hired Madonna's husband, Guy Richie, and used the Rolling Stones singing "Jumpin' Jack Flash" to create a memorable TV commercial showing a young boy fantasizing about being able to drive the Corvette. General Motors received complaints from parents and organizations indicating that it was inappropriate for GM to show a clearly underage driver, driving recklessly, even if it was a fantasy. GM responded quickly by withdrawing the commercial from the airwaves. How could this problem have been prevented? Perhaps, GM should have screened the ads to a variety of audiences, not just the target audience for the vehicle. The only thing that is certain is that one person's opinion or maybe even a work group's opinion is insufficient in dealing with complex decisions.

It is not our purpose to suggest that you ought to go along with management or the group on business ethics issues. Honesty and open discussion of ethical issues are important to successful ethical decision making. We believe that most companies and businesspeople try to make ethical decisions. However, because there is so much difference between individuals, ethical conflict is inevitable. If you manage and supervise others, it will be necessary to maintain ethical policies for your organization and report misconduct that occurs. This means that ethics is not just a personal matter.

Regardless of how a person or organization views the acceptability of a particular activity, if society judges it to be wrong or unethical, then this larger view directly affects the organization's ability to achieve its goals. Not all activities deemed unethical by society are illegal. But if public opinion decries or consumers protest against a particular activity, the result may be legislation that restricts or bans a specific business practice. For instance, concern about teen smoking prompted the government to regulate the placement of cigarette advertising and curb the use of characters and approaches designed to appeal to children. Public concern and outrage at the growth in cigarette smoking among minors spurred much of this intervention. Besieged by mounting negative opinion, numerous class-action lawsuits, and a landmark settlement with forty-six states, Philip Morris USA, producer of the world's best-selling cigarette, was forced to modify its marketing strategies, in particular to avoid marketing its products to minors. The company now uses the Internet, TV commercials, school publications, and print ads to encourage teenagers not to smoke. Philip Morris has spent over $600 million on youth smoking-prevention advertising, providing grants to youth-development organizations, producing tools and resources to help parents talk to their children about the hazards of smoking, and supporting youth access prevention initiatives to help keep cigarettes out of children's hands.[44]

If a person believes that his or her personal ethics severely conflict with the ethics of the work group and of superiors in an organization, that individual's only alternative may be to leave the organization. In the highly competitive employment market of the twenty-first century, quitting a job because of an ethical conflict requires courage and, possibly, the ability to survive without a job. Obviously, there are no easy answers for resolving ethical conflicts between the organization and the individual. Our goal is not to tell you what you should do. But we do believe that the more you know about how ethical decision making occurs within organizations, the more opportunity you will have to influence decisions positively and resolve ethical conflict more effectively.

SUMMARY

Corporate culture refers to the set of values, beliefs, goals, norms, and ways of solving problems that the members (employees) of an organization share. These shared values may be formally expressed or unspoken. Corporate cultures can be classified in several ways, and a cultural audit can be conducted to identify an organization's culture. If an organization's culture rewards unethical behavior, people within the company are more likely to act unethically. A company's failure to monitor or manage its culture may foster questionable behavior.

Leadership—the ability or authority to guide others toward achieving goals—has a significant impact on the ethical decision-making process because leaders have the power to motivate others and enforce both the organization's rules and policies and their own viewpoints. A leader must not only gain the respect of his or her followers but also provide a standard of ethical conduct. Leaders exert power to influence the behaviors and decisions of subordinates. There are five power bases from which a leader may influence ethical behavior: reward power, coercive power, legitimate power, expert power, and referent power. Leaders also attempt to motivate subordinates; motivation is an internal force that focuses an individual's behavior toward achieving a goal. It can be created by the incentives that an organization offers employees.

The structure of an organization may create opportunities to engage in unethical behavior. In a centralized organization, decision-making authority is concentrated in the hands of top managers, and little authority is delegated to lower levels. In a decentralized organization, decision-making authority is delegated as far down the chain of command as possible. Centralized organizations tend to be more ethical than decentralized ones because they enforce more rigid controls such as codes of ethics and corporate policies on ethical practices. However, unethical conduct can occur in both types of structures.

In addition to the values and customs that represent the culture of an organization, individual groups within the organization often adopt their own rules and values and even create subcultures. The main types of groups are formal groups—which include committees, work groups, and teams—and informal groups. Informal groups often feed an informal channel of communication called the "grapevine." Group norms are standards of behavior that groups expect of their members. They help define acceptable and unacceptable behavior within a group and especially define the limits on deviating from group expectations. Sometimes group norms conflict with the values and rules prescribed by the organization's culture.

Sometimes an employee's own personal ethical standards conflict with what is expected of him or her as a member of an organization and its corporate culture. This is especially true given that an organization's ethical decisions are often resolved by committees, formal groups, and informal groups rather than by individuals. When such ethical conflict is severe, the individual may have to decide whether to leave the organization.

IMPORTANT TERMS FOR REVIEW		
differential association	relatedness needs
whistle-blowing	growth needs
reward power	centralized organization
coercive power	decentralized organization
legitimate power	formal group
expert power	informal group
referent power	group norm
motivation	

A REAL-LIFE SITUATION*

As Gerard sat down in his expensive new chair, he was worried. What had he gotten himself into? How could things have gone so wrong so fast? It was as if he'd been walking and some truck had blindsided him. Gerard had been with Trawlers Accounting, a medium-size firm, for several years. His wife, Vicky, had a job in the pharmaceutical industry, and their first child was due any day now. The doctor had told her that she would need to stop work early because hers was a high-risk pregnancy. So three months before her due date, she asked and received a four-month leave of absence. This was great, but the leave was without pay. Luckily, Gerard had received a promotion and now headed a department.

Some interesting activities were going on in the accounting industry. For example, Gerard's superior had decided that all CPAs would take exams to become registered investment advisers. The rationale for such a new development was simple. The firm could use its relationships with clients to increase investment revenues. Because of the long-term nature of these relationships with many firms and individuals as well as the implicit sense of honesty that CPAs must bring to their jobs, clients understood that a violation of so high a trust was unlikely—or so Gerard's boss argued. Many of the people in Gerard's department didn't like this new policy; however, some who had passed the exams increased their pay by 15 percent. During lunch, one of Gerard's financial friends engaged him heatedly.

"What you're doing, Gerard, is called unfair competition," the friend accused him. "For example, your CPAs have exclusive access to confidential client taxpayer information, which could give you insight into people's financial needs. Besides, you could easily direct clients to mutual funds that you already own in order to keep your own personal investments afloat. Also, if your people start chasing commissions and fees on mutual funds that go bad, your credibility will become suspect, and you won't be trusted.

Plus, your people will now have to keep abreast of financial, tax, and accounting changes."

When Gerard got to his office, he found that some of his people had been recommending a group of mutual funds that Trawlers had been auditing. Then someone from another of his company's accounting clients, CENA Mutual Funds, telephoned.

"What's the idea of having your people suggest PPI Mutual Funds when they are in direct competition with us?" the caller yelled. "We pay you a lot, Gerard, to do our accounting procedures, and that's how you reward us? I want to know by the end of the day if you are going to continue to push our competitor's product. I don't have to tell you that this will directly affect your department and you. Also, things like this get around the business circles, if you know what I mean."

With these words, the caller hung up on Gerard.

QUESTIONS • EXERCISES

1. Identify any ethical and legal issues of which Gerard needs to be aware.
2. Discuss the advantages and disadvantages of each decision Gerard has made and could make.
3. Discuss the issue of accounting firms going into the financial services market.
4. Discuss the type of groups that are influencing Gerard.

*This case is strictly hypothetical; any resemblance to real persons, companies, or situations is coincidental.

Check Your EQ

Check your EQ, or ethics quotient, by completing the following. Assess your performance to evaluate your overall understanding of the chapter material.

		Yes	No
1.	Decentralized organizations tend to put the blame for unethical behavior on lower-level personnel.	Yes	No
2.	Decentralized organizations give employees extensive decision-making autonomy.	Yes	No
3.	Corporate culture provides rules for behaving within the organization.	Yes	No
4.	An integrative culture shows high concern for performance and little concern for people.	Yes	No
5.	Coercive power works in the same manner as reward power.	Yes	No

ANSWERS: 1. No. That's more likely to occur in centralized organizations. 2. Yes. This is known as empowerment. 3. Yes. Values, beliefs, customs, and ceremonies represent what is acceptable and unacceptable in the organization. 4. No. That's an exacting culture. An integrative culture combines high concern for people and production. 5. No. Coercive power is the opposite of reward power. One offers rewards and the other punishment to encourage appropriate behavior.

Implementing Business Ethics in a Global Economy

PART FOUR

CHAPTER 8
Developing an Effective Ethics Program

Developing an Effective Ethics Program

CHAPTER OBJECTIVES

- ◆ To understand the responsibility of the corporation to be a moral agent
- ◆ To understand why businesses need to develop ethics programs
- ◆ To list the minimum requirements for an ethics program
- ◆ To describe the role of codes of ethics in identifying key risk areas for the organization
- ◆ To identify the keys to successful ethics training, including program types and goals
- ◆ To examine the ways that ethical standards are monitored, audited, and enforced and to understand the need for continuous improvement

CHAPTER OUTLINE

Victoria was starting to wonder about the implications of her actions as well as her company's strategy. She had begun working for Koke International (KI) after graduating from Pacific West University with degrees in both finance and marketing. KI was the leader in franchised home repair outlets in the United States. In twenty-five years, KI had grown from several stores in the Pacific Northwest to two hundred and fifty over much of the United States and Canada. Koke International came to dominate the markets that it entered by undercutting local competitors on price and quality. The lower prices were easy to charge because KI received large quantity discounts from its vendors. The franchise concept also helped create another barrier to entry for KI's competitors. By expanding rapidly, KI was able to spread the costs of marketing to many more stores, giving it still another differential advantage. This active nourishment of its brand image coupled with some technological advances such as just-in-time inventory, electronic scanners, and electronic market niching had sent KI's stock soaring. As a result, it had a 50 percent share of the market. Koke International had done such an excellent job of positioning itself in its field that articles in major business newspapers were calling it "the Microsoft of home improvements." The view was that "KI is going to continue to be a very profitable endeavor, with less expected direct competition in a slow-growth, high-margin market for the future."

Wendy, Victoria's boss, had brought her in on KI's next potential conquest: the New England states of Maine, Vermont, New Hampshire, Connecticut, and Massachusetts.

"This is the last big potential market," Wendy said at a planning session with her senior staff. "I want you to realize that when we launch into these states we're going to have to be ruthless. I'd like your suggestions as to how we're going to eliminate the competition."

One person spoke up: "We first need to recognize that there are only five major players (multiple-store chains), with Home Designs being the largest."

"The top corporate people want us to attack Maine, New Hampshire, and Vermont first and then make a secondary attack on the other two states," interjected Victoria.

"Our buildings are four months from completion," Wendy pointed out, "and the media blitz is due to start one month prior to the twenty-store grand opening. With that much exposed capital from our franchises, we need to make sure everything goes well. Vicky, have you completed your price analysis of all of the surrounding home repair stores?"

"Yes, and you're not going to like the news," Victoria replied. "Many of the stores are going to be extremely competitive relative to our normal pricing. In a few cases, they seem to have an edge."

Wendy turned to Ed. "Ed, how much cash flow/reserves have you been able to calculate from the five players?"

"Well, Wendy, it looks like if we slash our prices for about six months to a year, we could drive all but Home Designs into near bankruptcy, providing that our promotional campaign doesn't have a misstep."

"What about personnel, Frank?" Wendy cut in. "Have you done the usual research to see about hiring away the five players' key personnel?"

"Yes, but many won't go unless they get a 50 percent raise, which is way out of line with our other stores."

At this point, Wendy slammed her fist on the table and shouted, "I'm tired of hearing negative reports! It's our job to drive out the competition, so I want solutions!"

There was a long silence in the room. Wendy was noted for her quick temper and her quick firings when things didn't go as planned. She had been the first woman to make it this high in the company, and it wasn't the result of being overly pleasant.

"So this is what we're going to do," Wendy said softly. "Frank, you're going to hire those key people at a 50 percent increase. You're going to keep the unions away from the rest of the people. In eighteen months, when these overpriced employees have trained the others, we'll find some way of getting rid of them. Ed, you're going to lean on the players' bankers. See if we do business with them as well. See what other information you can squeeze out of them. Victoria, since you're the newest, I'm putting you in charge of breaking the pricing problem. I want you to come up with a unique pricing strategy for each of the twenty stores that will consistently undercut the competition for the next eighteen months, even if we have to lose money on everything in the stores! The franchisees will go with this once we explain the payout."

One of the newer staff asked, "If we're successful, doesn't that make us a monopoly in the area? Don't we have to worry about antitrust issues?"

Wendy raised her eyebrow a little and said, "We don't mention the word *monopoly* around here as if it were wrong. It took the Feds decades to break up AT&T. Microsoft was next on their list, and now it's MasterCard. We're in retail. No one has ever had problems with the Feds in this industry. By the time they deal with what we're doing, we will all be retired."

QUESTIONS • EXERCISES

1. Identify the issues of which Victoria needs to be aware.
2. Discuss the implications of each decision that Wendy made.
3. Discuss the issue of monopolies and whether they are right or wrong.

*This case is strictly hypothetical; any resemblance to real persons, companies, or situations is coincidental.

Programs that are designed to foster ethical decision making in business are controversial today because much unethical and illegal business conduct has continued to occur, even in organizations that have adopted such programs. Enron, for example, had a code of ethics and was a member of the Better Business Bureau, yet the company was ruined by unethical activities and corporate scandal. Many business leaders believe that ethics initiatives should arise naturally from a company's corporate culture and that hiring good employees will limit unethical conduct. Moreover, many business executives and board members often do not understand how organizational ethics can be systematically implemented. We believe, however, that a customized ethics and compliance program will help many businesses provide guidance so that employees from diverse backgrounds will understand what behaviors are acceptable (or unacceptable) within the organization. In business, many ethical issues are complex and require that organizations reach a consensus on appropriate action. Top executives and boards of directors must provide the leadership and a system to resolve these issues.

Business ethics programs have the potential to help top managers establish an ethical culture and eliminate the opportunity for unethical conduct. This chapter therefore provides a framework for developing an ethics program that is consistent with research, best practices, and the decision-making process described in Chapter 5, as well as the Federal Sentencing Guidelines for Organizations (FSGO) and the Sarbanes–Oxley Act in Chapter 4. These legislative reforms require both executives and boards of directors to assume responsibility and ensure that ethical standards are properly implemented on a daily basis.

In this chapter, we first provide an assessment of the corporation as an entity in society, and then we give an overview of why businesses need to develop an organizational ethics program. Next, we consider the factors that must be part of such a program: a code of conduct, an ethics officer and the appropriate delegation of authority, an effective ethics-training program, a system for monitoring and supporting ethical compliance, and continual efforts to improve the ethics program. Finally, we consider common mistakes made in designing and implementing ethics programs.

THE RESPONSIBILITY OF THE CORPORATION AS A MORAL AGENT

Increasingly, corporations are viewed not merely as profit-making entities but also as moral agents that are accountable for their conduct to their employees, investors, suppliers, and customers. Companies are more than the sum of their parts or participants. Because corporations are chartered as citizens of a state and/or nation, they generally have the same rights and responsibilities as individuals. Through legislation and court precedents, society holds companies accountable for the conduct of their employees as well as for their decisions and the consequences of those decisions. Publicity in the news media about specific issues such as employee benefits, executive compensation, defective products, competitive practices, and financial reporting contribute to a firm's reputation as a moral agent.

Viewed as moral agents, companies are required to obey the laws and regulations that define acceptable business conduct. However, it is important to acknowledge that they are not human beings who can think through moral issues. Because companies are not human, laws and regulations are necessary to provide formal structural restraints and guidance on ethical issues. Although individuals may attempt to abide by their own values and moral philosophy, as employees they are supposed to act in the company's best interests. Thus, the individual as a moral agent has a moral obligation beyond that of the corporation because it is the individual, not the company, who can think responsibly through complex ethical issues.[1] Figure 8–1 illustrates the basic causes of individual misconduct, the key reason why individuals engage in misconduct to do "whatever it takes to meet business targets."

Though obviously not a person, a corporation can be considered a societal moral agent that is created to perform specific functions in society and is therefore responsible to society for its actions. Because corporations have the characteristics of agents, responsibility for ethical behavior is assigned to them as legal entities as well as to individuals or work groups they employ. As Figure 8–1 indicates, a corporate culture without values and appropriate communication about ethics can facilitate individual misconduct. As such, companies may be punished for wrongdoing and rewarded for good business ethics. The FSGO holds corporations responsible for conduct they engage in as an entity. Some corporate outcomes cannot be tied to one individual or even a group, and misconduct can be the result of a collective pattern of decisions supported by a corporate culture. Therefore, corporations can be held accountable, fined, and even receive the death penalty when they are operating in a manner inconsistent with major legal requirements. Some organizations receive such large fines and negative publicity that they have to go out of business because there is no way to survive under these pressures. On the other hand, companies that have been selected as the top corporate citizens—such as Green Mountain Coffee Roasters, Hewlett-Packard,

| **FIGURE 8-1** | Root Causes of Misconduct |

SOURCE: "KPMG Forensic Integrity Survey 2005–2006,"
http://www.kpmginsiders.com/display_analysis.asp?cs _id=148597 (accessed March 9, 2006).

Advanced Micro Devices, and Motorola—receive awards and positive publicity for being responsible moral agents in our society.[2]

One major misunderstanding in studying business ethics is to assume that a coherent ethical corporate culture will evolve through individual and interpersonal relationships. Because ethics is often viewed as an individual matter, many reason that the best way to develop an ethical corporate culture is to provide character education to employees or to hire individuals with good character and sensitize them to ethical issues. This assumes that ethical conduct will develop through company-wide agreement and consensus. Although these assumptions are laudable and have some truth, the companies that are responsible for most of the economic activity in the world employ thousands of culturally diverse individuals who will never reach agreement on all ethical issues. Many ethical business issues are complex close calls, and the only way to ensure consistent decisions that represent the interests of all stakeholders is to require ethical policies. This chapter provides support for the belief that implementing a centralized corporate ethics program can provide a cohesive, internally consistent set of statements and policies representing the corporation as a moral agent.

THE NEED FOR ORGANIZATIONAL ETHICS PROGRAMS

To understand why companies need to develop ethics programs, consider the following exercise and judge whether each of the described actions is unethical or illegal:

1. You want to skip work to go to a baseball game, but you need a doctor's excuse, so you make up some symptoms so that your insurance company pays for the doctor's visit. (unethical, illegal)

2. While having a latte at Starbucks, you run into an acquaintance who works as a salesperson at a competing firm. You wind up chatting about future product prices. When you get back to your office, you tell your supervisor what you heard. (unethical, illegal)
3. You get fired from your company, but before leaving to take a position with another company, you take a confidential list of client names and telephone numbers that you compiled for your former employer. (unethical, illegal)
4. You receive a loan from your parents to make the down payment on your first home, but when describing the source of the down payment on the mortgage application, you characterize it as a gift. (unethical, illegal)
5. Your manager asks you to book some sales revenue from the next quarter into this quarter's sales report to help reach target sales figures. You agree to do so. (unethical, illegal)

You probably labeled one or more of these five scenarios as unethical rather than illegal. The reality is that all of them are illegal. You may have chosen incorrectly because it is nearly impossible to know every detail of the highly complex laws relevant to these situations. Consider that there are ten thousand laws and regulations associated with the processing and selling of a single hamburger. Unless you are a lawyer who specializes in a particular area, it is difficult to know every law associated with your job. However, you can become more sensitized to what might be unethical or, in this case, illegal. One reason why ethics programs are required in one form or another is to help sensitize employees to the potential legal and ethical issues within their work environments.

As we have mentioned throughout this book, recent ethics scandals in U.S. business have destroyed trust in top management and significantly lowered the public's trust of business. As a result, the chairman of the Securities and Exchange Commission (SEC) issued a challenge for "American organizations to behave more ethically than the law requires to help restore investors' trust."[3] According to a survey by Golin/Harris International, there are five top recommendations to CEOs for rebuilding trust and confidence in American firms. These are making customers the top priority, assuming personal responsibility and accountability, communicating openly and frequently with customers, handling crises more honestly, and sticking to the code of business ethics no matter what.[4] This is a recurring theme among primary stakeholders. As shown in Figure 8–2, 80 percent of investors want more transparency in firms.

Understanding the factors that influence the ethical decision-making process, as discussed in Chapter 5, can help companies encourage ethical behavior and discourage undesirable conduct. Fostering ethical decision making within an organization requires terminating unethical persons and improving the firm's ethical standards. Consider the "bad apple–bad barrel" analogy. Some people are simply "bad apples" who will always do things in their own self-interest regardless of their organization's goals or accepted standards of conduct. Eliminating such bad apples through screening techniques and enforcement of the firm's ethical standards can help improve the firm's overall behavior.[5] For example, ClearOne Communications Inc. fired its CEO and CFO after they were named as defendants in a complaint filed by the SEC. The SEC alleged that they directed sales personnel to push extra products on customers in

FIGURE 8-2	Most Investors Want Transparency

Do you think that large corporations provide enough information about how they operate?

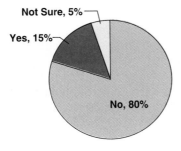

SOURCE: "TIAA-CREF Trust in America Survey of 1001 Respondents with Investments in Stocks, Bonds, or Other Investment Products," Snapshots, *USA Today,* January 5, 2006, B1.

addition to their orders so as to inflate sales and earnings.[6] In this case, the CEO and CFO not only allegedly directed employees to act unethically but also contributed to an unethical corporate culture.

Organizations also can become "bad barrels," not because the individuals within them are bad, but because the pressures to succeed create opportunities that reward unethical decisions. In the case of such bad barrels, the firms must redesign their image and culture to conform to industry and social standards of acceptable behavior.[7] Most companies attempt to improve ethical decision making by establishing and implementing a strategic approach to improving their organization's ethics. Companies as diverse as Texas Instruments, Starbucks, Ford Motor Company, and Johnson & Johnson have adopted a strategic approach to organizational ethics and also continuously monitor their programs and make improvements when problems occur.

To promote legal and ethical conduct, an organization should develop an organizational ethics program by establishing, communicating, and monitoring the ethical values and legal requirements that characterize its history, culture, industry, and operating environment. Without such programs, uniform standards and policies of conduct, it is difficult for employees to determine what behaviors are acceptable within a company. As discussed in Chapters 6 and 7, in the absence of such programs and standards, employees generally will make decisions based on their observations of how their coworkers and superiors behave. A strong ethics program includes a written code of conduct, an ethics officer to oversee the program, careful delegation of authority, formal ethics training, rigorous auditing, monitoring, enforcement, and revision of program standards. Without a strong program, problems likely will occur. Such is the case in Latin America where a survey by a Latin American business magazine found that Argentine businesses have the greatest number of ethical problems. In Latin America, there is no method, rule, or corporate internal policy that controls in absolute terms what business managers plan, execute, or do, and only 26 percent of all executives follow the values of the founder or owner of the business in which they are employed.[8]

Although there are no universal standards that can be applied to organizational ethics programs, most companies develop codes, values, or policies to provide guidance on business conduct. However, it would be naïve to think that simply having a code of ethics will solve all the ethical dilemmas that a company might face.[9] Indeed, most of the companies that have experienced ethical and legal difficulties in recent years have had formal ethics codes and programs. The problem is that top managers have not integrated these codes, values, and standards into their firms' corporate culture where they can provide effective guidance for daily decision making. Tyco, for example, had an ethics program and was a member of the Ethics and Compliance Officer Association. However, it was never active in that organization, and its top managers were involved in misconduct that sacrificed public confidence in the company. CEO Dennis Kozlowski allegedly used millions of dollars of company funds for personal use and was indicted for criminal tax avoidance schemes.[10] If a company's leadership fails to provide the vision and support needed for ethical conduct, then an ethics program will not be effective. Ethics is not something to be delegated to lower-level employees while top managers break the rules.

To satisfy the public's escalating demands for ethical decision making, companies need to develop plans and structures for addressing ethical considerations. Some directions for improving ethics have been mandated through regulations, but companies must be willing to have in place a system for implementing values and ethics that exceeds the minimum requirements.

AN EFFECTIVE ETHICS PROGRAM

Throughout this book, we have emphasized that ethical issues are at the forefront of organizational concerns as managers and employees face increasingly complex decisions. These decisions are often made in a group environment composed of different value systems, competitive pressures, and political concerns that contribute to the opportunity for misconduct. In a national survey by KPMG International, 74 percent of the more than four thousand workers surveyed indicated that they had observed violations of the law or of company standards in the previous twelve months.[11] When opportunity to engage in unethical conduct abounds, companies are vulnerable to both ethical problems and legal violations if their employees do not know how to make the right decisions.

A company must have an effective ethics program to ensure that all employees understand its values and comply with the policies and codes of conduct that create its ethical culture. Because we come from diverse business, educational, and family backgrounds, it cannot be assumed that we know how to behave appropriately when we enter a new organization or job. At the pharmaceutical company Merck, for example, all employees are expected to uphold the organization's corporate code of conduct. Merck's sixty thousand employees participate in an interactive ethical business practices program that exposes them to real-life situations they might encounter. According to Merck's chief ethics officer, "We want employees to know how Merck's values apply to their day-to-day activities so that they can adhere to these standards and model these values whenever and wherever they conduct Merck business."[12]

According to a study by the Open Compliance Ethics Group (OCEG), among companies with an ethics program in place for ten years or more, none have experienced "reputation damage" in the last five years—"a testament to the important impact these programs can have over time." Companies that have experienced reputation damage in the past are much further along compared to their peers in establishing ethics and compliance programs. Companies in the study spent an average of $5.8 million in total compliance or ethics efforts for every $1 billion in revenues.[13]

An Ethics Program Can Help Avoid Legal Problems

As mentioned in Chapter 7, some corporate cultures provide opportunities for or reward unethical conduct because their management lacks concern or the company has failed to comply with the minimum requirements of the FSGO (Table 8–1). In such cases, the company may face penalties and the loss of public confidence if one of its employees breaks the law. The guidelines encourage companies to assess their key risk areas and to customize a compliance program that will address these risks and satisfy key effectiveness criteria. The guidelines also hold companies responsible for the misconduct of their employees. The KPMG organizational survey found that about half of those surveyed felt that their company would not discipline workers guilty of an ethical infraction, and 57 percent said that they felt pressure to do "whatever it takes" to meet business goals.[14]

At the heart of the FSGO is a "carrot-and-stick" philosophy. Companies that act to prevent misconduct by establishing and enforcing ethical and legal compliance programs may receive a "carrot" and avoid penalties should a violation occur. The ultimate "stick" is the possibility of being fined or put on probation if convicted of a crime. Organizational probation involves using consultants on site to observe and monitor a company's legal compliance efforts as well as to report the company's progress toward avoiding misconduct to the U.S. Sentencing Commission. Table 8–2 shows the fines that have been imposed on sentenced organizations for leading offenses, including antitrust violations and fraud. The table compares two years of data; as can be seen from the table, fines for fraud, hazardous and toxic pollutants, and environmental water of-

TABLE 8–1	Minimum Requirements for Ethics and Compliance Programs

1. Standards and procedures, such as codes of ethics, that are reasonably capable of detecting and preventing misconduct

2. High-level personnel who are responsible for an ethics and compliance program

3. No substantial discretionary authority given to individuals with a propensity for misconduct

4. Standards and procedures communicated effectively via ethics training programs

5. Establishment of systems to monitor, audit, and report misconduct

6. Consistent enforcement of standards, codes, and punishment

7. Continuous improvement of the ethics and compliance program

SOURCE: Adapted from U.S. Sentencing Commission, *Federal Sentencing Guidelines Manual* (St. Paul: West, 1994), Chapter 8.

| **TABLE 8-2** | Mean and Median Fines Imposed on Sentenced Organizations in Four Offense Categories |

| | **Cases with Fine Imposed** | | | | | | | |
| | **Cases with Fine Imposed (2001)** | | | | **Cases with Fine Imposed (2003)** | | | |
Offense	**Total Number of Cases**	**Number**	**Mean Fine ($)**	**Median Fine ($)**	**Total Number of Cases**	**Number**	**Mean Fine ($)**	**Median Fine ($)**
Antitrust	16	12	20,980,184	3,999,744	13	10	6,243,940	2,837,500
Fraud	72	50	1,900,357	107,496	63	58	2,041,927	300,438
Environmental— water	31	29	744,863	100,000	24	22	805,188	200,000
Environmental— hazardous toxic pollutants	14	12	568,299	25,000	11	10	874,637	100

SOURCE: U.S. Sentencing Commission, *2003 Sourcebook of Federal Sentencing Statistics,* Table 52, www.ussc.gov/corp/03table52.pdf (accessed March 21, 2006).

fenses have increased, whereas fines for antitrust have decreased slightly. Thus, the government now views corporations as moral agents that are responsible for the conduct of their employees.

The FSGO also requires federal judges to increase fines for organizations that continually tolerate misconduct and to reduce or eliminate fines for firms with extensive compliance programs that are making due diligence attempts to abide by legal and ethical standards. Until the guidelines were formulated, courts were inconsistent in holding corporations responsible for employee misconduct. There was no incentive to build effective programs to encourage employees to make ethical and legal decisions. Now companies earn credit for creating ethics programs that meet a rigorous standard. The effectiveness of a program is determined by its design and implementation: It must deal effectively with the risk associated with a particular business and has to become part of the corporate culture.

An ethics program can help a firm avoid civil liability, but the company still bears the burden of proving that it has an effective program. A program developed in the absence of misconduct will be much more effective than one imposed as a reaction to scandal or prosecution. A legal test of a company's ethics program is possible when an individual employee is charged with misconduct. The court system or the U.S. Sentencing Commission evaluates the organization's responsibility for the individual's behavior during the process of an investigation. If the courts find that the company contributed to the misconduct or failed to show due diligence in preventing misconduct, then the firm may be convicted and sentenced.

The Sarbanes–Oxley Act of 2002, as discussed in Chapter 3, established new requirements for corporate governance to prevent fraudulent behavior in business. The heart of this act is an accounting oversight board that establishes financial reporting requirements including instituting a code of conduct for senior financial officers. This legislation covers many issues related to corporate governance including the role of board members relative to the oversight of ethics programs. It also requires public corporations to file their code of ethics with the accounting oversight board or explain why they do not have a code of ethics.

Values Versus Compliance Programs

No matter what their goals, ethics programs are developed as organizational control systems, the aim of which is to create predictability in employee behavior. Two types of control systems can be created. A **compliance orientation** creates order by requiring that employees identify with and commit to specific required conduct. It uses legal terms, statutes, and contracts that teach employees the rules and penalties for noncompliance. The other type of system is a **values orientation,** which strives to develop shared values. Although penalties are attached, the focus is more on an abstract core of ideals such as respect and responsibility. Instead of relying on coercion, the company's values are seen as something to which people willingly aspire.[15]

Research into compliance- and values-based approaches reveals that both types of programs can interact or work toward the same end but that a values orientation influences employees and creates ethical reasoning among employees. Values-based programs increase employees' awareness of ethics at work, their integrity, their willingness to deliver bad news to supervisors, and the perception that better decisions are made. Compliance-based programs are linked to employees' awareness of ethical issues at work, to their perception that decision making is better because of the program, and to their explicit knowledge of rules and expectations that makes decision making easier. In the final analysis, both orientations can be used to help employees and managers; however, it appears that a values-based program may be better for companies in the long run.

CODES OF CONDUCT

Most companies begin the process of establishing organizational ethics programs by developing **codes of conduct,** which are formal statements that describe what an organization expects of its employees. Such statements may take three different forms: a code of ethics, a code of conduct, and a statement of values.

A **code of ethics** is the most comprehensive and consists of general statements, sometimes altruistic or inspirational, that serve as principles and the basis for rules of conduct. A code of ethics generally specifies methods for reporting violations, disciplinary action for violations, and a structure of due process. A code of conduct is a written document that may contain some inspirational statements but usually specifies acceptable or unacceptable types of behavior. A code of conduct is more akin to a regulatory set of rules and, as such, tends to elicit less debate about specific actions. One problem with codes of conduct is that they tend to be developed without broad-based participation from stakeholders.[16] The final type of ethical statement is a **statement of values,** which serves the general public and also addresses distinct groups such as stakeholders. Values statements are conceived by management and are fully developed with

FIGURE 8-3	Presence of Written Standards of Conduct

A year-to-year comparison of the percentage of employees who are aware that their organizations have a written set of ethics standards.

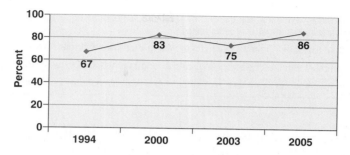

SOURCE: National Business Ethics Survey, *How Employees View Ethics in Their Organizations 1994–2005* (Washington, DC: Ethics Resource Center, 2005), 12.

input from all stakeholders. Despite our distinctions, it is important to recognize that these terms are often used interchangeably. According to an Ethics Resource Center survey, Figure 8–3 indicates that 86 percent of employees surveyed reported that their firm has written standards of ethical business conduct such as codes of ethics or conduct, policy statements on ethics, or guidelines on proper business conduct.[17]

Regardless of the degree of comprehensiveness, a code of ethics should reflect upper managers' desire for compliance with the values, rules, and policies that support an ethical culture. The development of a code of ethics should involve the president, board of directors, and chief executive officers who will be implementing the code. Legal staff should also be called on to ensure that the code has correctly assessed key areas of risk and that it provides buffers for potential legal problems. A code of ethics that does not address specific high-risk activities within the scope of daily operations is inadequate for maintaining standards that can prevent misconduct. Table 8–3 shows factors to consider when developing and implementing a code of ethics.

These codes may address a variety of situations, from internal operations to sales presentations and financial disclosure practices. Research has found that corporate codes of ethics often contain about six core values or principles in addition to more detailed descriptions and examples of appropriate conduct.[18] The six values that have been suggested as being desirable for codes of ethics include (1) trustworthiness, (2) respect, (3) responsibility, (4) fairness, (5) caring, and (6) citizenship.[19] These values will not be effective without distribution, training, and the support of top management in making these values a part of the corporate culture. Employees need specific examples of how these values can be implemented.

Codes of conduct will not resolve every ethical issue encountered in daily operations, but they help employees and managers deal with ethical dilemmas by prescribing or limiting specific activities. Many companies have a code of ethics, but it is not communicated effectively. A code that is placed on a website or in a training manual

TABLE 8-3	Developing and Implementing a Code of Ethics

1. Consider areas of risk and state the values as well as conduct necessary to comply with laws and regulations. Values are an important buffer in preventing serious misconduct.

2. Identify values that specifically address current ethical issues.

3. Consider values that link the organization to a stakeholder orientation. Attempt to find overlaps in organizational and stakeholder values.

4. Make the code understandable by providing examples that reflect values.

5. Communicate the code frequently and in language that employees can understand.

6. Revise the code every year with input from organizational members and stakeholders.

is useless if it is not reinforced every day. By communicating to employees both what is expected of them and what punishments they face if they violate the rules, codes of conduct curtail opportunities for unethical behavior and thereby improve ethical decision making. Fidelity Investment's code of ethics, for example, specifies that the sanctions for violating its code range from cautions and warnings to dismissal and criminal prosecution.[20] Codes of conduct do not have to be so detailed that they take into account every situation, but they should provide guidelines and principles that are capable of helping employees achieve organizational ethical objectives and addressing risks in an accepted way.

In the United States, Texas Instruments has gained recognition as having one of the nation's leading ethics programs. The company has won numerous ethics awards as well as being listed on the *Fortune* list of America's most admired company where it ranked number one in the semiconductor industry for three years. It was also on the *Business Ethics* "100 Best Corporate Citizens" list in the last four years. Texas Instruments is extremely focused on ethics and social responsibility, it ensures that its employees are educated in ethics, and it does this through its "Code of Ethics" booklet and the ethics quick test that is an integral part of everything that Texas Instruments does. It is not only large companies that need to develop an ethics and compliance program; small companies need to and are doing it too. Next, let's look at Honda Engineering and how they developed an ethics program.

Honda Engineering

Honda Engineering North America, Inc. has four hundred associates and sales of $100 million to $200 million per year. It provides engineering services such as designing, building and installing production tooling for Honda's plants in North America. There are many reasons why small companies should have an ethics program, especially to reduce the risk of compliance problems, because small companies usually have fewer internal controls and therefore have higher risks of compliance problems. It also gives small companies a competitive advantage; because their customers increasingly have an ethics program and want their suppliers to have one too. An ethics program can also improve hiring and reduce turnover because more and more employees become concerned about a corporation's ethical reputation when accepting a job offer. However, there are also problems that may not occur in a larger company; for example, there may be a limited or nonexistent budget, a leaner staff, cultural differences, and difficulty getting management buy-in.

Honda engineering was asked by its largest customer to establish an ethics program. The main concerns about implementing the program included concerns about the availability of workers and budget. Honda Engineering overcame these problems by using Honda of America (HAM) as a resource. They used HAM's code of conduct as a base and made minor changes to it using the same consultant as HAM. For code revisions, costs were kept low by not using a consultant. It has also been made available online, which reduces costs, and in a brochure format, which is only four pages. To address the worker-availability problem, Honda Engineering provided a toll-free number with a message, and they provided short, live training classes for all associates, which consisted of two hours for management and two hours for associates. All training was designed in-house with HAM support.

Honda Engineering runs an effective program by relying on the basic principles of building and maintaining trust. It does this though live training with frank discussions, asking the employees what they need, while maintaining independence and confidentiality. They use databases, surveys, and interviews with management to target the training and always follow up. Through effective communication, Honda Engineering ensures that employees are kept updated on changes to the code of conduct and any issues that arise. They send out an e-mail "Ethics@Work" a quarterly newsletter that is based on real situations and real concerns, Honda Engineering also addresses issues in the company newsletter. In this way, the company communicates the code to its employees while ensuring that employees know that it is everyone's responsibility to comply with the code at all times.[21]

ETHICS OFFICERS

Organizational ethics programs also must have oversight by high-ranking persons known to respect legal and ethical standards. These individuals—often referred to as **ethics officers**—are responsible for managing their organizations' ethics and legal compliance programs. They are usually responsible for (1) assessing the needs and risks that an organization-wide ethics program must address, (2) developing and distributing a code of conduct or ethics, (3) conducting training programs for employees, (4) establishing and maintaining a confidential service to answer employees' questions about ethical issues, (5) making sure that the company is in compliance with government regulation, (6) monitoring and auditing ethical conduct, (7) taking action on possible violations of the company's code, and (8) reviewing and updating the code. Ethics officers are also responsible for knowing thousands of pages of relevant regulations as well as communicating and reinforcing values that build an ethical corporate culture. According to the Ethics Resource Center survey, 65 percent of respondents reported that their firm has a designated office, person, or telephone line where they can get advice about ethics issues.[22] Corporate wrongdoings and scandal-grabbing headlines have a profound negative impact on public trust. To ensure compliance with state and federal regulations, many corporations are now appointing chief compliance officers and ethics and business conduct professionals to develop and oversee corporate compliance programs.[23]

The Ethics and Compliance Officer Association (ECOA) has over twelve hundred members, who are at the front lines of managing ethics programs.[24] The ECOA has members representing nearly every industry, they have members from more than 62 percent of the *Fortune* 100 companies, and they conduct business in more than 160 countries. In addition to U.S.–based organizations, members are based in Belgium, Canada, Germany, Great Britain, Greece, Hong Kong, India, Japan, the Netherlands, and Switzerland.[25] Ethics officers often move into their position from other jobs in their company rather than having formal ethics training. One-third of ECOA members have law degrees, one-fourth have financial backgrounds, and in some cases, they moved up through their companies' ranks and were selected because of their knowledge of the company and their ability to communicate and develop training programs. The financial reporting requirements of the Sarbanes–Oxley Act put more pressure on ethics officers to monitor financial reporting and the reporting of sales and inventory movements to prevent fraud in booking revenue and profits.[26]

In most firms, ethics officers do not report directly to the board of directors although that will likely change over the next few years. At Sun Microsystems, the ethics officer already reports to the board of directors, and employees can report concerns to someone outside the firm. If their concerns have merit, the outside help center can report directly to the appropriate board committee, which can request a full investigation. A Conference Board survey of one hundred senior ethics officers revealed that 60 percent indicated that their own board of directors is not sufficiently engaged in ethics issues. Fifty-seven percent said they have never engaged their board of directors in ethics training.[27]

ETHICS TRAINING AND COMMUNICATION

A major step in developing an effective ethics program is implementing a training program and communication system to educate employees about the firm's ethical standards. Figure 8–4 indicates that 69 percent of employees viewed that their organization provided ethics training by 2005. A significant number of employees report that they frequently find such training useful. Training can educate employees about the firm's policies and expectations, relevant laws and regulations, and general social standards. Training programs can make employees aware of available resources, support systems, and designated personnel who can assist them with ethical and legal advice. They can also empower employees to ask tough questions and make ethical decisions. Many companies are now incorporating ethics training into their employee and management development training efforts. At The Healthcare Company, for example, two hours of orientation training on the company's code of conduct is required for each employee within thirty days of employment, and a code of conduct refresher course is conducted for all employees annually.[28]

As we emphasized in Chapters 5 and 7, ethical decision making is influenced by corporate culture, by coworkers and supervisors, and by the opportunities available to engage in unethical behavior.[29] Ethics training can affect all three types of influence. Full awareness of the philosophy of management, rules, and procedures can strengthen both the corporate culture and the ethical stance of peers and supervisors. Such aware-

FIGURE 8-4 Presence of Ethics Training

The response of employees when asked if their organization provides ethics training.

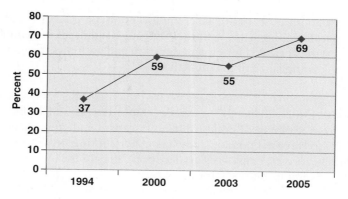

SOURCE: National Business Ethics Survey, *How Employees View Ethics in Their Organizations 1994–2005* (Washington, DC: Ethics Resource Center, 2005), 13.

ness, too, arms employees against opportunities for unethical behavior and lessens the likelihood of misconduct. Thus, the existence and enforcement of company rules and procedures limit unethical practices in the organization. If adequately and thoughtfully designed, ethics training can ensure that everyone in the organization (1) recognizes situations that might require ethical decision making, (2) understands the values and culture of the organization, and (3) can evaluate the impact of ethical decisions on the company in the light of its value structure.[30]

If ethics training is to be effective, it must start with a foundation, a code of ethics, a procedure for airing ethical concerns, line and staff involvements, and executive priorities on ethics that are communicated to employees. Managers from every department must be involved in the development of an ethics-training program. Training and communication initiatives should reflect the unique characteristics of an organization: its size, culture, values, management style, and employee base. It is important for the ethics program to differentiate between personal and organizational ethics. Discussions in ethical-training programs sometimes break down into personal opinions about what should or should not be done in particular situations. To be successful, business ethics programs should educate employees about formal ethical frameworks and models for analyzing business ethics issues. Then employees can base ethical decisions on their knowledge of choices rather than on emotions.

Some of the goals of an ethics-training program might be to improve employees' understanding of ethical issues and their ability to identify them, to inform employees of related procedures and rules, and to identify the contact person who could help them resolve ethical problems. In keeping with these goals, the purpose of the Boeing Corporation's "Boeing Ethics and Business Conduct" program is as follows:

◆ Communicate Boeing's values and standards of ethical business conduct to employees.

◆ Inform employees of company policies and procedures regarding ethical business conduct.

◆ Establish processes to help employees obtain guidance and resolve questions regarding compliance with the company's standards of conduct and values.

◆ Establish criteria for ethics education and awareness programs and for coordinating compliance oversight activities.[31]

Boeing also asks employees to take ethics refresher training each year. On the company's "Ethics Challenge" webpage, employees (as well as the general public) can select from a variety of ethical dilemma scenarios, discuss them with their peers, and select from several potential answers. After clicking on the answer they think is most ethically correct, employees get feedback: the company's own opinion of the correct response and its rationale for it.

Indeed, most experts agree that one of the most effective methods of ethics training is exercise in resolving ethical dilemmas that relate to actual situations that employees may face in their jobs. Lockheed Martin, for example, developed a training game called "Gray Matters" that includes dilemmas that can be resolved in teams. Each team member can offer his or her perspective, thereby helping other team members understand the ramifications of a decision for coworkers and the organization.

A relatively new training device is behavioral simulation, which gives participants a short, hypothetical ethical-issue situation to review. Each participant is assigned a role within a hypothetical organization and is provided with varying levels of information about the scenario. Participants then must interact to develop recommended courses of action representing short-term, mid-term, and long-term considerations. Such simulations re-create the complexities of organizational relationships as well as the realities of having to address difficult situations with incomplete information. They help participants gain awareness of the ethical, legal, and social dimensions of business decision making; develop analytical skills for resolving ethical issues; and gain exposure to the complexity of ethical decision making in organizations. Research indicates that "the simulation not only instructs on the importance of ethics but on the processes for managing ethical concerns and conflict."[32]

Top executives must communicate with managers at the operations level (in production, sales, and finance, for instance) and enforce overall ethical standards within the organization. Table 8–4 lists the factors crucial to successful ethics training. It is most important to help employees identify ethical issues and give them the means to address and resolve such issues in ambiguous situations. In addition, employees should be offered direction in how to seek assistance from managers, the ethics officer, or other designated personnel when resolving ethical problems.

Although training and communication should reinforce values and provide employees with opportunities to learn about rules, they represent just one part of an effective ethics program. Moreover, ethics training will be ineffective if conducted solely because it is required or because it is something that competing firms are doing. The majority of ethics officers surveyed by the Conference Board said that even ethics training would not have prevented the collapse of Enron due to accounting improprieties.[33]

TABLE 8–4	Keys to Successful Ethics Training

1. Help employees identify the ethical dimensions of a business decision.

2. Give employees a means to address ethical issues.

3. Help employees understand the ambiguity inherent in ethics situations.

4. Make employees aware that their actions define the company's ethical posture both internally and externally.

5. Provide direction for employees to find managers or others who can help them resolve ethical conflicts.

6. Eliminate the belief that unethical behavior is *ever* justifiable by stressing that

   ◆ stretching the ethical boundaries results in unethical behavior.

   ◆ whether discovered or not, an unethical act is just that.

   ◆ an unethical act is *never* in the best interests of the company.

   ◆ the firm is held responsible for the misconduct of its members.

SOURCE: Adapted from Walter W. Manley II, *The Handbook of Good Business Practice,* 1992. Reprinted with permission of Thomson Publishing Services, Andover, Hampshire, England.

Enron executives knew they had the support of Arthur Andersen, the firm's auditing and accounting consulting partner, as well as that of law firms, investment analysts, and in some cases, government regulators. Enron's top managers therefore probably thought that their efforts to hide debt in off-balance-sheet partnerships would not be exposed.

In the Conference Board survey, 56 percent of ethics officers responded that they do not survey their employees to assess the effectiveness of their ethics programs, and 54 percent do not have ethics measurements as part of their performance appraisal systems.[34] Both of these activities could help determine the effectiveness of a firm's ethics training. If ethical performance is not a part of regular performance appraisals, this sends the message that ethics is not an important component of decision making. For ethics training to make a difference, employees must understand why it is conducted, how it fits into the organization, and what their own role in implementing it is.

SYSTEMS TO MONITOR AND ENFORCE ETHICAL STANDARDS

An effective ethics program employs a variety of resources to monitor ethical conduct and measure the program's effectiveness. Observing employees, internal audits, surveys, reporting systems, and investigations can assess compliance with the company's ethical code and standards. An external audit and review of company activities may sometimes be helpful in developing benchmarks of compliance. (We examine the process of ethical auditing in Chapter 9.)

To determine whether a person is performing his or her job adequately and ethically, observers might focus on how the employee handles an ethically charged situation. For example, many businesses employ role-playing exercises in training salespeople and managers. Ethical issues can be introduced into the discussion, and the results can be videotaped so that both participants and their superiors can evaluate the outcome of the ethics dilemma.

Questionnaires can serve as benchmarks in an ongoing assessment of ethical performance by surveying employees' ethical perceptions of their company, their superiors, their coworkers, and themselves, as well as gaining their ratings of ethical or unethical practices within the firm and industry. Then, if unethical conduct appears to be increasing, management will have a better understanding of what types of unethical practices may be occurring and why. A change in the company's ethics training may then be necessary.

The existence of an internal system by which employees can report misconduct is especially useful for monitoring and evaluating ethical performance. Many companies have set up ethics assistance lines—often called help lines—or help desks to offer support and give employees an opportunity to ask questions or report ethical concerns. A survey of *Fortune* 500 companies indicates that 90 percent offer toll-free help lines. It is interesting to note that Kenneth Lay, who was often a featured ethics speaker at conferences, did not offer employees at Enron a help line when he was Enron's CEO. Enron's auditor, Arthur Andersen, also had no help line.[35]

Although there is always some concern that employees may misreport a situation or abuse a help line to retaliate against a coworker, help lines have become widespread, and employees do use them. An easy-to-use help line or desk can serve as a safety net that increases the chance of detecting and responding to unethical conduct in a timely manner. Help lines serve as a central contact point where critical comments, dilemmas, and advice can be assigned to the person most appropriate for handling a specific case.[36] Figure 8–5 provides an overview of changes in employee propensity to report misconduct. Employees prefer to deal with ethical issues through their supervisor or man-

---

FIGURE 8–5   Percentage of Employees Nationally Who Report Misconduct

There were gains between 2000 and 2005 in the propensity of employees to report misconduct.

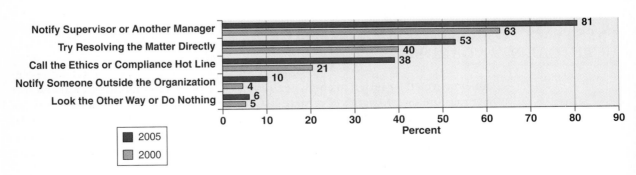

SOURCE: "KPMG Forensic Integrity Survey 2005–2006,"
http://www.kpmginsiders.com/display_analysis.asp?cs _id=148597 (accessed March 9, 2006).

ager or try to resolve the matter directly before using an anonymous reporting system such as a hot line.

Companies are increasingly using firms that provide professional case-management services and software. Software is becoming popular because it provides reports of employee concerns, complaints, or observations of misconduct, which can then be tracked and managed. It then allows the company to track investigations, analysis, resolutions, and documentation of misconduct reports. This helps prevent lawsuits, and the shared management and prevention can help a company analyze and learn about ethical lapses. However, it is important for companies to choose the right software for their company. They need to assess their current position and determine what they need going forward. Although only 10 to 15 percent of companies currently use some type of compliance management tool, many companies are moving toward the automated process that technology and software provide.

If a company is not making progress toward creating and maintaining an ethical culture, it needs to determine why and take corrective action, either by enforcing current standards more strictly or by setting higher standards. Corrective action may involve rewarding employees who comply with company policies and standards and punishing those who do not. When employees abide by organizational standards, their efforts should be acknowledged through public recognition, bonuses, raises, or some other means. On the other hand, when employees violate organizational standards, they must be reprimanded, transferred, docked, suspended, or even fired. If the firm fails to take corrective action against unethical or illegal behavior, the inappropriate behavior is likely to continue. In the Ethics Resource Center Survey, eight in ten employees who reported misconduct were dissatisfied with their organization's response because they did not believe that action taken by the organization was severe enough, suggesting that such corrective action is often not taken.[37]

Consistent enforcement and necessary disciplinary action are essential to a functional ethics or compliance program. The ethics officer is usually responsible for implementing all disciplinary actions for violations of the firm's ethical standards. Many companies are including ethical compliance in employee performance appraisals. During performance appraisals, employees may be asked to sign an acknowledgment that they have read the company's current ethics guidelines. The company must also promptly investigate any known or suspected misconduct. The appropriate company official, usually the ethics officer, needs to make a recommendation to senior management on how to deal with a particular ethical infraction. In some cases, a company may be required to report substantiated misconduct to a designated government or regulatory agency so as to receive credit. Under the FSGO, such credit for having an effective compliance program can reduce fines.[38]

Efforts to deter unethical behavior are important for companies' long-term relationships with their employees, customers, and community. If the code of ethics is aggressively enforced and becomes part of the corporate culture, it can effectively improve ethical behavior within the organization. If a code is not properly enforced, it becomes mere window dressing and will accomplish little toward improving ethical behavior and decisions.

Continuous Improvement of the Ethics Program

Improving the system that encourages employees to make more ethical decisions differs little from implementing any other type of business strategy. Implementation requires designing activities to achieve organizational objectives using available resources and given existing constraints. Implementation translates a plan for action into operational terms and establishes a means by which an organization's ethical performance will be monitored, controlled, and improved. Figure 8–6 indicates that about one-forth of organizations have implemented all six elements of a formal ethics program that would generally comply with suggestions of the FSGO and core practices that would be suggested by the ECOA. Note in Figure 8–6 that the majority of firms have at least part of the elements included in their ethics programs.

A firm's ability to plan and implement ethical business standards depends in part on how it structures resources and activities to achieve its ethical objectives. People's attitudes and behavior must be guided by a shared commitment to the business rather than mere obedience to traditional managerial authority. Encouraging diversity of perspectives, disagreement, and the empowerment of people helps align the company's leadership with its employees.

If a company determines that its ethical performance has been less than satisfactory, executives may want to reorganize how certain kinds of decisions are made. For example, a decentralized organization may need to centralize key decisions, at least for a time, so that upper managers can ensure that the decisions are ethical. Centralization may reduce the opportunities that lower-level managers and employees have to make unethical decisions. Executives can then focus on initiatives for improving the corporate culture and infuse more ethical values throughout the firm by rewarding positive behavior and sanctioning negative behavior. In other companies, decentralizing important decisions may be a better way to attack ethical problems so that lower-level managers, familiar with the forces of the local business environment and local culture

---

| **FIGURE 8–6** | Prevalence of Formal Program Elements |

One in four organizations across the United States has implemented all elements of a formal ethics program, as defined in the National Business Ethics Survey.

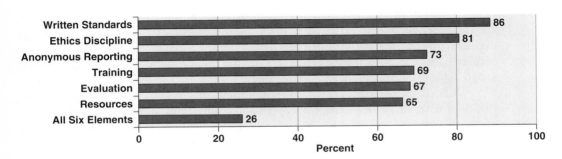

SOURCE: National Business Ethics Survey, *How Employees View Ethics in Their Organizations 1994–2005* (Washington, DC: Ethics Resource Center, 2005), 56.

and values, can make more decisions. Whether the ethics function is centralized or decentralized, the key need is to delegate authority in such a way that the organization can achieve ethical performance.

Common Mistakes in Designing and Implementing an Ethics Program

Many business leaders recognize that they need to have an ethics program, but few take the time to answer fundamental questions about the goals of such programs. As mentioned previously, some of the most common program objectives are to deter and detect unethical behavior as well as violations of the law; to gain competitive advantages through improved relationships with customers, suppliers, and employees; and, especially for multinational corporations, to link employees through a unifying and shared corporate culture. Failure to understand and appreciate these goals is the first mistake that many firms make when designing ethics programs.

A second mistake is not setting realistic and measurable program objectives. Once a consensus on objectives is reached, companies should solicit input through interviews, focus groups, and survey instruments. Finding out what employees might do in a particular situation and why can help companies better understand how to correct unethical or illegal behavior either reactively or proactively. Research suggests that employees and senior managers often know that they are doing something unethical but rationalize their behavior as being "for the good of the company." As a result, ethics program objectives should contain some elements that are measurable.[39]

The third mistake is senior management's failure to take ownership of the ethics program. Maintaining an ethical culture may be impossible if CEOs do not support an ethical culture. In recent years, many firms, particularly in the telecommunications industry, have falsified revenue reports by recording sales that never took place, shipping products before customers agreed to delivery, or recording all revenue from long-term contracts up front instead of over the life of the contracts in order to keep earnings high and boost their stock prices. In a number of cases, top executives encouraged such fraud because they held stock options or other bonus packages tied to the company's performance. Thus, reporting higher revenues ensured that they earned larger payoffs. Of the most highly visible accounting fraud cases brought by the SEC, more than half involved falsifying revenue records. For example, the SEC, along with the Department of Justice and a congressional committee, investigated whether Qwest improperly recorded revenues from the sale of fiber-optic capacity as immediate gains even though most of the deals involved long-term leases.[40] If top managers behave unethically, creating and enforcing an ethical culture will be difficult, if not impossible.

The fourth mistake is developing program materials that do not address the needs of the average employee. Many compliance programs are designed by lawyers to ensure that the company is legally protected. These programs usually yield complex "legalese" that few within the organization can understand. To avoid this problem, ethics programs—including codes of conduct and training materials—should include feedback from employees from across the firm, not just the legal department. Including a question-and-answer section in the program, referencing additional resources for guidance on key ethical issues, and using checklists, illustrations, and even cartoons can help make program materials more user friendly.

The fifth common mistake made in implementing ethics programs is transferring an "American" program to a firm's international operations. In multinational firms, executives should involve overseas personnel as early as possible in the process. This can be done by developing an inventory of common global management practices and processes and examining the corporation's standards of conduct in this international context.

A final common mistake is designing an ethics program that is little more than a series of lectures. In such cases, participants typically recall less than 15 percent the day after the lecture. A more practical solution is to allow employees to practice the skills they learn through case studies or small-group exercises.

A firm cannot succeed solely by taking a legalistic approach to ethics and compliance with sentencing guidelines. Top managers must seek to develop high ethical standards that serve as a barrier to illegal conduct. Although an ethics program should help reduce the possibility of penalties and negative public reaction to misconduct, a company must want to be a good corporate citizen and recognize the importance of ethics to success in business.

SUMMARY

Ethics programs help sensitize employees to potential legal and ethical issues within their work environments. To promote ethical and legal conduct, organizations should develop ethics programs by establishing, communicating, and monitoring ethical values and legal requirements that characterize the firms' history, culture, industry, and operating environment. Without such programs and such uniform standards and policies of conduct, it is difficult for employees to determine what behaviors a company deems acceptable.

A company must have an effective ethics program to ensure that employees understand its values and comply with its policies and codes of conduct. An ethics program should help reduce the possibility of legally enforced penalties and negative public reaction to misconduct. The main objective of the Federal Sentencing Guidelines for Organizations is to encourage companies to assess risk and then self-monitor and aggressively work to deter unethical acts and punish unethical employees. Ethics programs are developed as organizational control systems to create predictability in employee behavior. These control systems may have a compliance orientation—which uses legal terms, statutes, and contracts that teach employees the rules and the penalties for noncompliance—or a values orientation—which consists of developing shared values.

Most companies begin the process of establishing organizational ethics programs by developing codes of conduct, which are formal statements that describe what an organization expects of its employees. Variations of codes of conduct include the code of ethics and the statement of values. A code of ethics must be developed as part of senior management's desire to ensure that the company complies with values, rules, and policies that support an ethical culture. Without uniform policies and standards, employees will have difficulty determining what is acceptable behavior in the company.

Having a high-level manager or committee who is responsible for an ethical compliance program can significantly enhance its administration and oversight. Such ethics officers are usually responsible for assessing the needs of and risks to be addressed in an organization-wide ethics program, developing and distributing a code of conduct or ethics, conducting training programs for employees, establishing and maintaining a confidential service to answer questions about ethical issues, making sure the company is complying with government regulation, monitoring and auditing ethical conduct, taking action on possible violations of the company's code, and reviewing and updating the code.

Successful ethics training is important in helping employees identify ethical issues and in providing them with the means to address and resolve such issues. Training can educate employees about the firm's policies and expectations, available resources, support systems, and designated ethics personnel, as well as about relevant laws and regulations and general social standards. Top executives must communicate with managers at the operations level and enforce overall ethical standards within the organization.

An effective ethics program employs a variety of resources to monitor ethical conduct and measure the program's effectiveness. Compliance with the company's ethical code and standards can be assessed through observing employees, performing internal audits and surveys, instituting reporting systems, and conducting investigations, as well as by external audits and review, as needed. Corrective action involves rewarding employees who comply with company policies and standards and punishing those who do not. Consistent enforcement and disciplinary action are necessary for a functioning ethical compliance program.

Ethical compliance can be ensured by designing activities that achieve organizational objectives, using available resources and given existing constraints. A firm's ability to plan and implement ethics business standards depends in part on its ability to structure resources and activities to achieve its ethics and objectives effectively and efficiently.

In implementing ethics and compliance programs, many firms make some common mistakes including failing to answer fundamental questions about the goals of such programs, not setting realistic and measurable program objectives, failing to have its senior management take ownership of the ethics program, developing program materials that do not address the needs of the average employee, transferring an "American" program to a firm's international operations, and designing an ethics program that is little more than a series of lectures. Although an ethics program should help reduce the possibility of penalties and negative public reaction to misconduct, a company must want to be a good corporate citizen and recognize the importance of ethics to successful business activities.

IMPORTANT TERMS FOR REVIEW	compliance orientation values orientation code of conduct	code of ethics statement of values ethics officers

A REAL-LIFE SITUATION*

Jim, now in his fourth year with Cinco Corporation, was made a plant manager three months ago after completing the company's management-training program. Cinco owns pulp-processing plants that produce various grades of paper from fast-growing, genetically altered trees. Jim's plant, the smallest and oldest of Cinco's, is located in upstate New York, near a small town. It employs between 100 and 175 workers, mostly from the nearby town. In fact, the plant boasts about employees whose fathers and grandfathers have also worked there. Every year Cinco holds a Fourth of July picnic for the entire town.

Cinco's policy is to give each manager a free hand in dealing with employees, the community, and the plant itself. Its main measure of performance is the bottom line, and the employees are keenly aware of this fact.

Like all pulp-processing plants, Cinco is located near a river. Because of the plant's age, much of its equipment is outdated. Consequently, it takes more time and money to produce paper at Jim's plant than at Cinco's newer plants. Cinco has a long-standing policy of breaking in new managers at this plant to see if they can manage a work force and a mill efficiently and effectively. The tradition is that a manager who does well with the upstate New York plant will be transferred to a larger, more modern one. As a result, the plant's workers have had to deal with many managers and have become hardened and insensitive to change. In addition, most of the workers are older and more experienced than their managers, including Jim.

In his brief tenure as plant manager, Jim learned much from his workers about the business. Jim's secretary, Ramona, made sure that reports were prepared correctly, that bills were paid, and that Jim learned how to perform his tasks. Ramona had been with the plant for so long that she had become a permanent fixture. Jim's three foremen were all in their late 40s and kept things running smoothly. Jim's wife, Elaine, was having a difficult time adjusting to upstate New York. Speaking with other managers' wives, she learned that the "prison sentence," as she called it, typically lasted no longer than two years.

She had a large calendar in the kitchen and crossed off each day they were there.

One morning as Jim came into the office, Ramona didn't seem her usual stoic self.

"What's up?" Jim asked her.

"You need to call the EPA," she replied. "It's not really important. Ralph Hoad said he wanted you to call him."

When Jim made the call, Ralph told him the mill's waste disposal into the river exceeded Environmental Protection Agency (EPA) guidelines, and he would stop by next week to discuss the situation. Jim hung up the phone and asked Ramona for the water sample results for the last six months from upstream, from downstream, and at the plant. After inspecting the data and comparing them with EPA standards, he found no violations of any kind. He then ordered more tests to verify the original data. The next day Jim compared the previous day's tests with the last six months' worth of data and still found no significant differences and no EPA violations. As he continued to look at the data, however, something stood out on the printouts that he hadn't noticed before. All the tests had been done on the first or second shifts. Jim called the foremen of the two shifts to his office and asked if they knew what was going on. Both men were extremely evasive in their answers and referred him to the third-shift foreman. When Jim phoned him, he, too, was evasive and said not to worry—that Ralph would explain it to him.

That night Jim decided to make a spot inspection of the mill and test the wastewater. When he arrived at the river, he knew by the smell that something was very wrong. Jim immediately went back to the mill and demanded to know what was happening. Chuck, the third-shift foreman, took Jim down to the lowest level of the plant. In one of the many rooms stood four large storage tanks. Chuck explained to Jim that when the pressure gauge reached a certain level, a third-shift worker opened the valve and allowed the waste to mix with everything else.

"You see," Chuck told Jim, "the mill was never modernized to meet EPA standards, so we have to divert the bad waste here; twice a week it goes into the river."

"Who knows about this?" asked Jim.

"Everyone who needs to," answered Chuck.

When Jim got home, he told Elaine about the situation. Elaine's reaction was, "Does this mean we're stuck here? Because if we are, I don't know what I'll do!" Jim knew that all the managers before him must have had the same problem. He also knew that there would be no budget for installing EPA-approved equipment for at least another two years. The next morning Jim checked the EPA reports and was puzzled to find that the mill had always been in compliance. There should have been warning notices and fines affixed, but he found nothing.

That afternoon Ralph Hoad stopped by. Ralph talked about the weather, hunting, fishing, and then he said, "Jim, I realize you're new. I apologize for not coming sooner, but I saw no reason to because your predecessor had taken care of me until this month."

"What do you mean?" Jim asked.

"Ramona will fill you in. There's nothing to worry about. I know no one in town wants to see the mill close down, and I don't want it to either. There are lots of memories in this old place. I'll stop by to see you in another couple of months." With that, Ralph left.

Jim asked Ramona about what Ralph had said. She showed him a miscellaneous expense of $100 a month in the ledgers. "We do this every month," she told him.

"How long has this been going on?" asked Jim.

"Since the new EPA rules," Ramona replied. She went on to clarify Jim's alternatives. Either he could continue paying Ralph, which didn't amount to much, or he could refuse to, which would mean paying EPA fines and a potential shutdown of the plant. As Ramona put it, "Headquarters only cares about the bottom line. Now, unless you want to live here the rest of your life, the first alternative is the best for your career. The last manager who bucked the system lost his job. The rule in this industry is that if you can't manage Cinco's upstate New York plant, you can't manage. That's the way it is."

QUESTIONS • EXERCISES

1. Identify the ethical and legal issues of which Jim needs to be aware.
2. Discuss the advantages and disadvantages of each decision that Jim could make.
3. Identify the pressures that have brought about the ethical and legal issues.
4. What is Jim's power structure and leadership position at the plant?

*This case is strictly hypothetical; any resemblance to real persons, companies, or situations is coincidental.

Check Your EQ

Check your EQ, or Ethics Quotient, by completing the following. Assess your performance to evaluate your overall understanding of the chapter material.

	Yes	No
1. A compliance program should be deemed effective if it addresses the seven minimum requirements for ethical compliance programs.	**Yes**	**No**
2. The accountability and responsibility for appropriate business conduct rest with top management.	**Yes**	**No**
3. Ethical compliance can be measured by observing employees as well as through investigating and reporting mechanisms.	**Yes**	**No**
4. The key goal of ethics training is to help employees identify ethical issues.	**Yes**	**No**
5. An ethical compliance audit is designed to determine the effectiveness of ethics initiatives.	**Yes**	**No**

ANSWERS: 1. No. An effective compliance program has the seven elements of a compliance program in place and goes beyond those minimum requirements to determine what will work in a particular organization. 2. Yes. Executives in the organization determine the culture and initiatives that support ethical behavior. 3. Yes. Sometimes external monitoring is necessary, but internal monitoring and evaluation are the norm. 4. No. It is much more than that—it involves not only recognition but also an understanding of the values, culture, and rules in the organization as well as the impact of ethical decisions on the company. 5. Yes. It helps in establishing the code and in making program improvements.

Notes

Chapter 1

1. "Full Survey: Trust in Governments, Corporations and Global Institutions Continues to Decline," World Economic Forum, December 15, 2005, Geneva, Switzerland.
2. Michael Josephson, "The Biennial Report Card: The Ethics of American Youth," Josephson Institute of Ethics press release, www.josephsoninstitute.org/survey2004/ (accessed August 11, 2005).
3. "Teens Respect Good Business Ethics." *USA Today,* December 12, 2005, B1.
4. Marianne Jennings, "An Ethical Breach by Any Other Name," *Financial Engineering News,* January/February 2006.
5. Paul W. Taylor, *Principles of Ethics: An Introduction to Ethics,* 2nd ed. (Encino, CA: Dickenson, 1975), 1.
6. Adapted and reproduced from *The American Heritage Dictionary of the English Language,* 4th ed. Copyright © 2002 by Houghton Mifflin Company.
7. Wroe Alderson, *Dynamic Marketing Behavior* (Homewood, IL: Irwin, 1965), 320.
8. Ethics Resource Center, *2005 National Business Ethics Survey: How Employees Perceive Ethics at Work* (Washington, DC: Ethics Resource Center, 2005), 4, 28, 29.
9. "Krispy Kreme Problems," *[Fort Collins] Coloradoan,* August 11, 2005, D7.
10. Ronald Alsop, "Scandal-Filled Year Takes Toll on Firms' Good Names," *Wall Street Journal* online, February 12, 2003, http://online.wsj.com.
11. Julie Creswell, "Will Martha Walk?" *Fortune,* November 25, 2002, 121–124; Shelley Emling, "Martha Stewart Indicted on Fraud," *Austin American-Statesman* online, June 5, 2003, www.statesman.com; Constance L. Hays, "Stiff Sentence for ImClone Founder," *Austin American-Statesman* online, June 11, 2003, www.statesman.com.
12. Greg Farrell, "Hunt Is On for Notebook that Scrushy Denies Exists," *USA Today,* June 12, 2003, B1.
13. Jeffrey M. Jones, "Effects of Year's Scandals Evident in Honesty and Ethics Ratings," Gallup Organization press release, December 4, 2002, www.gallup.com/poll/releases/pr021204.asp.
14. John Lyman, "Who Is Scooter Libby? The Guy Behind the Guy," *Center for American Progress* (October 28, 2005).
15. Charles Piller, "Bell Labs Says Its Physicist Faked Groundbreaking Data," *Austin American-Statesman* online, September 26, 2002, www.austin360.com/statesman/.
16. Hwang Woo-Suk, http://en.wikipedia.org/wiki/Hwang_Woo-Suk (accessed June 27, 2006).
17. Mark Long, "Jimmy Johnson's Crew Chief Thrown Out of Daytona 500," *[Minneapolis–St. Paul] Star Tribune* online, February 13, 2006, http://www.startribune.com/694/story/244568.html.
18. Keith H. Hammonds, "Harry Kraemer's Moment of Truth," *Fast Company* online, November 2002, www.fastcompany.com/online/64/kraemer.html.
19. Archie B. Carroll and Ann K. Buchholtz, *Business and Society: Ethics and Stakeholder Management* (Cincinnati: South-Western, 2006), 452–455.
20. Alan R. Yuspeh, "Development of Corporate Compliance Programs: Lessons Learned from the DII Experience," in *Corporate Crime in America: Strengthening the "Good Citizenship" Corporation*

(Washington, DC: U.S. Sentencing Commission, 1995), 71–79.

21. Eleanor Hill, "Coordinating Enforcement Under the Department of Defense Voluntary Disclosure Program," in *Corporate Crime in America: Strengthening the "Good Citizenship" Corporation* (Washington, DC: U.S. Sentencing Commission, 1995), 287–294.

22. "Huffing and Puffing in Washington: Can Clinton's Plan Curb Teen Smoking?" *Consumer Reports* 60 (1995): 637.

23. Arthur Levitt, with Paula Dwyer, *Take on the Street* (New York: Pantheon Books, 2002).

24. Hill, "Coordinating Enforcement."

25. Richard P. Conaboy, "Corporate Crime in America: Strengthening the Good Citizen Corporation," in *Corporate Crime in America: Strengthening the "Good Citizenship" Corporation* (Washington, DC: U.S. Sentencing Commission, 1995), 1–2.

26. *United States Code Service* (Lawyers' Edition), 18 U.S.C.S. Appendix, Sentencing Guidelines for the United States Courts (Rochester, NY: Lawyers Cooperative Publishing, 1995), sec. 8A.1.

27. Anthony Bianco, William Symonds, and Nanette Byrnes, "The Rise and Fall of Dennis Kozlowski," *BusinessWeek*, December 17, 2002, 65–77.

28. "WorldCom CEO Slaps Arthur Andersen," CNN, July 8, 2002, www.cnn.com.

29. "Fraud Inc.," CNN/Money, http://money.cnn .com/news/specials/corruption/ (accessed February 5, 2002); "SEC Formalizes Investigation into Halliburton Accounting," *Wall Street Journal* online, December 20, 2002, http://online.wsj.com.

30. "Full Survey: Trust in Governments, Corporations and Global Institutions."

31. "Corporate Reform Bill Passed," CNN, July 25, 2002, www.cnn.com.

32. "Keeping an Eye on Corporate America," *Fortune*, November 25, 2002, 44–46.

33. Ethics and Compliance Officer Association homepage, "Membership," http://www.theecoa.org/ AboutMemb.asp (accessed March 6, 2006).

34. Chip Cummins. "Shell Trader, Unit Are Fined over Bogus Oil Trades," *Wall Street Journal*, January 5, 2006, C3.

35. Avi Shafran, "Aaron Feuerstein: Bankrupt and Wealthy," aish.com, June 30, 2002, www.aish.com/ societyWork/work/Aaron_Feuerstein_Bankrupt _and__Wealthy.asp.

36. Thomas L. Friedman, "A Green Dream in Texas," *New York Times* online, January 18, 2006, http://topi<<friedman.new.184.jpg>>cs.nytimes .com/top/opinion/editorialsandoped/oped/ columnists/thomaslfriedman/index.html?inline= nyt-per (accessed January 19, 2006).

37. Bernard J. Jaworski and Ajay K. Kohli, "Market Orientation: Antecedents and Consequences," *Journal of Marketing* 57 (1993): 53–70.

38. Ethics Resource Center, *2000 National Business Ethics Survey: How Employees Perceive Ethics as Work* (Washington, DC: Ethics Resource Center, 2000), 67.

39. "Wal-Mart Commits Additional $15 million to Katrina Relief," September 1, 2005, http:// walmartstores.com/GlobalWMStoresWeb/ navigate.do?catg=26&contId=4856 (accessed March 6, 2006).

40. Terry W. Loe, "The Role of Ethical Culture in Developing Trust, Market Orientation and Commitment to Quality" (PhD diss., University of Memphis, 1996).

41. Ethics Resource Center, *2000 National Business Ethics Survey*, 5.

42. John Galvin, "The New Business Ethics," SmartBusinessMag.com, June 2000, 99.

43. Ibid.

44. "Investors Prefer Ethics over High Return," *USA Today*, January 16, 2006, B1.

45. David Rynecki, "Here Are 8 Easy Ways to Lose Your Shirt in Stocks," *USA Today*, June 26, 1998, B3.

46. Zogby International Survey, reported in *Marketing News*, February 15, 2006, 3.

47. "Trend Watch," *Business Ethics*, March/April 2000, 8.

48. Marjorie Kelly, "Holy Grail Found. Absolute, Definitive Proof That Responsible Companies Perform Better Financially," *Business Ethics*, Winter 2004.

49. Kris Hudson, "Wal-Mart to Offer Improved Health-Care Benefits." *Wall Street Journal*, February 24, 2006, A2.

50. "Today's Briefing," *Commercial Appeal*, October 12, 2000, C1.

51. Nikebiz.com, "The Inside Story," http://www.nike .com/nikebiz/nikebiz.jhtml?page=24 (accessed March 6, 2006).

52. Loe, "The Role of Ethical Culture."

53. O. C. Ferrell, Isabelle Maignan, and Terry W. Loe, "The Relationship Between Corporate Citizenship

and Competitive Advantage," in *Rights, Relationships, and Responsibilities,* ed. O. C. Ferrell, Lou Pelton, and Sheb L. True (Kennesaw, GA: Kennesaw State University, 2003).

54. S. B. Graves and S. A. Waddock, "Institutional Owners and Corporate Social Performance: Maybe Not So Myopic After All," *Proceedings of the International Association for Business and Society,* San Diego, 1993; S. Waddock and S. Graves, "The Corporate Social Performance–Financial Performance Link," *Strategic Management Journal* 18 (1997): 303–319.

55. Melissa A. Baucus and David A. Baucus, "Paying the Payer: An Empirical Examination of Longer Term Financial Consequences of Illegal Corporate Behavior," *Academy of Management Journal* (1997): 129–151.

56. Healthsouth Statement Regarding Scrushy Press Conference, http://www.healthsouth.com/medinfo/home/app/frame?2=article.jsp,0,091505_Scrushy_Press (accessed March 7, 2006).

57. Kurt Eichenwald and N. R. Kleinfeld, "At Columbia/HCA, Scandal Hurts," *Commercial Appeal,* December 21, 1997, C1, C3.

58. Galvin, "The New Business Ethics."

59. Curtis C. Verschoor, "A Study of the Link Between a Corporation's Financial Performance and Its Commitment to Ethics," *Journal of Business Ethics* 17 (1998): 1509.

Chapter 2

1. Vikas Anand, Blake E. Ashforth, and Mahendra Joshi, "Business as Usual: The Acceptance and Perpetuation of Corruption in Organizations" *Academy of Management Executive* 18, no. 2 (2004): 39–53.

2. Debbie Thorne, O. C. Ferrell, and Linda Ferrell, *Business and Society* (Boston: Houghton Mifflin, 2003), 64–65.

3. "Enron 101," *BizEd* (May/June 2002): 40–46.

4. Lynn Brewer, Robert Chandler, and O. C. Ferrell, "Managing Risks for Corporate Integrity: How to Survive an Ethical Misconduct Disaster," (Mason OH: Texere/Thomson, 2006), 11.

5. Chad Terhune, "How Coke Beefed Up Results of a Marketing Test," *Wall Street Journal,* August 20, 2003, A1.

6. Betsy McKay and Chad Terhune, "Coca-Cola Settles Regulatory Probe; Deal Resolves Allegations by

SEC That Firm Padded Profit by 'Channel Stuffing,'" *Wall Street Journal,* April 19, 2005, A3.

7. Chad Terhune, "A Suit by Coke Bottlers Exposes Cracks in a Century-Old System," *Wall Street Journal,* March 13, 2006, A1.

8. Worth Civils, "Radio Shack Cleans House," *Wall Street Journal,* March 1, 2006, B1.

9. Brewer, Chandler, and Ferrell, "Managing Risks for Corporate Integrity," 11.

10. Adapted from Isabelle Maignan, O. C. Ferrell, and Linda Ferrell, "A Stakeholder Model for Implementing Social Responsibility in Marketing," *European Journal of Marketing* 39 (2005): 956–977.

11. Ibid.

12. Ibid.

13. Thorne, Ferrell, and Ferrell, *Business and Society.*

14. Isabelle Maignan and O. C. Ferrell, "Corporate Social Responsibility: Toward a Marketing Conceptualization," *Journal of the Academy of Marketing Science* 32 (2004), 3–19.

15. Ibid.

16. Ibid.

17. Amy Merrick, "Gap Report Says Factory Inspections Are Getting Better," *Wall Street Journal,* July 13, 2005, B10.

18. Maignan and Ferrell, "Corporate Social Responsibility."

19. G. A. Steiner and J. F. Steiner, *Business, Government, and Society* (New York: Random House, 1988).

20. Milton Friedman, "Social Responsibility of Business Is to Increase Its Profits," *New York Times Magazine,* September 13, 1970, 122–126.

21. "Business Leaders, Politicians and Academics Dub Corporate Irresponsibility 'An Attack on America from Within,'" *Business Wire,* November 7, 2002, via America Online.

22. Adam Smith, *The Theory of Moral Sentiments,* Vol. 2. (New York: Prometheus, 2000).

23. Theodore Levitt, *The Marketing Imagination* (New York: Free Press, 1983).

24. Norman Bowie, "Empowering People as an End for Business," in *People in Corporations: Ethical Responsibilities and Corporate Effectiveness,* ed. Georges Enderle, Brenda Almond, and Antonio Argandona (Dordrecht, Netherlands: Kluwer Academic Press, 1990), 105–112.

25. "1997 Cone/Roper Cause-Related Marketing Trends in 'Does It Pay to Be Ethical?'" *Business Ethics* (March–April 1997): 15.

26. Isabelle Maignan, "Antecedents and Benefits of Corporate Citizenship: A Comparison of U.S. and French Businesses," (PhD diss., University of Memphis, 1997).

27. "Leading the Way: Profiles of Some of the '100 Best Corporate Citizens' for 2002," *Business Ethics* online, May 16, 2002, www.business-ethics.com/newpage.htm.

28. Bruce Horovitz, "Whole Foods Setting Clean Energy Example," *USA Today,* January 16, 2006, www.Coloradoan.com (accessed January 16, 2006).

29. Ibid.

30. Steve Quinn, "Wal-Mart Green with Energy," *[Fort Collins] Coloradoan*, July 24, 2005, E1–E2.

31. Tobias Webb, James Rose, and Peter Davis, "ISO 26000 Indicates Immaturity: If Corporate Responsibility Is to Be Effective, Prominence Has to Be Given to Both Quantitative and Qualitative Analyses," *Ethical Corporation* (December 2005): 9.

32. Alex Frangos, "Timber Business Backs A New 'Green' Standard," *Wall Street Journal,* March 29, 2006, B6.

33. Ibid.

34. Archie B. Carroll, "The Pyramid of Corporate Social Responsibility: Toward the Moral Management of Organizational Stakeholders," *Business Horizons* 34 (1991): 42.

35. Isabelle Maignan, O. C. Ferrell, and G. Tomas M. Hult, "Corporate Citizenship: Cultural Antecedents and Business Benefits," *Journal of the Academy of Marketing Science* 27 (1999): 457.

36. Ronald Alsop, "Ranking Corporate Reputation," *Wall Street Journal,* December 6, 2005, B1.

37. *Dodge v. Ford Motor Co.*, 204 Mich.459, 179 N.W. 668, 3 A.L.R. 413 (1919).

38. Alfred Marcus and Sheryl Kaiser, "Managing Beyond Compliance: The Ethical and Legal Dimensions of Corporate Responsibility," *North Coast Publishers,* 2006, 79.

39. Ben W. Heineman, Jr., "Are You a Good Corporate Citizen?" *Wall Street Journal,* June 28, 2005, B2.

40. Jerry Markon, "Former Executive of Adelphia Plans to Plead Guilty," *Wall Street Journal,* November 14, 2002, A5.

41. Darryl Reed, "Corporate Governance Reforms in Developing Countries," *Journal of Business Ethics* 37 (2002): 223–247.

42. Bryan W. Husted and Carlos Serrano, "Corporate Governance in Mexico," *Journal of Business Ethics* 37 (2002): 337–348.

43. Maria Maher and Thomas Anderson, *Corporate Governance: Effects on Firm Performance and Economic Growth* (Paris: Organisation for Economic Co-operation and Development, 1999).

44. A. Demb and F. F. Neubauer, *The Corporate Board: Confronting the Paradoxes* (Oxford, Eng.: Oxford University Press, 1992).

45. Sandy Shore, "Ex-Qwest Exec Settlement Said Collapsed," *Associated Press,* January 20, 2006, http://accounting.smartpros.com/x51431.xml (accessed March 15, 2006).

46. Maher and Anderson, *Corporate Governance.*

47. Organisation for Economic Co-operation and Development, *The OECD Principles of Corporate Governance* (Paris: Organisation for Economic Co-operation and Development, 1999).

48. Louis Lavelle, "The Best and Worst Boards," *BusinessWeek,* October 7, 2002, 104–114.

49. Andrew Backover, "Overseer Confident WorldCom Will Come Back," *USA Today,* December 31, 2002, 8A.

50. Melvin A. Eisenberg, "Corporate Governance: The Board of Directors and Internal Control," *Cordoza Law Review* 19 (1997): 237.

51. Geoffrey Colvin, "CEO Knockdown," *Fortune,* April 4, 2005.

52. "Billionaire Warren Buffett Leaving Coca-Cola Board," *Atlanta Business Chronicle,* February 14, 2006, http://atlanta.bizjournals.com/atlanta/stories/2006/02/13/daily10.html.

53. James Covert, "Wal-Mart Urged to Review Controls," *Wall Street Journal,* June 2, 2005.

54. Amy Borrus, "Should Directors Be Nervous," *BusinessWeek* online, March 6, 2006 (accessed March 8, 2006).

55. John A. Byrne, with Louis Lavelle, Nanette Byrnes, Marcia Vickers, and Amy Borrus, "How to Fix Corporate Governance," *BusinessWeek,* May 6, 2002, 69–78.

56. "How Business Rates: By the Numbers," *BusinessWeek,* September 11, 2000, 148–149.

57. Kaja Whitehouse, "Investors Sue H-P over Size of Fiorina Severance Package," *Wall Street Journal,* March 8, 2006.

58. Sarah Anderson, John Cavanagh, Scott Klinger, and Liz Stanton, "Executive Excess 2005. Defense Contractors Get More Bucks for the Bang. 12th Annual CEO Compensation Survey," *Institute for Policy Studies, United for a Fair Economy,* August 30, 2005, http://www.faireconomy.org/

press/2005/EE2005_pr.html (accessed March 15, 2006).

59. Sarah Anderson, John Cavanagh, Ralph Estes, Chuck Collins, and Chris Hartman, *A Decade of Executive Excess: The 1990s Sixth Annual Executive.* Boston: United for a Fair Economy, 1999, online, June 30, 2006, http://www.faireconomy.org/.

60. Louis Lavelle, "CEO Pay, The More Things Change . . . ," *BusinessWeek,* October 16, 2000, 106–108.

61. Scott DeCarlo, "CEO Compensation: Special Report," *Forbes* online, April 21, 2005, www .Forbes.com.

62. Joann S. Lublin, "Boards Tie CEO Pay More Tightly to Performance," *Wall Street Journal,* February 21, 2006, A1.

63. Gary Strauss, "America's Corporate Meltdown," *USA Today,* June 27, 2002, 1A, 2A.

64. Phyllis Plitch, "Firms with Governance Disclosure See Higher Returns—Study," *Wall Street Journal* online, March 31, 2003, http://online.wsj.com/.

65. Adapted from Isabelle Maignan, O. C. Ferrell, Linda Ferrell, "A Stakeholder Model for Implementing Social Responsibility in Marketing," *European Journal of Marketing,* Sept./Oct. 2005, pp. 956–977. Reprinted with permission.

66. Marjorie Kelly, "Business Ethics 100 Best Corporate Citizens 2005," *Business Ethics* (Spring 2005): 20–25.

67. "Obesity Becomes Political Issue as Well as Cultural Obsession," Washington Wire, *Wall Street Journal* online, March 3, 2006, www.wsj.com (accessed March 21, 2006).

68. "Readers on Health Care," *Wall Street Journal* online, January 9, 2006, www.wsj.com (accessed March 21, 2006).

69. "Corporate Social Responsibility at Starbucks," http://www.starbucks.com/aboutus/csr.asp (accessed March 21, 2006).

70. Stephanie Armour, "Maryland First to OK 'Wal-Mart Bill' Law Requires More Health Care Spending," *USA Today,* January 13, 2006, B1.

71. Kris Hudson, "Wal-Mart to Offer Improved Health-Care Benefits," *Wall Street Journal,* February 24, 2006, A2.

Chapter 3

1. Joseph B. White and Lee Hawkins, Jr., "GM Will Restate Results for 2001 in Latest Stumble," *Wall Street Journal,* November 10, 2005, A1, A13.

2. John J. Fialka, "Top Oil Executives Defend Gas Prices Amid Scrutiny," *Wall Street Journal,* November 10, 2005, A4.

3. Eric H. Beversluis, "Is There No Such Thing as Business Ethics?," *Journal of Business Ethics* 6 (1987): 81–88. Reprinted by permission of Kluwer Academic Publishers, Dordrecht, Holland.

4. Carolyn Said, "Ellison Hones His 'Art of War' Tactics," *San Francisco Chronicle,* June 10, 2003, A1.

5. Michael Liedtke, "Oracle CEO to Pay $122M to Settle Lawsuit," Associated Press, *Washington Post* online, November 22, 2005, washingtonpost.com.

6. Beversluis, "Is There No Such Thing as Business Ethics?" 82.

7. Vernon R. Loucks, Jr., "A CEO Looks at Ethics," *Business Horizons* 30 (1987): 4.

8. Peter Lattman, "Boeing's Top Lawyer Spotlights Company's Ethical Lapses," *Wall Street Journal* online. Law Blog, January 30, 2006, http://blogs.wsj .com/law/2006/01/31/boeings-top-lawyer-rips -into-his-company (accessed March 31, 2006).

9. David Whelan, "Only the Paranoid Resurge," *Forbes,* April 10, 2006, 42–44.

10. Sarah Lueck and Anna Wilde Mathews, "Former FDA Head Held Shares in Regulated Firms as Late as '04," *Wall Street Journal,* October 26, 2005, A2.

11. "The Company We Keep: Why Physicians Should Refuse to See Pharmaceutical Representatives," *Annals of Family Medicine* 3, no. 1, (2005): 82–85.

12. "GAO Document B-295402," Lockheed Martin Corporation, February 18, 2005; "Decision; Matter of: Lockheed Martin Corporation," February 18, 2005, http://www.gao.gov/decisions/bidpro/ 295402.htm.

13. John Byrne, "Fall from Grace," *BusinessWeek,* August 12, 2002, 50–56.

14. Press release: "A World Built on Bribes?" March 2005, http://www.transparency.org/pressreleases _archive/2005/2005.03.16.gcr_relaunch.html.

15. Ira Winkler, *Corporate Espionage: What It Is, Why It's Happening in Your Company, What You Must Do About It* (New York: Prima, 1997); Ira Winkler, *Spies Among Us: How to Stop the Spies, Terrorists, Hackers, and Criminals You Don't Even Know You Encounter Every Day* (Indianapolis: Wiley, 2005); Kevin D. Mitnick and William L. Simon, *The Art of Intrusion: The Real Stories Behind the Exploits of Hackers, Intruders and Deceivers* (Indianapolis: Wiley, 2005).

16. "U.S. Equal Employment Opportunity Commission: An Overview," U.S. Equal Employment Opportunity Commission, www.eeoc.gov/overview.html (accessed February 4, 2003).

17. Bureau of the Census, *Statistical Abstract of the United States,* 2001 (Washington, DC: Government Printing Office, 2002), 17.

18. Randall Smith, "African-American Broker Sues Alleging Bias at Merrill Lynch," *Wall Street Journal,* December 1, 2005, C3.

19. John C. Hendrickson, "EEOC Charges Sidley & Austin with Age Discrimination," Equal Employment Opportunity Commission, January 13, 2005, http://www.eeoc.gov/press/1-13-05.html.

20. Sue Shellenberger, "Work and Family," *Wall Street Journal,* May 23, 2001, B1.

21. "What Is Affirmative Action?" HR Content Library, October 12, 2001, www.hrnext.com/content/view.cfm?articles_id=2007&subs_id=32.

22. "What Affirmative Action Is (and What It Is Not)," National Partnership for Women & Families, www.nationalpartnership.org/content.cfm?L1=202&DBT=Documents&NewsItemID=289&Header-Title=Affirmative%20Action (accessed February 4, 2003).

23. "What Is Affirmative Action?"

24. "What Affirmative Action Is (and What It Is Not)."

25. Debbie Thorne McAlister, O. C. Ferrell, and Linda Ferrell, *Business and Society: A Strategic Approach to Social Responsibility,* 2nd ed. (Boston: Houghton Mifflin, 2005), 255–259.

26. Joe Millman, "Delayed Recognition; Arab-Americans Haven't Put Much Effort into Advancing Their Rights as a Minority. Until Relatively Recently, That Is." *Wall Street Journal,* November 14, 2005, R8.

27. See http://www.eeoc.gov/stats/harass.html for EEOC statistics.

28. Paula N. Rubin, "Civil Rights and Criminal Justice: Primer on Sexual Harassment Series: NIJ Research in Action," October 1995, http://www.ncjrs.org/txtfiles/harass.txt.

29. *Zabkowicz v. West Bend Co.,* 589 F. Supp. 780,784, 35 EPD Par. 34, 766 (E.D. Wis. 1984).

30. Iddo Landau, "The Law and Sexual Harassment," *Business Ethics Quarterly* 15, no. 2 (2005): 531–536.

31. "Enhancements and Justice: Problems in Determining the Requirements of Justice in a Genetically Transformed Society," *Kennedy Institute Ethics Journal* 15, no. 1, (2005): 3–38.

32. "EEOC Settles Sexual Harassment and Retaliation Case for $1 Million," June 29, 2004, http://www.epexperts.com/print.php?sid=1515.

33. William T. Neese, O. C. Ferrell, and Linda Ferrell, "An Analysis of Mail and Wire Fraud Cases Related to Marketing Communication: Implications for Corporate Citizenship," working paper, 2003.

34. "Snapshot," *USA Today,* October 3, 2002.

35. Paul Davies, "Former Refco Officers Are Sued," *Wall Street Journal,* November 15, 2005, C3.

36. Matt Kranz, "More Earnings Restatements on Way," *USA Today,* October 25, 2002, 3B.

37. Nicole Bullock, "Qwest's Credit Ratings Reflect Risks Despite Recent Debt Swap," *Wall Street Journal,* December 30, 2002, B4.

38. Cassell Bryan-Low, "Accounting Firms Face Backlash over the Tax Shelters They Sold," *Wall Street Journal* online, February 7, 2003, http://online.wsj.com.

39. "WorldCom Finds Another $3.3B in Errors," CNN, August 8, 2002, www.cnn.com/2002/BUSINESS/asia/08/08/US.worldcom.biz/index.html.

40. *Gillette Co. v. Wilkinson Sword, Inc.,* 89-CV-3586, 1991 U.S. Dist. Lexis 21006, *6 (S.D.N.Y. January 9, 1991).

41. *Am. Council of Certified Podiatric Physicians & Surgeons v. Am. Bd. of Podiatric Surgery, Inc.,* 185 F.3d 606, 616 (6th Cir. 1999); *Johnson & Johnson-Merck Consumer Pharms. Co. v. Rhone-Poulenc Rorer Pharms., Inc.,* 19 F.3d 125, 129–30 (3d Cir. 1994); *Coca-Cola Co. v. Tropicana Prods., Inc.,* 690 F.2d 312, 317 (2d Cir. 1982).

42. Jeff Bater, "FTC Says Companies Falsely Claim Cellphone Patches Provide Protection," *Wall Street Journal* online, February 21, 2002, http://online.wsj.com.

43. Archie B. Carroll, *Business and Society: Ethics and Stakeholder Management* (Cincinnati: South-Western, 1989), 228–230.

44. "Netgear Settles Suit over Speed Claims," *Wall Street Journal,* November 28, 2005, C5.

45. "AT&T Settles Lawsuit Against Reseller Accused of Slamming," *Business Wire,* via America Online, May 26, 1998.

46. "Newsletter; Federal Trade Commission Report: ID Theft #1 Complaint," February 2005, http://www

.machine-solution.com/_Article+FTC+ID+Theft
.html.

47. "Retail Theft and Inventory Shrinkage," *What You Need to Know about . . . Retail Industry,* http://retailindustry.about.com/library/weekly/02/aa021126a.htm (accessed February 6, 2003).

48. Daryl Koehn, "Consumer Fraud: The Hidden Threat," University of St. Thomas, www.stthom.edu/cbes/commentary/HBJCONFRAUD.html (accessed February 6, 2003).

49. Robert Tomsho, "Two Plead Guilty to Fraud Charges Related to Charter One Acquisition," *Wall Street Journal,* November 4, 2005.

50. Anna Wilde Mathews, "Copyrights on Web Content Are Backed," *Wall Street Journal,* October 27, 2000, B10.

51. "Today's Briefing," *Commercial Appeal,* November 15, 2000, C1.

52. Electronic Protection Information Center, http://www.epic.org/crypto/ (accessed June 10, 2006).

53. Nora J. Rifon, Robert LaRose, and Sejung Marina Choi, "Your Privacy Is Sealed: Effects of Web Privacy Seals on Trust and Personal Disclosures," *Journal of Consumer Affairs* 39, no. 2 (2002): 339–362.

54. Steven Ward, Kate Bridges, and Bill Chitty, "Do Incentives Matter? An Examination of On-line Privacy Concerns and Willingness to Provide Personal and Financial Information," *Journal of Marketing Communications* 11, no. 1 (2005): 21–40.

55. "Electronic Monitoring and Surveillance Survey: Many Companies Monitoring, Recording, Videotaping—and Firing—Employees," *New York Times,* May 18, 2005, via http://www.amanet.org/press/amanews/ems05.htm.

56. "Sonera Executive Is Arrested in a Widening Privacy Probe," *Wall Street Journal* online, November 22, 2002, http://online.wsj.com.

57. "Privacy (Employee)," Business for Social Responsibility, www.bsr.org/ (accessed February 6, 2003).

58. John Galvin, "The New Business Ethics," SmartBusinessMag.com (June 2000): 97.

59. "Ethical Issues in the Employer–Employee Relationship," *Society of Financial Service Professionals,* www.financialpro.org/press/Ethics/es2000/Ethics_Survey_2000_Report_FINAL.cfm (accessed February 6, 2003).

60. Mitch Wagner, "Google's Pixie Dust," *InformationWeek,* issue 1061 (2005): 98.

61. Stephenie Steitzer, "Commercial Web Sites Cut Back on Collections of Personal Data," *Wall Street Journal,* March 28, 2002, http://online.wsj.com.

62. Christopher Conkey, "FTC Goes After Firm That Installs Spyware Secretly," *Wall Street Journal,* October 6, 2005, D4.

63. Eve M. Caudill and Patrick E. Murphy, "Consumer Online Privacy: Legal and Ethical Issues," *Journal of Public Policy & Marketing* 19 (2000): 7.

64. Galvin, "The New Business Ethics," 98.

65. Steitzer, "Commercial Web Sites Cut Back on Collections of Personal Data."

66. Christopher Conkey, "Credit-Card Use Is Up Despite Concern About Fraud," *Wall Street Journal,* October 6, 2005, D2.

67. Sarah Ellison, "Why Kraft Decided to Ban Some Food Ads to Children," *Wall Street Journal,* October 31, 2005, A1.

Chapter 4

1. "The Year in Global Corporate Responsibility. A Round-up of 2005's Biggest Business Ethics Stories," Ethical Corporation, December 2005, 6–7.

2. "Marsh to Cut 2,500 Jobs; Impact in Orlando Uncertain," *Orlando Business Journal* online, March 3, 2005, http://www.bizjournals.com/orlando/stories/2005/02/28/daily42.html (accessed June 27, 2006).

3. "Drug Firms Agree to Settle Lawsuit over Cardizem," *Wall Street Journal,* January 28, 2003, A1.

4. Stephen Scheibal, "Civic Group Takes Issue with Chain Bookstore," *Austin American-Statesman* online, December 11, 2002, www.austin360.com/statesman/.

5. Gary Martin, "Clear Channel Accused of Stifling Competition, Bullying Musicians," *Austin American-Statesman* online, January 31, 2003, www.austin360.com/statesman/; Yochi J. Dreazen and Joe Flint, "FCC Eases Media-Ownership Caps, Clearing the Way for New Mergers," *Wall Street Journal* online, June 3, 2003, http://online.wsj.com.

6. Gregory T. Gundlach, "Price Predation: Legal Limits and Antitrust Considerations," *Journal of Public Policy & Marketing* 14 (1995): 278.

7. Quoted in "Software Publishers Association Applauds Department of Justice Antitrust Competition

Action; Department Acts in Support of Software Industry Competition Principles," PRNewswire.com, May 18, 1998.

8. "Store Files Antitrust Lawsuit Against Microsoft," PRNewswire.com, May 18, 1998.

9. Don Clark, Mark Wigfield, Nick Wingfield, and Rebecca Buckman, "Judge Approves Most of Pact, in Legal Victory for Microsoft," *Wall Street Journal* online, November 1, 2002, http://online.wsj.com; Kim Peterson, Brier Dudley, and Bradley Meacham, "Microsoft Settles with California for $1 Billion," *Seattle Times,* January 11, 2003, A1, A10.

10. Lawrence Gordon, Martin Loeb, William Lucyshyn, and Robert Richardson, "10th Annual CSI/FBI 2005 Computer Crime and Security Survey," Computer Security Institute with the San Francisco Federal Bureau of Investigation's Computer Intrusion Squad. http://www.cybercrime.gov/FBI2005.pdf. (accessed June 27, 2006).

11. "A Child Shall Lead the Way: Marketing to Youths," *Credit Union Executive,* May–June 1993, 6–8.

12. "Federal Web Sites Ignore Children's Privacy Law," *Commercial Appeal,* October 7, 2000, A7.

13. Otto Krusius, "From Out of the Mouses of Babes," *Kiplinger's,* November 2000, 32.

14. Bureau of Labor Statistics, "Highlights of Women's Earnings in 2001," U.S. Department of Labor, May 2002, available at www.bls.gov/cps/cpswom2002 .pdf.

15. "Jury Finds Wal-Mart Guilty of Forcing Unpaid Overtime," *Wall Street Journal* online, December 20, 2002, http://online.wsj.com.

16. "Wal-Mart Key Topics: Wage and Hour Litigation," http://www.walmartfacts.com/keytopics/default .aspx#a49 (accessed March 16, 2006).

17. Michael Arndt, Wendy Zellner, and Peter Coy, "Too Much Corporate Power," *BusinessWeek,* September 11, 2000, 149.

18. Dave Bryan, "Royal Caribbean Guards Against Pollution," *USA Today* online, www.usatoday .com/life/travel/lt092.htm (accessed October 13, 2000).

19. John Yaukey, "Discarded Computers Create Waste Problem," *USA Today* online, www.usatoday.com/ news/ndsmonl4.htm (accessed October 13, 2000).

20. Andrew Park, "Stemming the Tide of Tech Trash," *BusinessWeek,* October 7, 2002, 36A–36F.

21. "Corporate Reform Bill Passed," CNN, July 25, 2002, www.cnn.com.

22. Penelope Patsuris, "The Corporate Scandal Sheet," *Forbes* online, August 26, 2002, www.forbes.com/ home/2002/07/25/accountingtracker.html.

23. Nelson D. Schwartz, "The Looting of Kmart, Part 2," *Fortune,* February 17, 2003, 30; Elliot Blair Smith, "Probe: Former Kmart CEO 'Grossly Derelict,'" *USA Today,* January 27, 2003, B1.

24. David McHugh, "Business Wants to Restore Public Trust," America Online, January 28, 2003.

25. Amy Borrus, "Learning to Love Sarbanes–Oxley," *BusinessWeek,* November 21, 2005, 126–128.

26. Stephen Taub, "SEC:1300 'Whistles' Blown Each Day: Most Tips Concerning Accounting Problems at Public Companies; 'A Tremendous Source of Leads,'" CFO.com, August 3, 2004, http://www.cfo.com/ article.cfm/3015607 (accessed March 15, 2006).

27. Julie Homer, "Overblown: In the Wake of Sarbanes–Oxley, Some Serious Misconceptions Have Arisen About What Blowing the Whistle Actually Means," CFO.com, October 1, 2003.

28. David Katz, "A Tough Act to Follow: What CFOs Really Think About Sarbox—and How They Would Fix the *!#& Thing," CFO.com, March 15, 2006, http://www.cfo.com/article.cfm/5598373 (accessed March 16, 2006).

29. Tim Reason, "Feeling the Pain: Are the Benefits of Sarbanes–Oxley Worth the Cost?" CFO.com, May 2005, http://www.cfo.com/article.cfm/3909558 (accessed March 15, 2006).

30. "Sarbanes–Oxley Act Improves Investor Confidence, but at a Cost," *CPA Journal,* October 2005, http://www.nysscpa.org/cpajournal/2005/1005/ perspectives/p19.htm (accessed March 16, 2006).

31. Tricia Bisoux, "The Sarbanes–Oxley Effect," *BizEd,* July/August 2005, 24–29.

32. Ibid.

33. James C. Hyatt, "Birth of the Ethics Industry," *Business Ethics* (Summer 2005): 20–27.

34. Amy Borrus, "Learning to Love Sarbanes–Oxley," *BusinessWeek,* November 21, 2005, 126–128.

35. Win Swenson, "The Organizational Guidelines' 'Carrot and Stick' Philosophy, and Their Focus on 'Effective' Compliance," in *Corporate Crime in America: Strengthening the "Good Citizenship" Corporation* (Washington, DC: U.S. Sentencing Commission, 1995), 17–26.

36. *United States Code Service* (Lawyers' Edition), 18 U.S.C.S. Appendix, Sentencing Guidelines for the United States Courts (Rochester, NY: Lawyers Cooperative Publishing, 1995), sec. 8A.1.

37. O. C Ferrell and Linda Ferrell, "Current Developments in Managing Organizational Ethics and Compliance Initiatives," University of Wyoming, white paper, Bill Daniels Business Ethics Initiative 2006.

38. Ibid.

39. Lynn Brewer, "Capitalizing on the Value of Integrity: An Integrated Model to Standardize the Measure of Non-financial Performance as an Assessment of Corporate Integrity," in *Managing Risks for Corporate Integrity. How to Survive an Ethical Misconduct Disaster,* ed. Lynn Brewer, Robert Chandler, and O. C. Ferrell (Mason, OH: Thomson/Texere, 2006), 233–277.

40. Poulomi Saha, "Enabling Customers: McDonalds New Packaging Initiative Has Been Welcomed by Anti-obesity Campaigners," *Ethical Corporation,* December 2005, 13–14.

41. Ingrid Murro Botero, "Charitable Giving Has 4 Big Benefits," *Business Journal of Phoenix* online, January 1, 1999, www.bizjournals.com/phoenix/stories/1999/01/04/smallb3.html.

42. "2004 Contributions: $248.52 Billion by Source of Contributions," Giving USA Foundation–American Association of Fundraising Counsel (AAFRC) Trust for Philanthropy/Giving USA 2005, http://www.aafrc.org/gusa/chartbysource.html (accessed June 27, 2006).

43. Marjorie Kelly, "100 Best Corporate Citizens 2005," *Business Ethics* (Spring 2005): 25.

44. "Wal-Mart Giving," Walmartfacts.com http://www.walmartfacts.com/community/walmart-foundation.aspx (accessed March 17, 2006).

45. Steve Hilton, "Bisto: Altogether now, 'Aah . . . ,'" *Ethical Corporation,* December 2005, 50.

46. "McDonald's Employees Honor Ray Kroc's Birthday by Giving Back to Communities Nationwide," PRNewswire.com (accessed October 13, 2000).

47. "CSR Case Study: The Home Depot: Giving Back to Communities," Interdepartmental Working Group on Corporate Social Responsibility (CSR), http://www.fivewinds.com/uploadedfiles_shared/CSRHomeDepot.pdf (accessed March 17, 2006).

48. "About Home Depot, Community Relations Quick Facts, Declaration of Independence Road Trip," http://www.independenceroadtrip.org/Media/faqsheets_homedepot.html (accessed March 17, 2006).

49. Swenson, "The Organizational Guidelines' 'Carrot and Stick' Philosophy."

Chapter 5

1. Thomas M. Jones, "Ethical Decision Making by Individuals in Organizations: An Issue-Contingent Model," *Academy of Management Review* 16 (February 1991): 366–395; O. C. Ferrell and Larry G. Gresham, "A Contingency Framework for Understanding Ethical Decision Making in Marketing," *Journal of Marketing* 49 (Summer 1985): 87–96; O. C. Ferrell, Larry G. Gresham, and John Fraedrich, "A Synthesis of Ethical Decision Models for Marketing," *Journal of Macromarketing* 9 (Fall 1989): 55–64; Shelby D. Hunt and Scott Vitell, "A General Theory of Marketing Ethics," *Journal of Macromarketing* 6 (Spring 1986): 5–16; William A. Kahn, "Toward an Agenda for Business Ethics Research," *Academy of Management Review* 15 (April 1990): 311–328; Linda K. Trevino, "Ethical Decision Making in Organizations: A Person-Situation Interactionist Model," *Academy of Management Review* 11 (March 1986): 601–617.

2. Jones, "Ethical Decision Making," 367, 372.

3. Donald P. Robin, R. Eric Reidenbach, and P. J. Forrest, "The Perceived Importance of an Ethical Issue as an Influence on the Ethical Decision-Making of Ad Managers," *Journal of Business Research* 35 (January 1996): 17.

4. "Lead Attorneys in Enron Shareholder Litigation: Wall St. Banks Operated Giant Ponzi Scheme," Corporate Governance Fund Report, August 14, 2002, www.cgfreport.com/NewsFlashMilberg.htm.

5. Roselie McDevitt and Joan Van Hise, "Influences in Ethical Dilemmas of Increasing Intensity," *Journal of Business Ethics* 40 (October 2002): 261–274.

6. Anusorn Singhapakdi, Scott J. Vitell, and George R. Franke, "Antecedents, Consequences, and Mediating Effects of Perceived Moral Intensity and Personal Moral Philosophies," *Journal of the Academy of Marketing Science* 27 (Winter 1999): 19.

7. Ibid.

8. Ibid.

9. Ibid., 17.

10. "2005 Draft Remarks of Attorney General Alberto Gonzales," Adelphia Victims Press Conference, http://www.usdoj.gov/ag/speeches/2005/draft_remarks_ag042505.htm (accessed February 11, 2006).

11. T. W. Loe, L. Ferrell, and P. Mansfield, "A Review of Empirical Studies Assessing Ethical

Decision-Making in Business," *Journal of Business Ethics* 25 (2000): 185–204.

12. Michael J. O'Fallon, and Kenneth D. Butterfield, "A Review of the Empirical Ethical Decision-Making Literature: 1996–2003," *Journal of Business Ethics* 59 (July 2005): 375–413; P. M. J. Christie, J. I. G. Kwon, P. A. Stoeberl, and R. Baumhart, "A Cross-Cultural Comparison of Ethical Attitudes of Business Managers: India, Korea and the United States," *Journal of Business Ethics* 46 (September 2003): 263–287; G. Fleischman and S. Valentine, "Professionals' Tax Liability and Ethical Evaluations in an Equitable Relief Innocent Spouse Case," *Journal of Business Ethics* 42 (January 2003): 27–44; A. Singhapakdi, K. Karande, C. P. Rao, and S. J. Vitell, "How Important Are Ethics and Social Responsibility? A Multinational Study of Marketing Professionals," *European Journal of Marketing* 35 (2001): 133–152.

13. R. W. Armstrong, "The Relationship Between Culture and Perception of Ethical Problems in International Marketing," *Journal of Business Ethics* 15 (November 1996): 1199–1208; J. Cherry, M. Lee, and C. S. Chien, "A Cross-Cultural Application of a Theoretical Model of Business Ethics: Bridging the Gap Between Theory and Data," *Journal of Business Ethics* 44 (June 2003): 359–376; B. Kracher, A. Chatterjee, and A. R. Lundquist, "Factors Related to the Cognitive Moral Development of Business Students and Business Professionals in India and the United States: Nationality, Education, Sex and Gender," *Journal of Business Ethics* 35 (February 2002): 255–268.

14. J. M. Larkin, "The Ability of Internal Auditors to Identify Ethical Dilemmas," *Journal of Business Ethics* 23 (February 2000): 401–409; D. Peterson, A. Rhoads, and B. C. Vaught, "Ethical Beliefs of Business Professionals: A Study of Gender, Age and External Factors," *Journal of Business Ethics* 31 (June 2001): 225–232; M. A. Razzaque and T. P. Hwee, "Ethics and Purchasing Dilemma: A Singaporean View," *Journal of Business Ethics* 35 (February 2002): 307–326.

15. J. Cherry and J. Fraedrich, "An Empirical Investigation of Locus of Control and the Structure of Moral Reasoning: Examining the Ethical Decision-Making Processes of Sales Managers," *Journal of Personal Selling and Sales Management* 20 (Summer 2000): 173–188; M. C. Reiss and K. Mitra, "The Effects of Individual Difference Factors on the Acceptability of Ethical and Unethical Workplace Behaviors,"

Journal of Business Ethics 17 (October 1998): 1581–1593.

16. O. C. Ferrell and Linda Ferrell, "Role of Ethical Leadership in Organizational Performance," *Journal of Management Systems* 13 (2001): 64–78.

17. James Weber and Julie E. Seger, "Influences upon Organizational Ethical Subclimates: A Replication Study of a Single Firm at Two Points in Time," *Journal of Business Ethics* 41 (November 2002): 69–84.

18. Sean Valentine, Lynn Godkin, and Margaret Lucero, "Ethical Context, Organizational Commitment, and Person-Organization Fit," *Journal of Business Ethics* 41 (December 2002): 349–360.

19. Bruce H. Drake, Mark Meckler, and Debra Stephens, "Transitional Ethics: Responsibilities of Supervisors for Supporting Employee Development," *Journal of Business Ethics* 38 (June 2002): 141–155.

20. Ferrell and Gresham, "A Contingency Framework," 87–96.

21. R. C. Ford and W. D. Richardson, "Ethical Decision-making: A Review of the Empirical Literature," *Journal of Business Ethics* 13 (March 1994): 205–221; Loe, Ferrell, and Mansfield, "A Review of Empirical Studies."

22. National Business Ethics Survey, *How Employees Perceive Ethics at Work* (Washington, DC: Ethics Resource Center, 2000), 30.

23. Vault editors, "Pens and Post-Its Among Most Pilfered Office Supplies, Says New Vault Survey," Vault.com, November 16, 2005, http://www.vault.com/nr/newsmain.jsp?nr_page=3&ch_id=420&article_id=25720773.

24. Jeffrey L. Seglin, "Forewarned Is Forearmed? Not Always," *New York Times* online, February 16, 2003, www.nytimes.com/2003/02/16/business/your-money/16ETHI.html; Barbara Ley Toffler, *Final Accounting: Ambition, Greed and the Fall of Arthur Andersen* (New York: Broadway Books, 2003).

25. National Business Ethics Survey, 30.

26. R. Eric Reidenbach and Donald P. Robin, *Ethics and Profits* (Englewood Cliffs, NJ: Prentice-Hall, 1989), 92.

27. "Small Virtues: Entrepreneurs Are More Ethical," *Business Week* online, March 8, 2000, www.businessweek.com/smallbiz/0003/ib3670029.htm?scriptFramed.

28. Constance E. Bagley, "The Ethical Leader's Decision Tree," *Harvard Business Review*, January–February 2003, 18.

29. John Byrne, "How Al Dunlap Self-Destructed," *BusinessWeek,* July 6, 1998, 44–45.

30. "Sunbeam Ex-CEO 'Chainsaw Al' Dunlap Settles SEC Case," Securities Class Action Clearinghouse, Stanford Law School press release, September 4, 2002, http://securities.stanford.edu/news-archive/2002/20020904_Settlement03_Roland.htm.

31. Daniel J. Brass, Kenneth D. Butterfield, and Bruce C. Skaggs, "Relationship and Unethical Behavior: A Social Science Perspective," *Academy of Management Review* 23 (January 1998): 14–31.

32. Andrew Kupfor, "Mike Armstrong's AT&T: Will the Pieces Come Together?" *Fortune,* April 26, 1999, 89.

33. From *Managing Risks for Corporate Integrity: How to Survive an Ethical Misconduct Disaster* 1st edition by Brewer, Chandler, and Ferrell. Copyright © 2006. Reprinted with permission of South-Western, a division of Thomson Learning: ww.thomsonrights.com. Fax 800 730-2215.

34. J. M. Burns, *Leadership* (New York: Harper & Row, 1985).

35. Royston Greenwood, Roy Suddaby, and C. R. Hinings, "Theorizing Change: The Role of Professional Associations in the Transformation of Institutionalized Fields," *Academy of Management Journal* 45 (January 2002): 58–80.

36. "WorldCom Chief Outlines Initial Turnaround Strategy," *Wall Street Journal* online, January 14, 2003, http://online.wsj.com.

37. Stephen R. Covey, *The 7 Habits of Highly Effective People* (New York: Simon & Schuster, 1989).

38. Archie B. Carroll, "Ethical Leadership: From Moral Managers to Moral Leaders," in *Rights, Relationships and Responsibilities,* Vol. 1, ed. O. C. Ferrell, Sheb True, and Lou Pelton (Kennesaw, GA: Kennesaw State University, 2003), 7–17.

39. Andy Serwer, "Wal-Mart: Bruised in Bentonville," *Fortune* online, April 4, 2005, www.fortune.com/fortune/subs/print/0,15935,1044608,00.html.

40. Thomas I. White, "Character Development and Business Ethics Education," in *Rights, Relationships and Responsibilities,* Vol. 1, ed. O. C. Ferrell, Sheb True, and Lou Pelton (Kennesaw, GA: Kennesaw State University, 2003), 137–166.

41. Carroll, "Ethical Leadership," 11.

42. Keith H. Hammonds, "Harry Kraemer's Moment of Truth," *Fast Company* online, November 2002, www.fastcompany.com/online/64/kraemer.html.

43. Carroll, "Ethical Leadership," 11.

44. Chad Terhune, "Pepsi, Vowing Diversity, Isn't Just Image Polish, Seeks Inclusive Culture," *Wall Street Journal,* April 19, 2005, B1.

45. Carroll, "Ethical Leadership," 12.

46. Steve Quinn, "Wal-Mart Green with Energy," *[Fort Collins] Coloradoan,* July 24, 2005, E1.

47. Brent Smith, Michael W. Grojean, Christian Resick, and Marcus Dickson, "Leaders, Values and Organizational Climate: Examining Leadership Strategies for Establishing an Organizational Climate Regarding Ethics," *Journal of Business Ethics,* as reported at "Research @ Rice: Lessons from Enron—Ethical Conduct Begins at the Top," Rice University, June 15, 2005, www.explore.rice.edu/explore/NewsBot.asp?MODE=VIEW&ID=7478&SnID=878108660.

48. "New Belgium Brewing: Environmental and Social Responsibilities," New Belgium Brewing Company, www.newbelgium.com (accessed August 25, 2005); Greg Owsley, "The Necessity for Aligning Brand with Corporate Ethics," in *Fulfilling Our Obligation: Perspectives on Teaching Business Ethics,* ed. Sheb L. True, Linda Ferrell, and O. C. Ferrell (Kennesaw, GA: Kennesaw University Press, 2005), 127–139.

49. Herb Baum and Tammy Kling, "The Transparent Leader," in LeaderPoints, Centerpoints for Leaders, December 2004, www.centerpointforleaders.org/newsletters/dec04.html.

50. Monica Langley, "Course Correction: Behind Citigroup Departures: A Culture Shift by CEO Prince," *Wall Street Journal,* August 24, 2005, A1.

Chapter 6

1. James R. Rest, *Moral Development Advances in Research and Theory* (New York: Praeger, 1986), 1.

2. "Business Leaders, Politicians and Academics Dub Corporate Irresponsibility 'An Attack on America from Within,'" *Business Wire,* November 7, 2002, via America Online.

3. Abhijit Biswas, Jane W. Licata, Daryl McKee, Chris Pullig, and Christopher Daughtridge, "The Recycling Cycle: An Empirical Examination of Consumer Waste Recycling and Recycling Shopping Behaviors," *Journal of Public Policy & Marketing* 19 (2000): 93.

4. "Court Says Businesses Liable for Harassing on the Job," *Commercial Appeal,* June 27, 1998, A1.

5. Richard Brandt, *Ethical Theory* (Englewood Cliffs, NJ: Prentice-Hall, 1959), 253–254.

6. J. J. C. Smart and B. Williams, *Utilitarianism: For and Against* (Cambridge, UK: Cambridge University Press, 1973), 4.

7. C. E. Harris, Jr., *Applying Moral Theories* (Belmont, CA: Wadsworth, 1986), 127–128.

8. Penelope Patsuris, "The Corporate Accounting Scandal Sheet," *Forbes* online, August 26, 2002, www.forbes.com/*2002/*07/*25/*accountingtracker.html; Debra Solomon, "Adelphia Plans to Dismiss Deloitte," *Wall Street Journal,* June 10, 2002, A3.

9. Immanuel Kant, "Fundamental Principles of the Metaphysics of Morals," in *Problems of Moral Philosophy: An Introduction,* 2nd ed., ed. Paul W. Taylor (Encino, CA: Dickenson, 1972), 229.

10. Example adapted from Harris, *Applying Moral Theories,* 128–129.

11. Gerald F. Cavanaugh, Dennis J. Moberg, and Manuel Velasquez, "The Ethics of Organizational Politics," *Academy of Management Review* 6 (1981): 363–374; U.S. Bill of Rights, www.law.cornell.edu/constitution/constitution.billofrights.html (accessed February 17, 2003).

12. Marie Brenner, "The Man Who Knew Too Much," *Vanity Fair,* May 1996, available at www.jeffreywigand.com/*insider/*vanityfair.html (accessed February 17, 2003).

13. Norman E. Bowie and Thomas W. Dunfee, "Confronting Morality in Markets," *Journal of Business Ethics* 38 (2002): 381–393.

14. Kant, "Fundamental Principles," 229.

15. Thomas E. Weber, "To Opt In or Opt Out: That Is the Question When Mulling Privacy," *Wall Street Journal,* October 23, 2000, B1.

16. C. R. Bateman, J. P Fraedrich, and R. Iyer, "The Integration and Testing of the Janus-Headed Model Within Marketing," *Journal of Business Research* 56 (2003): 587–596; J. B. DeConinck and W. F. Lewis, "The Influence of Deontological and Teleological Considerations and Ethical Culture on Sales Managers' Intentions to Reward or Punish Sales Force Behavior," *Journal of Business Ethics* 16 (1997): 497–506; J. Kujala, "A Multidimensional Approach to Finnish Managers' Moral Decision-Making," *Journal of Business Ethics* 34 (2001): 231–254; K. C. Rallapalli, S. J. Vitell, and J. H. Barnes, "The Influence of Norms on Ethical Judgments and Intentions: An Empirical Study of Marketing Professionals," *Journal of Business Research* 43 (1998): 157–168; M. Shapeero, H. C. Koh, and L. N. Killough, "Underreporting and Premature Sign-Off in Public Accounting," *Managerial Auditing Journal* 18 (2003): 478–489.

17. William K. Frankena, *Ethics* (Englewood Cliffs: Prentice-Hall, 1963).

18. R. E. Reidenbach and D. P. Robin, "Toward the Development of a Multidimensional Scale for Improving Evaluations of Business Ethics," *Journal of Business Ethics* 9, no. 8 (1980): 639–653.

19. Patrick E. Murphy and Gene R. Laczniak, "Emerging Ethical Issues Facing Marketing Researchers," *Marketing Research* 4, no. 2 (1992): 6–11.

20. T. K. Bass and Barnett G. Brown, "Religiosity, Ethical Ideology, and Intentions to Report a Peer's Wrongdoing," *Journal of Business Ethics* 15, no. 11 (1996): 1161–1174; R. Z. Elias, "Determinants of Earnings Management Ethics Among Accountants," *Journal of Business Ethics* 40, no. 1 (2002): 33–45; Y. Kim, "Ethical Standards and Ideology Among Korean Public Relations Practitioners," *Journal of Business Ethics* 42, no. 3 (2003): 209–223; E. Sivadas, S. B. Kleiser, J. Kellaris, and R. Dahlstrom, "Moral Philosophy, Ethical Evaluations, and Sales Manager Hiring Intentions," *Journal of Personal Selling & Sales Management* 23, no. 1 (2003): 7–21.

21. Manuel G. Velasquez, *Business Ethics Concepts and Cases,* 4th ed. (Upper Saddle River, NJ: Prentice-Hall, 1998), 132–133.

22. Ibid.

23. Adapted from Robert C. Solomon, "Victims of Circumstances? A Defense of Virtue Ethics in Business," *Business Ethics Quarterly* 13, no. 1 (2003): 43–62.

24. Ian Maitland, "Virtuous Markets: The Market as School of the Virtues," *Business Ethics Quarterly* (January 1997): 97.

25. Ibid.

26. Stefanie E. Naumann and Nathan Bennett, "A Case for Procedural Justice Climate: Development and Test of a Multilevel Model," *Academy of Management Journal* 43 (2000): 881–889.

27. Joel Brockner, "Making Sense of Procedural Fairness: How High Procedural Fairness Can Reduce or Heighten the Influence of Outcome Favorability," *Academy of Management Review* 27 (2002): 58–76.

28. "Wainwright Bank and Trust Company Award for Social Justice Inside and Out," *Business Ethics,* November/December 1998, 11.

29. John Fraedrich and O. C. Ferrell, "Cognitive Consistency of Marketing Managers in Ethical Situa-

tions," *Journal of the Academy of Marketing Science* 20 (1992): 245–252.

30. Manuel Velasquez, Claire Andre, Thomas Shanks, S. J., and Michael J. Meyer, "Thinking Ethically: A Framework for Moral Decision Making," *Issues in Ethics* (Winter 1996): 2–5.

31. Lawrence Kohlberg, "Stage and Sequence: The Cognitive Developmental Approach to Socialization," in *Handbook of Socialization Theory and Research,* ed. D. A. Goslin (Chicago: Rand McNally, 1969), 347–480.

32. Adapted from Kohlberg, "Stage and Sequence."

33. Clare M. Pennino, "Is Decision Style Related to Moral Development Among Managers in the U.S.?" *Journal of Business Ethics* 41 (2002): 337–347.

34. A. K. M. Au and D. S. N. Wong, "The Impact of Guanxi on the Ethical Decision-Making Process of Auditors—An Exploratory Study on Chinese CPA's in Hong Kong," *Journal of Business Ethics* 28, no. 1 (2000): 87–93; D. P Robin, G. Gordon, C. Jordan, and E. Reidenback, "The Empirical Performance of Cognitive Moral Development in Predicating Behavioral Intent," *Business Ethics Quarterly* 6, no. 4 (1996): 493–515; M. Shapeero, H. C. Koh, and L. N. Killough, "Underreporting and Premature Sign-Off in Public Accounting," *Managerial Auditing Journal* 18, no. 6 (1996): 478–489; N. Uddin and P. R. Gillett, "The Effects of Moral Reasoning and Self-Monitoring on CFO Intentions to Report Fraudulently on Financial Statements," *Journal of Business Ethics* 40, no. 1 (2002): 15–32.

35. David O. Friedrichs, *Trusted Criminals, White Collar Crime in Contemporary Society* (Belmont, CA: Wadsworth, 1996).

36. Kari & Associates, White Collar Crime website, http://www.karisable.com/crwc.htm (accessed March 9, 2006).

37. M. David Ermann and Richard J. Lundman, *Corporate and Governmental Deviance-Problems of Organizational Behavior in Contemporary Society* (New York: Oxford University Press, 1996).

38. H. J. Eysenck, "Personality and Crime: Where Do We Stand?" *Psychology, Crime & Law* 2, no. 3 (1996): 143–152; S. J. Listwan, *Personality and Criminal Behavior: Reconsidering the Individual,* UMI Digital Dissertations Abstracts, 2000, http://wwwlib.umi.com/dissertations/.

39. J. M. Rayburn and L. G. Rayburn, "Relationship Between Machiavellianism and Type A Personality and Ethical-Orientation," *Journal of Business Ethics* 15, no. 11 (1996): 1209–1219.

40. Quoted in Marjorie Kelly, "The Ethics Revolution," *Business Ethics,* Summer 2005, 6.

41. O. C. Ferrell and Larry G. Gresham, "A Contingency Framework for Understanding Ethical Decision Making in Marketing," *Journal of Marketing* 49 (2002): 261–274.

42. Thomas I. White, "Character Development and Business Ethics Education," in *Fulfilling Our Obligation: Perspectives on Teaching Business Ethics,* ed. Sheb L. True, Linda Ferrell, and O. C. Ferrell (Kennesaw, GA: Kennesaw State University Press. 2005), 165.

43. Ibid., 165–166.

Chapter 7

1. Richard Gibson, "McDonald's Faces the Costly Issue of Employee Rudeness," Dow Jones News Service, http://www.s-t.com/daily/07-01/07-15-01/b03bu066.htm (accessed March 30, 2006).

2. Richard L. Daft, *Organizational Theory and Design* (Cincinnati: South-Western, 2007).

3. Stanley M. Davis, quoted in Alyse Lynn Booth, "Who Are We?" *Public Relations Journal* (July 1985): 13–18.

4. T. E. Deal and A. A. Kennedy, *Corporate Culture: Rites and Rituals of Corporate Life* (Reading, MA: Addison-Wesley, 1982), 4.

5. G. Hofstede, "Culture's Consequences: International Differences," in *Work-Related Values* (Beverly Hills, CA: Sage, 1980), 25.

6. N. M. Tichy, "Managing Change Strategically: The Technical, Political and Cultural Keys," *Organizational Dynamics* (Autumn 1982): 59–80.

7. J. W. Lorsch, "Managing Culture: The Invisible Barrier to Strategic Change," *California Management Review* 28 (1986): 95–109.

8. "Transforming Our Culture: The Values for Success," Mutual of Omaha, www.careerlink.org/emp/mut/corp.htm (accessed February 19, 2003).

9. William Clay Ford, Jr., "A Message from the Chairman," Ford Motor Company, www.ford.com/en/ourCompany/corporateCitizenship/ourLearningJourney/message (accessed February 19, 2003); "GM and Ford: Roadmaps for Recovery," *BusinessWeek* online, March 14, 2006, http://www .businessweek.com/print/investor/content/

mar2006/pi20060314_416862.htm (accessed March 30, 2006).

10. "Southwest Airlines Adopt-a-Pilot Educational Program Encourages School-to-Career Path," PR Newswire, February 6, 2006, www.southwest.com/about_swa/press/prindex.html (accessed March 30, 2006).

11. N. K. Sethia and M. A. Von Glinow, "Arriving at Four Cultures by Managing the Reward System," in *Gaining Control of the Corporate Culture* (San Francisco: Jossey-Bass, 1985), 409.

12. Gigi Stone, "Are Pension Cuts Snuffing Out Workers' Dreams?" February 19, 2006, http://abcnews.go.com/WNT/PersonalFinance/story?id=1636508 (accessed March 30, 2006).

13. "Southwest Airlines Fact Sheet," Southwest Airlines, http://www.southwest.com/about_swa/press/factsheet.html#Fun%20Facts (accessed March 30, 2006).

14. "UPS Once Again 'America's Most Admired,'" February 21, 2006, http://pressroom.ups.com/pressreleases/current/0,1088,4653,00.html and http://www.ups.com/content/us/en/about/facts/worldwide.html (accessed March 30, 2006).

15. "US: U.S. Foodservice Auditors Committed Misconduct—SEC," Reuters, February 16, 2006, www.corpwatch.org/article.php?id=13287; www.hoovers.com/u.s.-foodservice (accessed March 31, 2006).

16. Peter Lattman, "Boeing's Top Lawyer Spotlights Company's Ethical Lapses," January 31, 2006, http://blogs.wsj.com/law/2006/01/31/boeings-top-lawyer-rips-into-his-company/ (accessed March 31, 2006).

17. Microsoft "Mission and Values," updated February 17, 2005, www.microsoft.com/mscorp/mission (accessed March 31, 2006).

18. "America's Most Admired Companies," *Fortune,* March 6, 2006, 65.

19. Christopher Lawton, "Judge Sanctions Gateway for Destroying Evidence," *Wall Street Journal,* March 31, 2006, A3.

20. Isabelle Maignan, O. C. Ferrell, and Thomas Hult, "Corporate Citizenship, Cultural Antecedents and Business Benefit," *Journal of the Academy of Marketing Science* 27 (1999): 455–469.

21. R. Eric Reidenbach and Donald P. Robin, *Ethics and Profits* (Englewood Cliffs, NJ: Prentice-Hall, 1989), 92.

22. E. Sutherland and D. R. Cressey, *Principles of Criminology,* 8th ed. (Chicago: Lippincott, 1970), 114.

23. O. C. Ferrell and Larry G. Gresham, "A Contingency Framework for Understanding Ethical Decision Making in Marketing," *Journal of Marketing* 49 (1985): 90–91.

24. Edward Wong, "Shuttle Insulator Admits to Shortcuts," *Austin American-Statesman* online, February 18, 2003, http://austin360.com/statesman.

25. James S. Bowman, "Managerial Ethics in Business and Government," *Business Horizons* 19 (1976): 48–54; William C. Frederick and James Weber, "The Value of Corporate Managers and Their Critics: An Empirical Description and Normative Implications," in *Research in Corporate Social Performance and Social Responsibility,* ed. William C. Frederick and Lee E. Preston (Greenwich, CT: JAI Press, 1987), 149–150; Linda K. Trevino and Stuart Youngblood, "Bad Apples in Bad Barrels: A Causal Analysis of Ethical Decision Making Behavior," *Journal of Applied Psychology* 75 (1990): 38.

26. Richard Lacavo and Amanda Ripley, "Persons of the Year 2002—Cynthia Cooper, Coleen Rowley, and Sherron Watkins," *Time* online, December 22, 2002, www.time.com/personoftheyear/2002; Thomas S. Mulligan, "Whistle Blower Recounts Enron Tale," *Los Angeles Times* online, March 16, 2006, http://www.latimes.com/business/la-fi-enron16mar16,1,5771701.story?ctrack=1&cset=true (accessed April 3, 2006).

27. Mulligan, "Whistle Blower Recounts Enron Tale."

28. John W. Schoen, "Split CEO–Chairman Job, Says Panel," MSNBC.com, January 9, 2003, www.msnbc.com/news/857171.asp (accessed June 27, 2006)

29. "Former Wal-Mart Exec Files Complaints," CNN/Money, May 24, 2005, www.money.cnn.com.

30. "Making Your Whistleblower Case Succeed: Basic Workings of Whistleblower Complaints," www.jameshoyer.com/practice_qui_tam.html?se=Overture (accessed April 5, 2006).

31. Paula Dwyer and Dan Carney, with Amy Borrus, Lorraine Woellert, and Christopher Palmeri, "Year of the Whistleblower," *BusinessWeek,* December 16, 2002, 106–110.

32. Darren Dahl, "Learning to Love Whistleblowers," *Inc.,* March 2006, 21–23.

33. John R. P. French and Bertram Ravin, "The Bases of Social Power," in *Group Dynamics: Research and*

Theory, ed. Dorwin Cartwright (Evanston, IL: Row, Peterson, 1962), 607–623.

34. Lynn Brewer, Robert Chandler, and O. C. Ferrell, *Managing Risks for Corporate Integrity* (Mason, OH: Thomson/Texere, 2006), 35.

35. "Ex-Worldcom Comptroller Gets Prison Time," "Ex-Worldcom CFO Gets Five Years," CNN/ Money, August 11, 2005, www.money.cnn.com (accessed August 11, 2005).

36. Lyman W. Porter, "Job Attitudes in Management: II. Perceived Importance of Needs as a Foundation of Job Level," *Journal of Applied Psychology* 47 (1963): 141–148.

37. Clayton Alderfer, *Existence, Relatedness, and Growth* (New York: Free Press, 1972), 42–44.

38. Louis P. White and Long W. Lam, "A Proposed Infrastructural Model for the Establishment of Organizational Ethical Systems," *Journal of Business Ethics* 28 (2000): 35–42.

39. Gary Edmondson, Kate Carlisle, Inka Resch, Karen Anhalt, and Heidi Dawley, "Human Bondage," *BusinessWeek,* November 27, 2000, 147–160.

40. Stanley Holmes, "Cleaning Up Boeing," *Business- Week* online, March 13, 2006, http://www .businessweek.com/print/magazine/content/ 06_11/ b3975088.htm?chan=gl (accessed April 6, 2006).

41. Spencer Ante, "They're Hiring in Techland," *Busi- nessWeek* online, January 23, 2006, http://www .businessweek.com/print/technology/content/jan 2006/tc20060123_960426.htm (accessed April 6, 2006).

42. Joseph A. Belizzi and Ronald W. Hasty, "Supervising Unethical Sales Force Behavior: How Strong Is the Tendency to Treat Top Sales Performers Leniently?" *Journal of Business Ethics* 43 (2003): 337–351.

43. John Fraedrich and O. C. Ferrell, "Cognitive Consistency of Marketing Managers in Ethical Situations," *Journal of the Academy of Marketing Science* 20 (1992): 243–252.

44. Michael Connor, "Philip Morris: More Spent on Health Ads," Yahoo! News, May 23, 2000, http:// dailynews.yahoo.com/h/nm/2000523/bs/ tobacco_engle_1.html; "Philip Morris U.S.A. Expresses Confidence in Its Youth Smoking Prevention Advertising Based on Extensive Research Findings," Business Wire, May 29, 2002, via www .findarticles.com, "About Youth Smoking Prevention," Phillip Morris, http://www.philipmorrisusa .com/en/policies_practices/ysp/about_ysp.asp (accessed April 6, 2006).

Chapter 8

1. Bob Lewis, "Survival Guide: The Moral Compass— Corporations Aren't Moral Agents, Creating Interesting Dilemmas for Business Leaders," *InfoWorld,* March 11, 2002, via www.findarticles.com.

2. Marjorie Kelly, "Business Ethics 100 Best Corporate Citizens 2006," *Business Ethics* (Spring 2006), 22.

3. "SEC Chief Donaldson Pushes Ethics," MSNBC News, February 28, 2003, www.msnbc.com/news/ 878994.asp.

4. "62% of Americans Tell CEOs 'You're Not Doing Enough to Restore Trust and Confidence in American Business,'" Golin/Harris International press release, June 20, 2002, www.golinharris.com/news/ releases.asp?ID=3788.

5. Linda K. Trevino and Stuart Youngblood, "Bad Apples in Bad Barrels: Causal Analysis of Ethical Decision Making Behavior," *Journal of Applied Psychology* 75 (1990): 378–385.

6. Kara Wetzel, "SEC Files Complaint Against ClearOne," *Wall Street Journal* online, January 15, 2003, http://online.wsj.com/.

7. Trevino and Youngblood, "Bad Apples in Bad Barrels."

8. "AmericaEconomia Annual Survey Reveals Ethical Behavior of Businesses and Executives in Latin America," AmericaEconomia, December 19, 2002, via www.prnewswire.com.

9. Constance E. Bagley, "The Ethical Leader's Decision Tree," *Harvard Business Review* (February 2003): 18–19.

10. "Ex-Tyco CFO Indicted for Tax Evasion," CNN/ Money, February 19, 2003, http://money.cnn .com/; "A Guide to Corporate Scandals," MSNBC .com, www.msnbc.com/news/wld/business/brill/ Corporate Scandal_DW.asp (accessed February 26, 2003).

11. "Fast Fact," *Fast Company,* September 2000, 96.

12. Merck & Co., Inc., 1999 Annual Report, 29.

13. "How Am I Doing?" *Business Ethics* (Fall 2005): 11.

14. "KPMG Integrity Survey 2005–2006," http://www .us.kpmg.com/RutUS_prod/Documents/9/ ForIntegritySurv_WEB.pdf (accessed March 24, 2006).

15. Gary R. Weaver and Linda K. Trevino, "Compliance and Values Oriented Ethics Programs: Influences on Employees' Attitudes and Behavior," *Business Ethics Quarterly* 9 (1999): 315–335.

16. Peter R. Kendicki, "The Options Available in Ethics Programs," *National Underwriter*, November 12, 2001, 57–58.

17. National Business Ethics Survey, *How Employees View Ethics in their Organizations 1994-2005* (Washington DC: Ethics Resource Center, 2005), 12.

18. Mark S. Schwartz, "A Code of Ethics for Corporate Code of Ethics," *Journal of Business Ethics* 41 (2002): 37.

19. Ibid.

20. "2002 Fidelity Investments Code of Ethics Summary," Fidelity Investments, http://personal .fidelity.com/myfidelity/InsideFidelity/index.html (accessed March 3, 2003).

21. Cate Whitfield, Staff Administrator, Honda Engineering N.A. Inc. "A Small Company Case Study," Annual Business Ethics and Compliance Conference, 2005.

22. National Business Ethics Survey, *How Employees View*, 56.

23. "USSC Commissioner John Steer Joins with Compliance and Ethics Executives from Leading U.S. Companies to Address Key Compliance, Business Conduct and Governance Issues," *Society for Corporate Compliance and Ethics*, PR Newswire, October 31, 2005.

24. Allynda Wheat, "Keeping an Eye on Corporate America," *Fortune*, November 25, 2002, 44–45.

25. "About the ECOA," At A Glance, http://www .theecoa.org/AboutEOA.asp (accessed June 27, 2006).

26. Wheat, "Keeping an Eye on Corporate America."

27. "Top Corporate Ethics Officers Tell Conference Board That More Business Ethics Scandals Are Ahead; Survey Conducted at Conference Board Business Ethics Conference," PR Newswire, June 17, 2002, via www.findarticles.com.

28. "Ethics, Compliance, and Corporate Responsibility," HCA Healthcare, http://ec.hcahealthcare.com (accessed March 3, 2003).

29. O. C. Ferrell and Larry Gresham, "A Contingency Framework for Understanding Ethical Decision Making in Marketing," *Journal of Marketing* 49 (1985): 87–96.

30. Diane E. Kirrane, "Managing Values: A Systematic Approach to Business Ethics," *Training and Development Journal* 1 (1990): 53–60.

31. "Ethics and Business Conduct," www.boeing.com/ companyoffices/aboutus/ethics/index. htm (accessed February 25, 2003), courtesy of Boeing Business Services Company.

32. Debbie Thorne LeClair and Linda Ferrell, "Innovation in Experiential Business Ethics Training," *Journal of Business Ethics* 23 (2000): 313–322.

33. "Top Corporate Ethics Officers Tell Conference Board."

34. Ibid.

35. Janet Wiscombe, "Don't Fear Whistle-Blowers: With HR's Help, Principled Whistle-Blowers Can Be a Company's Salvation," *Workforce*, July 2002, via www.findarticles.com.

36. Mael Kaptein, "Guidelines for the Development of an Ethics Safety Net," *Journal of Business Ethics* 41 (2002): 217.

37. National Business Ethics Survey, *How Employees View*, 32.

38. Curt S. Jordan, "Lessons in Organizational Compliance: A Survey of Government-Imposed Compliance Programs," *Preventive Law Reporter* (Winter 1994): 7.

39. Lori T. Martens and Kristen Day, "Five Common Mistakes in Designing and Implementing a Business Ethics Program," *Business and Society Review* 104 (1999): 163–170.

40. Anne C. Mulkern, "Auditors Smelled Trouble," *Denver Post*, October 2, 2002, A1.